Baseball Research Journal

Volume 50, Number 2
Fall 2021

Published by the Society for American Baseball Research

BASEBALL RESEARCH JOURNAL, Volume 50, Number 2

Editor: Cecilia M. Tan
Interior design and production: Lisa Hochstein
Copyediting assistance: King Kaufman, Keith DeCandido
Proofreader: Norman L. Macht
Fact checker: Clifford Blau

Front cover art and design: Gary Cieradkowski, Studio Gary C (studiogaryc.com)

Published by:
Society for American Baseball Research, Inc.
Cronkite School at ASU
555 N. Central Ave. #416
Phoenix, AZ 85004

Phone: (602) 496–1460
Web: www.sabr.org
Twitter: @sabr
Facebook: Society for American Baseball Research

Printed in the United States of America
Distributed by the University of Nebraska Press

ISBN: 978-1-970159-39-4 (paper)
ISBN: 978-1-970159-38-7 (e-book)

Contents

STATS AND STUDIES

From the Editor

By the time you read this, the 2021 World Series champion will have been crowned. But right up to the morning of game 161 the possibility of a four-way tie in the American League still loomed. In the end, none of the wacky tie-breaking scenarios came to pass. At best, what "didn't happen" is relegated to a footnote on the season, while what did actually occur is, naturally, what will be principally recorded and remembered.

But I still like to think about "what if." Part of the fun of baseball is the anticipation, the prediction of what might happen at each step of the game. Dreaming of "what if" is baked into the way many of us participate in the game as spectators: what if the batter hits a home run? what if the relief pitcher comes in, throws one pitch, and gets the groundball double play that snuffs the rally? It *could* happen.

It's one reason I like to keep score when I'm at the game: so I can look down at my scorecard and predict what might happen. Like one day when Bill Nowlin and I were at a game at Fenway to work the SABR Boston community table. The year was 2006, and David Ortiz's reputation for walk-off hits had already been established, but hadn't yet grown to legendary proportions. The Red Sox went into the ninth inning down two runs. The scorecard showed that if two men got on and two men made out, Ortiz would get a chance to bat. I pointed this out to Bill. In those days, shortly after the Red Sox had won the championship in 2004, old school Red Sox fans were still slow to shed their pessimistic ways. Bill was skeptical. Me, though, being a transplanted Yankees fan? I am optimistic by nature. I nudged him. "Just think. It *could* happen."

And it did. Big Papi hit a three-run walk-off homer, beating the Texas Rangers, 5–4.[1] We call those moments "magic" because it feels like we willed it to happen, like prayers were answered, like a miracle occurred. The magic of sports is that the game creates these moments, and *some* of them pan out. We didn't get any of the tiebreaker scenarios for a game 163, but Aaron Judge did have the very first walk-off hit of his career to break a 0–0 tie in the bottom of the ninth inning to prevent it. He picked a good time for it... because of course he didn't pick the time at all.

This is why I don't believe sabermetrics or analytics takes the romance out of the game. Sure, we can analyze and make predictions all we want. But no spreadsheet can tell you whether David Ortiz was going to hit a home run or strike out in the bottom of the ninth on June 11, 2006. No formula can calculate whether Tyler Wade was going to trip and fall or slide home safely on October 3, 2021.[2] No machine-learning algorithm can tell us if Cody Bellinger (or his father[3]) is going to rob a homer.[4] What analytics can do for the average fan (or broadcaster) is help understand the context that the action takes place in, and to *anticipate* the action.

But the action is still the action. Sometimes the outcome will be what we expect. Other times, it'll be what we only dared to hope for.

Dare to hope, my friends. Hope for the chance for your team's slugger to turn the tide with one swing, whether literally or as a metaphor. And I hope you enjoy this issue of the *BRJ*, which is larger than usual—because so many SABR members are producing quality research that a backlog is forming.

Maybe many folks had extra time on their hands during quarantine, but I feel one reason submissions are up is that we are in a golden age for research, whether one is looking back at history or forward through predictions. The Newspapers.com benefit of SABR membership (accessible to all members through SABR.org) has borne fruit, as have the continued expansions of online accessible libraries and resources. Many of us now have more computing power in our pockets than a university computer science department had just a few decades ago. Perhaps most importantly, though, we have so many ways to connect with other researchers, to bounce ideas, refine techniques, find leads and lost gems, and to support each other. All these elements add to the mix.

And SABR members are not going to run out of topics to research any time soon. You inspire me, each and every one.

– Cecilia M. Tan
October 2021

1. Retrosheet, Texas at Boston, June 11, 2006: https://www.retrosheet.org/boxesetc/2006/B06111BOS2006.htm.
2. Baseball Reference, Tampa Bay at New York AL, October 3, 2021: https://www.baseball-reference.com/boxes/NYA/NYA202110030.shtml.
3. MLB, "2000 WS Gm2: Bellinger snags Zeile's fly at the wall," YouTube video, 1:09, November 3, 2014: https://www.youtube.com/watch?v=YexGoJlr9N8.
4. Jack Harris, "How Cody Bellinger's father celebrated his son's home run-robbing catch is so 2020," *Los Angeles Times*, October 8, 2020: https://www.latimes.com/sports/dodgers/story/2020-10-08/cody-bellinger-catch-father-texas-padres-mlb-playoffs-padres-nlds.

Ryan Zimmerman and the Walk-Off Home Run

Steven C. Weiner

"The pressure is on him, man. It's not on me. I'm supposed to get out."
— Ryan Zimmerman[1]

Baseball games are filled with moments of great theater. What do we expect before the curtain rises? Perhaps a great pitching duel, or a milestone performance by a favorite player, perhaps even the major league debut of the game's next potential superstar. The possibilities are endless. The beauty of the game is that the many possible story lines we contemplate fail to reveal even a hint as to what might actually unfold on the field.

The drama might build slowly and treat us to a great pitching performance. For example, the possibility of witnessing a no-hitter is confirmed only when the last batter in the last inning makes the last out and the pitcher is mobbed on the field.

The most dramatic and emphatic of plays, the walk-off home run, must also wait for the last batter in the last inning. Every home team fan thinks of nothing less when its possibility arises. The reaction to a walk-off home run is as predictable as it is sudden. As the ball leaves the playing field and the batter circles the bases, the exuberance of the fans is immediate. The visiting team quickly leaves the field, while the home team emerges from the dugout, excited and victorious, to surround home plate as the umpires stand by stoically just to make sure that the batter touches every base. Game over, celebration begins!

The term "walk-off" didn't enter the baseball lexicon until 1988 as noted by author Paul Dickson. "The term was coined by Oakland Athletics pitcher Dennis Eckersley for that lonely stroll from the mound after a pitcher gives up the winning run (Gannett News Service, July 30, 1988)."[2]

Eckersley's use of the term had a rather negative connotation, referencing the losing pitcher as he leaves the field after yielding the home run. It is quite likely that he was referring to the Oakland versus Seattle game at the Kingdome on July 29, 1988. Eckersley came into the game in the 10th inning seeking his 31st save of the season with the A's leading, 3–2. Instead, Steve Balboni hit a three-run game-winning home run for the Mariners and the walk-off began.

To the chagrin of some, common usage of this terminology has evolved to highlight the achievement of the batter, regardless of how the walk-off was achieved. Larry Granillo's study, "Walking Off," defines a walk-off victory as "a run-scoring event in the bottom half of the last inning of the game that gives the home team a winning margin."[3] An article in *Sports Illustrated* in 2000 noted, "Like crabgrass invading someone's lawn, "walk-off!" has taken root in sports lingo and gotten out of control. The term should appear in quotes and be followed by an exclamation point because, without TV's dime-a-dozen talking heads repeating it endlessly and effusively, there would be no "Aaron Boone wins the game with a walk-off!" Instead, we would simply (and gracefully) call a game-ending home run what we've always called it: a game-ending home run."[4] The home run is not the only play given the designation: these days it's not unusual for a game to be ended by a "walk-off single," a "walk-off walk," or even a "walk-off balk."[5]

The history of major league baseball's walk-off home runs is rich and no player personifies that recent history better than Ryan Zimmerman. The arrival of Zimmerman as a Washington National virtually coincided with baseball's return to the nation's capital after a 33-season absence. The Nationals selected Zimmerman as the fourth player overall in the June 2005 amateur player draft. He spent the summer moving from Class A to Class AA minor league baseball, batting .336 and earning a September call-up for his major league debut. Zimmerman played in 20 games for the Nationals and batted .397, leaving a first and certainly lasting impression on teammates and fans alike.

There have been 1,084 walk-off home runs in the 16 seasons 2005–20.[6] Since 2005, when the Montreal

Expos franchise relocated to Washington, DC, Ryan Zimmerman has more game-ending home runs (11) than any other major league player, assuring his place among the career leaders as summarized in Table 1.

Table 1. Career walk-off home run leaders

Jim Thome	13
Jimmie Foxx	12
Mickey Mantle	12
Stan Musial	12
Albert Pujols	12
Frank Robinson	12
Babe Ruth	12
Ryan Zimmerman	11
David Ortiz	11
Tony Pérez	11

All eleven games that have ended with a Ryan Zimmerman walk-off home run are noted in Table 2, along with the name of the author who has chronicled each game for SABR's Baseball Games Project.[7] Let's recap four of them, covering several different types of games and circumstances.

Table 2. SABR Baseball Games Project – Ryan Zimmerman's Walk-off Home Runs

1. **June 18, 2006** – Ryan Zimmerman hits his first walk-off home run (Peebles)
2. **July 4, 2006** – Nationals' Ryan Zimmerman provides the walk-off fireworks (Peebles)
3. **May 12, 2007** – Another holiday, another Ryan Zimmerman walk-off homer (Peebles)
4. **March 30, 2008** – Ryan Zimmerman sends D.C. fans home happy with walk-off homer in Nationals Park debut (Sharp)
5. **September 6, 2009** – Ryan Zimmerman hits fifth career walk-off home run (Peebles)
6. **July 6, 2010** – Ryan Zimmerman hits sixth career walk-off home run (Peebles)
7. **July 31, 2010** – Twice in a month: 'Mr. Walk-Off' Ryan Zimmerman sends Nationals fans home happy (Peebles)
8. **August 19, 2011** – Ryan Zimmerman's walk-off grand slam beats Phillies (Weiner)
9. **July 26, 2013** – Ohlendorf's pitching, Zimmerman's walk-off homer lift Nationals over Mets (Peebles)
10. **May 19, 2015** – 'Mr. Walk-Off' Ryan Zimmerman's 10th-inning blast beats Yankees (Weiner)
11. **August 22, 2018** – Ryan Zimmerman's 11th walk-off home run, a play in two acts (Weiner)

HAPPY FATHER'S DAY, MR. ZIMMERMAN!

Father's Day weekend 2006 brought New York Yankees fans from everywhere for a three-game interleague series between the Nationals and Yankees in creaky old RFK Stadium. Ironically, the Yankees' last game in this same ballpark on September 30, 1971, against the American League rival Washington Senators, ended in the chaos of a swarming crowd on the field and a forfeit victory for the Yankees.[8] Baseball was gone from RFK Stadium until the 2005 season.

Fittingly, Ryan Zimmerman's parents, Keith and Cheryl Zimmerman, were among the Father's Day crowd (45,157), the largest since the Nationals had played their first home game in 2005 against the Arizona Diamondbacks.[9] As the Nationals came to bat in the bottom of the eighth inning, Yankees starter Chien-Ming Wang, on his way to leading the major leagues in wins (19) in 2006, was seemingly in control. The Yankees had a 2–1 lead and Wang had yielded only four singles through seven innings and thrown only 80 pitches.

After walking two batters in the eighth inning, perhaps Wang was tiring. When Wang finished the scoreless eighth with a 96-pitch count, Yankees manager Joe Torre seemed determined not to use his premier closer, Mariano Rivera, for a third game in a row. Rivera had won the first game of the series and lost the second one.

But Keith Zimmerman expressed a premonition about what was to come next for his eldest son, Ryan.[10] After Marlon Anderson singled to right in the ninth inning with one out, Zimmerman came to bat as the potential winning run. If a tiring Wang left a pitch up in the strike zone, Zimmerman was ready to pounce. He did just that on the very first pitch, sending it over the left-field fence into the bullpen for his first-ever walk-off hit.

SABR author Laura Peebles described Zimmerman's trot around the bases: "The usually reserved Zimmerman smiled and raised his arm in triumph as he circled the bases, throwing away his batting helmet as he approached his teammates ready to mob him at home plate."[11] After all, this was a first. Dating all the way back to his Little League days, Zimmerman had never ended a game in that fashion. "No walk-off, nothing," he noted later. "No single. Nothing."[12] His walk-off home run was the first at RFK Stadium since the Nationals had become the new tenants a year earlier. The fans demanded a curtain call and got one. Indeed, there would be more such occasions to come.

INAUGURATING A NEW BALLPARK

A better script could not have been written for the Opening Night play at Nationals Park on March 30, 2008,

TOPPS, INC

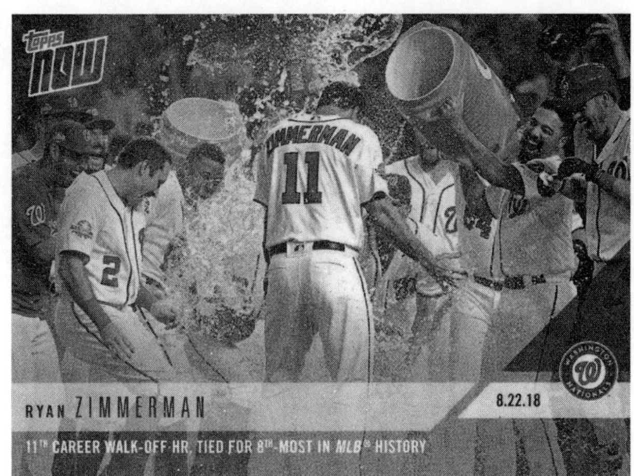

Topps commemorated Zimmerman's 11th career walk-off with a collectible card.

especially for the closing act. The Nationals successfully lobbied Major League Baseball and ESPN to open the season one day before the scheduled Opening Day, highlighting a spanking new ballpark to a nationally televised audience.[13]

The pre-game festivities had all the trappings of an Opening Night: flags unfolded across the field, F-16s roaring through the skies overhead, and esteemed mezzo-soprano Denyce Graves singing the National Anthem. The honor of handing a baseball to President Bush for the first pitch belonged to Ryan Zimmerman, by now the face of the franchise. President Bush, former owner of the Texas Rangers, threw that pitch—a ball, high and tight—to Nationals manager Manny Acta.[14]

The Nationals were swept up in the excitement of the night in the very first inning. Cristian Guzman lined a single to right on Braves starter Tim Hudson's first pitch and raced to third on an errant pick-off throw. With two outs, Nick Johnson's double and Austin Kearns's single gave the Nationals an early 2–0 lead. Braves pitching—Hudson, Will Ohman, and Peter Moylan—would not allow another batter to reach base until the fateful ninth inning.

Meanwhile, Chipper Jones cut the Nationals lead in half, 2–1, when he hit a solo home run off starter Odalis Pérez in the fourth inning. In the top of the ninth inning, the Braves tied the score against Nationals reliever Jon Rauch. Mark Teixeira's double eventually led to an unearned run when pinch runner Martín Prado scored on a passed ball.

After 24 consecutive batters had been retired, including two in the bottom of the ninth inning, Ryan Zimmerman came to bat. All this game needed was a rousing conclusion. As Nick Johnson moved into the on-deck circle and Kearns grabbed a bat in the dugout, veteran Dimitri Young had a premonition. "Put it down, he told Kearns, You won't need it."[15] He was right. Zimmerman hit Peter Moylan's 1-and-0 fastball into the left-center stands for his fourth career game-ending home run and another curtain call. "Storybook ending," said Mark Lerner, the Nationals' managing principal owner. "It was the end of a perfect day. You can't write a script like that."[16]

THE 38th PITCH

It's August 19, 2011, and you are in first place by 8½ games in the National League's East Division. It's the bottom of the ninth inning and your team is ahead, 4–2. For Phillies manager Charlie Manuel, it was time to call on his closer, Ryan Madson, for a third consecutive game. His 23rd save on the previous night sealed a 4–1 victory for the Phillies over the Arizona Diamondbacks.

The inning began and ended with classic confrontations of pitcher versus batter, requiring the best of skills by both combatants. To open the ninth, Madson was facing ex-teammate Jayson Werth for the first time in his career. Werth was known for being able to work a pitch count to advantage. Werth was well on his way to leading the National League in 2011 with 4.37 pitches per plate appearance.[17] Werth was quickly down 0-and-2 in the count. Over the next eight pitches, Werth fouled off five in between taking three balls. Finally, with the count 3–2, Werth lined a 95-mph fastball into left field for a single.

Was Madson unnerved by Werth's at-bat? Three more singles wrapped around an intentional walk and a sacrifice bunt tied the score at 4–4. With two outs and the bases loaded, Ryan Zimmerman came to the plate. It was well past midnight since a rain delay had been called only five minutes after the first pitch, which lasted over two hours. Only a fraction of the original crowd (37,841) remained to anticipate the possibilities of what might happen next.

Ryan Madson was now in uncharted territory. He had already thrown 32 pitches in the inning. The last time he had thrown that many pitches in a relief outing had come nearly three years earlier, in this very same ballpark.[18] What did happen next? Bases loaded, two outs, full count. On Madson's 38th pitch of the inning, Zimmerman expected fastball and got one, inside at 92 mph. He deposited it down the left-field line, a grand slam, the eighth walk-off home run of his career and a Nationals 8–4 win.[19]

Zimmerman understood, as did Jayson Werth, the pressure of these pitcher-versus-batter confrontations. "The way I've always been taught is, the pressure is on the pitcher," Zimmerman said. "Obviously, I want to get a hit as much as anyone else. But if you kind of put it into that mindset, it puts the pressure on him, keeps you calm. The key thing is to try and not do too much."[20]

A PLAY IN TWO ACTS

As dramatic and emphatic as the walk-off home run may be, ambiguity can prevail. Is it a game-ending home run or a game-tying double?

On August 22, 2018, it's the bottom of the ninth inning and the Nationals trail, 7–6, as the Phillies bring in Seranthony Dominguez to close out the game. The Nationals were down to their last out after Bryce Harper flied out to short left and Anthony Rendon flied a first pitch to right. Juan Soto's double down the right-field line gave the fans what they wanted—Ryan Zimmerman coming to the plate as the winning run.

But this play took a strange turn. In act one, Zimmerman hit Dominguez's 2-and-1 offering just barely over the right-field wall. He reacted as if he had just hit his 11th walk-off home run, but the blast was initially ruled a double, with Soto scoring to tie the game at 7–7. The umpires went to video replay to review the initial call while Zimmerman stood on second base. When the home-run signal came from the umpires, act two began. The exuberant, 19-year-old Soto started running from home plate toward Zimmerman, who had resumed his home run trot. Soto just wanted to start an early celebration, but manager Dave Martinez thought about the rules and said, "If he touches Ryan, he's out. I was screaming bloody murder."[21] Several other media outlets also reported Martinez's conclusion as correct.[22] Soto got the message and retreated to home plate to await the arrival of "Mr. Walk-Off" with his 11th career game-ending home run and an 8–7 Nationals win.[23]

According to MLB umpire Gerry Davis, Martinez's assertion is incorrect because the ball was dead when Zimmerman resumed his home run trot.[24] "While the ball is dead no player may be put out, no bases may be run and no runs may be scored, except that runners may advance one or more bases as the result of acts which occurred while the ball was alive (such as, but not limited to, a balk, an overthrow, interference, or a home run or other fair ball hit out of the playing field." (Section 5.06(c)—Dead Balls, Official Rules of Major League Baseball, 2019: 31).

For the record book, this walk-off home run was Zimmerman's fifth when his team was trailing at the time, tied for the most in major-league history with Babe Ruth, Frank Robinson, and Fred McGriff.[25]

MR. WALK-OFF

Ryan Zimmerman was called "Mr. Walk-Off" on MASN, the network that carries Nationals games, after hitting his 10th game-ending home run against the New York Yankees on May 19, 2015.[26] Following the game, Dan Steinberg, columnist for the *Washington Post*, explored the nickname's background and discovered it was first used in 2008 by blogger William F. Yurasko following Zimmerman's fourth walk-off home run.[27] Yurasko had attended the game marking the opening of Nationals Park. Yurasko exclaimed on his blog right after the game that "Ryan Zimmerman sent a telegram to the baseball world this evening: 'I am Mr. Walkoff.'"[28]

The name stuck in print media as well. One month after Zimmerman hit his ninth walk-off home run in 2013 against the New York Mets,[29] the cover story photo and banner for the Nationals in-game program, *Inside Pitch*, greeted fans for a late August homestand, "Mr. Walk-Off."[30] During the Nationals' stretch run to secure a spot in the 2019 postseason playoffs, *Nationals Magazine* writer Michael Bradley reminded fans of "The Legend of Mr. Walk-Off." He wrote that Zimmerman is focused on one thing in these clutch situations, "making the man delivering the ball worry about what happens if he surrenders the hit that gives Washington a victory."[31]

Retrosheet data through the 2020 season provide us with a statistical glimpse of Ryan Zimmerman's performance and success in the most dramatic of circumstances.[32] The career .279 hitter's batting line when a walk-off situation confronts him is noted in Table 3.

Table 3. Ryan Zimmerman's career batting in walk-off situations, 2005–20

AB	R	H	2B	3B	HR	RBI	BB	SO	BA
109	11	33	4	0	11	35	17	23	.303

It is not surprising that Zimmerman's career has been publicly acclaimed for his propensity to end games with a home run (Table 4). In addition to 11 walk-off home runs, Zimmerman also knocked in the winning run in the last plate appearance in six other games with four singles, a walk, and a sacrifice fly. His 17 walk-off events place him in a tie for 24th place for the 1937–2020 seasons. How does that compare to others? Coincidentally, two of his former managers, Frank Robinson (27) and Dusty Baker (25), are the leaders, but Albert Pujols (21) was the only player active in 2020 with more walk-off events than Zimmerman.

Table 4. Walk-off home runs, 2005–20

1	**Ryan Zimmerman**	**11**
2	David Ortiz	8
2	Jason Giambi	8
2	Adam Dunn	8
2	Albert Pujols	8

Analysis of batting averages suggests at least one way to examine the performance of players in walk-off situations. How might we judge, even qualitatively, the performance of Ryan Zimmerman in comparison to his peers in this most dramatic, pressure-filled circumstance of batter versus pitcher?

From 2005 through 2020, 16 players recorded at least 100 at-bats in walk-off situations. Of those players, only five recorded higher batting averages in walk-off situations than in their other at-bats and only two recorded batting averages higher than .300 in doing so, Nick Markakis and Ryan Zimmerman (Table 5).

Table 5. Higher batting average (BA) in walk-off situations 100 AB min, 2005-2020

Player	AB	H	HR	TOT*	BA w-o	BA other
Nick Markakis	109	42	2	10	.385	.286
Ryan Zimmerman	109	33	11	17	.303	.278
Albert Pujols	139	41	8	16	.295	.289
José Reyes	109	32	0	4	.294	.283
Jay Bruce	100	29	5	12	.290	.244

* TOT = total walk-off events

In Table 6, Zimmerman's performance in these pressure-filled at-bats is compared to three contemporaries from the top 10 list of career leaders in walk-off home runs. Jim Thome was inducted into the Hall of Fame in 2018 and Pujols and Ortiz are likely headed there in the future. Zimmerman is keeping good company with some true home run hitters as suggested by each player's 162-game career home run average. The 162-game home run averages for Babe Ruth (46), Barry Bonds (41), and Hank Aaron (37) provide a broader appreciation of Zimmerman's accomplishments.

Table 6. Career performance in walk-off situations

Player	AB	H	HR	TOT*	BA w-o	BA other	HR-AVG*
Jim Thome (1991–2012)	135	30	13	14	.222	.277	39
Albert Pujols (2001–20)	164	47	12	21	.287	.299	37
Ryan Zimmerman (2005–20)	**109**	**33**	**11**	**17**	**.303**	**.278**	**26**
David Ortiz (1997–2016)	97	33	11	20	.340	.285	36

* TOT = total walk-off events; HR-AVG = 162-game HR average

Pitcher versus batter remains the most fundamental confrontation in baseball. Any interest to assess batter performance more quantitatively in walk-off situations will require the review and analysis of pitcher performance under those same circumstances.

Player introductions are a lasting tradition of any Opening Day at the ballpark as the respective teams take their places along the infield foul lines. When Ryan Zimmerman took his spot along the first-base line for the 2019 Opening Day ceremonies at Nationals Park, we were reminded of his baseball accomplishments. The capacity crowd heard the introduction clearly, "Number 11, Mr. Walk-Off, Ryan Zimmerman."[33] A fitting title. ■

Acknowledgments

The author thanks fellow SABR members, Laura H. Peebles, Andrew Sharp and Tom Ruane for their contributions to this work. Peebles and Sharp authored SABR Games Project essays identified, discussed and referenced here. Ruane provided Retrosheet data for analysis of walk-off home runs and the career performance of Ryan Zimmerman and other players in game-ending situations. Baseball-Reference.com, which appropriately acknowledges "Mr. Walk-Off" as one of Ryan Zimmerman's nicknames, served as a rich resource for baseball-related data and information. Thank-yous are deserved for colleagues involved in many ways with the SABR Baseball Games Project for their hard work, inspiration and camaraderie.

Notes

1. Amanda Comak, "Zimmerman's walk-off grand slam lifts Nats to 8–4 comeback win over Phillies," *Washington Times*, August 20, 2011.
2. Paul Dickson, *The Dickson Baseball Dictionary*, 3rd Edition (New York: W.W. Norton & Company, 2009), 919.
3. Larry Granillo, "Walking Off," BaseballAnalysts.com, August 27, 2009, accessed March 29, 2018, baseballanalysts.com/archives/2009/08/walking_off.php.
4. Jeff Pearlman, "Walk-off! Crazy A Simple Turn of Phrase by Dennis Eckersley in 1993 Has Become an Overused Appellation for a Game-Ending Dinger," SI.com, July 17, 2000, accessed November 12, 2020, si.com/vault/2000/07/17/walk-off-crazy-a-simple-turn-of-phrase-by-dennis-eckersley-in-1993-has-become-an-overusedappellation-for-a-game-ending-dinger.
5. On August 18, 2018, Dylan Floro balked in the winning run in the 10th inning and the Seattle Mariners beat the Los Angeles Dodgers, 5–4. It was the 22nd walk-off balk in MLB history. (Nick Greene, "The Walk-Off Balk is Actually a Great Way to Lose a Baseball Game," Slate.com,

August 19, 2018, accessed July 24, 2021, slate.com/culture/2018/08 /walk-off-balk-the-sea>le-mariners-beat-the-los-angeles-dodgers-5-4-on-friday-thanks-to-a-mostpeculiar-play.html.)

6. Tom Ruane, emails to author, October 14, 2020, March 13, 2021.
7. SABR Baseball Games Project, sabr.org/gamesproject.
8. Shirley Povich, "The Senators' Final Game," *Washington Post*, October 1, 1971.
9. Laura H. Peebles, "April 14, 2005: 'Baseball is back in Washington, DC!' as Nationals win home opener," SABR Baseball Games Project, sabr.org/gamesproj/game/april-14-2005-baseball-is-back-in-washington-dc-asnationals-win-home-opener.
10. Barry Svrluga, "Zimmerman's Homer Lifts Nationals over Yankees," *Washington Post*, June 19, 2006.
11. Laura H. Peebles, "June 18, 2006: Ryan Zimmerman hits his first walk-off home run," SABR Baseball Games Project, sabr.org/gamesproj/game/june-18-2006-ryan-zimmerman-hits-his-first-walk-off-home-run.
12. Svrluga.
13. Barry Svrluga, "First Game at Nationals' New Ballpark Is Set 13 for March 30," *Washington Post*, December 15, 2007, E2.
14. Dave Sheinin and Daniel LeDuc, "A Storybook Ending," *Washington Post*, March 31, 2008.
15. Andrew Sharp, "March 30, 2008: Ryan Zimmerman sends D,C, fans home happy with walk-off homer in Nationals Park debut," SABR Baseball Games Project, sabr.org/gamesproj/game/march-30-2008-ryan-zimmermansends-d-c-fans-home-happy-with-walk-off-homer-in-nationals-park-debut.
16. Dave Sheinin and Daniel LeDuc,
17. "MLB Player Batting Stats–2011," ESPN.com, accessed July 8, 2017, espn.com/mlb/stats/batting/_/year/2011/league/nl/sort/pitchesPerPlateAppearance/type/expanded.
18. The Phillies lost to the Nationals, 9–7, on September 3, 2008, at Nationals Park. Madson threw 32 pitches in two innings that included striking out the side in the sixth inning. In his first major-league start against the Chicago White Sox on June 8, 2004, Madson threw 37 pitches in two-thirds of an inning and was taken out of the game. It was his only start of the 2004 season.
19. Steven C. Weiner, "August 19, 2011: Ryan Zimmerman's walk-off grand slam beats Phillies," SABR Baseball Games Project, sabr.org/gamesproj/game/august-19-2011-ryan-zimmermans-walk-off-grand-slam-beatsphillies.
20. Adam Kilgore, "Nationals vs. Phillies: Ryan Zimmerman hits walk-off grand slam to cap Washington's improbable rally," *Washington Post*, August 20, 2011.
21. "Zimmerman hits 2-run HR in 9th, Nationals beat Phillies 8–7," USAToday.com, October 29, 2020, accessed November 12, 2020, usatoday.com/story/sports/mlb/2018/08/22/zimmerman-hits-2-run-hr-in-9th-nationalsbeat-phillies-8-7/37575047.
22. Chelsea Janes, "Ryan Zimmerman lifts Nationals to walk-off win over Phillies," WashingtonPost.com, August 22, 2018, accessed November 12, 2020, washingtonpost.com/sports/nationals/ryan-zimmerman-liftsnationals-to-walk-off-win-over-phillies/2018/08/22/39b6c696-a64a-11e8-97ce-cc9042272f07_story.html; Jamal Collier, "Zim hits 2-run walk-off HR vs. Phils after review," MLB.com August 22, 2018, mlb.com/news/ryanzimmerman-hits-2-run-walk-off-homer-c291475236.
23. Steven C. Weiner, "August 22, 2018: Ryan Zimmerman's 11th walk-off home run, a play in two acts," SABR Baseball Games Project, sabr.org/gamesproj/game/august-22-2018-ryan-zimmermans-11th-walk-off-homerun-a-play-in-two-acts.
24. Gerry Davis, personal communication with author, June 29, 2019.
25. Charlotte Carroll, "Nationals Win on Ryan Zimmerman's Replay-Reviewed Walk-Off Homer," SI.com, August 22, 2018, accessed November 12, 2020, si.com/mlb/2018/08/22/ryan-zimmerman-walkoff-homer-nationals.
26. Steven C. Weiner, May 19, 2015: 'Mr. Walk-Off' Ryan Zimmerman's 10th-inning blast beats Yankees," SABR Baseball Games Project, sabr.org/gamesproj/game/may-19-2015-mr-walk-off-ryan-zimmermans-10th-inningblast-beats-yankees.
27. Dan Steinberg, "How Ryan Zimmerman got his 'Mr. Walk-Off' nickname," *Washington Post*, May 20, 2015.
28. William F. Yurasko, "Ryan Zimmerman is Mr. Walkoff," March 31, 2008, accessed November 12, 2020, yurasko.net/wfy/2008/03/ryan-zimmerman-is-mr-walkoff.html.
29. Laura H. Peebles, "July 26, 2013: Ohlendorf's pitching, Zimmerman's walk-off homer lift Nationals over Mets," SABR Baseball Games Project, sabr.org/gamesproj/game/july-26-2013-ohlendorfs-pitching-zimmermanswalk-off-homer-lift-nationals-over-mets.
30. "Mr. Walk-Off," *Inside Pitch* 6 (2013).
31. Michael Bradley, "Ryan Zimmerman, The Legend of Mr. Walk-off," *Nationals Magazine* 15 (August/September 2019): 20–28.
32. Ryan Zimmerman opted not to play during the 2020 season due to the coronavirus pandemic. He returned to the Nationals active roster for the 2021 season.
33. The author watched and listened from Section 208 on March 28, 2019. The Mets won an old-fashioned pitchers' duel, 2–0. Max Scherzer struck out 12 and Jacob DeGrom struck out 10.

The Hammer Hits the Road

A New Look at Henry Aaron's Home Run Record

Eric Marshall White

"Although he never hit more than 47 home runs in a season..." was a common refrain in the eulogies that marked Henry Aaron's passing on January 22, 2021. Intended as a nod to Aaron's workmanlike virtue, the suggestion that his peak fell short of the more spectacular feats of other sluggers set up the inevitable pivot to the main point, that his 23-year climb to the top of the all-time home run list highlighted two even greater virtues: superlative consistency and longevity.[1] Developed over several decades, the popular image of "Quiet Henry" wielding his relentless hammer underpins our understanding of Aaron's legacy within baseball history and American folklore.[2] The underlying facts are not in question: Aaron's career did exemplify longevity; his performance was remarkably consistent; his best seasonal home run total (47 in 1971) did not threaten any records; and of course he did later eclipse Babe Ruth's career record for home runs. Nevertheless, the common wisdom regarding Aaron is misleading. It is framed so that the titanic breadth of his career-long achievement must provide necessary compensation for the supposedly low ceiling under which he performed. Thus, Aaron's career is remembered as a somewhat quiet, deceptively plodding marathon that lacked the flashy brilliance of more supercharged careers.[3] In fact, the notion that Aaron did not have what it takes to hit 50 or more home runs in a season understates his true greatness, because it bows unnecessarily to the inflated feats of less-worthy competitors against whom his peak ability has been compared unfavorably. A fresh examination of overlooked but essential evidence, considered in proper context, reveals that the common wisdom falls prey to statistical illusions and analytical pitfalls that have distorted our perceptions of Aaron's unique strengths and have misdirected our assessments of his career.

"ONLY 47" HOME RUNS

Following decades of rampant home run proliferation, it became possible for the compiler of Aaron's obituary in *The New York Times* to remark that the Hall-of-Famer's "highest total was only 47, in 1971."[4] It should go without saying that 47 is historically an impressive number of home runs for a single season: People do not complain that Lou Gehrig hit "only" 47 home runs in his legendary 1927 campaign. The fact that Aaron never surpassed 47 home runs should not be particularly remarkable or disquieting: other famous sluggers who failed to exceed the same threshold include Reggie Jackson (47), Ernie Banks (47), Eddie Mathews (47), Joe DiMaggio (46), Willie McCovey (45), Johnny Bench (45), Carl Yastrzemski (44), Ted Williams (43), Duke Snider (43), Mel Ott (42), Rogers Hornsby (42), and Stan Musial (39). During Aaron's lengthy career, from 1954 to 1976, only eight players managed to exceed 47 home runs in one year, although they did it on thirteen occasions.[5] However, eight of those performances tacked on a mere homer or two, and even though Roger Maris once managed to exceed Aaron's top mark by 14 home runs, that did not put him significantly closer to Ruth's career mark.

There are multiple problems with the suggestion that Aaron's failure to exceed 47 home runs in a season made him a long shot to challenge Ruth's home run record. First, a single-season high-water mark does not define a player's greatness. If it did, then Maris would already be in the Hall of Fame while Aaron, with his peak of "only" 47 home runs, might still be just another popular underdog candidate. A single season is an extremely limited sample. One can remove any one of seventeen different Aaron seasons and he still would have 715 or more home runs. Strong decades matter more than epic seasons. Most career records for counting statistics, even Babe Ruth's, have required about twenty years of high-rate accumulation. There is nothing especially insightful about the idea that Aaron needed longevity to break an all-time record when that is a given for anyone. Aaron's excellent *rate* put him over the top. His totals for two or three seasons were excellent; his totals for four, five, and six or more seasons were prodigious. Before Aaron's retirement, only Ruth, Foxx, Killebrew, Gehrig, and Mays had hit more home runs in any ten-year run, and only Ruth exceeded Aaron's since-broken National League record of 573 home runs in fifteen seasons. Clearly, the traditional unit of the single season is not the best indicator of Aaron's ability to hit quantities of home runs quickly, and the common wisdom has made too much of the perception that Aaron's ability to compile home runs in a given year was relatively modest.

A second point to consider is that 1971 was not really Aaron's most impressive home run season. That year, he hit 16 home runs on the road to go with 31 in Atlanta's Fulton County Stadium, where the ball carried well because the field was 1,050 feet above sea level. It was an amazing accomplishment for a 37-year-old in 495 at bats—compare Ernie Banks, who won an MVP award in 1958 with 30 home runs at Wrigley Field and 17 on the road over 617 at bats—but Aaron had several better years. In three campaigns during which he connected for 44 or 45 round-trippers (1957, 1962, and 1963), his home numbers were held down by difficult hitting conditions, including chilly weather, in Milwaukee's County Stadium. But he blasted 26, 27, and 25 road home runs in those seasons (with 83 *road* RBIs in 1957!), leading the league each year.

Aaron also had a pair of 44-homer seasons during his tenure in Atlanta in which he twice hit 23 on the road, finishing second to Donn Clendenon's amazing total of 25 in 1966 and pacing the league for the fourth time in 1969. Moreover, he connected for 20 home runs in his road games during the 1958 pennant-winning season, hit 19 in both 1959 and 1960, and collected 15 or more in six other seasons. These were Ruthian feats in any context and in any era.

One might even argue that Aaron's seasonal home run rate was a more important component of his assault on Ruth's record than his longevity was.[6] Plenty of players have played for twenty or more seasons, but only three (Aaron, Ruth, and Barry Bonds) have averaged 35 home runs over two decades. Mays played 22 seasons but came up well short of this pace. Aaron played 23 seasons, but he needed only twenty seasons plus three games to break Ruth's record. His home run pace, seen in proper context, was by no means a modest one. It was historic.

A TALE OF TWO CITIES

As Bill James pointed out in his *Historical Baseball Abstract* (1986), some of the tranquil consistency in Aaron's home run ledger is a statistical illusion caused by park effects: "At his peak, Aaron would have hit 50 home runs, and probably more than once, had he been playing in an average home run park." Aaron

NATIONAL BASEBALL HALL OF FAME LIBRARY, COOPERSTOWN, NY

Aaron found the home-run-hitting conditions in Atlanta more favorable than in Milwaukee.

considered Milwaukee's County Stadium a "fair" (meaning symmetrical) ballpark where he could "see the ball well," but it played large, meaning it tended to contain long drives that were home runs elsewhere, resulting in 185 home runs from Aaron's bat in Milwaukee versus 213 on the road during his first twelve seasons (1954–65).[7] Whereas Aaron was held to four 40-homer campaigns in Milwaukee between ages 20 and 31, Atlanta's "Launching Pad" boosted his gradually waning power production during his later years (1966–74), giving life to one or more of the four 40-homer campaigns that he enjoyed between ages 32 and 40. Naturally, a ballpark cannot cause baseballs to exit all by themselves—Aaron still had to hit hundreds of balls high and far and fair in Atlanta—but in the hope of taking full advantage of the thin air he began to lay off outside pitches more and adjusted his swing for greater pull and loft, doing so far more effectively than any of his rivals did.

Park-neutral performance is more indicative of home run-hitting ability than simply asking whether a player was able to hit more than 47 in a season.[8] Therefore, it is significant that at the time of his retirement, Aaron had compiled six seasons with at least 20 home runs on the road, the second-most in baseball history (tied with Mays and Killebrew). Ruth, as usual, was in a league of his own with 13 such seasons; Schmidt later reached seven. Listed below are all the players active before or during Aaron's career (that is, by 1976) who accumulated at least 100 home runs in road games during their five best seasons in that category; for purposes of ranking, ties are broken by career road home run totals (Table 1).

In this contest of park-neutral skill, Aaron is not just a steady also-ran, to be found near the bottom of this fast company, nor is he in the middle of the pack. The guy who never hit more than 47 home runs in a season is up there at the top of the list, behind only Ruth. Indeed, he leads all competitors from baseball's post-integration, pre-steroid era. Who knew?

Even when the five-year durability criterion is eased back to a player's top four seasons, which favors not the tortoise but the hare, this presents no problem for Aaron, who holds onto third place (101 road home runs), just one behind the surprisingly lethal Mathews (102), and just two home runs per year short of The Babe's best efforts (109). Conversely, as we increase the number of sample seasons to six and beyond, Aaron pulls away from the pack and eventually surpasses even Ruth, ending with 370 lifetime road home runs. While Aaron's lofty ranking may be surprising, it is a testament to his top-tier proficiency on the road that he was able to climb to the very precipice of the all-time record in his twentieth season. For two decades he had been greater than recognized, and his numbers, seen in proper context, were better than all but Ruth's.

NATIONAL BASEBALL HALL OF FAME LIBRARY, COOPERSTOWN, NY

Aaron entering 1973 having surpassed Willie Mays in career home runs. Synchronized by age, Hank had always been ahead of Willie's road home run pace.

AARON IN COMPARISON TO THE 50-HOMER CLUB

At the time of Aaron's retirement in 1976, only eight players besides Babe Ruth had ever hit 50 home runs in a single season. According to those who perceived Aaron's peak of 47 home runs to be a relatively modest total, it was these eight men—or men very much like them—who should have been the likeliest candidates to break Ruth's lifetime record for home runs. Two of them, Mays and Mantle, reached the big leagues at young ages, twice hit 50 + home runs, and lasted long enough to become legitimate threats to Ruth's record before falling off the pace. (Their road performances will be discussed in greater detail below.)

However, the six remaining members of the club were never realistic record challengers. Whereas Ruth, Mays, and Mantle (like Aaron) performed within the normal expectations for home-park leniency, the rest of the 50-home run club, with one notable exception, was essentially the product of drastic home-park

Table 1. Hitters (1900–76) with 100+ Road Home Runs in Their Five Best Seasons

Player	Total	HR Road	Road AB/HR	Road HR Top 5 Seasons	Total
1. Babe Ruth	714	367	11.9	32, 27, 25, 25, 25	134
2. Henry Aaron	755	370	17.3	27, 26, 25, 23, 23	124
3. Eddie Mathews	512	275	16.2	30, 26, 24, 22, 21	123
4. Willie Mays	660	325	17.4	29, 28, 22, 21, 21	121
5. Harmon Killebrew	573	282	14.9	28, 25, 23, 23, 21	120
6. Lou Gehrig	493	242	17.1	27, 23, 22, 22, 22	116
7. Mike Schmidt	548	283	15.3	29, 23, 21, 21, 21	115
8. Mickey Mantle	536	270	15.3	30, 25, 21, 20, 19	115
9. Joe DiMaggio	361	213	16.2	27, 24, 23, 21, 18	113
10. Jimmie Foxx	534	235	18.1	27, 22, 20, 19, 18	106
11. Willie Stargell	475	254	16.1	27, 22, 20, 19, 18	106
12. Rocky Colavito	374	181	18.5	27, 22, 21, 18, 18	106
13. Reggie Jackson	563	275	17.9	25, 21, 21, 20, 18	105
14. Roger Maris	275	153	17.5	31, 26, 18, 16, 14	105
15. Ted Williams	521	273	14.0	26, 20, 20, 20, 18	104
16. Willie McCovey	521	257	16.7	23, 23, 22, 18, 18	104
17. Dave Kingman	442	225	15.0	23, 22, 21, 20, 18	104
18. Frank Howard	382	196	16.7	26, 21, 20, 18, 17	102
19. Boog Powell	339	189	18.0	23, 23, 21, 17, 16	100

advantages. Here are their home-road splits and their rates of home and road home runs per 600 at bats (Table 2).

Table 2. The 50-Homer Club through 1976: Home/Road Splits

	Home-Road	Home	Road
Player	**Home-Road Split**	**HR/600**	**HR/600**
1. Babe Ruth	347 / 367	52	50
2. Willie Mays	325 / 335	38	35
3. Mickey Mantle	266 / 270	40	39
4. Jimmie Foxx	299 / 235	46	33
5. Ralph Kiner	210 / 159	49	36
6. Johnny Mize	212 / 147	40	27
7. Hank Greenberg	205 / 126	47	29
8. Roger Maris	122 / 153	30	34
9. Hack Wilson	137 / 107	34	27

Jimmie Foxx played in twenty campaigns but did most of his damage (503 home runs) in the thirteen seasons from 1929 to 1941. He took tremendous advantage of Shibe Park and Fenway Park, compiling home-road splits of 31/27 in 1932, 31/17 in 1933, and 35/15 in 1938. His 235 road home runs are a more accurate measure of his muscles than the 299 that he hit in friendly ballparks. Even with his enormous home-field advantage, Foxx was no match for Aaron, who outpaced him with 533 home runs across fourteen seasons and pulled away with nine more productive campaigns. Although The Beast's 58 home runs in 1932 dwarfed Aaron's 47 in 1971, his road totals are far less impressive, and the nine-homer difference in their pinnacle seasons ultimately had little impact on the final tally, which Aaron won by a margin of 221 home runs.

Ralph Kiner took enormous advantage of Kiner's Korner at Forbes Field, with peak years of 51 home runs in 1947 and 54 in 1949, featuring home-road splits of 28/23 and 29/25. Overall, he collected 369 home runs in a career that lasted ten seasons. But this pales in comparison to Aaron, who never topped 47 home runs in a season, but who could choose from eight different ten-season spans in which he hit 370 or more home runs, topped off with a total of 386 round-trippers from 1962 to 1971. Thus, we may ask, why should Kiner-esque totals of 54 or 51 home runs be considered such a big deal when Aaron was so quick to make up the difference, and more?

Johnny Mize, Hank Greenberg, and Hack Wilson entered the 50-homer club with performances that were boosted significantly by accommodating home parks: Mize clobbered 51 home runs in 1947, with 29 at the short-cornered Polo Grounds and a personal-best 22 on the road; Greenberg chased Ruth with 58 home runs in 1938, smashing a record 39 at cozy Briggs Stadium in Detroit and a career-high 19 on the road; and Hack Wilson hit 56 home runs in 1930, with 33 leaving the friendly confines of Wrigley Field and 23 on the road, by far his top total.[9] Their career-best road totals would have represented good seasons for Aaron, but nothing out of the ordinary. The fact that Aaron repeatedly outperformed Foxx, Kiner, Mize, Greenberg, and Wilson on the road reveals that he was truly a greater power threat than these 50-homer legends ever were, and it destroys the common wisdom that Aaron needed unusual longevity and a late boost from a friendly home park to compensate for a lack of transcendent brilliance.

As a side note, the great exception among the early 50-homer club members was the lone non-Hall of Famer, Roger Maris, another home run record-setter who became a victim of taunts and under-appreciation. Unlike the other eight, he alone managed to hit more home runs on the road than at home in his biggest season, 1961 (30/31). He also did it in his second-best season, 1960 (13/26), the summer *before* expansion, as well as by a wide margin across his injury-shortened career (122/153). The two-time Most Valuable Player was never a candidate to set any lifetime marks, but he was by no means a one-year wonder, just as he was not simply a home-park phenom. Unbeknownst to many except those reading this article, Maris still holds the all-time record for most home runs hit during consecutive pennant-winning seasons: 182.

KING OF THE ROAD

Aaron retired as the all-time leader in home runs hit on the road. Recognizing the importance of park-neutral performance, Bill James combined Aaron's road home run totals from consecutive seasons into two halves of a single road "season," creating a relentless career-long road trip in which the slugger produced an outstanding rookie campaign with 25 home runs, highs of 52, 46, and 42 home runs during the Milwaukee years, and highs of 39, 38, and 35 during the Atlanta years, even while never being able to enjoy the advantages of home cooking, lengthy stays, or friendly fans. Although James's method is artificial (requiring repetition of the first and last single seasons) it illustrates the main point: canceling out the disparate influences of Aaron's home parks, the road totals indicate a more natural career arc, with a true peak at age 28 in 1962 and with no notable spike at age 37 in 1971. The chart below recreates the James experiment and fills out some of Aaron's amazingly productive road statistics (Table 3).

In this light, it may be more meaningful to remember Aaron for the 52 home runs that he hit on the road at age 28 than for the 47 he actually hit while playing his home games in Atlanta at age 37. The only better consecutive-season home run performances on the road were by Ruth (1927–28) and Maris (1960–61), with 57 each; Ruth again (1926–27) with 56; Mathews (1953–54) with 54; and Jim Gentile (1961–62) with 53.[11] Matching Aaron's high of 52 were Ruth (1920–21) and Mike Schmidt (1979-80). Next came Mays with his twin peaks of 50, Ruth (1928–29) with 50; Gehrig (1930–31) with 49, Ruth yet again (1921–22 and 1929–30) with two instances of 48, and Joe DiMaggio (1936–37) with 48 in his rookie and sophomore road trips. Meanwhile, some very big names, including six players who hit 50 home runs in normal seasons, are missing from this company. While George Foster hit 47 road home runs in 1976–77, edging Aaron's second-best effort (46) from 1957–58, Kiner topped out at 45 in 1949–50; Foxx at 44 in 1932–33; Mize at 37 in 1947–48; Wilson at 37 in 1929–30; and Greenberg at 36 in 1938-39.

Road totals indicate that Hammerin' Hank Aaron, with his peak totals of 52 in 1962–63 and 46 in 1957–58, was genuinely more productive on a seasonal scale than these legends were.

For career-long comparisons, the same consecutive-season road home run chart can be compiled for Mays, Mantle, and others. Remarkably, both Aaron and Mays averaged one home run every 17 at bats on the road, so here Aaron's longevity took the prize.[12] Mays also had a slower start, caused by time away during the the Korean War. If Aaron, not Mays, had lost most of two prime years to military service, then Mays might have been the second man to reach 700 home runs.[13] Once back, Mays quickly reached a peak of 50 road home runs in 1954–55, fell back to the low 30s for a spell, then surged to 50 again in 1964–65. Aaron, meanwhile, reached a loftier pinnacle (52), won 17 of their head-to-head races, enjoyed more 30+ home run seasons, and did not fade as quickly. Memories of Aaron sneaking up on Mays in pursuit of various offensive milestones in the early 1970s helped

Table 3. Consecutive-Season Road Numbers Combined into Single-Season Approximations

Age	AARON	G	AB	R	H	TB	HR	Total	RBI	Avg.	Slug.
20	[1954	61	253	42	78	138	12	12	51	.308	.545]
20	1954–55	137	572	96	170	293	25	37	99	.297	.512
21	1955–56	154	633	101	206	341	24	61	100	.325	.539
22	1956–57	151	625	110	219	390	37	98	135	.350	.624
23	1957–58	150	633	127	214	399	46	144	138	.338	.630
24	1958–59	152	651	120	223	403	39	183	121	.343	.619
25	1959–60	151	636	109	204	377	38	221	125	.321	.593
26	1960–61	154	623	110	197	352	34	255	121	.316	.565
27	1961–62	157	622	121	211	395	42	297	140	.339	.635
28	1962–63	160	635	128	212	416	52	349	145	.334	.655
29	1963–64	156	634	115	208	359	38	387	120	.328	.566
30	1964–65	147	584	101	183	299	26	413	97	.313	.512
31	1965–66	150	588	111	172	316	36	449	111	.293	.537
32	1966–67	156	626	111	173	328	39	488	117	.276	.524
33	1967–68	157	629	94	170	303	28	516	92	.270	.482
34	1968–69	151	593	94	168	314	35	551	93	.283	.530
35	1969–70	148	545	103	167	316	38	589	105	.306	.580
36	1970–71	149	516	95	163	289	31	620	97	.316	.560
37	1971–72	138	480	78	142	257	31	651	81	.296	.535
38	1972–73	122	412	75	116	228	31	682	79	.282	.553
39	1973–74	114	359	61	94	189	25	707	71	.262	.526
40	1974–75	126	422	46	104	173	17	724	66	.246	.410
41	1975–76	114	384	32	93	143	12	736	46	.242	.372
42	[1976	45	137	8	31	48	4	740	10	.226	.350]
Totals:	23 years	3300	12,792	2188	3918	7066	740	–	2360	.306	.552

lock in the notion that Aaron's success came from a strong late push. Make note, however, that when their road home run performances are synchronized by age, Mays was never ahead of Aaron's pace (Table 4).

Switch-hitting Mickey Mantle was park-proof, wielding enough power to propel the ball out of any arena in any direction. Yankee Stadium's "Death Valley" in left-center may have cost him a home run or two per year, but most of his at bats took aim at right field, where there was a short porch. Away from Yankee Stadium, Mantle hit 185 home runs batting lefty and only 85 righty, but with rates of one home run per 15 at bats each way.[14] Compared to Aaron, Mantle had seven fewer combined road seasons with 30+ home runs, peaked with "only" 47 home runs (1960–61), had his last great season at age 29, and finished with a road total of 540 home runs—200 behind a road warrior who never set foot in Atlanta. Whereas Mantle started ahead of Aaron's pace by making his debut at 19, Aaron's closure of the gap was relentless. He pulled ahead of Mantle during their epic age-28 seasons (52 vs. 47) and passed him for good at age 30 (Mays finally passed Mantle when they were both 34).

Other famous sluggers, including Gehrig, Foxx, Banks, Killebrew, McCovey, Jackson, and Schmidt, were never able to match Aaron's pace, early or late. Mel Ott started fast as a teenager but was not the same level of threat on the road. Both Joe DiMaggio and Ted Williams went ahead at early ages, but already by 1940 Joe was falling behind the pace Aaron would set (further proof of Aaron's amazing start).[15] Ted lost his lead when he gave up his 1943 season to military service.[16] Even if Joe and Ted had remained in the lineup during the war years, matching Aaron's combined road home run totals at the same ages would have been a very tall order. Either way, they eventually would have fallen short of both Ruth and Aaron.

Aaron's greatest challengers are actually Ruth and Mathews. Ruth began his career as a pitcher before converting to being a full-time power hitter, and thus in our game of age-synchronized longball, Aaron will have already hit more than 500 home runs before Ruth catches *him* at age 33. The Babe will pull as many as 45 road home runs ahead, but then fall half-a-dozen short after his retirement.

Mathews took the opposite approach, getting off to the fastest start of the century and holding off Aaron's assault until their age-31 seasons. Aaron's good friend and Milwaukee teammate paced his league in road home runs (in actual seasons) four times, with a high

Table 4. Comparing Aaron, Mays, and Mantle: Consecutive-Season Home Runs, by Age

Aaron / Mays Age	Aaron Road HR Total	Mays Consecutive Seasons	Mays Road HR / Seasons	Mays Road HR Total	Mantle Age	Mantle Consecutive Seasons	Mantle Road HR / Seasons	Mantle Road HR Total
20	12	1951	7	7	19	1951	6	6
20	37	1951–52	9	16	19	1951–52	18	24
21	61	1952–53	2	18	20	1952–53	25	49
22	98	1953–54	21	39	21	1953–54	26	75
23	144	1954–55	50	89	22	1954–55	31	106
24	183	1955–56	45	134	23	1955–56	43	149
25	221	1956–57	34	168	24	1956–57	45	194
26	255	1957–58	31	199	25	1957–58	41	235
27	297	1958–59	31	230	26	1958–59	34	269
28	349	1959–60	35	265	27	1959–60	30	299
29	387	1960–61	36	301	28	1960–61	47	346
30	413	1961–62	40	341	29	1961–62	44	390
31	449	1962–63	39	380	30	1962–63	21	411
32	488	1963–64	40	420	31	1963–64	26	437
33	516	1964–65	50	470	32	1964–65	29	466
34	551	1965–66	49	519	33	1965–66	22	488
35	589	1966–67	30	549	34	1966–67	24	512
36	620	1967–68	20	569	35	1967–68	20	532
37	651	1968–69	17	586	36	1968	8	540
38	682	1969–70	19	605				
39	707	1970–71	22	627				
40	724	1971–72	14	641				
41	736	1972–73	7	648				
42	740	1973	2	650				

of 30 in 1953, but tailed off during the pitching-dominated Sixties. In some ways the third baseman's consecutive-season road performance is more impressive than Mantle's. Canceling out eight seasons in which they compiled equal home run totals, Mathews still had seasons of 54, 42, 40 and 33 to compare to Mantle's 47, 31, 30, and 26, and he ended up with 10 home runs to spare, although Mantle edged him slightly on power rates (Table 5).

WHO WERE THE GREATEST HOME RUN HITTERS?

It would seem perfectly easy to state outright that Babe Ruth was the greatest slugger in baseball history, based on his eye-popping home-run hitting feats at home, on the road, during his peak, and across his career. Some may argue that the racially segregated competition that Ruth faced, and the less challenging conditions under which he played, argue against his top standing. While it seems plausible that paunchy, libertine Ruth, transported through time, might have kept pace with Williams, Musial, and DiMaggio during the 1940s if he could hit at night, it becomes even harder for many to picture him competing at the same level against Mays, Mantle, and Aaron in subsequent decades, facing fresh-armed relief specialists after coast-to-coast travel. Others may dismiss these doubts. No one is dismissing The Babe's abilities in his own time, but it is no less reasonable to question how his numbers would hold up under the greater competitive pressures of later eras than it is to insist on their eternally unchallengeable superiority.

Here one must also consider Josh Gibson (1911–47), whose plaque in Cooperstown asserts that he "hit almost 800 home runs in [Negro] league and independent baseball." Even if this could be documented, the moundsmen he faced across those endless summers ranged in quality from certified immortals to local volunteers. Given that Gibson was hitting titanic home runs at Yankee Stadium by age 19 but died of a stroke at age 35, one must accept that even a player of his conspicuous talent could have spent no more than 17 seasons in the retroactively integrated major leagues. As history has shown, it is difficult enough to average 35 home runs per year across twenty years in order to reach 700, as Ruth and Aaron did; the argument that Gibson, a catcher by trade, would have maintained the even higher rate necessary to reach the same plateau in seventeen seasons (17 seasons × 42 home runs = 714 total) enters the realm of hypotheticals and wishful thinking.

Table 5. Comparing Aaron, Ruth, and Mathews: Consecutive-Season Home Runs, by Age

Aaron / Ruth Age	Aaron Road HR Total	Ruth Consecutive Seasons	Ruth Road HR / Seasons	Ruth Road HR Total	Mathews Age	Mathews Consecutive Seasons	Mathews Road HR/ Seasons	Mathews Road HR Total
20	12	1914–15	3	3	20	1952	14	14
20	37	1915–16	6	9	20	1952–53	44	58
21	61	1916–17	4	13	21	1953–54	54	112
22	98	1917–18	12	25	22	1954–55	45	157
23	144	1918–19	31	56	23	1955–56	43	200
24	183	1919–20	45	101	24	1956–57	41	241
25	221	1920–21	52	153	25	1957–58	33	274
26	255	1921–22	48	201	26	1958–59	40	314
27	297	1922–23	43	244	27	1959–60	42	356
28	349	1923–24	44	288	28	1960–61	34	390
29	387	1924–25	36	324	29	1961–62	29	419
30	413	1925–26	38	362	30	1962–63	23	442
31	449	1926–27	56	418	31	1963–64	25	467
32	488	1927–28	57	475	32	1964–65	28	495
33	516	1928–29	50	525	33	1965–66	23	518
34	551	1929–30	48	573	34	1966–67	18	536
35	589	1930–31	45	618	35	1967–68	12	548
36	620	1931–32	44	662	36	1968	2	550
37	651	1932–33	34	696				
38	682	1933–34	21	717				
39	707	1934–35	13	730				
40	724	1935	4	734				
41	736							
42	740							

Many exclude Barry Bonds from consideration because they believe his natural skills fell short. From 1986 to 1998, over the course of 1,898 games, Bonds tallied 411 home runs, establishing firmly (through age 34) that he had the ability to hit as many as 46 home runs in a season while leading his league only once and averaging 32 per season. Aaron, reaching age 34 in the "Year of the Pitcher," already had hit 510 home runs while pacing his league four times and averaging 34 per season. To that point Bonds's home run ability looked superficially like that of Reggie Jackson or Willie McCovey, although in historical context it was more like that of Eddie Murray or Andre Dawson, who each likewise led in home runs once, albeit during an era that was far friendlier to pitchers. Then, in the seasons in which he turned 35, 36 and 37, Bonds showed a startling upswing in power: he smashed 34 home runs in only 355 at bats in 1999; reached a new career high with 49 in 480 at bats in 2000; and then more than doubled what had been his career home run percentage per plate appearance (5.4%) with 73 in only 476 at bats (11%) in 2001, the first of four straight MVP seasons. Understandably, it is widely suspected that Bonds's late-career power increase resulted from the use of performance-enhancing drugs. If so, his record belongs to a different category of evidence that is not directly comparable to Aaron's.

Henry Aaron was a supremely well-qualified candidate to break Ruth's career home run record from the day he reached the major leagues. He started fast at a very young age, upped his game as he realized the value of his power swing in the late Fifties, surged even higher at his physical peak around age 28, made the most of a golden opportunity in Atlanta, and worked hard to take care of himself as he aged.[17] To repeat the point, the "Launching Pad" did not transform Aaron into something he was not meant to be. Atlanta's thinner air merely gave him back the home runs that he had lost in Milwaukee—plus umpteen more spread over nine seasons there—so that he was able to speed past Ruth's record in April 1974 instead of in August 1974.

The fact that Aaron succeeded where all others had failed attests to his unique ability, adaptability, determination, and courage in the face of multiple death threats from racists. Although biased or uninformed members of the press and public during the early 1970s dismissed him as an unworthy interloper within Ruth's mythic realm, in truth they could easily have questioned the legitimacy of the legendary records of Ruth, Cy Young, Ty Cobb, and others that were set under conditions of competitive imbalance and social injustice. The standard Aaron set in 1974, although since broken, ranked among the most worthy and legitimate of all of baseball's major records.

CONCLUSION

No single season can define Henry Aaron's greatness as a home run hitter. The sustained dominance that he demonstrated as a home run hitter in neutral parks was second only to Babe Ruth's in the pre-steroid game, and it was unsurpassed during the integrated era in which he played. Ruth and Aaron were genuine 700+ home run talents, combining innate longevity, raw power, and peak ability like no one else. Mays and Williams came the closest to joining this rare company. Gibson passed from the earth far too early, and even the mighty Mantle could not keep pace. Neither could later stars like Albert Pujols, Ken Griffey Jr., and Jim Thome, not to mention the allegedly substance-enhanced sluggers of recent memory. Aaron thus emerges (again) as a true home run king: he was able to hit great quantities of home runs regardless of the ballpark, and he set a high bar for production that few could match in the short run, and none (save for Bonds) could match in the long run. His signature achievement was not one of workmanlike consistency, but rather an unbeatable combination of legendary staying power elevated by genuine and heretofore under-appreciated excellence. ■

Notes

1. In an article published under various headlines by numerous Associated Press newspapers on January 23, 2021, Paul Newberry wrote: "Aaron was numbingly consistent, which explains how he broke Ruth's record without ever hitting more than 47 homers in a season." Kevin Sweeney, "Remembering Hank Aaron: A Look at His Most Impressive Stats, Feats," *Sports Illustrated* (SI.com), January 22, 2021, wrote: "What allowed Aaron to surpass Babe Ruth was his longevity and consistency as much as his dominance. Aaron never hit more than 50 home runs in a single season and reached 45 just once, in 1971." In fact, Aaron hit 45 home runs in 1962 and 47 in 1971.
2. "While Henry Aaron never hit more than 47 home runs in one big-league season, the righthanded-hitting slugger rode remarkable consistency and career longevity to a place atop the all-time homer chart." "Daguerreotypes," (*The Sporting News*, 1990), 174.
3. "It was a marathon with Hank, it wasn't a sprint [...] He's in the pack but you think he'll never break out." Denzel Washington, quoted in *Home Run: My Life in Pictures* (Total Sports, 1999), v.
4. Richard Goldstein, "Hank Aaron, Home Run King Who Defied Racism, Dies at 86," *The New York Times*, January 22, 2021: "He won the National League's single-season home run title four times, though his highest total was only 47, in 1971."
5. All home run statistics are available online at Baseball-Reference.com; a handy printed source is *The Home Run Encyclopedia* (Society for American Baseball Research, 1996).
6. Eddie Collins, Bobby Wallace, Rickey Henderson, Pete Rose, Rick Dempsey, and Omar Vizquel all played in more seasons than Aaron did, yet they hit 714 home runs *combined*. After Aaron's 755, the next-best home run total in a 23-year career is Carl Yastrzemski's 452; and after

Aaron's 47, the next-best seasonal mark for a 23-year man is 44, also by Yaz (he hit 17 away from Fenway Park).

7. Quotations from Hank Aaron, with Lonnie Wheeler, *I Had a Hammer* (Harper Collins, 1991), 159. Eddie Mathews hit 211 home runs in Milwaukee versus 241 away, while Joe Adcock hit 104 there and 135 away. Thus, Aaron "lost" fewer home runs to County Stadium than they did.
8. Road statistics, by themselves, are somewhat biased in that the hitter has not had the opportunity, or the chore, of playing an equitable portion of games in his own home park. As an example, for the sake of fairness, we could convert Ted Williams's results at the seven road parks he visited into seven-eighths of his total and add back one-eighth of his home results, all multiplied by two, to recreate a full career of balanced competition: thus, $273 \times \frac{7}{8} = 239$ home runs on the road; $248 \times \frac{1}{8} = 31$ home runs at home; $239 + 31 = 270$ adjusted home runs; $270 \times 2 = 540$ career home runs.
9. Greenberg and Mize lost prime years to military service in World War II. Another factor that limited Greenberg's road totals is the fact that he never got to hit in Briggs/Tiger Stadium as a visitor. Foxx, for example, hit 9 home runs in 11 games in Detroit in 1932 and 7 more in 1937.
10. In Aaron's actual rookie season, he hit 12 home runs on the road but only one in Milwaukee. All 13 were hit either in tie games or with the Braves behind in the score.
11. Two of these historic combined seasons, as well as Mantle's top pairing, coincided at least partially with the American League's expansion in 1961. Aaron's top mark included the National League expansion year of 1962.
12. These statistics were calculated from road at-bat totals available online at Baseball-Reference.com.
13. According to Aaron's autobiography *Aaron* (Crowell, 1974), written with Furman Bisher, 64–65, he had been drafted and was due to report for duty in October 1954, but the season-ending broken ankle he suffered on September 5 (on a sliding triple that completed a 5-for-5 doubleheader) put him on the deferred list; thus he enjoyed an uninterrupted career.
14. In Yankee Stadium, Mantle hit 76 home runs (one every 19.51 at bats) righthanded, and 190 home runs (one every 13.12 at bats) lefthanded; thus, his switch-hitting effectively neutralized the impediment that DiMaggio faced there (one every 22.7 at bats).
15. Yankee Stadium's mercilessly lopsided blueprint held the brilliant centerfielder to 148 home runs in pinstripes, yet he was lethal with 213 home runs during his visits to other towns—fourth all-time when he retired, a mere 22 behind Foxx and 29 behind Gehrig, despite a much shorter career. Given back the three war years and situated in a normal home park, his superior rate per at bat would have put him second only to Ruth upon his early retirement, with about 500 career home runs.
16. On a road home runs-per-at-bat basis, Williams ranks immediately behind Ruth. Although Fenway Park nudged his .344 lifetime batting average up a few points, Williams hit 273 of his 521 home runs away from home (that is, 25 more homers in 68 fewer at bats). Alas, he missed so much playing time to his military service across two wars that his road numbers, impressive as they are, cannot begin to tell the whole story.
17. Craig Wright, *Pages from Baseball's Past*: "Aaron Becomes a Home Run Hitter" (online by subscription, February 8, 2021), reinforces Aaron's recollection that his surprising success on the "Home Run Derby" television show in December 1959 played a positive role.

Ball Four at 50 and the Legacy of Jim Bouton

Robert Elias and Peter Dreier

Amidst the current upsurge of social activism among professional athletes, it is worth recalling the enormous contribution of Jim Bouton, one of the most politically outspoken sports figures in American history. Among professional team sports, baseball may be the most conservative and tradition-bound, but throughout its history, rebels and mavericks have emerged to challenge the status quo in baseball and the wider society, none more so than Bouton. During his playing days, Bouton spoke out against the Vietnam War, South African apartheid, the exploitation of players by greedy owners, and the casual racism of the teams and his fellow players.[1] When his baseball career ended, he continued to use his celebrity as a platform against social injustice.

Bouton's baseball memoir, *Ball Four*—published in 1970—may be the most influential sports book ever written.[2] It was the only sports book to make the New York Public Library's 1996 list of *Books of the Century*.[3] *Time* magazine lists *Ball Four* as one of the 100 greatest non-fiction books of all time.[4] But the baseball establishment ignored the 50th anniversary of this revolutionary book. Even after the COVID-19-shortened 2020 season, neither the Hall of Fame nor Major League Baseball planned any celebration.

Bouton—who died in 2019 at age 80—wrote *Ball Four* after his best days as a hard-throwing All-Star pitcher with the New York Yankees were over and he was trying to make a comeback as a knuckleball pitcher. He wanted athletes to speak out for themselves, to refuse to conform, and to defy complacency. Following his own advice, he was an early supporter of anti-Vietnam War presidential candidate Eugene McCarthy in 1968 and he served as a Democratic Party convention delegate for anti-war presidential candidate George McGovern in 1972.[5]

In *Ball Four*, Bouton accused organized baseball of hypocrisy: portraying a squeaky clean image while ignoring burning social issues. Bouton condemned baseball's support for the Vietnam War. He attacked icons such as the Reverend Billy Graham, disputing his claim that communists had organized anti-war protests. While Baseball Commissioner Bowie Kuhn said he couldn't remember any players being ostracized for anti-war statements, Bouton recounted being repeatedly heckled for his anti-war views by players and fans: "They wanted to know if I was working for Ho Chi Minh."[6]

Ball Four—funny, honest, and well-written—revealed aspects of major league baseball that sportswriters and previous ballplayer memoirs had ignored. Bouton expressed his outrage at owners who exploited players and at players who showed disrespect for the game he loved. He didn't hold back naming names or describing the lives and antics of ballplayers both on and off the field. It portrayed laudable characters and accomplishments, but also aspects of players' heavy drinking, crass language and behavior, pep pills and drug use, conservative political views, questionable baseball smarts, anti-intellectualism, womanizing, voyeurism, and extramarital affairs. It described boys being boys: human, fun-loving, vulnerable, and sometimes immature. That is, ballplayers were normal young men, with some special skills, but otherwise not necessarily idealistic heroes, as they had been portrayed by most sports reporters. Exposing what had always been under wraps generated a firestorm of protest from players, management, and sportswriters.[7]

Ball Four is ostensibly a diary of Bouton's 1969 season as a pitcher with the lowly Seattle Pilots and Houston Astros, but the most memorable and controversial parts of the book deal with his years with the Yankees. Decades before baseball was rocked by scandal over PEDs, Bouton disclosed players' widespread use of amphetamines (aka "greenies."). One of the most controversial parts of the book was his revelation that his Yankees teammate Mickey Mantle, whom sportswriters viewed as baseball's golden boy, was an alcoholic who often blasted towering home runs while nursing a hangover. As Bouton told *Fresh Air* host Terry Gross during a 1986 radio interview, his portrayal of Mantle "wasn't really even so much as a put-down of Mickey Mantle as it was a story of what a great athlete he was."[8]

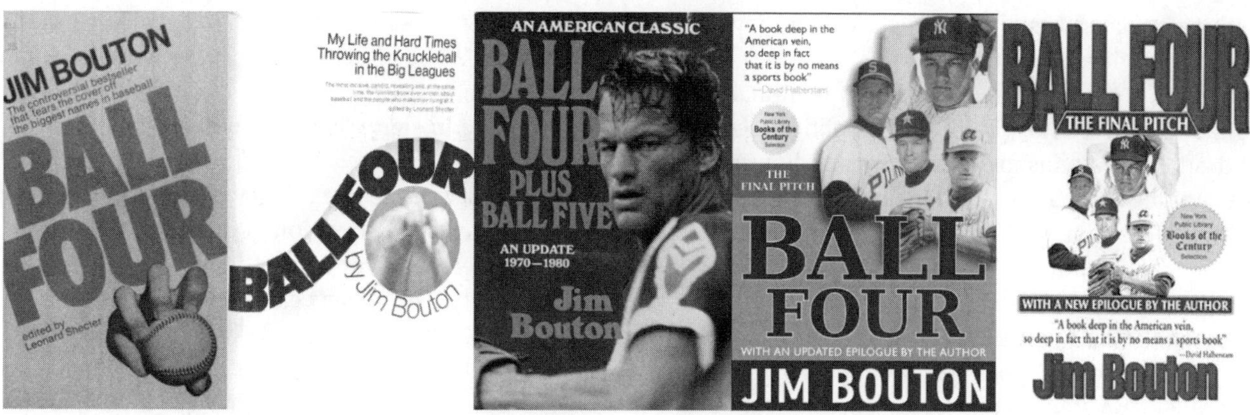

Since the book's original publication in 1970, Ball Four has been updated, expanded, reprinted, and republished numerous times.

Bouton acknowledged with candor that he was a participant, not just an onlooker, in these activities. And he described his clashes with his coaches and team executives, over salary disputes and his desire to use his knuckleball as his main pitch, as well as his outspoken views about politics. "Baseball, football—they've always felt the need to be patriotic," Bouton observed, "to be on the side of America and might, supporting wars no matter what, and so going against that conservative bent, to have a break in their ranks: This was a little too much for them."[9]

In the past half-century since *Ball Four*'s publication, many athletes and writers have sought to outdo each other with "tell-all" books highlighting tales of drugs and sex among pro athletes, but they lack Bouton's skills as a sociological observer and political renegade.[10] Bouton was not above recounting juvenile hijinks among himself and fellow players, but he reserved most of his outrage for major league baseball's, and America's, corporate and political establishment.

Even before he gained notoriety for *Ball Four*, Bouton was not the typical ballplayer. In his free time, he painted watercolors and made costume jewelry. He and his first wife adopted a Korean mixed-race child at a time when few couples did so. Bouton not only complained about his own salary, he was also a "clubhouse lawyer" and stood up for fellow players if management cheated them. In the book, Bouton claimed that he "wanted to nail those guys [management] because they stole money from the players."[11] By illuminating his own salary battles with the Yankees and their dirty tricks in dealing with him and other players, Bouton revealed baseball's unfair labor conditions.

As a white professional athlete in the late '50s and 1960s, he was unusually curious about the world around him and the burgeoning movements for social change. In the book, Bouton described a visit he and fellow ballplayer Gary Bell made to the University of California campus in Berkeley. They:

> ...walked around and listened to speeches—Arab kids arguing about the Arab-Israeli war, Black Panthers talking about Huey Newton, and the usual little old ladies in tennis shoes talking about God. Compared with the way everybody was dressed Gary and I must have looked like a couple of narcs. So some of these people look odd, but...anybody who goes through life thinking only of himself with the kinds of things that are going on in this country...well, he's the odd one. Gary and I are really the crazy ones...We're concerned about getting the Oakland Athletics out...about making money in real estate, and about ourselves and our families. These kids, though, are genuinely concerned about...Vietnam, poor people, black people...and they're trying to change them. What are Gary and I doing besides watching?...I wanted to tell everybody, Look, I'm with you, baby. I understand. Underneath my haircut I really understand that you're doing the right thing.'[12]

By today's standards, the book is quite tame. But at the time, it was shocking. As Mitchell Nathanson explains in his biography, *Bouton: The Life of a Baseball Original*,[13] Bouton's fellow ball players were outraged that he had broken the code by revealing stories from the locker rooms and hotel rooms. Many fans were upset by Bouton's revelations about the private lives of their favorite players. Bouton was excoriated by baseball officials, including Commissioner Kuhn, who called it "detrimental to baseball" and tried to force Bouton to sign a statement saying that the book was a total fiction. Bouton was attacked by sportswriters, who viewed their job as protecting the integrity of the game and the private lives of the players whom they relied on for interviews and stories.

Through extensive interviews with Bouton, as well as his family, friends, ballplayers, political activists, and others, Nathanson shows why and how Bouton was unique among the thousands of pro athletes who came before him. Today, we are less shocked when athletes speak out about social and political issues. The Trump era triggered an upsurge of activism and outrage among pro athletes, led by players like NFL quarterback Colin Kaepernick, MLB relief pitcher Sean Doolittle, NBA star LeBron James, soccer great Megan Rapinoe, tennis star Naomi Osaka, and many others. Some have been successful at raising consciousness and engendering debate while being shut out of their sports or dropped from teams—like Kaepernick and the NFL's Chris Kluwe—while others have maintained their status as stars. James raised millions of dollars to ensure voting rights leading up to the November 2020 election. Players on championship NFL, NBA, and MLB teams, as well as the World Cup-winning women's soccer team, refused invitations to celebrate their victories with Trump at the White House. Pro athletes responded to the murder of George Floyd and the police shooting in Kenosha, Wisconsin, of Jacob Blake. NBA, WNBA, and MLB teams refused to play scheduled games to protest the Blake shooting.

In his time, Bouton was not alone in his views, but the many other celebrated athletes who shared his beliefs kept them to themselves. The handful of exceptions included basketball stars Bill Russell and Elgin Baylor, boxer Muhammed Ali, tennis great Arthur Ashe, baseball star Roberto Clemente, and Olympic track stars John Carlos and Tommie Smith. But Bouton was rare in two respects. He was white and, except for a few spectacular years with the Yankees, he was not a major star.

Ball Four revolutionized sports writing, forever changing how journalists cover sports and how fans think about their favorite teams and players. The book's critics focused on how it assaulted the sanctity of the locker room. But for MLB owners, Bouton's real threat was challenging their economic power and, more broadly, America's unequal economic system and the undue influence of big corporations. Bouton loved baseball, but not the baseball establishment which, he believed, took advantage of powerless, unorganized, and under-educated athletes. In a clubhouse discussion one day when Bouton was still with the Yankees, his teammates claimed a fair minimum salary should range between $7,000 and $12,000. Bouton was scolded when he proposed $25,000, but he pointed out that: "...everyone in this room has a PhD in hitting or pitching. We're in the top 600 in the world at what we do. In an industry that makes millions of dollars, and we have to sign whatever contract they give us? That's insane."[14]

Playing before the ascendancy of the Major League Baseball Players Association, Bouton revealed that major leaguers led lives with little financial or professional security. The owners cared about nothing except their profits. They kept salaries indecently low, and traded or demoted even the most loyal players. At the time, under major league contract terms, ballplayers were little more than indentured servants, with no ability to negotiate with their team owners for better salaries, benefits, or working conditions. Salary negotiations were a farce, and most players couldn't make a living on their baseball pay, despite generating millions in profits for owners.[15] Except for the superstars, ballplayers led a vagabond, insecure existence. By disclosing these conditions, Bouton thought fellow ballplayers would appreciate him blowing the whistle. Instead, they complained about him violating their privacy and tarnishing their reputations.

By the late 1960s, however, the Major League Baseball Players Association (MLBPA) was beginning its assault on their peonage. In 1968, two years after Marvin Miller joined the union as executive director, the MLBPA negotiated the first-ever collective-bargaining agreement in professional sports. Minimum salaries increased from $6,000 to $10,000. Two years later, the MLBPA established players' rights to binding arbitration over salaries and grievances. Most importantly, Bouton helped overturn the renewal clause that prevented players from offering their services to the highest bidder. In 1970, with union support, outfielder Curt Flood filed a lawsuit against Major League Baseball for trading him without his consent, which he claimed violated federal antitrust laws. "Marvin Miller called me up," Bouton recalled, "and said, 'We'd like to have you put *Ball Four* in testimony against the owners.'" The union had been accumulating "stories about ballplayers being taken advantage of by the owners." Miller claimed that *Ball Four* "played a significant role in the removal of baseball's reserve clause."[16]

In 1972, the US Supreme Court ruled against Flood, but in 1975, Miller persuaded pitchers Andy Messersmith and Dave McNally to play that season without a contract, and then file a grievance arbitration. The arbitrator ruled in their favor, paving the way to free agency, which allows players to choose which team they want to work for, veto proposed trades, and bargain for the best contract. By then Bouton was out of the majors, but it was part of his legacy. While Bouton's book became a bestseller, he paid dearly in baseball, temporarily blacklisted from playing and excluded from ballparks such as Yankee Stadium.[17]

Born in Newark, New Jersey, in 1939, Bouton attracted attention as a pitcher after moving to the Chicago suburbs in his teens. He studied painting briefly at the Art Institute of Chicago, attended Western Michigan University for a year, and signed a contract with the New York Yankees in 1958. After three years in the minor leagues, he made the Yankees roster in 1962. In 36 appearances, including 16 starts, he went 7–7 with a 3.99 ERA, and got a World Series ring when the Yankees beat the San Francisco Giants in the Fall Classic.

Bouton's agitations for fair treatment by management began years before the idea of writing a book began to flicker. After earning the MLB minimum ($7,000 according to *Ball Four*, though other sources list the minimum at $5,000) as a rookie, Bouton asked for a raise. He was offered a tiny bump, if he "made the team." Bouton was incredulous: "What do you mean if I make the team?" he asked Yankees executive Dan Topping. "I was with the team the whole year; why wouldn't I make it? Why would you even want to plant that kind of doubt in the mind of a rookie pitcher?"[18]

Resorting to the usual ploy, Topping reminded Bouton that he'd be making more money in October since the Yankees always made the World Series. Bouton said: "Fine, I'll sign a contract that guarantees me $10,000 more at the end of the season if we don't win the pennant." Instead, Topping offered the same contract, regardless whether Bouton made the team, and Bouton again refused. Yankees General Manager Roy Hamey called Bouton, yelling that he'd be making the biggest mistake of his life if he didn't sign. Bouton hung up on him. Topping tried again, and they settled for a bigger but still meager raise.[19]

In 1963, a six-month hitch in the Army kept Bouton out of the rotation until mid-May, but he nevertheless had a sensational season, going 21–7 with a 2.53 ERA plus 10 relief appearances. He emerged as one of baseball's top young pitchers and appeared in that season's All-Star Game. The Los Angeles Dodgers beat the Yankees in the World Series by winning four straight games. Bouton pitched superbly in game three, giving up only four hits and one run in seven innings, but he was bested by Dodger hurler Don Drysdale, who threw a three-hit shutout.

After that season, Bouton claimed he deserved a much bigger raise, but again the Yankees stonewalled. Bouton asked the Yankees to double his salary to $21,000. GM Ralph Houk refused, offering $18,500 instead. Bouton told *The New York Times*, "Right now I wouldn't even say we were in the same neighborhood." Houk threatened to reduce his salary by $100 each day he held out and report to spring training camp. With few alternatives, Bouton signed for $18,500.[20] He might not have even gotten that had he not broken the taboo against discussing one's salary with teammates and the press. He told the angry Houk that he talked to reporters to "let them know I'm being reasonable" in his salary requests. Many writers began to take his side.

Bouton repeated his pitching success in 1964, finishing 18–13 with a 3.02 ERA. He led the league in starts and won two World Series games. But besides his salary demands, Bouton began speaking out on social issues, and his teammates and Yankees management began regarding him as a flake. They found him too intelligent and outspoken for his own good, an outside agitator disturbing the status quo. He typically sat at the back of the team bus, reading! He was considered a free thinker, "which in those days was one step away from being a Communist, to conservative sports minds," observed sportswriter Ron Kaplan.[21]

The Yankees tolerated this until Bouton suddenly became a marginal performer in 1965. Probably from overuse the previous two years, Bouton began having arm problems and slipped to 4–15 with a 4.82 ERA as the Yankees dropped to sixth place. His ERA bounced back in 1966 to 2.69, but poor run support held his won-loss record to 3–8.

Bouton and his liberal opinions had become expendable. After opening the 1967 season with the Yankees, the club demoted him to their Syracuse farm team, where he posted a 3.36 ERA but only a 2–8 record.[22] He made it back to the majors in August, pitching much better, and made the Yankees roster again the next year.

His tenure with the Yankees was already in jeopardy when the South African Non-Racial Olympic Committee (SAROC) approached him in early 1968 to sign a petition protesting the ban on non-white athletes on that country's team, scheduled to play in the Olympic Games in Mexico City. In a country that was 80% black, the team was 100% white. Bouton became friendly with SANROC's executive secretary—South African anti-apartheid activist Dennis Brutus—who Bouton called "the greatest man I ever met."[23]

"We need fellow athletes to stand up for us and change this injustice," Bouton argued. Signing the petition, he thought, was a "no brainer."[24] Bouton believed

NATIONAL BASEBALL HALL OF FAME LIBRARY, COOPERSTOWN, NY

After his 1962 rookie year, and years before he ever considered writing a book, Bouton made waves by asking for better contract terms from the New York Yankees. (The Yankees did not accede.)

his would be one of hundreds of signatures from major leaguers, but only a few, including his teammate Ruben Amaro, signed. The poor response appalled Bouton. A planned press conference was cancelled, but the two ballplayers traveled to Mexico City anyway, only to be rebuffed by the Olympic Committee. "They knew all about the discrimination against the black South African athletes," Bouton observed, "and they simply didn't care. They were a bunch of pompous racists. It was sickening."[25] He wrote about the issue and his ordeal for *Sport* magazine later that year.[26]

The Yankees sold Bouton mid-season to the expansion Seattle Pilots, a team that wouldn't begin play until 1969. Bouton finished out the 1968 season with the Triple-A Seattle Angels, teaching himself how to throw a knuckleball because he had lost the velocity on his fast ball.

During his time with the Yankees, Bouton had taken notes. Bouton had befriended sportswriter Leonard Shecter, who encouraged him to keep it up while playing for the Pilots (and later, the Astros).[27] When the Pilots played in New York, Bouton would visit Shecter's apartment and the two men would look over Bouton's notes, which he wrote on envelopes, toilet paper, hotel stationery, and airplane airsick bags. (Bouton's notes are now housed at the Library of Congress). These notes and sessions ultimately produced *Ball Four*.

Shecter was Bouton's collaborator and co-author, not his ghost-writer. Bouton was busy trying to make his baseball comeback, but, as Nathanson notes, he was already glimpsing the possibility of a second career as a writer and journalist. Overall, Bouton pitched in 80 games that season, almost all in relief. He had reason to believe he'd resurrected his career.

In 1969, Bouton supported students protesting the war and signed anti-war petitions. He spoke against the Vietnam War at a rally in New York's Central Park. Eager to participate and recruit other athletes, Bouton observed: "What I'm doing now, with the Moratorium group, is no major concerted effort. I'm just feeling some players out. But it is not like Jim Bouton is trying to rouse guys. A lot of them feel the same way I do, about the war and about other types of involvement. And there are many who want to express these feelings." He added, "We're always being used for telling kids to stay in school, to brush their teeth. Why can't we tell them how we feel about things like the Vietnam War? And athletes do have influence."[28]

Bouton was also bothered by his teammates' racism and the institutional racism of the teams and the leagues. He was repulsed by the segregation in spring training (mostly held in Florida) and during the season in Southern cities. He was angered watching Emmett Ashford—who in 1966 became the first black major league umpire—being repeatedly ridiculed by his white colleagues. More than a decade after Jackie Robinson broke baseball's color line in 1947, Bouton witnessed his teammates subject Elston Howard, the Yankees' first black player, to endless humiliations.[29]

A handful of baseball players did use their celebrity to express their political views. For example, following Martin Luther King's assassination in April 1968, Pittsburgh Pirates stars Roberto Clemente and Maury Wills urged their teammates to refuse to play on Opening Day and the following day, when America would be watching or listening to King's funeral. At a team meeting, the players unanimously endorsed the idea and persuaded the Houston Astros players, whom they were scheduled to play, to join them. Players on other teams followed their lead. Commissioner William Eckert, his back against the wall, reluctantly moved all Opening Day games to April 10. But such rebellions were rare, especially among white players.

Bouton was part of Houston's starting rotation through May, making his last start on May 24. *Ball Four* came out in June 1970. Bouton struggled to regain his place in the rotation, but the backlash against the book didn't help.

A few ballplayers defended Bouton's book. Cy Young Award winner Mike Marshall said, "I thought it was a celebration. I thought it was funny, and made us look far better than we were. It made us look human, and vulnerable, and struggling, all the things we were."

But most players didn't see it that way. They viewed Bouton as a "rat," revealing their foibles, weaknesses, and indiscretions. Bouton wasn't the very first to write a candid diary, but he may as well have been. He was following in the footsteps of another pitcher-turned-writer, Jim Brosnan, who published *The Long Season* in 1960.[30] Chronicling his experience of splitting the 1959 season between the St. Louis Cardinals and the Cincinnati Reds, Brosnan avoided the usual, sanitized portrayal, addressing some issues normally confined to the clubhouse. Although former major leaguer and sports broadcaster Joe Garagiola called the strait-laced Brosnan a "kooky beatnik,"[31] *The Long Season* offered relatively tame revelations. While Brosnan broke ground and began lifting the veil, Bouton's book was more irreverent and forthright, and engendered a stronger backlash.

When Bouton faced the Cincinnati Reds, Pete Rose shouted: "Fuck you, Shakespeare."[32] In three successive anti-Bouton articles, *New York Daily News* sportswriter Dick Young portrayed Bouton as a "social leper" and a "commie in baseball stirrups."[33] To him, Bouton had committed the cardinal sin: he tarnished baseball icon Mickey Mantle, by suggesting that maybe it wasn't Mantle's injuries that shortened his career but rather his drinking problem and skirt-chasing until all hours of the morning.[34]

The Houston Astros management forbade their radio and TV announcers from mentioning the book.[35] American League president Joe Cronin called *Ball Four* "unforgivable."

Commissioner Kuhn demanded a meeting with Bouton. Before that meeting, however, Bouton got a boost from a positive book review by *New York Times* sportswriter Robert Lipsyte: "Bouton should be given baseball's most valuable salesman of the year award. His anecdotes and insights are enlightening, hilarious, and most important, unavailable elsewhere. They breathe new life into a game choked by pontificating statisticians, image-conscious officials, and scared ballplayers."[37]

Not all fans turned against Bouton. On the day of the meeting with Kuhn, two college freshmen, Steve Bergen and Richard Feuer, appeared outside Kuhn's office, protesting with placards reading: "Jim Bouton is a Real Hero," "No Punishment for Exposing the Truth," and "Kuhn: Stop Repression and Harassment."[38]

Like other young antiwar activists and students of the time, they viewed Kuhn as an example of the establishment trying to shut up their generation. According to Bergen: "...[Dick] Young's comments smacked of the same authoritarian putdown of kids growing up in the '60s. Bouton was a hero for being willing to tell the truth about an aspect of society... the whole '60s movement was about questioning authority."[39]

Players union executive director Marvin Miller, union attorney Richard Moss, and Shecter joined Bouton at the meeting with Kuhn. The commissioner claimed that Bouton was undermining baseball, but Bouton responded: "You're wrong... People will be more interested in baseball, not less... People are turned off by the phony goody-goody image." Kuhn said Bouton owed "it to the game because it gave you what you have," but Bouton protested: "I always gave baseball everything I had. Besides, baseball didn't give me anything. I earned it."[40]

Kuhn ordered Bouton to release a statement saying he falsified or exaggerated his stories, but Bouton refused. When Kuhn told him to regard the meeting as a warning, Miller shot back: "A warning against what...against writing about baseball?... You can't subject someone to future penalties on such vague criteria."[41] Kuhn told Bouton that he was going to issue a statement threatening players with punishment for any further writing like *Ball Four*. He told Bouton that he should remain silent. Again, Bouton refused. The controversy helped turn the book into a bestseller.[42]

New York Congressman Richard Ottinger claimed the Commissioner's actions were "part of a growing mood of repression in the country" that indicated "an intolerable arrogance [by] the official baseball establishment." Ottinger threatened to approach the House Judiciary Committee about Kuhn's denial of individual rights.[43]

Meanwhile, Bouton's pitching was not improving. After being demoted to the Oklahoma City minor league team, he had two more bad starts in Triple A and decided to retire from playing, but the far-reaching effects of *Ball Four* were just beginning.

Bouton's book helped change sports writing. While the old-timers condemned Bouton, younger people who read *Ball Four* became sportswriters *because* of the book. A new wave of writers abandoned the deification of ballplayers and instead looked for unconventional angles. In *The New Yorker*, Roger Angell described the book as "a rare view of a highly complex public profession seen from the innermost inside, along with an even more rewarding inside view of an ironic and courageous mind." According to Stephen Jay Gould, a Harvard paleontologist and baseball writer, *Ball Four* inaugurated a "post-modern Boutonian revolution," revealing that "heroes were not always what they were thought to be, questioning the masculine ideal in the professional game, and encouraging the reader to look beyond the media's interpretations." George Foster of the *Boston Globe* called the book a "revolutionary manifesto." *New York Times* writer David Halberstam observed that Bouton "has written...

a book deep in the American vein, so deep in fact that it is by no means a sports book..... [A] comparable insider's book about, say, the Congress of the United States, the Ford Motor Company, or the Joint Chiefs of Staff would be equally welcome."

As MLB historian John Thorn later observed, *Ball Four* was "a political work, and a milestone in the generational divide that characterized the 1960s. It is the product of a widespread rebellion against both authority and received wisdom."[44] According to writer Nathan Rabin: "The times were changing outside the ballpark, but the major-league mindset seemed stuck somewhere in the mid-'50s. The old guard still ruled with crew cuts, knee-jerk patriotism, reactionary politics, and a near-religious belief in... maintaining the status quo."[45]

MLB officials pressured, if not required, players to wear their hair short to counter the hippies of the period. According to Bouton: "If the choice for a pinch hitter or a relief pitcher was between a long-haired guy and a short-haired guy, the [latter] would get into the game." But, Bouton explained, in the broader society, everything was being called into question. "All the assumptions...rules...ways of doing things, [the era] tossed them all up in the air, and forced people to take another look....I don't think it occurred to me that, 'Gee, all these other people are kicking up a fuss, maybe I should write a book that does the same thing.' [B]ut you are a part of your environment."

According to sociologist Elizabeth O'Connell, *Ball Four* may have advanced the cause of women by challenging America's masculine ideal. Previous sports books were hagiographies, "reinforcing Horatio Alger myths of self-made men who through dedication and determination were able to rise above their circumstances and become American heroes." Instead, *Ball Four* portrays many players as adolescent adults who never matured: what psychologists call the "Peter Pan Syndrome." "It's an emasculating text, presenting players as boys who never grew up," according to O'Connell. "By opening the clubhouse doors to the public and allowing the reader to see the reality of ballplayers' lives, Bouton contradicted the concept of the male athletic body symbolizing strength of character."[46]

With his baseball career apparently ended in 1970, Bouton became a television sportscaster in New York for WABC and then WCBS. Not surprisingly, he was also regarded as a maverick in his new profession. He refused to waste time reading the scores of games during his newscasts, recognizing that fans could get those in the newspaper. Rather than catering to the high-profile professional teams, he focused instead on lower level and lesser known sports, and didn't just report but also participated, such as in roller derby matches or rodeo events. He urged people to play sports rather than merely watch them.

In 1971, Bouton published a second book, *I'm Glad You Didn't Take It Personally*, mostly describing the reaction to *Ball Four*.[47] Bouton made no apologies and expressed his view that sports should be part of ongoing consciousness-raising: "[A]thletes and entertainers have a special obligation to take a stand on issues of the day. In our profession, we tend to be tranquillizers for a whole nation. We contribute to a false feeling of well-being [when instead] we have a responsibility to let people know that, even though we are playing games, we are also aware of problems outside the ball fields."

Bouton kept pitching in various adult leagues in New Jersey in the early 1970s, while continuing his journalism career. Then, in 1973, he got a phone call from actor Elliott Gould, with whom he had become friends after they met at an anti-war rally in New York and played pick-up basketball games together. Gould told him that he'd persuaded director Robert Altman to give Bouton the part in the film *The Long Goodbye* that Stacy Keach had been slated to play before he got sick. Bouton got respectful reviews for his acting debut. (The film was also noteworthy for an uncredited appearance by an unknown body-builder named Arnold Schwarzenegger). In 1976, Bouton also starred in a TV sitcom called *Ball Four*, playing a ballplayer named "Jim Barton" who was also a writer with a preoccupation with his teammates' personal lives. The show was canceled after only five episodes.

But Bouton gave up his lucrative television career and budding acting career to pursue a baseball comeback. "I decided that my day to day happiness is more important," he explained at the time.[48] In 1975 he joined the Portland Mavericks in the independent Northwest League, earning $400 a month, the same as his teammates. He went 4–1 with a 2.20 ERA. The Knoxville Sox in the Southern League signed Bouton in 1977, but things didn't go well. His pitching improved when he moved to Durango in the Mexican League, and he finished the year back with the Portland Mavericks, compiling a 5–1 record. That success brought him back to the Southern League in 1978, this time with the Savannah Braves. He pitched well, going 11–9 with a 2.82 ERA. Bouton pitched so well that the Atlanta Braves called him up later in the 1978 season, and at age 38, his comeback was complete, eight years after his initial retirement. He started five games and

was 1–3 with a 4.97 ERA. Bouton could have returned with Atlanta in 1979, but he retired instead, having nothing left to prove to himself. In ten major league seasons he was 62–63 with a 3.57 ERA. He continued pitching competitively into his fifties.

When Bouton pitched for Portland in 1977, players were chewing tobacco and getting sick. One of his teammates, Rob Nelson, observed: "Too bad there isn't something that looks like tobacco but tastes good like gum." Bouton responded: "Hey, that's a great idea. Shredded gum in a pouch, call it Big League Chew and sell it to every ballplayer in America."

Bouton didn't think any more about it, but after returning home at the end of the season, he remembered it and called up Nelson. Bouton put in the start-up money, contacted an attorney, and sold the idea to the Wrigley Chewing Gum Company. A big hit, the company has sold more than 800 million pouches since 1980 and it won a health and safety award from *Collegiate Baseball Magazine* for creating the first healthful alternative to chewing tobacco, no doubt sparing many ballplayers from mouth cancer. Bouton also coauthored a baseball murder mystery, *Strike Zone*.[49] He would go on to update *Ball Four* three times, publishing new editions in 1981, 1990, and 2001, each time adding to his story.

Over the years, Bouton tried several times to make peace with Mickey Mantle, but not until Bouton sent a condolence note after Mantle's son Billy died of cancer in 1994 did Mantle contact him. The two former teammates reconciled not long before Mantle's death in 1995.[50] For almost 30 years, the Yankees barred Bouton from participating in their annual Old Timers games. But in 1998, the Yankees ended their boycott, finally inviting Bouton back for that celebration. Bouton pitched one inning, enjoying an emotional reunion with fans and some old teammates.

But Bouton wasn't finished protesting. In 2000, a Cuban boy, Elian Gonzalez, and his mother shipwrecked trying to enter the US from Cuba, and she drowned. The Clinton administration took custody of Gonzalez, intending to return him to his father, who wanted his son back with him in Cuba. But right-wing Cubans in Miami—a powerful political force—wanted him kept in the US as a rebuke of Fidel Castro. Several Cuban ballplayers launched a one-day walkout to oppose the return, and Commissioner Bud Selig backed the move. Having previously rejected political activism by ballplayers, MLB was suddenly claiming its support was a matter of "social responsibility."

Bouton called out MLB's hypocrisy. MLB had consistently refused to speak out against injustices such as

In 1978, eight years after his initial retirement from major league baseball, Bouton made a comeback with the Atlanta Braves.

NATIONAL BASEBALL HALL OF FAME LIBRARY, COOPERSTOWN, NY

the Vietnam War and South African apartheid and was now pretending to take a stand. The players were "once again exhibiting typically sheeplike behavior," Bouton observed. "Cuban players are not acting from political courage but from fear of reprisal from their own community."[51]

In 2001, Bouton learned that an old ballpark in Pittsfield, near his home in western Massachusetts, would be abandoned in favor of a new field, to be built in the city's downtown. Wahconah Park wasn't just any ballfield. It was (and still is) one of the oldest minor league ballparks in the US and among the few remaining wooden grandstand fields. Although the ballpark was built in 1919, ballgames had been played on that spot as far back as 1892. Bouton decided to step in to save the stadium, and renovate it not with public money but by selling shares to ensure ownership by local fans of the team. The plan generated strong public support, but local media, politicians, and business leaders wanted taxpayers to fund a new ballpark on the site of an abandoned General Electric factory that the federal government had determined was a toxic waste dump.

Pursuing his campaign, Bouton discovered that in the previous 15 years, $16 billion of taxpayer money had been spent on new stadiums, replacing more than 100 older, beloved ballparks, "because baseball's powers-that-be can get away with it. They have a monopoly, granted by the federal government, and they use it to bludgeon local governments to bid against each other for the right to teams."

"These owners are capitalists who don't want capitalism," Bouton explained. "When sports owners don't have to use their own money to build stadiums and make enormous profits—when American taxpayers subsidize these wealthy owners—it's massive corporate welfare."[52]

To address not only his Wahconah Park experience but also these broader ballpark issues in the US, Bouton turned his extensive notes into a book, *Foul Ball: My Life and Hard Times Trying to Save An Old Ballpark*.[53] He had a contract with a publisher, PublicAffairs, and was ready to launch a 16-city tour to promote the book in 2002. Before publication, however, the publisher told Bouton he would have to delete his discussion of General Electric or the book would be dead. Shocked at the publisher's complicity, Bouton instead created his own publishing company, Bulldog Press, and released the book on his own in 2003 at a considerable cost to himself. Lyons Press published an updated version in 2005.

Local political and business leaders in Pittsfield undermined Bouton's restoration and public ownership plan. The town ultimately lost minor league baseball, but he still fought to keep the game alive at the old ballpark. From baseball historian John Thorn, Bouton learned that Pittsfield had the additional attraction of having been one of the oldest places where baseball was known to have been played in the US, dating back to 1791. In response, Bouton helped create the Vintage Base Ball Federation, bringing nineteenth century baseball rules, uniforms, and atmosphere to cities and towns across the nation. Bouton arranged a vintage baseball game at Wahconah Park on July 3, 2004, when a record crowd of 5,000 fans watched a contest between the Pittsfield Hillies and the Hartford Senators. ESPN Classic telecast the game live for over four hours, billing it as "America's Pastime: Vintage Baseball Live." The network commentators included baseball historians John Thorn and David Pietrusza, *Bull Durham* actor Tim Robbins, as well as Bouton and former major league pitcher Bill "Spaceman" Lee. Bouton and Lee each pitched an inning in the game.

Despite his setback in Pittsfield, Bouton remained active on the stadium issue. After the Montreal Expos became the Washington Nationals in 2005, the new owners persuaded Washington city officials to subsidize construction of a new stadium, Nationals Park. Bouton was outraged, claiming it was bad enough that a profitable ball club would rip off the public but it was even more appalling in an economically troubled city: "How anyone could walk through the public schools of Washington, DC, and then say that paying for a new professional baseball stadium should be that city's priority, amazes me."[54]

In 2004 Bouton appeared in Brooklyn to support the Prospect Heights Action Coalition in its efforts to block another taxpayer-funded stadium proposal that would destroy historic buildings.[55] With the support of New York City's political establishment, including Mayor Michael Bloomberg, billionaire developer Bruce Ratner's company Forest City Ratner sought to bulldoze homes and small businesses belonging to hundreds of families to make way for what eventually became the Atlantic Yards project, which included Barclays Center, an indoor arena that is now the home to the NBA's Nets, the New York Islanders of the National Hockey League, and the New York Liberty of the Women's National Basketball Association.

Calling the proposal's tax abatement provision "corporate welfare," Bouton decried the same "fuzzy financing" and "secret meetings" he had encountered in Pittsfield. "You're not alone, this is an issue nationwide," Bouton told the crowd. "If this stadium gets built, 20 years from now you'll hear: 'These [celebrity architect] Frank Gehry stadiums are out of date. So we're going to be leaving Brooklyn for another place with a [post-9/11 World Trade Center architect, Daniel] Libeskind stadium.' Don't let it happen."

The same year, after the US launched an illegal, preemptive attack on Iraq, Bouton spoke out against the war. "I opposed it," recalled Bouton, "because although the US had the means to be successful militarily...[w]e didn't have nearly enough understanding of that country's language and culture, just like in Vietnam. In the US, our rocket science is way ahead of our social science."[56]

Handicapped by a stroke in 2012, Bouton announced in 2017 that he had cerebral amyloid angiopathy, a brain disease. He died two years later at age 80 at his home in western Massachusetts.

Bouton did not set out to be a literary or political revolutionary. As he recalled, he grew up as a "conservative kid"[57] and viewed himself as an "old fashioned guy." He ended *Ball Four* observing: "You spend a good piece of your life gripping a baseball and in the end it turns out that it was the other way around all the time."[58] ■

Notes

1. Karl E.H. Seigfried, "Jim Bouton, Pray for Us," *The Wild Hunt*, August 24, 2019 https://wildhunt.org/2019/08/column-jim-bouton-pray-for-us.html.
2. Jim Bouton, with Leonard Shecter, *Ball Four: My Life and Hard Times Throwing the Knuckleball in the Big Leagues* (New York: The World Publishing, 1970).
3. New York Public Library, *Books of the Century*, https://www.nypl.org/voices/printpublications/books-of-the-century.
4. *Time Magazine*, "All-Time Greatest Non-Fiction Books" https://www.goodreads.com/list/show/12719.Time_Magazine_s_All_TIME_100_Best_Non_Fiction_Books. In contrast, in 2001 the Baseball Reliquary, a Pasadena-based non-profit organization that Bouton called "the people's hall of fame," inducted him into its Shrine of the Eternals and in 2009 hosted a celebration of *Ball Four*'s 40-year anniversary that

included Bouton and his former Seattle Pilots teammates Greg Goossen and Tommy Davis.
5. William Ryczek, *Baseball on the Brink: The Crisis of 1968* (Jefferson, NC: McFarland, 2017), 95.
6. John Thorn, "Jim Bouton Interviewed," *Our Game*, July 16, 2019, https://ourgame.mlblogs.com/jim-bouton-interviewed-2d0930e2ecb9.
7. Joan Mellen, "Jim Bouton," in *Cult Baseball Players—The Greats, the Flakes, the Weird, and the Wonderful*, ed. Danny Peary (New York: Simon & Schuster, 1990), 160.
8. Terry Gross, "Jim Bouton Destroys Illusions About Baseball," *Fresh Air*, December 8, 1986. https://freshairarchive.org/segments/jim-bouton-destroys-illusions-about-baseball.
9. Stan Grossfeld, "Jim Bouton Still as Opinionated as Ever," *Boston Globe*, July 18 2014, https://www.bostonglobe.com/sports/2014/07/17/catching-with-ever-opinionated-jim-bouton/ynmwU7CYTMS2qveyeSh3KJ/story.html.
10. Anthony D. Bush, "Knuckleball on Paper: Jim Bouton's Effect on Sports Autobiographies" Presented at Society of American Baseball Research Seymour Medal Conference, Cleveland. April 17, 1999, www.gpc.peachnet.edu/~dbush/bouton.htm.
11. Mellen, "Jim Bouton," 161.
12. Jim Bouton, *Ball Four: The Final Pitch* (New York: Turner Publishing, 2014), 147–48.
13. Mitchell Nathanson, *Bouton: The Life of a Baseball Original* (Lincoln: University of Nebraska Press, 2020).
14. Mellen, "Jim Bouton," 158.
15. Even star players didn't earn enough during the season to make ends meet. In his Hall of Fame Induction speech, Nolan Ryan mentioned working in a gas station during the winter. Jim Palmer got an $11,000 World Series bonus after the Orioles won the 1966 World Series, and still had to take a job in a department store selling suits to cover "groceries, hot water, and electricity." Loren Kantor, "When Ballplayers Had Offseason Jobs," Medium, August 13, 2020. https://medium.com/buzzer-beater/whenballplayers-had-offseason-jobs-66bba31cecb2.
16. Marvin Miller, *A Whole Different Ballgame* (Chicago: Ivan Dee Publishers, 2004), 85.
17. Matt Schudel, "Jim Bouton, Baseball Pitcher Whose 'Ball Four' Gave Irreverent Peak Inside the Game, Dies at 80," *Washington Post*, July 10, 2019. https://www.washingtonpost.com/local/obituaries/jim-bouton-baseball-pitcher-whose-ball-four-gave-irreverent-peek-inside-the-game-dies-at-80/2019/07/10/f73acf52-b4e5-11e7-9e58-e6288544af98_story.html.
18. John Florio and Ouisie Shapiro, *One Nation Under Baseball: How the 1960s Collided with the National Pastime.* (Lincoln, NE: University of Nebraska Press, 2017), 38.
19. Florio and Shapiro, *One Nation Under Baseball*, 39.
20. Ryczek, *Baseball on the Brink*, 101–02.
21. Ron Kaplan, "The Legacy of *Ball Four*," Huffington Post, May 25, 2011, https://www.huffingtonpost.com/ron-kaplan/the-legacy-of-ball-four_b_709682.html.
22. Jim Bouton, "Returning to the Minors," *Sport*, April 1968: 30.
23. Dave Zirin, "A Q&A With the Late, Great Jim Bouton," *The Nation*, July 12, 2019, https://www.thenation.com/article/jim-bouton.
24. Zirin, "A Q&A With the Late, Great Jim Bouton."
25. Steve Treder, "THT Interview: Jim Bouton," *The Hardball Times*, January 10, 2006, https://www.fangraphs.com/tht/the-tht-interview-jim-bouton.
26. Jim Bouton, "A Mission in Mexico," *Sport.* August 1969: 35.
27. Leonard Shecter, "Jim Bouton—Everything In Its Place," *Sport*, March 1964: 71–73.
28. All-Star pitcher Tom Seaver was another white ballplayer who spoke out against the Vietnam war. See Kelly Candaele and Peter Dreier, "Tom Seaver's Major League Protest," *The Nation*, September 11, 2020. https://www.thenation.com/article/society/tom-seaver-vietnamprotest.
29. David Keyser, "Baseball Ball Four," *Harvard Crimson*, October 13, 1970, http://www.thecrimson.com/article/1970/10/13/baseball-ball-four-world-publishing-company.
30. Jim Brosnan, *The Long Season* (New York: Harper & Row, 1960).
31. Steve Chawkins, "Jim Brosnan Dies at 84; Relief Pitcher Wrote Inside Look at Baseball," *Los Angeles Times*, July 6, 2014, https://www.latimes.com/local/obituaries/la-me-jimbrosnan-20140707-story.html.
32. Stan Hochman, "Life Writes Bouton a New Ending to 'Ball Four'," *Philadelphia Daily News,* December 7, 2020. Retrieved May 12, 2020.
33. Dick Young, "Young Ideas" *Daily News*, May 28, 1970: C26; Ryczek, *Baseball on the Brink*, 181.
34. Florio and Shapiro, *One Nation Under Baseball*, 183.
35. Jim Bouton, *I'm Glad You Didn't Take It Personally* (New York: William Morrow, 1971), 137.
36. John Florio and Ouisie Shapiro, *One Nation Under Baseball: How t he 1960s Collided with the National Pastime* (Lincoln: University of Nebraska Press, 2017), 183.
37. Robert Lipsyte, "Sports of the Times," *The New York Times*, June 22, 1970: 67.
38. Florio and Shapiro, *One Nation Under Baseball*, 186–87.
39. Florio and Shapiro, *One Nation Under Baseball*, 187.
40. Florio and Shapiro, *One Nation Under Baseball*, 188.
41. Florio and Shapiro, *One Nation Under Baseball*, 189.
42. Ryczek, *Baseball on the Brink*, 178–79.
43. Florio and Shapiro, *One Nation Under Baseball*, 190.
44. John Thorn, "Jim Bouton: An Improvisational Life," *Our Game.* December 16, 2016, https://ourgame.mlblogs.com/jim-bouton-an-improvisational-life-5237aa5d438a.
45. Nathan Rabin, "Jim Bouton's *Ball Four*," April 17, 2009, https://www.avclub.com/jimbouton-s-ball-four-1798216529.
46. Elizabeth O'Connell, "Now Batting, Peter Pan: Jim Bouton's *Ball Four* and Baseball's Boyish Culture," in *The Cooperstown Symposium on Baseball and American Culture, 2007–2008*, ed. William Simons (Jefferson, NC: McFarland and Company, 2009), 61–78; see also: Ron Briley, *Class at Bat, Gender on Deck* and *Race in the Hole: A Line-Up of Essays on Twentieth Century Culture and America's Game* (Jefferson, NC: McFarland, 2003), 308.
47. Jim Bouton, with Leonard Shecter, *I'm Glad You Didn't Take It Personally* (New York: William Morrow, 1971).
48. Paul Goldman, Peter Dreier, and Mimi Goldman, "Jim Bouton Follows His Dream," *In These Times*, September 28–October 4, 1977
49. Jim Bouton and Eliot Asinof, *Strike Zone* (New York: Viking, 1994).
50. Zirin, "A Q&A With the Late, Great Jim Bouton."
51. Miles Seligman, "The Boy-cotts of Summer," *Village Voice*, May 20, 2000, https://www.villagevoice.com/2000/05/02/sports-27.
52. Ted Miller, "Jim Bouton Still Brings It With Gusto from the Inside," *Seattle Post-Intelligencer*, June 30, 2006, https://www.seattlepi.com/sports/baseball/article/Jim-Bouton-stillbrings-it-with-gusto-from-the-1207789.php.
53. Jim Bouton, *Foul Ball: My Fight to Save An Old Ballpark.* (Great Barrington, MA: Bulldog Publishing, 2010).
54. Treder, "THT Interview: Jim Bouton."
55. Deborah Kolben, "Jim Bouton Cries 'Foul' Over Arena," *Brooklyn Paper*, January 10, 2004, https://www.brooklynpaper.com/jim-bouton-cries-foul-over-arena.
56. Treder, "THT Interview: Jim Bouton."
57. Florio and Shapiro, *One Nation Under Baseball*, 183.
58. Bouton, *Ball Four: The Final Pitch*, 397.

The Trials, Tribulations, and Challenges of Al Kaline

Francis Kinlaw

Although Al Kaline obviously deserved the many accolades he received as an exceptional athlete with admirable personal characteristics, misconceptions have long existed regarding the severity of challenges he faced in his youth and during his 22-year professional baseball career. This article will address a litany of circumstances that he encountered and explain how he overcame most of them. Before discussing specific instances, however, the causes of those misconceptions should be identified.

Viewing Kaline's career in retrospect, it may be observed that the stage for the troubling episodes that would occur later in his career was set in 1955 when, as a 20-year-old with a bothersome physical issue, he posted the highest batting average in the American League. As a result of that remarkable achievement, waves of compliments from baseball luminaries and scribes flowed forth and registered with people across the baseball spectrum. Those plaudits frequently included a comparison with Joe DiMaggio that would create unrealistic expectations of his potential. Immediate linkage with the legend of the Yankee Clipper, along with other premature declarations of greatness and minimization of facts that failed to fit into a storybook narrative, would adversely affect evaluations of Kaline's performance for at least a decade as he achieved stardom but failed to win another batting title or bring a pennant to Detroit.

Consider these statements regarding Kaline's talent and promise, all from respected sources, starting with the scout who signed him to a major-league contract:

- "He was the kind of prospect a scout sees in his dream." —*Tigers scout Ed Katalinas*[1]
- "He was the prospect that a scout creates in his mind and then prays that someone will come along to fit the pattern." —*Katalinas*[2]
- "Kaline, the slender but slick bonus baby from Baltimore, is the hottest item on the [Tigers'] squad...The way he is performing will make it practically impossible for (manager Fred) Hutchinson to keep him out of his outfield. Kaline has slapped out nine hits in 16 tries for a sparkling .563 average...He is the fastest man in camp. He is an excellent fielder. His throwing arm is strong. Despite his age, his baseball savvy is sound."
  —*Lyall Smith, sports editor of the* Detroit Free Press, *March 1954 during Kaline's first spring training with the Tigers*[3]
- "[Kaline] can run and he can throw. Now he is proving that...he can hit. He got his 100th hit of the [1954 season] before mid-August, and that's not bad for a youngster who one season ago was battling for his high school team in Baltimore. At 19 ...he looks fragile but then so does a scalpel."
  —*Smith in the* Free Press *describing the very young prospect to readers, many of whom had yet to see him play*[4]
- "He's going to be one of the great right-handed hitters of baseball, if he isn't that already."
  —*Ted Williams, 1955*[5]
- "Kaline is a graceful, right-handed swinger, who also is one of the best right fielders in the league. He is equipped with a fine arm, good speed, and has excellent judgment on the bases...He joined the Tigers, upon payment of a $30,000 bonus, directly after his graduation from high school. Two and a half years later, he has reached a salary bracket that might very well match that tidy bonus." —*Hy Goldberg, journalist and editor of* Who's Who in the Big Leagues[6]
- "Even in the major leagues, players are conscious that there are a few who are involved in a different game, whose skill level is unattainable to most others. Kaline was one of these."
  —*George Cantor,* Detroit Free Press[7]
- "At 19, [Kaline] was Detroit's regular right fielder and acclaimed the best glove man to field that spot

in Tiger history. At 20, he had led the American League in batting and was named the player of the year...With credentials like these, Sid Keener up in Cooperstown was already dusting off a cubicle in the Hall of Fame for the slender clouter...In style and ease of performance he is the closest approximation we have to the flawless rhythm of Joe DiMaggio on a baseball diamond."

—*Murray Olderman, sports cartoonist and writer*[8]

- "Comparisons with Joe DiMaggio...were inevitable. Both players were smooth and graceful. Both made the game look easy."

  —*Jim Hawkins,* Detroit Free Press[9]

- "[Kaline] played the game so smoothly, with such class that he was the closest thing to DiMaggio that I ever saw."

  —*Ted Williams, 1992*[10]

- "Kaline was probably one of the best of all time. He could do it all. I thought he was another Joe DiMaggio."

  —*Joe DeMaestri, former major-league infielder*[11]

- "In [the late 1950s], Kaline was as complete a player as Joe DiMaggio [had been]."

  —*Gus Zernial, former major-league outfielder and teammate of Kaline in 1958 and 1959*[12]

- "[Kaline]...had great instincts in the outfield. He was smooth and graceful."

  —*Ernie Harwell*[13]

Yearbooks published annually by the National Baseball Hall of Fame and Museum after Kaline's induction invariably praised the Tigers' star as "a model of consistency who got the job done with a minimum amount of fanfare."[14] The accuracy of that statement—along with the frequent use of descriptive adjectives such as "graceful" and "smooth" regarding his style of play—resulted in cursory examinations by media sources into the difficulties he faced throughout his playing career. Rarely was Kaline's chronic physical ailment described as clearly it was by journalists Daniel Okrent and Steve Wulf when they wrote that he "played with such grace that most Tigers fans never realized he also played in pain because of a bone condition that left him with what he called 'a constant toothache in my left foot.'"[15]

One prominent Detroit writer who initially misgauged Kaline's immense talent would later admit that the term "easy" should never have been associated with Kaline's performance. Joe Falls wrote in 1965:

> I've seen Kaline play almost every game he has played for the Detroit Tigers, and I didn't care too much for him in those early years. He was too good. Everything was too easy for him. He was making $30,000 before he could vote. He was a kid in a Cadillac. Nobody should have it that easy...But as the years wore on...I began to realize what I should have realized in the beginning—that he was not the greatest player in the world, that everything was not as easy as it looked. I finally realized that Kaline had to work for what he got out of life.[16]

Falls would repeat his contention when Kaline was elected to the Hall of Fame, writing, "Everyone said what a nice thing it was because Kaline always made the game look so easy. It was never easy for him."[17]

In 1980, author Art Hill concisely summarized the career of the Tigers' star by writing, "Kaline...was born a star; he made himself a superstar."[18] The baseball great did so by overcoming a variety of environmental, physical, and psychological challenges with a persistence often unappreciated by those who saw him play.

POVERTY AND HEALTH CONCERNS

Fate threw punches at Kaline long before he attained legendary status on Baltimore's sandlots and as a high school athlete, but a lack of devoted parents was not one of them. Nicholas and Naomi Kaline raised Al and his two older sisters in a row house in the working-class Westport section of Baltimore, about one mile from the current site of Oriole Park at Camden Yards.[19] Both parents consistently encouraged their son's love of baseball. The strong emotional support that Al received from his father in regard to his baseball development came naturally (his dad and his dad's five brothers had played semipro baseball in their younger days), but the family struggled financially. Nicholas Kaline earned a meager living as a broom maker, and Naomi scrubbed floors and worked in a factory that produced pills.[20] Jack Olsen of *Sports Illustrated* described the Kaline family as "poor, proud, and hungry" in a 1964 article.[21]

As his family contended with financial difficulties, Kaline himself had to deal with a troubling physical condition. At the age of eight, Kaline was diagnosed with osteomyelitis (a chronic bone disease) in his left foot. Doctors removed two inches of bone from the foot, but jagged scars and a permanent deformity unfortunately resulted.[22] Despite the procedure, two toes on his left foot remained extended and the young boy found it necessary to reduce persistent pain by shifting his weight to his toes or by running on the side of his foot.[23] Periodic treatments involving X-ray therapy were required to keep the disease in check.[24]

By the time Kaline signed his initial baseball contract with the Tigers in June 1953, the health of his parents had also become a concern. His mother's eyesight was failing and surgery would be required to save it,[25] while his father's condition would later be described as "never too healthy."[26] In 1955, Kaline would reveal to writer Hal Middlesworth that his dad "was not real well and neither is Mom."[27] When Kaline inked that first contract with Detroit, he used the money to pay off the mortgage on his parents' home and to pay for his mother's operation before proceeding to move on to the next phase of his life.[28]

"BONUS BABY" AMONG MEN

By signing with the Detroit club upon graduation from Southern High School, the 18-year-old began a journey into major league baseball that was available to only a select group of prospects. Tigers scout Ed Katalinas had dedicated himself to signing Kaline during his high school years in the face of competing expressions of interest from the Brooklyn Dodgers, St. Louis Cardinals, and Philadelphia Phillies.[29] After Katalinas convinced Tigers farm director John McHale and club president Walter O. "Spike" Briggs that Kaline would be worth the necessary financial cost, Briggs authorized a bonus payment of $15,000 as well as a $6,000 salary for the next two years.[30] While the terms of this agreement did provide Kaline with badly needed cash, a "Bonus Rule" adopted by major league baseball in 1952 to restrict bidding wars for amateur players would dictate the path of his development and progression in the short term.

The Bonus Rule stipulated that any prospect signed to a bonus of $4,000 or more was required to spend his first two years in professional baseball on a major league roster.[31] As promising as Kaline's future seemed to be, several key people within the Tigers' organization reserved judgment regarding his future as a big leaguer because bonus baby Frank House had failed to deliver positive results (to later signees, Bob Miller and Reno Bertoia, would also fail).[32] McHale would later admit that the Kaline matter was approached with a five-year plan in mind: "Under the bonus arrangement we knew that we had to keep him on the roster for two years. When that period was up he could be sent out [to the minors] without bothering with waivers. We thought that it would take at least two more seasons in the minors, probably with our Triple-A club in Buffalo, before he could possibly be ready for the majors."[33]

On the day of Kaline's signing, the Tigers were in the American League's cellar (nearly 30 games out of first-place) with a record of 15–43. The club's front office was receiving harsh criticism from fans for a failure to acquire talented players.[34] McHale would recall, "It was a tough time for us. We felt that we had to do something on the spectacular side to prove to our fans that we were hustling and trying hard to correct a bad situation."[35]

Kaline played sparingly in 1953 as he began the process of adapting to life in the company of older and more experienced players. The Tigers initially evaluated Kaline as a second baseman or shortstop until the organization's signing of infielder Reno Bertoia in late August of 1953 caused Kaline to be shifted to the outfield.[36] He was pleased to receive valuable guidance from manager Fred Hutchinson and advice from veteran players. A few years later he would say, "Nobody resented my getting all that money. In fact, the two guys I beat out for a job in 1954—Pat Mullin and Steve Souchock—were nicest to me."[37] He also gave credit to former teammate Johnny Pesky and third base coach Billy Hitchcock for helping him during the adjustment process.[38]

During spring training in 1954, Hutchinson confirmed that Kaline had made a good first impression and told reporters, "I've got to be shown that he can't play in the big leagues right away."[39] The manager did not offer assurances that Kaline would be an everyday player but, when expected starter Souchock suffered a broken wrist while playing in the Cuban League prior to spring training, Kaline's door of opportunity flew open.

Kaline played in 138 games in 1954 and posted a batting average of .276. Some criticism came his way for a lack of power: he homered only four times and drove in only 43 runs, and 114 of his 139 hits were singles. However, he distinguished himself in right field with solid overall fielding and by registering 16 assists with a strong and accurate arm.

He was adapting to life in the big leagues, and the stage was being set for stardom.

MISINTERPRETED DEMEANOR

Kaline was a very private man playing a very prominent role in a very public profession. Bucky Harris, who succeeded Hutchinson as the Tigers' manager prior to the 1955 season, described Kaline's personality as "pleasant and cooperative, but extremely reticent."[40] Lyall Smith of the *Detroit Free Press* wrote that he was "as hard to pump for a story as a deep well with a broken handle."[41] Such opinions were reflected on a broader basis in a poll published by *The Sporting News* early in 1954 when writers who had covered American League teams during the 1953 season identified the young Kaline as the "Least Talkative Tiger."[42] He was extremely uncomfortable with public speaking, avoiding it whenever possible.

Jack Olsen of *Sports Illustrated* would write in 1964, "Talking to Kaline is like making funeral arrangements."[43] Joe Falls of the *Detroit News* recalled that Kaline "was surly in (his) early years. He swung a sharp bat and spoke with a sharp tongue. If you had any questions, you approached him with apprehension."[44]

Others, such as the authors of an article in a 1959 publication by *Sport* magazine, sought to analyze the reason for Kaline's perceived persona: "An emotionless young man with green eyes and a sallow face, Kaline may suffer from the look he has. He looks like a brooder...He feels he should hit the ball every time he is up, and when he doesn't he is disappointed. People see the exterior of this disappointment, the kick at the water bucket, the grumbled answer to a question, the pout that is on his face."[45]

The reticence was transferred into the clubhouse. George Cantor, a long-time Detroit reporter and columnist, described Kaline as "a private man, one who remained well within himself. Friendly but always holding back some private corner...He had no speeches to make when the clubhouse doors were closed, no inspirational messages to impart. He led by the way he played."[46] Former Tigers infielder Jake Wood has spoken similarly, referring to his teammate as "the Silent Assassin" who "didn't say much, but displayed a fierce competiveness on the field."[47]

Despite a reluctance to share details about his life, Kaline generally maintained satisfactory relations with the press, and his status as a gentleman was never questioned.[48] As one of his sport's genuine stars, he lived up to another statement by a sportswriter who knew him well: "Kaline was special—but only in the field. Off the field, he was just another guy. A guy who couldn't be less impressed with himself."[49]

STARDOM BRINGS HIGH EXPECTATIONS

Highly motivated to excel in the major leagues while possessing a reserved personality, Kaline would quickly learn in 1955 that avoiding the limelight would be impossible. His three home runs against the Kansas City Athletics in the Tigers' sixth game of the season nearly matched his total of four round-trippers during the 1954 season and served notice that Kaline's efforts during the off-season to increase his strength had been successful. (He had also added 22 pounds to his previously slender frame.) By the end of April, he had recorded a 14-game hitting streak and posted a batting average of .429. Fans of the Tigers began to believe that he would avoid the fate of other young Detroit players—such as Dick Wakefield, Hoot Evers, and Johnny Groth—who had in recent years seemed primed to become stars only to have to settle for more ordinary status.[50]

NATIONAL BASEBALL HALL OF FAME LIBRARY, COOPERSTOWN, NY

In a poll by The Sporting News, *baseball writers pegged Al Kaline as the "Least Talkative Tiger."*

Kaline's onslaught continued into the summer. At the end of July he was leading the American League in batting average, hits, runs scored, runs batted in, and home runs. He did go hitless for a short time in mid-September, but he bounced out of that temporary slump on a weekend in Cleveland with six hits against a solid pitching combination of Bob Lemon, Mike Garcia, and Ray Narleski. One week later, he secured a unique place in baseball history by becoming (with a mark of .340) the youngest player to win an American League batting title.

For Kaline, however, the euphoria of the 1955 season created the high and sometimes unrealistic expectations mentioned previously in this article. In the years that followed, he would often repeat words he spoke to Olsen in 1964: "The worst thing that happened to me in the big leagues was the start that I had. [That] put the pressure on me."[51]

The burden felt by the new star can be understood by taking into account the opinions that have been cited, as well as the following:

- "He can't miss. He's got that extra-special look."
  —*Joe DiMaggio*[52]

- "He won't fall far short of Joe DiMaggio."
  —*Paul Richards, manager, Chicago White Sox and Baltimore Orioles*[53]
- "I will take Kaline over Mantle or any other young outfielder you can name. This kid is going down with the great ones of all time."
  —*Fred Hutchinson*[54]
- "I'm disappointed when he doesn't get a hit. He's got me spoiled."
  —*Bucky Harris, Kaline's second manager in the major leagues*[55]
- "He seems to have absorbed five years' experience in two. We move the ball around on him and we haven't found a spot yet that he can't get at."
  —*Casey Stengel, manager, New York Yankees*[56]

The pressures faced by the shy 20-year-old may be summarized by referring to an unrestrained comment that appeared in a widely-read 1956 publication: "Among an illustrious collection of Tiger batting kings—Ty Cobb, Harry Heilmann, Heinie Manush, Charlie Gehringer, and George Kell—Kaline in 1955 became the youngest Tiger to achieve the distinction, a scant one day younger than Cobb was when he won the first of his 12 titles. With all the years stretching out before him, something approaching Cobb's remarkable record is not beyond the realm of possibility."[57]

After capturing one batting title, the emerging Tigers star was already being compared to Ty Cobb! It is no wonder that Detroit's new hero might have, at times, considered his sudden rise in status to be unfortunate.

NATIONAL BASEBALL HALL OF FAME LIBRARY, COOPERSTOWN, NY

During his career, Kaline suffered from both chronic conditions (osteomyelitis, low blood pressure) and acute injuries (including fractures to his collarbone, cheekbone, and arm).

INJURIES

Kaline dealt with a long list of aches, pains, and serious injuries along his path to the Hall of Fame. His first significant injury occurred during the 1954 season when he pursued a fly ball into the right-field corner of Detroit's Briggs Stadium and collided with a wall that protruded into the playing field. The impact had two effects: a knee injury that caused him to be hospitalized for five days, and the ordered removal of seats by Tigers president "Spike" Briggs to prevent a subsequent injury to his organization's valuable asset.[58]

Two abscessed teeth were removed during spring training in 1956 and, during the regular season, he fought a virus and injured a shoulder. He was plagued in 1957 by a sore shoulder, a bad foot, and general exhaustion. His left cheekbone was fractured in mid-June of 1959 when, after hitting into an apparent double play, he was nailed in the face by Baltimore second baseman Billy Gardner's relay throw to first base.

In 1960, a combination of an injured left knee and low blood pressure caused Kaline's production to drop to its lowest point since 1954. (Medication was prescribed to address the latter issue.)

The most publicized and memorable injury of Kaline's career—one that reversed the Tigers' fortunes in a tight pennant race—occurred in Yankee Stadium on May 26, 1962, and was viewed by a national television audience. Kaline executed a tumbling, game-ending catch of an Elston Howard drive into right field with the Tigers clinging to a 2–1 lead. If the sensational catch had not been made, Hector Lopez of the Yanks (running from first base) would have almost certainly scored the tying run. The catch, however, came at an enormous cost, and a diagnosis of a fractured right collarbone led winning pitcher Hank Aguirre to lament that "we won the game and lost the season."[59] The player who had been leading the American League in RBIs and who had been tied for the home run lead the day before would remain out of action until late July.

In 1963, a knee injury suffered in late May continued to hinder Kaline throughout the season and likely curtailed his opportunity to record a second batting title. After contending with Boston's Carl Yastrzemski for the league's highest average, the pain in Kaline's knee worsened in the month of September, as he batted only .254 to end the season with a .312 average. The Red Sox star batted .326 during that month—and .321 overall—to capture the honor.

The effects of osteomyelitis in Kaline's left foot that had plagued him since childhood grew extremely bothersome in 1964 and 1965. His big toe was curled almost completely over the toe next to it, and by the end of the 1965 season—a year in which he also missed 18 games due to a pulled rib cartilage[60]—the resulting pain had intensified to such a degree that surgery was again required to reset bones in the foot.[61]

While avoiding misery from the effects of osteomyelitis had been beyond Kaline's control, he did bear responsibility for an impulsive act that caused a major injury during the tight 1967 American League pennant race. After striking out against Cleveland's Sam McDowell on June 27, Kaline slammed his bat into the bat rack in the Detroit dugout and fractured a finger. He missed the next 26 games and the Tigers went on to finish the season in a second-place tie with the Minnesota Twins, one game behind Boston. Kaline regretted his uncharacteristic display of emotion: "I wanted to do so much to help the ball club...I didn't do my job...I was very embarrassed about the whole thing afterwards."[62] He also termed his outburst "the dumbest thing I ever did."[63]

A disappointing blow of a different kind occurred in the Tigers' world championship year of 1968 when a pitch from the Oakland Athletics' Lew Krause broke a bone in Kaline's right arm on May 25, sidelining him for five weeks.

Age and an accumulation of past physical activity took a toll on Kaline as he entered the final stage of his playing career. This progressive development had been observed by writer Joe Falls as early as 1967 when he wrote that the Detroit star "will play when he is tired, but the inevitable happens. It affects his play. The plain fact is that Kaline is not a very strong player and he gets tired."[64]

Occasionally taking days off likely prevented serious injuries in the twilight years of Kaline's career, but nagging injuries continued to occur. A pulled muscle in his left leg hindered his performance in 1972, and a rib problem and other ailments kept him out of action for all but 91 games in 1973.

The physical pain in which Mickey Mantle played is frequently mentioned in sports literature, and the admirable wartime service of men such as Ted Williams and Bob Feller obviously affected their baseball records significantly. In the same vein, it should be noted that Kaline missed more than 500 games during his career—more than three full seasons—and that most of those absences occurred for physical reasons.[65]

UNSYMPATHETIC FANS AND WRITERS

The high expectations linked to Kaline's potential and the effects of his occasional injuries combined to produce an undesirable and perhaps unavoidable by-product: criticism of performance. The first indication of this phenomenon became apparent as early as 1956 when Kaline's statistics declined from "extraordinary" in 1955 to "well above average" in the following year. In the words of an article that appeared in *Sport* magazine, "People in Detroit expect him to become nothing less than the Tigers' greatest outfielder since Ty Cobb."[66]

This gap between what fans wanted to happen and the results that Kaline could deliver would be observed at other times during the next decade. Events during the 1964 season—when foot, ankle, and knee injuries forced Kaline to miss 17 games and appear only as a pinch hitter in eight other contests[67]—demonstrated how some Tigers fans were unable to accept Kaline's limitations. As frustration was fueled by their team's lack of success, boos were directed at an already disappointed player.[68]

Developments from the 1965 season that preceded Kaline's aforementioned foot surgery again provided evidence of a disconnect between athletic effort and public expectation. Due to an assortment of nagging injuries as well as persistent pain in his left foot, Kaline's batting average dropped to .281—still the highest among Detroit's players but his lowest mark in five seasons. Some people in and around the Motor City questioned Kaline's desire, but that group did not include a key executive in the Tigers' front office. General manager Jim Campbell stood steadfastly on the Kaline bandwagon, having proclaimed in 1964 that he had never seen the outfielder give less than everything he had.[69]

ANNOYING CONTROVERSIES

For a man who remained on playing fields and in the public eye for so many years, Kaline became engaged in few contentious situations. Two instances, however, attracted unwelcome attention from the Detroit press and temporarily affected his image.

The first situation originated as a routine salary negotiation after Kaline had posted a batting average of .314, hit 27 home runs, and driven in 128 runs in 1956. With a difference of only $3,000 existing between Kaline's requested salary of $30,000 and the Tigers' offer,[70] the bargaining process went awry in December of 1956 when Briggs (working under a new club management group headed by Fred Knorr) responded to a question at an advertising club's luncheon in downtown Detroit by stating, "Al thinks he's as good as Mickey Mantle and wants more money than Mantle. I

Kaline would spend his entire major league career with the Detroit Tigers, spanning 1953 through 1974.

don't agree with him, and he's not going to get it. After all, his batting average went down last year, and he didn't lead the American League in anything. We have offered Kaline a bigger raise than he got last year, and that's that."[71]

The discord was resolved on January 29, 1957, when newly promoted player personnel director McHale invited Kaline to meet while Briggs was in Daytona Beach, Florida. The deal was closed after a short conversation between McHale and Kaline and a routine telephone call to Briggs.[72]

Kaline reportedly received his desired salary of $30,000 but his popularity in working-class Michigan suffered a temporary setback.[73] Furthermore, the Detroit press displayed its critical side. Lee Greene of *Sport* magazine reported that when Kaline batted .295 in 1957, "'I-told-you-so' clippings began to turn up. People said that the kid wasn't using his great skills to proper advantage. Sympathetic phrases like 'pressing too much,' 'swinging too hard,' and 'too anxious' gave way to quotes such as 'spoiled by success,' 'less than a superstar,' and 'the personality of a squeezed lemon.'"[74]

The second controversy revolved around an investment of money rather than Kaline's acquisition of it. The seeds of this story were planted in that same winter of 1956–57 when Kaline and hockey legend Gordie Howe of the Detroit Red Wings accepted opportunities to join businessman Frank Carlin in an automobile parts design business called the Michigan Automotive Products Corporation—also known as Mapco. Kaline was officially the firm's vice president, but his primary role was to perform public relations functions. When the enterprise quickly proved to be successful, the trio of business associates formed a separate entity (the Howe-Kaline-Carlin Corporation) for the purpose of serving as a manufacturers' representative.[75]

This business arrangement was working fine until Carlin persuaded Kaline and Howe to invest in racehorses as a legal means of reducing their tax liability relating to profits generated from the automotive endeavor. A separate business venture (HKC Stables) was thus formed in the winter of 1959–60 to maintain horses that would race at a track in Toledo, Ohio.[76]

Accounts of Kaline's involvement in a sport linked closely to gambling were revealed in May of 1960, and the news was not received favorably by the baseball establishment or baseball fans. Kaline's initial comments were unapologetic: "Sure, I'm part owner of a string of horses. What's all the excitement about? I happen to like racing. I like horses. I go out to tracks quite a bit when we aren't playing ball because it relaxes me. For that matter, so do club owners, managers, coaches, everybody. I don't see what all the fuss is about."[77]

Within a short time, however, Kaline reconsidered his stance in the matter and sold his interest in HKC Stables to Carlin.[78] (Kaline's name had not appeared on HKC Stables' application to Michigan's Racing Commission, nor had he contributed financially.)[79] He offered a qualified apology for his brief entry into the world of horse racing, saying that he was "sorry I got everybody so shook up, but I've got nothing to be ashamed of. This was only an investment. But I think it is best for everybody that I drop out of the racing thing. After all, my life is baseball, and I don't want to embarrass anybody connected with the game."[80]

Headlines relating to the deal disappeared from the newspapers and the issue was formally resolved, but Kaline continued to hear from patrons in the bleachers of Briggs Stadium. He would later recall that "they even remembered the names of those horses until the end of the 1960 season!"[81]

MOVING RELUCTANTLY TO CENTER FIELD

Kaline patrolled right field for the Tigers almost exclusively from the time of his emergence as a big league star until a pitch by Bill Fischer of the Washington Senators struck and bruised the right arm of regular center fielder Harvey Kuenn on April 30, 1959. With Kuenn temporarily out of action, a decision was made to move Kaline to the middle of the outfield. Kaline performed so well in his new position that he (rather than Mickey Mantle) was selected in a poll of players, managers, and coaches as the starting center fielder in the first of two All-Star games played in 1959. When Kuenn (who had been installed in right field upon his return to the lineup) was traded to Cleveland in April 1960 for right fielder Rocky Colavito, Kaline remained in center for another season.

While Kaline had the talent to excel in center field and never rebelled against doing so, he made it clear on several occasions that he preferred right field. One statement, published in May 1967, succinctly expressed his feelings: "To me center field is a lot of work...right field is like driving a car. I guess it's because I've been doing it so long...I don't know whether it's the mental pressures of it, the fact that I have to do some work for the guys alongside me... I just don't enjoy it as much as right field."[82]

Three Detroit managers—Bill Norman, Jimmy Dykes, and Joe Gordon—had determined that Kaline's value to the club would be maximized by keeping him in center field, but that need was eliminated on December 7, 1960, with the acquisition of experienced center fielder Billy Bruton from the Milwaukee Braves. Kaline was elated that new manager Bob Scheffing would assign him to his former spot on the diamond in 1961.

THE FIRING OF BOB SCHEFFING

Kaline was also pleased that Scheffing had been chosen to manage the Tigers in 1961, and his admiration for his new skipper would increase in their time together. As the Detroit team challenged the Yankees for the 1961 American League pennant, Kaline observed that Scheffing was "a master of handling guys on the bench...You get down in the dumps when you're not playing, and Scheffing treats [everyone] perfectly."[83] Kaline also said that Scheffing was "a real man, liked by his players. He left you alone as long as you did your job. He was a father-type manager."[84]

Given these statements of praise, Kaline was naturally displeased and angry when Scheffing was fired (along with his entire coaching staff) on June 17, 1963, after the Tigers had lost seven consecutive games. Kaline directed kind words to Scheffing upon his departure, saying, "I really can't thank him enough for what he's done for me."[85]

Years later, Kaline continued to speak highly of a man he genuinely liked when he recalled that Scheffing "was the only guy who came to me and told me what he wanted me to do."[86]

ROCKY RELATIONSHIP WITH CHARLIE DRESSEN

Kaline's interactions with Scheffing's successor Charlie Dressen would not be nearly as cordial. Unlike Scheffing, who had proclaimed that he wouldn't trade Kaline for Mantle or Mays,[87] several of the new skipper's comments about his best player were more critical. For example, after managing Kaline for more than a full season, Dressen told reporters, "I've got to go on what I see. I have to see Kaline play some more."[88]

The personalities of the player and manager differed in fundamental ways, but open hostility was avoided by both men. There was, rather, an inconsistency in their relationship. Kaline became upset in 1964 when he was required to participate in early-morning workouts during spring training, but he was appreciative at season's end when Dressen suggested that more rest—such as sitting out second games of doubleheaders—would be provided in 1965.[89]

Kaline and several of his teammates experienced difficulty in dealing with a manager whose actions and attitudes could change in a heartbeat. Despite occasional conflicts, however, Kaline credited Dressen for having a solid knowledge of baseball and for his attention to the fine points of the game.[90]

The relationship was suddenly altered during spring training in 1965 when something much more important than Dressen's personal nature changed in a heartbeat: the condition of the manager's heart. After suffering a coronary blockage on March 7, the skipper returned to the dugout on May 31.[91] He resumed managerial duties the following year, but a second heart attack occurred on May 16, 1966.[92] Bob Swift, who had filled in for Dressen during the latter's absence in 1965, replaced his former boss—but only until he left the club for health reasons of his own in July 1966. Diagnosed soon thereafter with terminal lung cancer, Swift was succeeded by coach Frank Skaff for the remainder of the 1966 campaign.[93]

The erratic Dressen-Kaline saga thus concluded with a depressing series of events that placed an emotional toll on Kaline and his teammates.

TRADE RUMORS

Kaline gained an identity soon after his initial signing in 1953 as a significant person within the Detroit community. So, having made his home in the Detroit area and expressed a desire to remain there throughout his career,[94] he became concerned whenever credible speculation about trades included his name. At least six trade discussions are known to have taken place:

- In the winter following the 1956 season, Vice President Charles Comiskey of the White Sox offered a total of $250,000 in players and cash for Kaline, but the offer was refused by the Tigers' front office.[95]

- George Weiss (the general manager of the Yankees) asked Tigers GM John McHale during the 1958 World Series whether Kaline might be available in a trade. Within a few days, as word of the conversation spread, McHale admitted that the conversation had occurred and teased reporters about whom the Yankees might send to Detroit. He did not, however, state firmly that Kaline was unobtainable by other clubs.[96]
- Mickey Mantle and Whitey Ford pulled Kaline aside in 1959 and informed him that they had heard that the Yankees had offered Moose Skowron and a couple of minor leaguers to the Tigers in exchange for his services. However, any possibility of the rumored trade's consummation vanished on July 25 when Skowron's left wrist was fractured in a collision at first base with the Tigers' Coot Veal.[97]
- The Yankees again probed the Tigers' willingness to trade Kaline in 1964 with Roger Maris in the role of primary trade bait. The Bengals rebuffed this proposal, even after it was reported that a second player might be offered by the Bronx Bombers. Rumors had been flying around the baseball world for months that Dressen and some individuals in Detroit's front office might entertain a reasonable exchange involving Kaline, but owner John Fetzer made it known that he considered Kaline to be essential to Tigers pennant hopes in the years ahead.[98]
- During professional baseball's winter meetings of 1966, the Los Angeles Dodgers offered several top prospects to Tigers general manager Jim Campbell for Kaline. Campbell immediately declined this deal.[99]
- It was reported during that same off-season that Campbell had offered to send Kaline and pitcher Dave Wickersham to the Minnesota Twins for ace hurler Jim Kaat and outfielder Jimmie Hall.[100] Kaline realized that the Tigers needed to improve at several positions, but he resented the fact that conversations about the trade had begun a short time after he had been asked—and had agreed—to move back to center field (from his preferred position in right field) to benefit the Detroit team.[101] The Twins rejected Campbell's proposed swap.

RESENTMENT (OR JEALOUSY) BY TEAMMATES

Although Kaline's substantial value to the Tigers reduced his chances of being traded, his esteemed status within the organization also produced significant disparities between his annual salaries and those of other Detroit players. Even as they recognized Kaline's superiority on the field, some teammates resented the differences in pay. A few were privately critical of his reserved nature and even questioned whether his importance to the club was overrated.[102]

Rocky Colavito did not, however, suppress his feelings about his salary as compared to Kaline's. He engaged in a shouting match with Campbell during one negotiation and asked the GM, "Who is Kaline, a little tin god?"[103] The use of anger did not succeed as a negotiating tactic. Although the *Detroit Free Press* reported on March 5, 1962, that Colavito would be receiving more money than Kaline during the season ahead, Campbell emphatically denied that account.[104]

In truth, the Tigers' management did establish Kaline's pay as the benchmark against which salaries of other team members were based.[105] Former Tigers slugger Willie Horton accepted the fact that "he could never make more [money] than Kaline."[106] Players who attempted to employ an aggressive approach during negotiations with Campbell were frequently asked whether they believed that they were better players than the team's star.[107] Consequently, a few players—in hushed tones—referred to Kaline as "the Salary Cap."[108]

Although Kaline's salaries (like those of all other players from his era) were essentially established by club management, annual comparisons of his pay with that of his teammates would be criticized in 1995 by Marvin Miller, the former executive director of the Major League Baseball Players Association. Miller remarked that the circumstances relating to Kaline's compensation "did a disservice to other players by limiting their salaries."[109]

INTERNAL CONFLICT

Each challenge that has been mentioned in this article resulted from either a situation beyond Kaline's control, perceptions about personal qualities that were difficult to change, or decisions made (or, in regard to trade rumors, not made) by other people. One more mountain to be climbed apparently existed, however, within Kaline's own mind and psyche.

Such a theory based on psychological factors may be considered because Kaline exhibited a smaller ego than most superstars while competing aggressively on baseball diamonds for 22 years. He never relished attention or acclaim as many of his peers did, readily admitting his limitations and stating occasionally that some other renowned players were more talented.

Consider this comment to Jack Olsen of *Sports Illustrated* in 1964:

> Everybody said this guy's another Ty Cobb, another Joe DiMaggio...What they didn't know is I'm not that good a hitter. They kept saying I do everything with ease. But it isn't that way. I have to work as hard if not harder than anybody in the league...They threw all this pressure on my shoulders and I don't think it's justified and I don't think it's fair to compare anybody with Cobb. I'll tell you something else: I'm not in the same class with players like Mays or Musial or Henry Aaron, either. Their records over the last five seasons are much better than mine.[110]

A similar remark appeared in an authorized biography published in 2010: "My hitting is all a matter of timing. I don't have the strength that Mantle or Mays have. I've got to have my timing down perfect or I'm finished...To say that I'm like [Cobb] is the most foolish thing that anybody can make a comparison on."[111]

While these comments provide insight into Kaline's view of himself in comparison to other prominent players, the effects of psychological reservations on his self-esteem should not be exaggerated. His response to a question in 1968 is revealing. Asked how he felt about not quite being a superstar (like Mays, Mantle, Aaron, Frank Robinson, or Carl Yastrzemski), Kaline replied, "My makeup isn't one of a superstar. I think the guys you mentioned are certainly better players than I am and are possibly a little more exciting. And these fellows have all played in World Series, which is a big thing for your stature. But I think I can hold my own with all these guys in everything but home runs and possibly batting average in some cases. There is a very thin line between them and myself."[112]

CONCLUSION

When the many obstacles that Al Kaline encountered prior to and during his playing career are placed under a spotlight, assumptions that his road to stardom was a smooth one are shown to be false. Rather, as he suffered the misfortune of being "a child who was thrust full-blown into a world in which nothing he ever did was good enough and excellence brought its own torments,"[113] he was forced to overcome many difficulties on his journey from the heart of Baltimore to the National Baseball Hall of Fame. Along the way, his public image blended well with the culture of a basically blue-collar city in the Midwestern region of the United States, and he became a Detroit institution as challenges were met and usually conquered.

Noting the superstar's many years in the public eye, author Tom Stanton was prompted to write: "Through race riots, through the assassinations of King and the Kennedys, through Vietnam death counts on the morning news, through the crimes of our president, through times of turmoil and uncertainty, Kaline [was] there, every season."[114]

That extraordinary longevity—along with impressive character traits, determination, and considerable talent—ultimately enabled Kaline to conquer various forms of adversity and earn lasting praise as one of baseball's greatest and most admired competitors. ■

Notes

1. William M. Anderson, *The Detroit Tigers: A Pictorial Celebration of the Greatest Players and Moments in Tigers' History*, Detroit: Wayne State University Press, 1999, 174.
2. Nick Waddell, "Al Kaline," SABR Baseball Biography Project, accessed September 9, 2021. https://sabr.org/bioproj/person/al-kaline.
3. *Detroit Free Press* staff, *Mr. Tiger: The Legend of Al Kaline, Detroit's Own*, Chicago: Triumph Books, 2020, 73–74.
4. Lyall Smith, "Kaline's a Real Tiger: Teenage Regular Captures Detroit," *Detroit Free Press*, condensed in *Baseball Digest*, October 1954, 49.
5. Jim Hawkins, *Al Kaline: The Biography of a Tigers Icon*, Chicago: Triumph Books, 2010, 63.
6. "Pacemaker of the American League," *Who's Who in the Big Leagues*, ed. by Hy Goldberg, New York: Dell Publishing Company, 1956, 38.
7. George Cantor, *The Tigers of '68: Baseball's Last Real Champions*, Dallas: Taylor Publishing Company, 1997, 160.
8. Murray Olderman, "Al Kaline," *Sports All-Stars Baseball 1958*, June 1958, 38.
9. Hawkins, 63.
10. Glenn Liebman, "Here's What Hall of Famers Say About Each Other," *Baseball Digest*, June 1992, 64.
11. Danny Peary, Ed., *We Played the Game: 65 Players Remember Baseball's Greatest Era, 1947–1964*, New York: Hyperion Books, 1994, 312.
12. Peary, 415.
13. *Detroit Free Press* staff, *Ernie: Our Voice of Summer*, Chicago: Triumph Books, 2010, 79.
14. Bill Guilfoile, Ed., *National Baseball Hall of Fame and Museum Yearbook 1981*, 72; also Bill Guilfoile, Ed., *National Baseball Hall of Fame and Museum Yearbook 1983*, 18.
15. Daniel Okrent and Steve Wulf, *Baseball Anecdotes*, New York: Oxford University Press, 1989, 244.
16. Joe Falls, "Al Kaline Matures Again," *Sport*, October 1965, 29, 81.
17. Joe Falls, "Baseball Never Came Easy for Al Kaline," *The Sporting News*, August 16, 1980, 17.
18. Art Hill, *I Don't Care If I Never Come Back: A Baseball Fan and His Game*, New York: Simon & Schuster, 1980; referenced by Joe Falls, *The Detroit Tigers: An Illustrated History*, New York: Prentice Hall Press, 1989, 108.
19. Tom Stanton, *The Final Season: Fathers, Sons, and One Last Season in a Classic American Ballpark*, New York: St. Martin's Press, 2001, 119.
20. Jay Jaffe, "Remembering Al Kaline, Mr. Tiger (1934–2020)," FanGraphs, accessed April 11, 2020. https://blogs.fangraphs.com/remembering-al-kaline-mr-tiger-1934-2020.
21. Jack Olsen, "The Torments of Excellence," *Sports Illustrated*, May 11, 1964, 35.
22. Olsen.

23. Waddell.
24. Hal Middlesworth, "Kaline: Bat King at 20," *Baseball Digest*, January-February 1956, 49.
25. Olsen, 36.
26. Middlesworth, 40.
27. Middlesworth.
28. Olsen, 36.
29. Waddell.
30. Hawkins, 31.
31. Sam Zygner, "Phillies Bonus Babies, 1953–57," *The National Pastime: From Swampoodle to South Philly*, Philadelphia: Society of American Baseball Research, 2013, 92.
32. Editors of *Sport Magazine*, "Al Kaline: Nobody Calls Him a Morning Glory Now," *Baseball's Best Hitters*, 1957, 52.
33. Tommy Devine, "Kaline Can Be King in Detroit," *Sport*, August 1955, 60.
34. Devine, 35.
35. Devine.
36. Watson Spoelsta, "Keen Play of Kuenn Tigers' Top '53 Tale," *The Sporting News*, September 16, 1953, 8.
37. Lee Greene, "They Don't Knock Kaline Any More," *Sport*, May 1960, 59.
38. David Laurila, "A Conversation with Hall of Famer Al Kaline, 1934–2020," FanGraphs.com, accessed April 11, 2020. https://blogs.fangraphs.com/a-conversation-with-hall-of-famer-al-kaline-1934-2020.
39. Watson Spoelstra, "Kid Kaline Winning His Stripes as Tiger Regular on Clouting," *The Sporting News*, March 31, 1954, 11.
40. Devine, 62.
41. Lyall Smith, "Kaline's a Big Man Now," *Baseball Digest*, May 1955, 85.
42. C.C. Johnson Spink, "The Low-Down on Majors' Big Shots," *The Sporting News*, January 6, 1954, 1.
43. Olsen, 41.
44. Joe Falls, "Al Kaline Matures Again," *Sport*, October 1965, 29.
45. Editors of *Sport Magazine*, "Al Kaline: He Has Everything to be a Hero," *Who's Best in Sports: 1959*, 39.
46. Cantor, 160.
47. Jim Sargent, *The Tigers and Yankees in '61*, Jefferson, NC: McFarland & Company, 2016, 1.
48. Falls, "Al Kaline Matures Again," 81.
49. Falls, 29, 81.
50. Greene, 57.
51. Olsen, 36.
52. Greene.
53. Middlesworth, 39.
54. Greene, 57.
55. Greene.
56. "Al Kaline: He Has Everything to be a Hero," 39.
57. "Al Kaline: The Fiercest Tiger Since Cobb," *Dell Sports: Baseball Stars*, 1956, Vol. 1, #7, 4.
58. Waddell.
59. Cantor, 94.
60. Bill James, *The Bill James Historical Baseball Abstract*, New York: Villard Books, 1986, 618.
61. Hawkins, 131.
62. Jerry Green, "Al Kaline Sounds Off On His 15 Years of Pain and Joy," *Sport*, May 1968, 87.
63. Patrick Harrigan, *The Detroit Tigers: Club and Community, 1945–1995*, Toronto: University of Toronto Press, 1997, 117.
64. Joe Falls, "Victim of Versatility," *Baseball Digest*, May 1967, 56.
65. Waddell.
66. Irv Goodman, "How the Tigers Are Building a Winner," *Sport*. July 1957, 71.
67. "Hobbled Tiger," *Dell Sports*, Vol. 1, #44, May 1965, 51.
68. "Hobbled Tiger," 51.
69. Olsen, 42.
70. Greene, 60. See also Watson Spoelstra, "Tiger Prexy Turns on Extinguisher in Kaline Pay Flareup," *The Sporting News*, January 16, 1957, 11.
71. Hawkins, 85.
72. "Kaline Signs $30,000 Pact with Spike Away in Florida," *The Sporting News*, February 6, 1957, 6.
73. *The Sporting News* dated February 6, 1957 stated that Kaline's salary would be $30,000 but, according to SABR member Michael Haupert's research of contracts of Hall of Fame members, the amount of Kaline's contract for the 1957 season was $29,000 rather than $30,000. https://www.baseball-reference.com/players/k/kalinal01.shtml. See also Jaffe, "Remembering Al Kaline, Mr. Tiger (1934–2020)."
74. Greene, 58.
75. Hawkins, 84.
76. Hawkins, 111.
77. Hawkins.
78. Hawkins, 112.
79. Walter Spoelstra, "Bye-Bye to Bangtails: Kaline 'Retires' as Race-Track Tycoon," *The Sporting News*, June 1, 1960, 17.
80. Hawkins.
81. Joe Falls, "Meet the New Kaline," *Baseball Digest*, April 1961, 35.
82. Falls, "Victim of Versatility," 55.
83. Sargent, 93.
84. Hawkins, 104.
85. Hawkins, 123.
86. Hawkins.
87. Watson Spoelstra, "Dressen-Kaline Peace Pact Big Plus for Tigers," *The Sporting News*, December 12, 1964, 12.
88. Watson Spoelstra, "'No Deal,' Tigers Reply to All Offers for Kaline," *The Sporting News*, October 3, 1964, 17.
89. Watson Spoelstra, "Kaline Accepts $5,000 Slash; Freehan Signs," *The Sporting News*, January 16, 1965, 10.
90. Hawkins, 126.
91. Watson Spoelstra, "Sick Dressen Pulls Fast One; Swift in Tiger Driver's Seat," *The Sporting News*, March 20, 1965, 8; "Doctor Gives Green Light; Dressen Rejoining Tigers," *The Sporting News*, May 22, 1965, 13; Fred T. Smith, *Tiger Facts*, Lathrup Village, MI: Fred T. Smith, Russ Entwistle, and John Duffy, 1986, 186.
92. Watson Spoelstra, "Stricken Dressen Keeps Close Tabs on Bengals," *The Sporting News*, May 28, 1966, 16.
93. Smith, 190.
94. Joe Falls, "The Al Kaline Mystery," *Sport*, February 1964, 82.
95. Edgar Munzel, "Chisox Set Up Tall Goal for Harshman—20 Victories in '57," *The Sporting News*, January 16, 1957, 15.
96. Hawkins, 102.
97. Hawkins, 103.
98. "Hobbled Tiger," 51. See also Watson Spoelstra, "'No Deal,' Tigers Reply to All Offers for Kaline," 17.
99. Cantor, 160.
100. Joe Falls, "Turmoil on the Tigers: Does It Still Exist?," *Sport*, June 1967, 92.
101. Falls, "Turmoil on the Tigers."
102. These players (referred to in writings by George Cantor and Jim Hawkins, both of the *Detroit Free Press*) were not identified by those authors, nor were the players' identities revealed in *The Sporting News* or other major baseball publications in the late 1960s or early 1970s.
103. Cantor, 109.
104. Harrigan, 136.
105. Hawkins, 210.
106. Harrigan, 137.
107. Cantor, 167.
108. Cantor, 159.
109. Harrigan, 137.
110. Olsen, 36, 38.
111. Hawkins, 70.
112. Green, 86.
113. Olsen, 35.
114. Stanton, 121.

Besting Honus Wagner

The Forgotten Season of Cy Seymour

Tom Nardacci

When James Bentley "Cy" Seymour of the Reds stepped into the batter's box on August 2, 1905, in Cincinnati, he was battling Pittsburgh Pirates great Honus Wagner for the National League batting crown. At start of play that Wednesday afternoon Wagner, 31, was batting .356, and Seymour, 32, was at .357.[1] Wagner had won the title in each of the previous two seasons and would win it in the succeeding four. Seymour, though, was no stranger to the NL batting race. He had previously challenged for the title in 1903, ultimately finishing fifth behind Wagner's .355 average.

On this day, a struggling Brooklyn squad faced the Reds at Cincinnati's League Park, also called the "Palace of the Fans." Brooklyn, owned by Charles Ebbets, had finished the previous decade with its second league championship, but since then had steadily been falling in the standings. The Superbas, though, had come to Cincy fresh off a 1–0 victory over Wagner's Pirates. In contrast, their hosts had lost an incredible eight in a row to the indomitable New York Giants. The Reds were eager to snap their skid.

In the top of the 13th, light-hitting Brooklyn shortstop Charlie Babb had doubled down the right-field line, was sacrificed to third, then scored on a bobbled bunt. With that, Brooklyn had taken a 7–6 lead.[2]

Leading off the Reds' half of the inning was lefty-batting Seymour. The veteran hitter's gray eyes were sharp and he was tall, of medium-build.[3] Cy already had stroked two singles and a triple over the first nine innings before working a walk in the 10th.[4]

The first offering from Brooklyn pitcher Harry McIntire was crushed, as Seymour drove the ball on a line over first base and sprinted around the bases. Speedy outfielder Harry Lumley bolted for the ball at the crack of the bat, hoping to intercept it near the right-field line. He had no chance; the ball was simply moving too fast and he chased it into the far corner in right. Before Lumley could get the ball back to the infield, Seymour had crossed home plate and was on his way to the dugout. In one swing, Seymour had tied the score, 7–7. McIntire, appearing exhausted, yielded three more singles, and the Reds pushed across the second run of the inning to win, 8–7.[5]

Seymour and Wagner, "The Flying Dutchman," would battle through the rest of the summer and into October, but with his four hits against Brooklyn that August afternoon, Seymour never trailed in the batting race the rest of the season.

A WILD START

"Cy" Seymour had been on the baseball scene for some time when the 1905 season began. He had played amateur, professional, and semipro baseball before joining the New York Giants as a pitcher in 1896. The Albany, New York, native played first in Plattsburgh, New York, near the Canadian border, then in Springfield, Massachusetts.[6] Because of Seymour's wildness on the mound, some batters feared him as much as a cyclone. "He had speed to burn and probably has as much stuff on the ball as any lefthander in the history of the game with the possible exception of 'Rube' Waddell," wrote Fred Lieb. "But 'Cy' never could tell where his fast ball would go," he added. "If he had luck, it would dart over the corners of the plate as intended."[7] His career in baseball would indeed carve a path befitting his pseudonym.

In 1898, Seymour won 25 games pitching for the Giants and led the National League in both strikeouts (239) and walks (213). In fact, he led the league in walks three straight years: 1897, 1898, and 1899. In his first five years with the Giants, he occasionally played other positions and batted part time, including two years in which he batted over .300.[8]

In 1901 and 1902, Seymour played for Baltimore in the upstart American League, where he was managed by John McGraw. McGraw converted him from pitcher to outfielder and full-time batsman. When John T. Brush bought the Baltimore team and broke it up, a few players—such as pitcher Joe "Iron Man" McGinnity and catcher Roger Bresnahan—went with McGraw to New York, while Joe Kelley and Seymour jumped to Cincinnati, a team in which Brush held interests. New York viewed Seymour as the "most desirable" player in

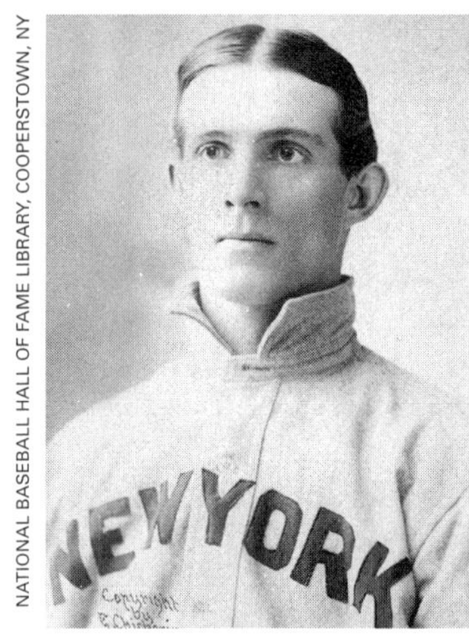

Seymour's career included two stints with the Giants and a season-plus in Baltimore. He moved to Cincinnati when the Orioles were broken up midway through the 1902 season.

Baltimore and wanted him, but ultimately, the player split was part of a "peace agreement" among the owners.[9] In 1903, Seymour posted top-five numbers in batting average, hits, triples, and home runs.[10] The 1905 season would prove to be his best and one of the best ever in the game of baseball.

OPENING DAY 1905

In 1905, 5,855,062 people attended major league baseball games.[11] The Deadball Era of the sport was steadily turning baseball into America's National Pastime. The beginning of the twentieth century, from 1901 until 1920, was a time of great prosperity in the country. America was an established world power. American industry, finance, and ingenuity were all booming, and its railroads had finally connected the nation from coast to coast. People were becoming consumers, buying telephones and phonographs. The age of the automobile had arrived. Americans were flocking to electrified cities and looking for entertainment. The sport of baseball fit the bill, and business magnates and city leaders started to work together to build stadiums to satisfy the growing populace.

Excitement was high in Cincinnati on Opening Day, Friday, April 14, as the Reds welcomed a fearsome rival, the Pittsburgh Pirates, a squad that featured many players who had participated in the first—and, to that point, only—AL-NL World Series in 1903.

"This afternoon at League Park the baseball season is scheduled to burst into bloom," wrote sportswriter Jack Ryder in *The Cincinnati Enquirer*. "At the end of the session the hope of every fan in Redland is that Manager [Joe] Kelley's grand conglomeration of earnest workers will be off in the lead. The Pirates will have a few well-wishers, however, for several car loads of Smoketown enthusiasts are at this moment wending their way hither to lend aid and encouragement to Fred Clarke's lusty crew."[12]

More than 15,000 fans watched the Reds lose, 9–4. The star batters for each team, Wagner and Seymour, were held hitless. In that season-opening series, the Pirates won three of four.[13]

In the first month of the season, Wagner's Pirates finished with an 8–4 record, a half-game behind the Giants. The Reds, at a pedestrian 6–6, were fourth of the eight teams in the league. For his part, Seymour put together a six-game hitting streak at the end of April, and his batting average stood at .347 to Wagner's .346.[14] Seymour inching ahead of Wagner thanks to a hitting streak would become a theme in 1905.

PLAYING AGAINST THE GREATS

Cincinnati opened the month of May by winning two of four at home with the Cubs, including eking out a victory over Mordecai "Three-Fingered" Brown, who was on the verge of establishing a reputation as one of baseball's best pitchers. Seymour went 0-for-3 with a walk.[15]

After that, the Reds traveled to Pittsburgh, hoping to fare better on the road against their rival. "The Reds found the Pirates just as hard to beat on their own grounds as they were in the opening series of the season on the old home field and lost the first game here today before a large crowd, which gathered at Exposition Park to welcome Clarke's crew home from their Eastern trip," wrote Ryder of the *Enquirer*.[16] It was Seymour's poor defense in the fourth inning that gave the Pirates the run they needed to win. He had thrown errantly to the wrong base and in the process hit a runner with the ball, which allowed a third run to score in the inning. Although the former pitcher had a terrific arm, Seymour had a reputation as an erratic fielder. In 1903, the converted center fielder had accumulated an incredible 36 errors, leading all outfielders. In 1905, he finished second-worst with 21.[17]

Seymour tried to atone for his mistake at the plate. He had a hot bat, hitting two singles and a double. He also stole third and scored. Although he saved his team from a shutout, the Reds came up short, losing, 4–2. Wagner had a single and a run scored because of another Reds error. In the series, Pittsburgh once again bested Cincinnati, three games to one.[18]

Seymour's hitting remained consistent, with a 10-game hitting streak from May 11 to May 24. On May 23, the Reds visited the Polo Grounds to face the juggernaut New York Giants and the game's most dominant pitcher, Christy Mathewson. The Giants sat at an astounding 24–6, while the Reds had dropped below the .500 mark at 13–16. Mathewson, six-foot-one and broad-shouldered, had won 30 games in each of the previous two seasons, and 1905 would be one of his finest. "Big Six" would finish the year 31–9 with a 1.28 ERA, leading the Giants to a 105-win season and a world championship.[19]

In 1912, still in the midst of his great career, Mathewson wrote and published *Pitching in a Pinch*, an autobiographical insider's look at the game. He devoted key sections in Chapter 1, "The Most Dangerous Batters I Faced," to Seymour, including the following:

> "Cy" Seymour, formerly the outfielder of the Giants, was one of the hardest batters I ever had to pitch against when he was with the Cincinnati club and going at the top of his stride. He liked a curved ball, and could hit it hard and far, and was always waiting for it. He was very clever at out-guessing a pitcher and being able to conclude what was coming. For a long time whenever I pitched against him I had "mixed 'em up" literally, handing him first a fast ball and then a slow curve and so on, trying to fool him in this way. But one day we were playing in Cincinnati, and I decided to keep delivering the same kind of a ball, that old fast one around his neck, and to try to induce him to believe that a curve was coming. I pitched him nothing but fast ones that day, and he was always waiting for a curve. The result was that I had him in the hole all the time, and I struck him out three times. He has never gotten over it. Only recently I saw Seymour, and he said: "Matty, you are the only man that ever struck me out three times in the same game.[20]

On that Tuesday afternoon, Seymour could muster only a single to keep his second significant hitting streak of the season alive one more day. Matty held the Reds scoreless and struck out eight, yielding three harmless singles.[21]

To close out May, the Reds split a two-game series with the Pirates, then beat Chicago three games to one. In Pittsburgh, the first game of the series, on Saturday, May 27, was a "swatfest" for the home team, with Wagner getting three of the Pirates' 12 hits. Had he not slipped running the bases, his deep drive to left in the fifth inning would have been a home run instead of a triple. His single to center in the seventh was fumbled by Seymour, a miscue that allowed another run to score and closed out an 8–3 Pirates victory. At the plate, Seymour singled and scored a run.[22]

The second game was a different story, as the rivals traveled to Cincy for the Sunday rematch. The Reds routed the Bucs, 12–3, and Seymour singled and scored twice as part of the romp. Wagner singled twice before being ejected in the seventh inning for arguing with an umpire. With Seymour on first, Reds right fielder Jimmy Sebring grounded to Pirates second baseman Claude Ritchey, who flipped the ball to Wagner. The shortstop, however, was out of position, a few feet off the bag, when he received the toss and then threw too high to first. Both runners were ruled safe. The hulky "Dutchman" vehemently protested and had his finger in umpire Bob Emslie's face when he got tossed.[23]

On the last day of May, the Reds capped their home series against Chicago by taking both games of the midweek doubleheader. Costly errors in both games by normally reliable Cubs middle infielders shortstop Joe Tinker and second baseman Johnny Evers contributed to their team's misery. Each made two miscues in the first game, a batters' battle that yielded 21 hits between the two clubs. The Reds had built a comfortable 5–0 lead by the fifth and looked to make it a runaway, but the scrappy Cubs clawed their way back. By the seventh, the score was tied, 8–8. The Cubs added two more runs in the eighth after "Three-Fingered" Brown was brought in to close out the contest. He held the Reds scoreless in the eighth and started the ninth by striking out Seymour, who earlier had hit his fourth triple of the year and scored. Brown then walked the next two batters before getting the second out. After Brown walked player-manager Kelley to load the bases, Tinker muffed an easy grounder, allowing the Reds to score two and tie the game. Brown then yielded a hit, and the game was over, with the Reds winning, 11–10.[24]

Game two of the doubleheader was tame by comparison. In the bottom of the first, Reds second baseman Miller Huggins walked, took second on teammate Tommy Corcoran's safe bunt, then advanced to third on a sacrifice by Seymour. A wild pitch allowed Huggins to score and give the Reds the lead. The Reds scored in the fifth when Evers muffed a grounder. With the bases loaded for the Cubs in the eighth, Evers tied the game by singling home teammates Frank Chance and Billy Maloney. The Reds scored a run in the ninth to win the game, 3–2.[25]

Seymour closed out May batting .327, with Wagner at .321. The Reds maintained their middling status at 19–19, followed by the Cubs at 20–21. The Giants stood as tall as their star pitcher; at 30–9 they had surged well ahead of the second-place Pirates, who stood at 23–17.[26]

AN 18-GAME HITTING STREAK

In June, Seymour and Wagner continued their torrid hitting. Wagner hit safely in 23 of his 25 games, and Seymour hit safely in 22 of 25. Between June 7 and June 25, Seymour had his third significant hitting streak of the season: 18 straight games.[27] In the five-game series that opened that month against the St. Louis Cardinals, Seymour collected seven hits, including a day when he hit a home run and had five runs batted in.[28]

Seymour's June streak coincided with a planned 16-game homestand against Eastern opponents: Brooklyn, Philadelphia, Boston, and New York. In game two of the homestand, the Reds made easy work of their foes, beating Brooklyn, 11–2. In the first inning, Seymour blooped a single to center, scoring Huggins and first baseman Shad Barry. Seymour's two RBIs and his own run scored later in the inning would've been all the home team needed, but the center fielder added a second hit and second run.[29] In game three, the Reds completed a sweep of Brooklyn, with Seymour adding two more hits, marking three straight multihit games.[30]

The Reds, who welcomed the surging Philadelphia Phillies next, lost the opener of the four-game series but then won three straight. In the second game, Seymour went 4-for-4, adding another double and triple. For the series, he was 8-for-13, a torrid .615 batting average. During his June hitting streak, Seymour added five triples, bringing his season total to nine. By contrast, for the Phillies, future batting champ Sherry Magee, a 20-year-old left fielder in his second season, went a paltry 1-for-17 during the series.[31]

The Beaneaters, Boston's National League team, faced the red-hot Reds next and lost all four games. In game one, the teams garnered 11 hits each during the contest, which the Reds won in 10 innings.

The best play of the series, a defensive gem by Seymour, happened in the sixth inning of the third game. After Boston's Jim Delehanty tripled, Rip Cannell lined a shot to center, which Seymour, in perfect position, easily grabbed. Delehanty tagged and raced home. Jack Ryder of the *Enquirer* captured the moment: "Almost as soon as the ball had touched his hands it was on its way to the plate as fast as the bat had sent it out. Cy had gauged the distance exactly right, and had applied speed to burn. The ball sailed into Schlei's waiting mitt on the first bound, fully three steps ahead of the hustling Delehanty. The Admiral took no chances, but stood square in the path, and made the runner dodge, tagging him as he went by."[32]

Despite his penchant for committing errors, Seymour had a reputation for throwing out runners at the plate on fly balls. The double play occurred with Boston leading, 2–1, giving the Reds the jolt they needed to pull out the victory. With the Reds up, 4–2, Seymour opened the eighth with a triple, then scored on a single to close out the day's scoring. The Reds beat Boston pitcher Vic Willis, a future Hall of Famer who had won 20 games four times in his career in Boston and would move on to Pittsburgh and win 20 games in four more seasons. In the fourth and final game against Boston, Seymour added his second home run of the season on a long drive to the right-field corner in the seventh inning.[33]

The Reds' hot streak propelled them to a 31–24 record in the National League, a half-game behind Pittsburgh. The Giants, still in first with a seven-game cushion, were the next Eastern team to come to Cincinnati. The series was a chance for the Reds to make a move in the pennant chase, though the Giants' top-flight pitchers posed a serious threat to Seymour's June hitting streak.

In game one, the Reds continued their roll, beating up four Giants pitchers for 17 runs. Pitching in relief, future Hall of Famer McGinnity gave up four runs in one-third of an inning in the fourth before being yanked by McGraw. For his part, Seymour scored three runs and drove in three while collecting three hits. It was the Reds' eighth straight win.[34] In game two, Giants pitcher Red Ames finally slowed down the Reds' offense in an 8–3 victory. The 22-year-old earned the win to raise his record to 11–2 en route to one of the best W-L records of his career. Seymour picked up a single to keep his hitting streak alive and was having a great day defensively, nabbing five flies. But in the ninth, he rushed a ball hit by Giants catcher Frank Bowerman, and it went through his legs all the way to the fence, turning a single into four bases and a run.[35]

In game three, the Giants scored four first-inning runs, and the Reds simply could never catch up. On the day, Seymour bagged two hits, including a long drive to center that he turned into a triple, and drove in two of the Reds' three runs. Seymour had failed to run out a grounder to the pitcher in the first, which resulted in a double play. In the field, Seymour snagged a fly ball in the fifth and immediately gunned down Giants third baseman Art Devlin, who couldn't get back to first in time. With the 6–3 victory, Mathewson boosted his record to 11–3, while the loss started a tumble for the Reds in the standings.[36] In the final game of the series, McGinnity got his revenge on the Reds, holding down Cincinnati in a 2–1 victory. Seymour had two singles, including a hit to lead off the ninth, but his teammates couldn't advance him. Still, he had collected at least one hit in 15 straight games.[37]

The Reds then traveled to Pittsburgh and easily beat the Pirates, 8–2, in a lively Saturday afternoon contest. Wagner had two hits in the game, and Seymour had a single to continue his hit streak, but when he threw his glove in the seventh to object to a Pirates' runner being called safe at second base, he was ejected.[38]

In Chicago, the Reds dropped three of four games to close out the month. In the first game, about 12,000 Sunday fans watched the Cubs score 18 runs and tally 34 total bases in an absolute drubbing of the Reds. The only notable hits for Cincinnati were a triple by Huggins and a double by Seymour.[39] The Cubs beat the Reds badly again in the second game, 9–1. Seymour slammed a double, his 20th of the year, to right field to maintain his June hit streak.[40] In the third contest, Reds rookie Orval Overall hurled a 6–0 shutout. Seymour walked once but failed to produce a hit in three official at bats, ending his hitting streak at 18 games. He then went 0-for-5 the following day as the Reds lost again, 13–5.[41]

In the final four games of the month, Seymour went 3-for-15 (.200), and his average stood at .351. Because of a doubleheader in St. Louis, Wagner had played an extra game over that same stretch, and he closed the month on a tear, batting 15-for-26 (.577). The Dutchman raised his average 20 points to end June at .377. Wagner found himself in a familiar position: leading the league.[42] Could Seymour hit well enough the rest of the year to overtake the perpetual champ? Sporting pages around the country started to report that there was a battle brewing for the batting crown.[43]

A 21-GAME HITTING STREAK

Almost as if perfectly scripted, July started with a four-game series between Cincinnati and Pittsburgh. It had to be fate that after two games without a hit, Seymour would start his fourth noteworthy hitting streak of the 1905 season in Pittsburgh. Beginning on July 2 and ending on July 29, this streak would last 21 games.[44]

The series between Cincinnati and Pittsburgh was ultimately led by players who were not named Cy Seymour nor Honus Wagner. Seymour batted 5-for-15 (.333) and collected two more doubles. Wagner was 3-for-14 (.214) and added two more stolen bases, bringing his total to 27. Pittsburgh won three of the four games.[45] In the National League, the Giants continued to set the pace and had the best record in baseball at 50–20. The Pirates trailed by seven games and stood at 43–27. The Reds were starting to fall completely out of the race; they were 35–33, 14 games back and struggling to stay above .500.

Seymour really picked up his pace when the club hosted St. Louis at home before traveling to Boston and then Philly. He batted .429 over the next 13 games, in which the Reds went 7–6 to remain just above .500. Seymour's latest hitting streak was at 17 games, seven of which were multihit affairs. He added four more doubles and another triple.[46]

The Reds closed out July with an eight-game series against the Giants, the first four games to be played at the Polo Grounds in New York and then four in Ohio. Manager McGraw rolled out his pitchers in the following order for the home games: McGinnity, Mathewson, Ames, and Hooks Wiltse.

McGinnity held firm in game one, and the Giants picked up the win, 4–3. Seymour continued his streak,

Seymour at Cincinnati's Palace of the Fans.

NATIONAL BASEBALL HALL OF FAME LIBRARY, COOPERSTOWN, NY

reaching base twice on singles in the sixth and ninth innings. With runners on base earlier in the second inning, "Iron Man" had issued an intentional pass to Seymour rather than allowing him to hit because, as the *Enquirer*'s Ryder reported, "McGinnity saw the fire in Seymour's eye and let him walk."[47] In game two, Mathewson gave up nine hits but held the Reds to two runs while his team scored seven. Seymour had a triple off Matty and also smacked a single in four at bats. In game three, the Giants squeaked out a win for Ames, 6–5, and "Iron Man" lived up to his nickname when he came in for two innings to close out the victory. Seymour had a single and three RBIs. The Reds almost erased the deficit in the eighth, but fell short. In the last game at the Polo Grounds, the Giants' bats came alive and they won easily, 9–3, sweeping the series. Seymour went 1-for-5 with a single in the first to extend his hitting streak to 21 games. During his July streak, Seymour batted .402. The Reds, however, went 8–13 during the span.[49]

In the opener of the series at League Park, Mathewson shut out the Reds, and Seymour went 0-for-4 with two strikeouts against him to end his last notable hitting streak that year.

Unfortunately for the Reds, the remaining three home games against the Giants had the same result as at the Polo Grounds—Cincy lost them all. New York had completed an incredible eight-game sweep of the Reds. Cincinnati finished the month having lost more ground in the National League, going 12–18.[50]

During Seymour's 21-game hitting streak, Wagner fell off his torrid pace, batting .299. The Pirates, though, went 17–7 between July 2 and July 27. By the last day of July, Wagner was leading all National League batters with a .356 average. But Seymour had successfully battled back and sat right behind him at .355.[51]

OVERTAKING WAGNER

Seymour started August on a tear. He collected 13 hits in the first five games, including a triple and the homer in the 13th inning in the August 2 game against Brooklyn.[52] In fact, through the first three games against Brooklyn, he had what would have been a run of eight straight at-bats with a hit if only one had not been ruled an error.[53] The Reds picked up four wins in the five-game series and then, with Philadelphia in town, swept the Phillies in a four-game set.

The opening game against Philly was a slugfest; the Reds scored five runs in the first inning. Huggins started things out by slamming a hard shot to third. When the third baseman threw wildly, Huggins ended up on third. A triple by Barry brought in Huggins, and a single by Kelley scored Barry. Seymour then laid down a perfect bunt toward third and beat the throw to first. Shortstop Tommy Corcoran loaded the bases by reaching on an error, and two runners scored before the final out of the inning. In the sixth, Seymour singled with the bases loaded, scoring two more en route to a 13–7 victory.[54]

Seymour's hot August start raised his batting average 19 points, and he overtook Wagner. Wagner would fight his way back through the remainder of the season, but Seymour would never lose the batting lead after his torrid first week of the month.[55]

Cincinnati played Boston for the next seven games, with four in Boston and three at home, then went back to Philadelphia for three more games. Over that stretch, the Reds went 6–4, while Seymour's hitting cooled, and he collected only 11 hits in 38 at bats (a .289 average) and merely one RBI. The Reds then headed to the Polo Grounds for a Thursday doubleheader and were blanked by Mathewson in the first game, losing 8–0 and only getting two hits off him. Seymour was 0-for-4 as Mathewson improved his record to 22–7. The second game ended in a 6-6 tie, with the game being called after the ninth because of darkness.[57] In that game, Seymour had two hits and a sacrifice. The Giants won the third game with McGinnity shutting out the Reds, 2–0. Seymour went 0-for-3.[58]

After that, Cincinnati traveled to Brooklyn and split a two-game series to end the month. After losing the opening contest, the Reds, powered by Seymour, won the second. In the latter game, Seymour hit a shot that cleared the right-field wall for his fourth home run of the season. And he ended the game with a sensational double play, throwing out a Brooklyn runner on his way to third after catching the second out of the ninth.[59]

As August faded, Seymour still maintained his lead in the race for the batting crown with a .361 average. Wagner was right behind at .357. At month's end, the Reds were 22½ games back and out of the pennant hunt. At 6½ games back, the Pirates were still chasing the dominant Giants.[60]

THE SEPTEMBER BATTLE

In September, Seymour kept hitting the ball consistently and playing like he had throughout August. He batted .387 and picked up 43 more hits, including five doubles, three home runs, and seven triples. He also stole nine bases. As a team, the Reds didn't keep up their star player's pace. They started the month miserably, losing two in Chicago to the Cubs, and then four out of five to St. Louis. Seymour batted .333 during the stretch and added a triple and home run in St. Louis. The Reds then traveled to Pittsburgh for a much-anticipated three-game series.[61]

"Premier Batters in the League/Seymour and Wagner Hook Up In Pittsburgh/Each Secured a Single, a Double and a Triple," proclaimed the three-deck September 8 headline on *The Cincinnati Enquirer*'s sports page.[62] The Thursday series opener the day before at Pittsburgh's Exposition Park did not disappoint. It was a "slugging contest" with the teams combining for 30 base hits, 43 total bases and 18 runs. The *Enquirer* zeroed in on the showcase matchup of the day: "A feature of the game was the batting duel between the two premier sluggers of the league, Cy Seymour and Hans Wagner. The result was a tie. Both men came to bat five times and each secured three hits—a single, a double and a triple. Each also secured two runs, so neither had any advantage on the day's work. Wagner also fielded beautifully, but Seymour did not have a chance to show what he could do in that time."[63]

Pittsburgh hit and scored at will and had a 10–3 lead heading to the eighth. Seymour singled and scored in the eighth, and in the ninth, he tripled to right with the bases loaded to drive in three. It wasn't enough, and the contest ended with the Pirates winning, 11–7. The victory moved the Pirates to within five games of the Giants.

In game two, though the Pirates rapped out 15 hits, they left plenty of runners on base, scoring only three times. The Reds scored at a better rate, crossing the plate eight times on 13 hits. Wagner walked three times and singled. Seymour got the better of the Dutchman, getting four hits, including two triples. His triple in the third drove home two runs. In the fifth, Huggins and Seymour executed a double steal that brought Huggins home. The report by the *Enquirer* noted: "The battle between the two main sluggers, Seymour and Wagner, was all the way of the Red biffer this afternoon. Cy was in fine trim, and his eye was never off the ball."[64]

The rubber match was all Pittsburgh, and this time the Pirates produced runs at a high rate, scoring 12 times on 19 hits. The Reds scored five on eight hits. Wagner finished with two singles, two runs scored, and one RBI. Seymour garnered three hits, including a double, and scored a run. The next day's *Pittsburgh Gazette* covered the status of the batting race between Seymour and Wagner and also made a point to say that the Pirates were playing better team ball and leading the league in hitting: "The race between Seymour and Wagner is one that any person who takes an interest in the game will watch from now to the finals of the season. The Reds' clever hitter is now 8 points ahead of the Pirates' slugger, while last week only 5 points separated them."[65]

On the Reds' next homestand, they beat the Cubs two out of three games before hosting the Pirates in a two-game Friday-Saturday series. The first game vs. Pittsburgh was tight, with both teams getting 11 hits. Seymour did his part for his team, going 2-for-4, scoring twice and stealing a base. Wagner edged him out on the day, going 2-for-4 as well, but contributing a triple. After his single in the first drove in Tommy Leach with the first run, Wagner easily stole second and third, then scored on a drive by Del Howard. The Bucs ultimately bested the Reds, 8–7.[66] In game two, Reds spitball ace Bob Ewing baffled the Pirates, shutting them out and holding them to six hits. Wagner had a single. Seymour's single in the first drove home Huggins, and although the Reds scored five more times, Cy's RBI was all that was needed to split the series. The *Enquirer* continued to follow the batting race closely, its headline proclaiming "Wagner and Seymour are Now Nip and Tuck," and reporting that "The National League race is rapidly drawing to a finish and a battle royal is 'on' for the honor of leading batsman. Wagner and Seymour are having a hot struggle."[67]

After losing two to the Cubs in Chicago, the Reds then won seven straight games against lowly Brooklyn and Boston. In the first game of a Sunday doubleheader against Brooklyn at home, Seymour hit home runs in his first two at bats. The slugger drove both balls deep to right and, on both occasions, teammate Barry was on base and scored ahead of him.[68] In the second game, Seymour beat out a bunt in the third.[69] Seymour closed out September by collecting a few more hits against Philadelphia while his team dropped two of three.[70]

September ended with Seymour leading the National League batting race with a .367 average to Wagner's .361. The former had collected 202 hits to that point to Wagner's 188.[71] With the season not yet over, the New York Giants had 102 wins and the Pirates 94. The Reds, at 74–72, were just above .500.

THE NATIONAL SPOTLIGHT

With the pennant race decided, National League partisans turned their attention to the batting race between Seymour and Wagner that had percolated all season. Cincinnati was slated to end the season on October 8, with all eight of its final games at home—first against the pennant-clinching New York Giants, then vs. the Philadelphia Phillies, and finally, like from out of a storybook, with a closing-day doubleheader against the Pirates and Wagner. Over eight days in

October, the Reds played magnificently: They won five, lost two, and tied one. And Seymour helped pace his team's strong close.[72]

Fifteen thousand fans showed up for the Reds' Sunday doubleheader with the Giants on October 1, and they were treated to two fine games. In the first game, McGinnity and Ewing both pitched all 10 innings, with the Giants victorious, 5–4. In the first inning, Seymour put the Reds ahead with a sharp hit to right-center that scored one. The Giants broke a 4–4 tie in the top of the tenth. When it was the Reds' turn in the bottom half, McGraw made a defensive switch in the outfield when he noticed a lot of Cincinnati's hits going to center. He directed speedy outfielder Sam Mertes to move from left field to center, with center fielder Mike Donlin moving to left. (Donlin would finish third in the 1905 batting race.) The first batter in the inning for the Reds, Shad Barry, singled past the second baseman. That brought up Cy, seeking his fourth hit of the day. As the *Enquirer*'s Ryder recounted, "Seymour, with three good marks already on his slate, raized [*sic*] a long fly ball to deep center that would undoubtedly have escaped Donlin, but Mertes just did get under it." McGraw's defensive switch and Mertes' great catch robbed Seymour and saved the first game for the Giants.[73] In the second game, the Reds scored three runs in the first, including one on Seymour's triple to deep center field, and one more in the fourth.

Seymour's race with Wagner would come down to the final series of the 1905 season, when their two teams met in Cincinnati.

The umpire called the game in the fifth inning because of darkness with the Reds up, 4–3.[74]

Two days later, the same teams played another doubleheader. The Reds won the first game, 4–2, and Seymour hit a long triple in the eighth, his 21st and final three-bagger of the season.[75] In the second game, Seymour got the Reds off to a hot start by smashing a line drive over center fielder Sammy Strang's head for a home run, which also scored Barry. The Giants scored three in the fourth to go ahead, 3–2. The Reds came right back to tie the score in the bottom of the inning on a walk to Barry and singles by Seymour and Corcoran. Seymour led off the sixth with a single and was forced out at second, but the Reds still managed to score a run to go up, 4–3. The Giants tied it when Bill Dahlen scored all the way from first after Seymour let a ball go through him and then, recovering it, juggled it. The game was called after the Reds failed to score in the bottom of the eighth to allow the Giants to catch their train. Notwithstanding that tie, the Reds won two of the three completed games and thus beat the Giants in a series for the first time all season.[76]

The closing weekend of the 1905 baseball season for the Reds at home included a Saturday doubleheader against St. Louis and then the much-anticipated contest on Sunday against Wagner and the Pirates to decide the year's batting race. In the Saturday series, Seymour positioned himself well for the finale, going 5-for-8 on the day. He smashed two doubles in the opener, further lifting his average, as the Reds split the series with the Cardinals.[77]

FINAL MATCHUP

The closing regular-season series, and the contest between Seymour and Wagner, drew 10,000 to the "Palace of the Fans." The *Pittsburgh Gazette* described the opening scene:

> Interest centered on Seymour and Wagner. They met and shook hands. Everybody cheered. Seymour thoughtfully wiped his eye and grinned. Wagner walked over and hefted Seymour's bat and sighed. Cy looked at Hans' stick, drew his form up in three-bagger posture and swung it mightily, then carefully laid it down. Services concluded, both took a chew of tobacco (from different plugs) and the game was on. Ten minutes later Seymour tried to tear Wagner's arm off with his first hit. When Wagner struck out his first time up, 10,000 fans yelled. Every swipe at the leather by either of the mighty pair caused craned attention until the last.[78]

Ironically, it was Seymour's defense that generated the greatest moment of the anticipated day, when he initiated a rare triple play in the seventh inning. Seymour caught a long fly off the bat of Pirates right fielder Bob Ganley and fired the ball home to nail Pirates catcher George Gibson trying to score. Reds catcher Schlei made the tag and then zipped the ball to third to nab Pirates pitcher Charlie Case, who was trying to advance from second base. With the Reds ahead, 2–1, the play saved the game. Seymour picked up two singles in the contest; Wagner was 0-for-3. Wagner was hit by a pitch in the eighth when the ball grazed his hand. The Reds added one more run and won, 3–1.[79]

In the second game, the final of the season for each club, both Seymour and Wagner collected two hits, but Cy was a little better on the day. Seymour's blooper over first base in the opening inning was lost in the sun by the Pirates infielders, allowing him to reach second. It was his 40th double of the season and would ensure that he led the league in that category. In the third, with two outs and the Reds trailing, 1–0, Huggins singled to center and then tried to steal second. Wagner, covering the bag from short, bobbled the throw from the Pirates catcher to keep the inning alive. Barry walked, and Seymour then smashed a hit to right field that scored Huggins. The Reds added two more runs in the fourth inning and then, with two outs, loaded the bases, bringing up Seymour.

Reds fans erupted. "The stands clamored for a homer and four more runs when the mighty Cy advanced to the plate," reported The *Cincinnati Enquirer*.[80] The Pirates thought the situation over and decided it was best to simply walk Seymour and force in a run rather than pitch to him. The *Cincinnati Enquirer* reported: "[Pitcher Ed] Kinsella and [Catcher Heine] Peitz, however, were afraid of the Main Slugger, for he was given a base on balls, forcing [catcher Gabby] Street over."[81] Shortstop Tommy Corcoran then flied out to end the inning. That ended the scoring for the day, and the Reds maintained the 4–1 lead to win. Wagner had two singles on the day, but it was not nearly enough to surpass Seymour.[82]

The *Pittsburgh Gazette* noted that the fate of the race favored Seymour: "There was scant chance today for Wagner to displace Seymour for the leadership, but even had there been, Cy would have triumphed, for in the test of the last day he doubled the inside count of the Carnegie Dutchman."[83]

UNSEATING WAGNER

In the end, Seymour was the 1905 National League batting champ. He finished the season with a .377 batting average, compared with Wagner's .363. In his last eight games in October, Seymour batted .567.[84]

Seymour also led the National league in hits (219), doubles, triples, and RBIs (121). His eight home runs were one shy of the lead, keeping him from winning what would one day be called the Triple Crown.

To beat out Honus Wagner during a decade in which "The Flying Dutchman" reigned as baseball's greatest player was no simple feat; 1900 through 1910 was the Wagnerian Era. Wagner won seven batting titles, with averages ranging from .381 to .339. In 1905, with his .363 average, Wagner was as dangerous a hitter as ever, though Seymour was just a notch better. That year, 1905, was the only year between 1900 and 1911 that Wagner didn't lead the league in at least one offensive category.[85]

PASSING OF A CYCLONE

Seymour's 1906 season got off to a slow start with the Reds, and McGraw, who had managed him in Baltimore, bought him for the princely sum of $12,000 halfway through the season.[86] (McGraw had tried in vain in 1905 to work out a deal to bring Seymour back to New York.) The change of scenery seemed to rejuvenate Seymour, who batted .320 for the Giants in the second half. Of the chance to play in New York again and his time in Cincinnati, Seymour said, "When I found that I was to be sold to the New York club a load seemed lifted off my shoulders. The bare announcement made me feel differently, and when I finally did join the New Yorks I knew that I was in my element again—that it was a change that I needed to bring me to form again." He added, "I was never disloyal to Cincinnati for a moment—but I simply could not do the work there that was expected of me, so this deal was the best thing that could have happened to me or the Reds."[87]

Seymour batted above .300 in eight of his 16 professional seasons and was a lifetime .303 batter.[88] For several seasons, he was one of the star players in the game. In 1906, writer Bozeman Bulger of New York's *Evening World* published his "All-American" list of the game's top players. He included Seymour as his center fielder.[89]

But Seymour's career came to an unceremonious close for a variety of reasons: a series of injuries, his frequent alcohol abuse, and his mercurial temperament, which led to a mix of on- and off-field incidents and several fallings-out with McGraw and other officials. He was suspended several times for instances labeled "unruly behavior" and drew the ire of team owners, league officials, and even newspaper editors throughout his career. Giants owner Andrew Freedman sent a missive to manager Buck Ewing on May 21, 1900, calling into question Seymour's "habits" and his "lack of condition."[90] In a January 31, 1906, letter from *Cincinnati Post* managing editor Ray Long to Reds team President August Hermann, Long complained that Seymour had threatened a photographer.[91] McGraw suspended Seymour for all of the Giants' spring training in 1909 for attacking coach Arlie Latham at the team hotel.[92]

Despite the abrupt end to his stardom, Seymour stayed around the game he loved until his untimely death. After he left the Giants in 1910, Seymour played minor league ball for two years. He first went back to Baltimore and then in 1912 was recruited to play for Newark by its manager, former rival "Iron Man" McGinnity.[93] Seymour briefly attempted a comeback at the age of 40 with the Boston Braves in 1913.[94] Later that year he wrote to Reds President Hermann on November 28, 1913, and pitched his services as a manager and called himself a "changed man" from what Hermann had known.[95]

During World War I, Seymour went to work in the New York shipyards and contracted tuberculosis. In 1918, at the age of 45, he played minor league ball again briefly for 13 games for Newark. He was also known to frequent Yankees and Giants practices at the Polo Grounds, including during the 1919 season.[96] Seymour died in his New York City home on September 20, 1919. He was 46 years old. Every major sports paper in the country carried at least a brief notice of his death, including in the places he played: Baltimore, Cincinnati, and New York. The *Pittsburgh Gazette Times* carried his headshot under the headline "Cy Seymour Passes Away" and listed among his accomplishments the 1905 batting-title victory over Wagner.[97]

Seymour is interred in a family plot at Albany Rural Cemetery. ■

Sources

In addition to the sources cited in the Notes, the author consulted the Baseball-Reference.com and Retrosheet websites for pertinent material and the box scores noted here.

Notes

1. Sports Reference LLC. Baseball-Reference.com - Major League Statistics and Information. https://www.baseball-reference.com/ (Date accessed December 2020) (https://www.baseball-reference.com/players/gl.fcgi?id=seymocy01&t=b&year=1905), (https://www.baseball-reference.com/players/gl.fcgi?id=wagneho01&t=b&year=1905).
2. Jack Ryder, "Broke that Long Losing Streak...Cy Seymour Makes A Season's Record by Pounding Out Five Clean Hits," *The Cincinnati Enquirer*, August 3, 1905, 4.
3. U.S. World War I draft card, James Bentley Seymour, September 12, 1918.
4. "Broke that Long Losing Streak," *The Cincinnati Enquirer*, August 3, 1905, 4.
5. "Broke that Long Losing Streak," *The Cincinnati Enquirer*, August 3, 1905, 4.
6. Bill Kirwin, "Cy Seymour," Society for American Baseball Research (SABR) Bio Project.
7. Frederick Lieb, "Seymour Too Wild to Pitch: But He Could Hit, As Major League Records Show," *Hartford Daily Courant*, January 19, 1924, 13.
8. Baseball-Reference.com (https://www.baseball-reference.com/players/s/seymocy01.shtml).
9. "Brooklyn Cannot Claim Joe Kelley," *The Cincinnati* Enquirer, July 19, 1902, 3.
10. Baseball-Reference.com (https://www.baseball-reference.com/players/s/seymocy01.shtml).
11. *The Reach Official American League Baseball Guide* (Philadelphia: A.J. Reach Company, 1906), 17.
12. Jack Ryder, "Baseball Season Opens Today," *The Cincinnati Enquirer*, April 14, 1905, 4
13. Jack Ryder, "Opening Scenes at League Park," *The Cincinnati Enquirer*, April 15, 1905, 3.
14. Baseball-Reference.com (https://www.baseball-reference.com/players/gl.fcgi?id=seymocy01&t=b&year=1905), (https://www.baseball-reference.com/players/gl.fcgi?id=wagneho01&t=b&year=1905).
15. Retrosheet (https://www.retrosheet.org/boxesetc/1905/B05030CIN1905.htm)
16. "Back in His Old Form...Cy Seymour Was the Only One of Kelley's Men Who Did Good Work With Bat," *The Cincinnati Enquirer*, May 6, 1905, 3.
17. Baseball-Reference.com (https://www.baseball-reference.com/players/gl.fcgi?id=seymocy01&t=f&year=1905).
18. Jack Ryder, "Back in His Old Form," *The Cincinnati Enquirer*, May 6, 1905, 3.
19. Baseball-Reference.com (https://www.baseball-reference.com/players/gl.fcgi?id=mathech01&t=p&year=1905).
20. Christy Mathewson (as told to John N. Wheeler), *Pitching in a Pinch* (New York: G.P. Putnam's Sons, 1912), 5–6.
21. Jack Ryder, "Four Home Runs Off Overall," *The Cincinnati Enquirer*, May 24, 4.
22. Ralph S. Davis, "Jack Harper Victim of Pirate Swatfest," *Pittsburgh Press*, May 28, 1905, 18.
23. Jack Ryder, "HOODOO...Demolished by the Reds," *The Cincinnati Enquirer*, May 29, 6.
24. Jack Ryder, "Rallied Twice in the Ninth," *The Cincinnati Enquirer*, June 1, 1905, 4.
25. "Rallied Twice in the Ninth," *The Cincinnati Enquirer*, June 1, 1905, 4.
26. Baseball-Reference.com (https://www.baseball-reference.com/boxes/?year=1905&month=05&day=31).
27. Baseball-Reference.com ((https://www.baseball-reference.com/players/gl.fcgi?id=seymocy01&t=b&year=1905).
28. Baseball-Reference.com (https://www.baseball-reference.com/players/gl.fcgi?id=seymocy01&t=b&year=1905).
29. Jack Ryder, "Cheered by President's Daughter," *The Cincinnati Enquirer*, June 9, 1905, 4.
30. Baseball-Reference.com (https://www.baseball-reference.com/players/gl.fcgi?id=seymocy01&t=b&year=1905).
31. Baseball-Reference.com (https://www.baseball-reference.com/players/gl.fcgi?id=mageesh01&t=b&year=1905).
32. Jack Ryder, "Half Dozen Now the Reds' Record," *The Cincinnati Enquirer*, June 18, 1905, 8.
33. Jack Ryder, "Bunted, Biffed, Banged, Bingled," *The Cincinnati Enquirer*, June 19, 1905, 3.
34. Jack Ryder, "Smashed Through Giants Defense," *The Cincinnati Enquirer*, June 20, 1905, 4.
35. Jack Ryder, "Broke Reds' Winning Streak," *The Cincinnati Enquirer*, June 21, 1905, 4.
36. Jack Ryder, "Bumped," *The Cincinnati Enquirer*, June 22, 1905, 4

37. Jack Ryder, "Quartet of Singles Off Overall," *The Cincinnati Enquirer*, June 23, 1905, 4.
38. Ralph S. Davis, "Pirates Walloped by Cincinnati Sluggers," 38 *The Pittsburgh Press*, June 25, 1905, 18.
39. "Selee's Men Hit Ball for 18 Bases," *Chicago Tribune*, June 26, 1905, 8.
40. Baseball-Reference.com (https://www.baseball-reference.com/players/gl.fcgi?id=seymocy01&t=b&year=1905).
41. Baseball-Reference.com (https://www.baseball-reference.com/players/gl.fcgi?id=seymocy01&t=b&year=1905).
42. Baseball-Reference.com (https://www.baseball-reference.com/players/gl.fcgi?id=wagneho01&t=b&year=1905).
43. George L. Moreland, "Seymour and Wagner Having a Close Race," *The Pittsburgh Press*, June 25, 1905, 18.
44. Baseball-Reference.com (https://www.baseball-reference.com/players/gl.fcgi?id=seymocy01&t=b&year=1905).
45. Baseball-Reference.com (https://www.baseball-reference.com/players/gl.fcgi?id=wagneho01&t=b&year=1905), (https://www.baseball-reference.com/players/gl.fcgi?id=seymocy01&t=b&year=1905).
46. Baseball-Reference.com (https://www.baseball-reference.com/players/gl.fcgi?id=seymocy01&t=b&year=1905).
47. Jack Ryder, "Iron Man Won His Own Game," *The Cincinnati Enquirer*, July 25, 1905, 4.
48. "Champions Defeat Cincinnati Again," *The New York Times*, July 28, 1905, 5.
49. Baseball-Reference.com (https://www.baseball-reference.com/players/gl.fcgi?id=seymocy01&t=b&year=1905).
50. Baseball-Reference.com (https://www.baseball-reference.com/boxes/?year=1905&month=07&day=31).
51. Baseball-Reference.com (https://www.baseball-reference.com/players/gl.fcgi?id=seymocy01&t=b&year=1905), (https://www.baseball-reference.com/players/gl.fcgi?id=wagneho01&t=b&year=1905).
52. "Brooklyns Lose a 13-Inning Game," *The Brooklyn Daily Eagle*, August 3, 1905, 11
53. Jack Ryder, "Thirteen Reds at Bat in First," *The Cincinnati Enquirer*, August 6, 1905, 10.
54. Jack Ryder, "Pounded Pitt Off the Rubber," *The Cincinnati Enquirer*, August 8, 1905, 4.
55. Baseball-Reference.com (https://www.baseball-reference.com/players/gl.fcgi?id=seymocy01&t=b&year=1905).
56. Baseball-Reference.com (https://www.baseball-reference.com/players/gl.fcgi?id=seymocy01&t=b&year=1905).
57. Jack Ryder, "Chased to the Tall Timber," *The Cincinnati Enquirer*, August 25, 1905, 4.
58. Baseball-Reference.com (https://www.baseball-reference.com/players/gl.fcgi?id=seymocy01&t=b&year=1905).
59. Jack Ryder, "Tired, Shooting the Chutes," *The Cincinnati Enquirer*, August 30, 1905, 4.
60. Baseball-Reference.com (https://www.baseball-reference.com/boxes/?year=1905&month=08&day=31).
61. Baseball-Referance.com (https://www.baseball-reference.com/players/gl.fcgi?id=seymocy01&t=b&year=1905).
62. Jack Ryder, "Premier Batters in the League. Seymour and Wagner Hook Up in Pittsburgh," *The Cincinnati Enquirer*, September 8, 1905, 4.
63. "Premier Batters in the League," *The Cincinnati Enquirer*, September 8, 1905, 4.
64. Jack Ryder, "Batted Pirate's Prize Pitchers," *The Cincinnati Enquirer*, September 9, 1905, 3.
65. "Batting Race is Still Close," *Pittsburgh Gazette*, September 10, 1905, Third Section, 2.
66. Jack Ryder, "Short Fell the Reds Rally," *The Cincinnati Enquirer*, September 16, 1905, 3.
67. "Close Race for the Batting Honors…Wagner and Seymour Are Now Nip and Tuck," *The Cincinnati Enquirer*, September 17, 1905, 34.
68. Jack Ryder, "RECRUITS…Seymour Drives Out Two Home Runs in Succession," *The Cincinnati Enquirer*, September 25, 1905, 3.
69. "RECRUITS," *The Cincinnati Enquirer*, September 25, 1905, 3.
70. Baseball-Reference.com. (https://www.baseball-reference.com/players/gl.fcgi?id=seymocy01&t=b&year=1905).
71. Baseball-Reference.com. (https://www.baseball-reference.com/players/gl.fcgi?id=seymocy01&t=b&year=1905).
72. Baseball-Reference.com. (https://www.baseball-reference.com/players/gl.fcgi?id=seymocy01&t=b&year=1905).
73. Jack Ryder, "Fifteen Rounds with Champs," *The Cincinnati Enquirer*, October 2, 1905, 3.
74. "Fifteen Rounds with Champs," *The Cincinnati Enquirer*, October 2, 1905, 3. "Through the Day Without Defeat,"
75. *The Cincinnati Enquirer*, October 4, 1905, 4.
76. "Through the Day Without Defeat," *The Cincinnati Enquirer*, October 4, 1905, 4.
77. Jack Ryder, "Seymour Boosts His Big Average," *The Cincinnati Enquirer*, October 8, 1905, 18.
78. "Pirates Lose Two: Seymour Leader," Pittsburgh Gazette, October 9, 1905, 7.
79. "'Cy' Seymour The 'Champeen' Hitter," *The Cincinnati Enquirer*, October 9, 1905, 3.
80. "'Cy' Seymour The 'Champeen' Hitter," *The Cincinnati Enquirer*, October 9, 1905, 3.
81. "'Cy' Seymour The 'Champeen' Hitter," *The Cincinnati Enquirer*, October 9, 1905, 3.
82. "'Cy' Seymour The 'Champeen' Hitter," *The Cincinnati Enquirer*, October 9, 1905, 3.
83. "Pirates Lose Two: Seymour Leader," *Pittsburgh Gazette*, October 9, 1905, 7.
84. Baseball-Reference.com (https://www.baseball-reference.com/players/gl.fcgi?id=seymocy01&t=b&year=1905).
85. Baseball-Reference.com (h#ps://www.baseball-reference.com/players/gl.fcgi?id=wagneho01&t=b&year=1905).
86. "Seymour Wears Red Sox No More, Cy Sold to Champion New York Giants," *The Cincinnati Enquirer*, July 13, 1906, 4.
87. "No Mystery About Cy Seymour's Batting," *The Scranton Truth*, July 31, 1906, 4.
88. Baseball-Reference.com (https://www.baseball-reference.com/players/s/seymocy01.shtml).
89. Bozeman Bulger, "Bulger Selects the All-Americans for 1906 Season," *The Evening World* (New York), September 22, 1906, 8.
90. Letter from Andrew Freedman to William Ewing, May 21, 1900. Baseball Hall of Fame Archives "Cy Seymour Clip File"
91. Letter from Ray Long to August Hermann, January 31, 1906. Baseball Hall of Fame Archives "Cy Seymour Clip File"
92. "Cy Seymour Fired Bodily," *Buffalo Evening News*, Sat, March 13, 1909
93. May Buy Cy Seymour, Joe McGinnity is Said to Have Dickered with Player," *The Baltimore Sun*, March 13, 1912, 10.
94. Baseball-Reference.com (https://www.baseball-reference.com/players/s/seymocy01.shtml).
95. Letter from J.B. Seymour to August 95 Hermann, November 28, 1913. Baseball Hall of Fame Archives "Cy Seymour Clip File"
96. "Seymour Funeral Today," *The New York Times*, September 22, 1919, 12.
97. "Cy Seymour Passes Away," *Pittsburgh Gazette Times*, September 22, 1919, 9.

The Elusive Fourth Out

What Teams Don't Know Will Bite Them

Stew Thornley

Your team clings to a lead in the late innings and is trying to get out of a first-and-third, one-out jam. Your pitcher gives up a long fly to right-center, and both runners take off. But your fleet center fielder seemingly saves the day. She sprints, leaps, extends, dives, and snags the drive inches off the ground. The runner from third has already crossed the plate, and the other one, beyond second base, stops and watches helplessly as the center fielder heaves the ball in. The relay goes to first, and the runner is doubled off for the third out.

You see the plate umpire point to home and hear the call, "The run scores!" What do you do?

You may respond as many—maybe even most—managers would: charge the umpire and scream, "How the fudge[1] does that run count? The runner from third didn't tag up!" As the umpire explains that the runner crossed the plate before the third out occurred, it finally dawns on you that you need to make an appeal play on the runner on third. You tell the umpire you want to appeal, but get the reply, "It's too late. Your infielders have already left the field." All that's left is to kick dirt on the umpire, expel a few more naughty words, get ejected, and possibly draw a suspension. After all, it's the umpire's fault that you don't know the rules, right?

What should you have done? Yell, but not at the umpire. Yell at your infielders to stay on the field. Next, tell the umpire you want to appeal. When all is reset and an appeal at third is properly performed, the runner will be called out and the run nullified.

This is the fourth-out play, as cited in what is now Rule 5.09(c): "Appeal plays may require an umpire to recognize an apparent 'fourth out.' If the third out is made during a play in which an appeal play is sustained on another runner, the appeal play decision takes precedence in determining the out."

Most appeals occur in non-inning-ending situations, when the appeal must be made before the next play or pitch. In the situation described here, however, a team loses the right to appeal once its infielders, including the pitcher, have left fair territory.

How often has the fourth-out occurred in the white/integrated major leagues? According to rules expert Rich Marazzi, never.[2]

FORCE PLAY OR NOT?

Beyond general ignorance of the rules by people who are paid to know them, many believe that a runner doubled off a base is a force out. It is not.[3] If a perceived force out ends an inning, a manager may think an appeal on another runner isn't necessary since a run cannot score when the third out is on a force.

This misperception can be costly even in situations in which a runner on third has correctly tagged up.

In a game on June 10, 2010, with Kansas City at Minnesota, the Twins had Nick Punto on third and Denard Span on second with one out in the third when Joe Mauer hit a long fly to center. The wind kept the ball in the park, and Mitch Maier caught it in front of the fence. Punto tagged and, as he started for home, saw that Span had taken off from second and was nearly at third. Punto turned and yelled at Span to retreat while he jogged toward the plate. Maier threw the ball to shortstop Yuniesky Betancourt to double off Span and end the inning. Punto, running at only a trot, was still a few steps short of the plate; thus, his run didn't count.

Two reporters, a television play-by-play announcer, and a Twins team official asked the official scorer if Punto's run would have counted had he crossed the plate before the third out. (It definitely would have.) After the game, Punto admitted that he didn't know the rule, that he thought his run wouldn't count regardless of whether he crossed the plate ahead of the third out. "I figured a double play is a double play, but it's not," Punto said. "You can go ahead and touch home plate there and get the run." The Twins lost this game, 9–8.[4]

A year later the Twins may have lost a run in a similar way. In a May 27, 2011, game against the Los Angeles Angels of Anaheim, Michael Cuddyer hit a long fly to right-center that was caught. Alexi Casilla tagged at third and only jogged toward home as he gestured to teammate Jason Kubel to get back to second. Kubel was doubled off for the third out before Casilla crossed the plate. The Twins lost this game, 6–5.

UNCERTAINTY AMONG UMPIRES

Even the umpires have required prompting on the rule. In a game at Arizona on April 12, 2009, the Los Angeles Dodgers had Andre Ethier on third and Juan Pierre on second with one out when Randy Wolf lined out to pitcher Dan Haren, who threw to shortstop Felipe Lopez. Rather than step on the base, Lopez chased Pierre down. By the time he tagged him for the third out, Ethier—who had been running on contact and hadn't tagged up—crossed the plate.

"That's the four-out play," said Dodgers coach Bob Schaefer to manager Joe Torre, referring to what the Diamondbacks should have then executed, but didn't. As Arizona left the field, Torre came out to confer with the umpires and remind them that Ethier's run counted. Torre knew that Ethier's failure to tag up was irrelevant unless and until the Diamondbacks appealed, and he credited Schaefer for that knowledge. "I remembered because he had put some of the rules on my desk this spring and we read them to the players a number of times last year."

What Torre and the Dodgers knew was something the Diamondbacks didn't. "I still don't really understand the rule," said Haren. Wrote Dylan Hernandez in the *Los Angeles Times*, "By reminding the officiating crew of an obscure rule unknown to most of the players at Chase Field, Torre essentially argued in the tying run in the Dodgers' 3–1 victory over the Arizona Diamondbacks."[5]

Confusion has reigned even in situations in which the runner on third *did* tag up, a scenario that would not have had the potential for a fourth out.

In a Baltimore at Cleveland game April 28, 2007, the Orioles had a 2–1 lead in the top of the third. With Nick Markakis on third and Miguel Tejada on first and one down, Ramon Hernandez flied out to Grady Sizemore in center field. Markakis tagged and came home as Sizemore threw to Ryan Garko at first base to double off Tejada. Plate umpire Marvin Hudson signaled that Markakis's run did not count, even though Markakis had clearly crossed the plate before the third out. Hudson waved it off because he did not think a run could score on such a play. Orioles bench coach Tom Trebelhorn knew the run should count but didn't say anything until after the fourth inning, when he had a short conference with the umpires. Crew-chief Ed Montague sent Bill Miller, one of the umpires, to check the rules. By the time Baltimore manager Sam Perlozzo came out at the end of the fifth inning, Miller had confirmed that the run should have counted. Montague called the press box and told Chad Broski, the official scorer, to add the run to Baltimore's total. Broski was aware of the situation but had to wait for word from the field to count the run. "When it happened, I thought the run should have counted but, of course, I have to go off the umpire's ruling," said Broski. "Most people in the press box were commenting on the baserunning error by Tejada and didn't know the rule. Not much happened in the box until the umpire called up and then changed it and I had to announce it. At that point I explained to them why the run counted." Cleveland lodged a protest as the score changed from 2–2 to 3–2 in favor of the Orioles. Cleveland scored twice in the last of the sixth for a 4–3 lead, but the Orioles rallied in the eighth and ninth to win, 7–4, a result that stuck when Cleveland's protest was denied three days later.[6]

In a game on June 26, 1935, St. Louis at Brooklyn, home plate umpire Charlie Moran misapplied the rules by denying a run to the Dodgers after Jim Bucher had tagged on a fly ball and scored before Jimmy Jordan was doubled off first for the third out. Manager Casey Stengel lodged a protest. However, Brooklyn won the game in extra innings, and league president Ford Frick did not have to rule on the matter. Ray J. Gillespie of the *St. Louis Star-Times* reported that Moran said the rule governing this type of play had changed, although the rules of the time do not back up Moran's decision. The *Brooklyn Times Union* referred to Moran's decision as "weird."[7]

The umpires were on top of the rules when the Yankees visited the Mets on June 28, 1998, but there

REUTERS

Umpire Ed Montague (pictured here with Lou Piniella of Seattle) had to send a member of his crew to check the rules in an April 2007 game in which Baltimore faced Cleveland.

was still turmoil over the usual conundrum of what a force is and what it isn't. With the score 1–1 in the last of the ninth, the Mets had Carlos Baerga on third and Brian McRae on first with one out. Luis Lopez flied out to Paul O'Neill. Baerga tagged and was running home when he saw McRae going to second. "I wanted to start yelling, but I was running too hard," said Baerga, avoiding the errors of Nick Punto and Alexei Casilla noted in earlier examples. The Yankees got the ball to Tino Martinez at first as McRae tried to get back. Baerga, after crossing the plate and starting to celebrate, saw first-base umpire Bruce Dreckman signal out. The Mets erupted, and coach Cookie Rojas had to restrain Baerga. Part of the protest may have been over whether or not Martinez had made a clean catch of Derek Jeter's relay, although it didn't matter since Baerga scoring ahead of what happened at first base ended the game.

If shortstop Alexi Casilla had hurried to cross the plate in a May 2011 game, might the Twins have avoided a 6–5 loss?

Plate umpire Frank Pulli conferred with Dreckman and, making the judgment that Baerga had crossed the plate before the final out, ruled that the run counted. "I don't know what he was waiting for," Mets manager Bobby Valentine said after the game, referring to Pulli's delayed ruling. "Maybe he just didn't want us to celebrate."[8]

Jeter and Martinez admitted not being familiar with the rule and even manager Joe Torre had to ask about it. Martinez was quoted by Ohm Youngmisuk in the *New York Daily News*: "I thought that if it's a force-out at first, I figured the game may go on, but I don't know the rule."[9]

WHAT'S THE SCORE?

A 2016 game in Detroit didn't have the final score correct until a day later. On June 24, Cleveland held a 7–4 lead over the Tigers, who had Ian Kinsler on second and Cameron Maybin on first with one out in the bottom of the ninth. Miguel Cabrera hit a long fly to center, where Rajai Davis juggled the ball and hung on for the catch. Kinsler and Maybin had taken off without tagging, and Cleveland relayed a throw home too late to get Kinsler at the plate. Chris Gimenez then threw to Mike Napoli at first to double off Maybin and end the game. Although Kinsler's run had no bearing on the game outcome, Cleveland could have saved reliever Cody Allen a run by then throwing to second for a fourth out on Kinsler. Not only did Cleveland not realize that—without the additional appeal, Kinsler's run counted—no one else did, and the final score reported in newspapers the next day was 7–4. A day later, Major League Baseball clarified that Kinsler, having crossed the plate before the third out, did score and the final was changed to 7–5.

Another game that had fans leaving without knowing the score also resulted in Lee Guetterman thinking he had a save. It happened when the Milwaukee Brewers failed to get the fourth out, resulting in a run for the New York Yankees, on July 1, 1989. In the last of the eighth, the Yankees had a 4–1 lead with Mike Pagliarulo on third and Bob Geren on first. The runners were off on a squeeze play as Wayne Tolleson popped up a bunt. Pitcher Jay Aldrich caught it and threw to first to double off Geren. Pagliarulo had crossed the plate, and plate umpire Larry Barnett signaled that the run counted. Milwaukee didn't appeal for a fourth out to nullify Pagliarulo's run. In addition to the Brewers not being aware of the situation, the same was true with the scoreboard operator, who did not put the run on the board. Everyone thought the Yankees had won, 4–1 only to learn later that the final was 5–1. Guetterman pitched the ninth and was originally credited with a save, since he had entered with what was thought to be a three-run lead. When the score was corrected, Guetterman's save was removed.

DID THE ASTROS MISS THE PENNANT?

Here's one that might have been...or maybe was. The best-of-five National League playoff series between Houston and Philadelphia in 1980 was wild, the final four games going into extra innings. Houston was on the verge of earning a trip to the World Series in game four—one that had everything, including protests lodged by both teams after a fourth-inning play with disagreements if there should have been one, two, or three outs called. Houston's Gary Woods had two baserunning mishaps, one when he was called out on appeal for leaving third base too early on a fly ball.

Less was said about a potential appeal later in the game. As with the fourth-inning play, this one centered on uncertainty about whether a batted ball had been trapped or cleanly caught.

The score was 2–2 in the top of the eighth. With one out, the Phillies had Pete Rose on third and Mike Schmidt on first when Manny Trillo hit a sinking fly to right. As Jeffrey Leonard rushed in to attempt a shoestring catch, Schmidt danced between the bases and finally took off for second when it appeared that Leonard had only trapped the ball. However, right-field umpire Bruce Froemming signaled out. Leonard heaved the ball to the plate, far too short and late to get Rose, racing home from third. Catcher Bruce Bochy then threw to Art Howe at first to double off a now-enraged Schmidt, who claimed Leonard had not made the catch. Froemming's call stood, the inning was over, but Rose's run counted, and Philadelphia had a 3–2 lead. Speculation emerged over whether Rose had properly tagged before coming home, but the Astros did nothing about it at the time.

Because of all the other strange events in the game, this play was glossed over in many news accounts. However, Jayson Stark of the *Philadelphia Inquirer* wrote, "Manny Trillo lined a 1–2 pitch to right that Jeff Leonard may or may not have shoestringed. Ump Bruce Froemming ruled he caught it, and Schmidt was doubled off first for the second sacrifice fly-double play of the day. But Rose had made sure. He waited until the ball came down, then tagged and scored." Stark quoted third-base coach Lee Elia: "I yelled to him [Rose], 'Tag up.' But he already was gonna do that. Only Pete Rose has the instincts to do that. A lot of people would overlook that. Pete was gonna make sure this was a 3–2 ball game."

On the other hand, the *Inquirer*'s Allen Lewis wrote,

> After Rose scored, the Astros decided that maybe Rose had left third base too soon and they could nullify the run by making the appeal, even though it would have been a fourth out. Rules allow for a fourth out in such cases, but no appeal was made.
>
> As [plate umpire Doug] Harvey explained, "I didn't immediately signal Rose's run scored before the third out, because I knew that an appeal could be made on Rose, although I didn't know if he tagged up. There is a possible appeal on the fourth out. They can do that, but they must do it correctly. If all the infielders leave the field, the appeal can no longer be made.... I walked toward [first base umpire Ed] Vargo and said, "The run counts if there's no appeal."

The oversight may have been costly. The Astros tied the score in the last of the ninth, only to lose in the 10th. The Phillies won again in 10 innings the next night to win the pennant, en route to the team's first-ever World Series championship. It took another 25 years for Houston to get to the World Series.[10]

THE 1957 GAME THAT BROKE THE RULE BOOK

In all of the situations so far cited, the rules are clear about a team forfeiting its right to appeal after the infielders have left the field. Through 1957, though, no such provision was in the rule book, only a reference to an "appeal before the next legal pitch." Hank Soar had to determine how to handle a situation in an August 22, 1957, game in Cleveland. The Red Sox were up, 10–0, with one out in the top of the ninth and had Gene Mauch on second and Pete Daley on first. Mike Fornieles hit a soft fly to short center. The runners took off, confident that the ball would drop safely, but shortstop Chico Carrasquel made a spectacular running catch. Carrasquel didn't see Mauch racing for the plate and, rather than step on second, threw to first to double off Daley.

Soar, working the plate, made no indication of Mauch scoring ahead of the third out. Between innings the Red Sox asked if Mauch's run counted. Soar told them, "We'll handle this. Just go away." After the first pitch of the bottom of the ninth, Soar turned toward the official scorer in the press box and yelled, "The run counts."

Asked after the game if he shouldn't have indicated in some way that Mauch's run counted, even if only tentatively, Soar said, "We couldn't without tipping off that he left his base too soon. On an appeal, it's up to the teams to call our attention to the play, not for us to call their attention to it." Cal Hubbard, the American League supervisor of umpires, said Soar handled the situation perfectly and did so even though the rules did not outline the proper method for dealing with such a situation. Hubbard said he would bring the question to the Rules Committee; the following year the rules were amended to acknowledge a potential fourth-out situation and clarify when a team forfeited the opportunity to appeal.[11]

Columnist Hal Lebovitz posed this hypothetical to Hubbard: same situation, only a 3–3 game with the Red Sox as the home team, batting in the last of the ninth.

> Again Mauch scores and again the Indians ignore it. Vic Wertz comes to bat in the top of the tenth. He hits the first pitch into the seats for a home run.
>
> But wait! The umpire is shouting, "The home run doesn't count," he yells. "The Red Sox win, 4 to 3, because Mauch's run became legal with that first pitch."
>
> "Yes," says Cal Hubbard. "That's what the umpire would have to do, all right. But I'd hate to be the umpire in that situation. All Hell would probably break loose."

Regardless of the lack of clarity in the 1957 rules, Hubbard emphasized that the burden was on the teams. "If they know the rules, they'll know what to do," he said. "If not, tough luck."

As many players and teams have demonstrated in the half-century that followed, they don't know the rules and it's often tough luck. ■

Acknowledgments

Thanks to Chad Broski and Rich Marazzi and to Society for American Baseball Research members Wayne McElreavy, Karen Brown, David McDonald, John Hernandez, Howard Elson, Lyle Spatz, Dwight Oxley, Dan Cichalski, Charlie Bevis, Bruce Slutsky, and Steve Gietschier along with Dave Smith and all the great folks at Retrosheet (https://www.retrosheet.org). [Note: The author of this article was the official scorer for both of the Twins games noted in 2010 and 2011; the description of those plays is based on his notes and recollection.]

Notes

1. Possibly not the exact word a manager would use here.
2. Marazzi is an author of books on baseball rules and a rules consultant to numerous major-league teams and sports networks. In email correspondence on January 25, 2021, Marazzi said he is not aware of such an event ever happening. He said Sam McDowell once told him a fourth out was executed in a Cleveland game although he hasn't been able to document it.
3. From the "Definition of Terms" section of the rule book regarding a force play: "Example: Not a force out. One out. Runner on first and third. Batter flies out. Two out. Runner on third tags up and scores. Runner on first tries to retouch before throw from fielder reaches first baseman, but does not get back in time and is out. Three outs. If, in umpire's judgment, the runner from third touched home before the ball was held at first base, the run counts."
4. John Shipley, "Sloppy Play Costs Twins," *St. Paul Pioneer Press*, June 11, 2010: 6D.
5. Dylan Hernandez, "Play It Out Strictly by the Rules: Torre's Appeal Leads to, Yes, Four Outs, Tying Run in Second Inning," *Los Angeles Times*, April 13, 2009, C1, C11.
6. Jeff Zrebiec, "Orioles Strike Last in Victory," *Baltimore Sun*, April 29, 2007: 1, 13D. Zrebiec, Jeff, "Indians' Protest Denied," *Baltimore Sun*, May 3, 2007: 7E; Email correspondence with Chad Broski, January 22, 2021.
7. Gillespie, Ray J., "Cards End Eastern Tour with Nine Victories and Eight Defeats: Mediocre Relief Pitching Permits Brooklyn to Win," *St. Louis Star-Times*, June 27, 1935: 23; McCullough, "Dodger Victory Averts Protest: Stengel Put Out of Game for Interpreting Rule Correctly," *Brooklyn Times Union*, June 27, 1935: 11. Rule 52 of the 1934 and 1935 *Official Base Ball Rules* notes that no run can score if the third out is forced. The definition of a force play in the rule book states, "A force-out can be made only when a base-runner legally loses the right to the base he occupies by reason of the batsman becoming a base-runner, and he is thereby forced to advance."
8. Barry Stanton, "A Funky Finish, But It's Finally All Over," *Home News Tribune* (New Brunswick, New Jersey), June 29, 1998: D2; Tom Withers, Associated Press, June 29, 1998.
9. Ohm Youngmisuk, "Tino Won't Concede," *New York Daily News*, June 29, 1998: 54; Jason Dumias, "Mets Find Consolation in a Strange Series Finish: Mound Gems Set Up a Confusing Ninth," and Claire Smith "Welcome to the Flushing Zoo," *The New York Times*, June 29, 1998: C1.
10. Jayson Stark, "Phils Come Up with a Surprise Ending in Wild and Crazy 5-3 Win over Astros," *Philadelphia Inquirer*, October 12, 1980: 1, 6F; Allen Lewis, "Triple Play? Ain't No Way," *Philadelphia Inquirer*, October 12, 1980: 1, 6F. Frank Mercogliano, in an April 11, 2015 post on the SID [Sports Information Directors] Scoring Assistance Facebook group, wrote of the play, "Leonard caught it and threw home to get Rose, who left way early and scored easily (he was sprinting home when the ball was caught)." However, television coverage (Game 4 of the 1980 playoffs is on YouTube: https://www.youtube.com/watch?v=-2kkfWU0zz4) does not show if Rose took off early.
11. In Rules 7.08(d), Rule 7.10, and Rule 7.10 in the Notes and Case Book Comments section in the 1957 rule book, appeals and a "fourth out" are covered but with no clarification on dealing with a situation when a half-inning has apparently ended. Beginning in 1958, Rule 7.10(d) specifies that "during a play which ends a half-inning, the appeal must be made before the defensive team leaves the field."
12. Hal Lebovitz, "Bosox Score on 4th-Out Puzzler When Indians Nip Wrong Runner: Mauch Leaves Base too Soon, But Tribe Fails to Appeal," *The Sporting News*, September 4, 1957: 29; Marazzi, Rich, *The Rules and Lore of Baseball*, New York: Stein and Day Publishers, 1980: 170–71.

Impact of the Varying Sac-Fly Rules on Batting Champs, 1931–2019

Herm Krabbenhoft

The official rules currently governing sacrifice flies in Major League Baseball have not always been in use, and have varied.[1] From 1908 through 1930, the official rules stipulated that a player who batted in a run with a flyout was credited with a sacrifice hit and not charged an at-bat. In fact, from 1926 through 1930, a player was also credited with a sacrifice hit when he hit a flyout that resulted in any baserunner advancing to any base. Then from 1931 through 1938, the official rules did *not* credit a batter with a sacrifice when he hit a flyout which permitted a runner to score (or advance to any base); i.e., an RBI flyout was scored as an at-bat, just like an RBI groundout. Then, for the 1939 season, the sacrifice on a fly was re-instituted, but only for RBI flyouts. The sacrifice fly was again eliminated for the 1940–53 seasons; batters were again charged with an at-bat when they hit an RBI flyout. Finally, the sacrifice fly rule that has been in operation from 1954 to the present restores the rule that batters who hit RBI flyouts are credited with a sac fly, and an RBI flyout is not charged as an at bat, just as a sacrifice bunt is not charged as an at-bat.

The back-and-forth character of the sacrifice fly rule (i.e., at-bat or no at-bat) has resulted in some interesting "What if?" situations. For instance, one of baseball's oldest (and at-one-time highly revered) batting metrics is batting average (BA, hits divided by at-bats), with the player with the highest batting average being regarded as the batting champion of his league.[2] But which players would have won baseball's batting crowns if the rule had been consistent since 1931? Specifically:

A. What if the current sacrifice fly rule had been in effect for the 1931–53 period?

B. What if the no-sacrifice-fly rule—the one in effect for the 1931–38 and 1940–53 periods—had continued to be in effect from 1954 to today?

RESEARCH PROCEDURE

To address Question A, I utilized Retrosheet to ascertain the number of RBI flyouts achieved by each player who was the league leader in BA as given on the relevant "League Leaders" pages for the seasons from 1931 through 1953. I examined the Retrosheet Play-By-Play (PBP) narratives for each game in which the player's Retrosheet Daily file indicated he had one or more runs batted in. I recorded the batting event for each RBI as follows: two-RBI single (S-2), one-RBI double (D-1), one-RBI groundout (GO-1), one-RBI flyout (FO-1), one-RBI walk (W-1), etc. I did the same for each player who finished with a BA within .020 of the leader's league-leading mark. With complete RBI flyout numbers then in hand, I was able to ascertain the values for a player's hypothetical BA (i.e., his BA computed with RBI flyouts treated as not being at-bats). With regard to Question B, the hypothetical BA was obtained using the official statistics for sacrifice flies and treating sac-flies as at-bats.

RESULTS

A. What if the Present Sac-Fly rule (No At-Bat) had been in effect for the 1931–53 period?

Table 1 summarizes the five times that a player did not win his league's batting title during the 1931–53 period because of the "no Sac-Fly" rule. As can be seen, nearly half of the players listed became Hall of Famers. Twice the "no Sac-Fly" rule precluded a player from winning the esteemed Triple Crown of batting.

Table 1. Hypothetical BA Champs if the 1954 Sac-Fly Rule Had Been Used for 1931–53 Period

Year League	Player (RBI Flyouts)	BA (Official)	BA (Hypothetical)
1932	Dale Alexander (2)	**.3673**	.3692
AL	**Jimmie Foxx (11)**	.3641	**.3711**
1935	Buddy Myer (7)	**.3490**	.3530
AL	**Joe Vosmik (9)**	.3489	**.3541**
1944	Lou Boudreau (6)	**.3271**	.3304
AL	Bobby Doerr (7)	.3248	.3297
	Bob Johnson (11)	.3238	**.3307**
1945	George Stirnweiss (3)	**.30854**	.31001
AL	**Tony Cuccinello (4)**	.30846	**.31156**
1949	George Kell (6)	**.3429**	.3469
AL	**Ted Williams (7)**	.3428	**.3470**

The first hypothetical change in a batting average king occurred in 1932. The actual 1932 AL batting champion was Dale Alexander, who compiled a batting average of .367 (144 hits in 392 AB).[3] Jimmie Foxx finished second with a .364 mark (213 hits in 585 AB). Had the current Sac-Fly rule been operative in 1932, Foxx would have won the batting crown. According to Retrosheet, two of Alexander's 60 RBIs came via flyouts, which when treated as non at-bats, would adjust his batting average to .3692. Foxx, meanwhile, had eleven RBI flyouts, which—if not counted as at-bats—yields an adjusted batting average of .3711. Since Double X was also the AL leader in home runs (58) and runs batted in (168), he would have won the batting Triple Crown.[4]

At the conclusion of the 1935 campaign, Buddy Myer emerged with the highest batting average: .3490 (215 hits in 616 AB). Joe Vosmik was runner-up: .3484 (216 hits in 619 AB).[5] Jimmie Foxx came in third: .346 (185 hits in 535 AB). However, Vosmik would have been the batting champ if the current Sac-Fly rule had been in effect. Myer had 7 RBI flyouts, which would have given him a hypothetical .3530 BA. Vosmik had 9 RBI flyouts, giving him a hypothetical .3541 BA. Foxx, with only one RBI flyout, would have ended up with .3464.

The 1944 campaign provides the next *possible* hypothetical change for the occupant of the batting throne. According to the official rules and records, Lou Boudreau compiled the highest qualifying batting average in the American League. With 191 hits in 584 at bats he fashioned a .3271 BA. Close behind were Bobby Doerr (.3248) and Bob Johnson (.3238). Had the current Sac-Fly rule been in effect, all three of these players would have had a higher batting average. According to the PBP details given on the Retrosheet website, Boudreau had six RBI flyouts (which afford an adjusted BA of .3304). Similarly, Doerr's seven RBI flyouts give him an adjusted BA of .3297. And, Johnson's eleven RBI flyouts provide him a modified BA of .3307. Thus, it appears that Johnson won our hypothetical batting title. However, there's an uncertainty connected with Boudreau's adjusted BA.

"Double X"—Jimmie Foxx—had 11 RBI flyouts in 1932, but only one in 1935. Would these achievements have changed the record books if today's sac fly rule were in place?

In addition to the six clearly-stated RBI flyouts given in the Retrosheet PBPs, there are three RBI plays with the following deduced descriptions:

1. **June 21 (at Detroit), first inning**. "Boudreau out on an unknown play [Peters scored, O'Dea to second]."
2. **July 1 (at Washington), fourth inning**. "Boudreau out on an unknown play [Hoag scored (unearned)]."
3. **September 20 (vs. Boston), fourth inning**. "Boudreau out on an unknown play [Rocco scored]."

Each of these deduced "out on an unknown play" events could be a groundout-RBI or a flyout-RBI. To ascertain which, if any, of these three "unknown plays" was an RBI flyout, I examined the game accounts in pertinent newspapers and found that Boudreau made infield outs in each of the first two games. Unfortunately, the newspaper text descriptions did not resolve the "unknown play" for the third game. Thus, if the "unknown play" was an infield out, Boudreau's adjusted BA would still be .3304 and Johnson's hypothetical .3307 BA would still be the highest. However, if the "unknown play" was an outfield flyout, then Boudreau's adjusted BA would be .3310, resulting in Boudreau retaining the batting crown.[6,7]

The 1945 AL batting race remains the closest race in history, with a slim .00008 separating the champion's .30854 batting average from the runner-up's .30846. George "Snuffy" Stirnweiss, playing in 152 games, amassed 195 hits in 632 at bats to carve out his league-leading .309 mark, while Tony Cuccinello accumulated 124 hits in 402 at bats in the 118 games he played for his second-place .308 BA. However, when one takes into account the RBI flyouts each man had, Cuccinello emerges with the higher hypothetical batting average. Cuccinello, with four RBI flyouts, has an adjusted BA of .31156, while Stirnweiss, with three RBI flyouts, has an adjusted BA of .31001.[8] The 1945 campaign was Cuccinello's final season of his 13-year big league career. Playing "full time" for the first time since 1940, he was basically a "war-time replacement player" during the 1943–45 seasons. Had the current Sac-Fly rule been operative in 1945, he would have been the first and only player to be a BA king in his final major-league season.

NATIONAL BASEBALL HALL OF FAME LIBRARY, COOPERSTOWN, NY

Dale Alexander won the 1932 batting title with an official batting average of .3673, but if sacrifice flies had not been counted as at-bats, he would have been edged out by Jimmie Foxx.

In 1949, the chase for the AL batting crown came down to the final day, October 2. Before that day's diamond action commenced, Boston's Ted Williams had the highest BA: .344. Detroit's George Kell was next at .341. As the day unfolded, Williams went 0-for-2 with a pair of walks in Boston's 5–3 loss to the pennant-clinching Yankees. The Splendid Splinter finished with a .3428 BA (194 hits in 566 AB). Kell's Tigers also did not fare well, dropping its game to Cleveland, 8–4. But Kell did well from the batter's box, collecting two hits in three at bats plus a walk, finishing at .3429 (179 hits in 522 at bats). What would have been the final result if the current Sac-Fly rule had been in place? Kell had six RBI flyouts on the year, which would have boosted his average to .3469 if they had not counted against his at-bats. However, Williams had seven RBI flyouts, which would have elevated his BA to .3470. Teddy Ballgame would have won his third consecutive batting crown and—since he also led the AL in homers (43) and RBIs (159, tied with teammate Vern Stephens)—he would have earned his third Triple Crown.

While there were a few other very close batting races during the 1931–53 period, such as the 1931 NL race (Chick Hafey at .3489 and Bill Terry at .3486) and the 1953 AL race (Mickey Vernon at .3372) and Al Rosen at .3356), but after adjustment the winner remained in the lead.[9,10] One other no-sac-fly-impacted batting average item is worth mentioning. In 1941, Ted Williams batted a lusty .406 (185 H in 456 AB), but had his eight RBI flyouts not been counted as at-bats, his batting average would have been .413.

B. What if the "no Sac-Fly" rule (1931–38 and 1940–53) had remained in effect to the present?

If the 1953 Sac-Fly rule had not been changed there would have been four different batting kings (Table 2). In 1970, Alex Johnson edged out Carl Yastrzemski for the AL batting title, .32899 to .32862. However, because Johnson had three sac-flies and Yaz had two, Johnson's adjusted BA would be .32739 while Carl's would be .32746 and Yastrzemski would have captured the batting throne by .00007 points. It would have been Yaz's fourth BA title. Similarly, Derek Jeter would have catapulted over both Manny Ramirez and Bill Mueller in 2003, Josh Harrison would have overtaken Justin Morneau in 2014, and Ketel Marte would have surpassed Christian Yelich in 2019 to earn hypothetical batting titles.

In addition to the hypothetical changes shown in Table 2, Carl Yastrzemski would have surfaced as the 1968 AL batting king with a sub-.300 mark. Yaz, who put together an official batting average of .301 (162 hits in 539 at bats), had four no-at-bat-sac-flies. Had those four sac-flies been at-bat RBI flyouts, his official batting average would have been reduced by three points, to a hypothetical .298.

Table 2. Hypothetical BA Champs if the 1953 Sac-Fly Rule Had Been Used for 1954–2019 Period

Year League	Player (SF)	BA (Official)	BA (Hypothetical)
1970	Alex Johnson (3)	**.3290**	.3274
AL	**Carl Yastrzemski (2)**	.3286	**.3275**
2003	Bill Mueller (6)	**.3263**	.3226
AL	Manny Ramirez (5)	.3251	.3223
	Derek Jeter (1)	.3237	**.3230**
2014	Justin Morneau (8)	**.3187**	.3137
NL	Josh Harrison (2)	.3154	**.3142**
2019	Cristian Yelich (3)	**.3292**	.3272
NL	Ketel Marte (2)	.3286	**.3275**

OTHER HYPOTHETICAL CHANGES

While the traditional batting averages and batting championships are/were historically considered important, they are certainly not viewed with esteem and utility by many of today's baseball analysts.[11] Perhaps the only traditional batting metric still considered at least somewhat worthwhile is slugging average (total bases divided by at bats), which has been included in the annual baseball guides such as *Spalding's Official Base Ball Guide* since 1924 for the National League, and since 1947 for the American League (for example, in *The Sporting News Official Baseball Guide*). In addition to ascertaining the hypothetical batting champions impacted by the varying sac-fly rules, I also determined the hypothetical slugging kings, as well as the hypothetical leaders in one of today's more-highly-valued and seemingly ubiquitous batting metrics, on-base-plus-slugging (OPS), which made its in-print debut

Tony Cucinello would have beaten George Stirnweiss for the 1945 AL batting crown had that season been played under today's sac fly rules.

in 1984.[12] Table 3 provides the information for the hypothetical slugging average leaders analogous to Table 1 (i.e., if the 1954 "yes-SF" rule had been utilized for the 1931–53 period). As can be seen, Hank Greenberg would have surpassed Jimmie Foxx in 1935, Bob Johnson would have overtaken Bobby Doerr in 1944, Vern Stephens would have supplanted George Stirnweiss in 1945, and Ralph Kiner would have leapfrogged over both Andy Pafko and Stan Musial in 1950. According to my research, there would not have been any hypothetical changes in the OPS leaders (and no change in the On-Base Average leaders[13]).

Table 3. Hypothetical SLG Kings if the 1954 Sac-Fly Rule Had Been Used for 1931–53 Period

Year League	Player (SF)	BA (Official)	BA (Hypothetical)
1935	Jimmie Foxx (1)	**.6355**	.6367
AL	**Hank Greenberg (9)**	.6284	**.6377**
1944	Bobby Doerr (7)	**.5278**	.5358
AL	**Bob Johnson (11)**	.5276	**.5389**
1945	George Stirnweiss (3)	**.4763**	.4785
AL	**Vern Stephens (9)**	.4729	**.4804**
1950	Stan Musial (3)	**.5964**	.5996
NL	Andy Pafko (4)	.5914	.5961
	Ralph Kiner (10)	.5905	**.6015**

Tables 4 and 5 present the corresponding adjusted SLG and OPS numbers analogous to Table 2, showing the leaders if the 1953 "no-SF" rule had been used 1954–2019. Joe Adcock would have fashioned a higher adjusted slugging average than Duke Snider in 1956. Similarly for Orlando Cepeda and Frank Robinson in 1961, Andres Galarraga and Darryl Strawberry in 1988, and Carlos Quentin and Alex Rodriguez in 2008. And, as shown in Table 5, Dave Winfield compiled a higher adjusted OPS than Dave Kingman in 1979. Likewise for Dale Murphy and Mike Schmidt in 1984, Mike Piazza and Barry Bonds in 1995, David Ortiz and Alex Rodriguez in 2007, and Giancarlo Stanton and Andrew McCutchen in 2014.

Table 4. Hypothetical SLG Kings if the 1953 Sac-Fly Rule Had Been Used for 1954–2019 Period

Year League	Player (SF)	SLG	SLG (Adjusted)
1956	Duke Snider (4)	**.5978**	.5934
NL	**Joe Adcock (2)**	.5969	**.5943**
1961	Frank Robinson (10)	**.6110**	.6000
NL	**Orlando Cepeda (3)**	.6085	**.6054**
1988	Darryl Strawberry (9)	**.5451**	.5362
NL	**Andres Galarraga (3)**	.5402	**.5376**
2008	Alex Rodriguez (5)	**.5725**	.5670
AL	**Carlos Quentin (3)**	.5708	**.5673**

Table 5. Hypothetical OPS Kings if the 1953 Sac-Fly Rule Had Been Used for 1954–2019 Period.

Year League	Player (SF)	OPS	OPS (Adjusted)
1979	Dave Kingman (8)	**.9558**	.9467
NL	**Dave Winfield (2)**	.9528	**.9509**
1984	Mike Schmidt (8)	**.91890**	.91090
NL	**Dale Murphy (3)**	.91888	**.91619**
1995	Barry Bonds (4)	**1.0086**	1.0040
NL	**Mike Piazza (1)**	1.0060	**1.0046**
2007	Alex Rodriguez (9)	**1.0672**	1.0574
AL	**David Ortiz (3)**	1.0664	**1.0631**
2014	Andrew McCutchen (6)	**.9525**	.9466
NL	**Giancarlo Stanton (3)**	.9497	**.9477**

CONCLUDING REMARKS

I emphatically declare that I am not advocating the changing of any official records impacted by the various rules regarding sacrifice flies. Jimmie Foxx (in 1932) and Ted Williams (in 1949) should not be granted Triple Crowns because officially there were no sacrifice flies in those seasons, and Dale Alexander and George Kell earned their batting crowns fair-and-square. Likewise, for all of the other players shown as official batting kings or classified as "hypothetical batting kings" in Tables 1 and 2 and the hypothetical slugging percentage kings and OPS leaders shown in Tables 3–5. ■

ACKNOWLEDGMENTS

It is a pleasure to thank Pete Palmer, Tom Ruane, and Dixie Tourangeau for their inputs and help with the research I carried out for this project, some of which was described previously in a presentation I made at the Baseball Records Committee Meeting at the SABR 45 Convention (Chicago, June 2015, "The Impact of the Sac-Fly Rule on Baseball Royalty...The Kings of the Percentage Crowns for Batters").

DEDICATION

I should like to dedicate this article to my good friend and fellow SABR member Art Neff. Thanks, Art, for your fantastic collaboration in documenting the uniform numbers of Detroit Tigers players (1931–2019) and all the great times we've shared at SABR meetings and ballgames as we achieved the feat of attending and scoring at least one game at every current major league ballpark through the 2019 season. All the best for you and Sue!

NOTES

1. John Schwartz, "The Sacrifice Fly," *The Baseball Research Journal*, 1981, 150–58.
2. "Spalding's Official Base Ball Guide, 1877," provides (pages 50–51) the "batting averages of players who have taken part in six or more championship games."
3. However, there has been some disagreement with the official position. For example, in its file of ML League Leaders for the 1932 season, for the AL BAVG, Retrosheet has the following rank-order list: ".364 Foxx PHI; .349 Gehrig NY; .367 Alexander DET-BOS; .342 Manush WAS." Both BAVG and Alexander are shown with plus (+) signs, directing the reader to the statement "Alexander was officially recognized as winning the batting title."
4. According to the Retrosheet Player Daily file for Jimmie Foxx for 1932, Foxx amassed a total of 168 RBIs, one RBI fewer than the 169 RBIs given in the AL's official DBD records. The discrepancy is attributable to the second game of the Boston vs. Philadelphia double header on August 13: The official DBD records mistakenly show Foxx credited with one (1) RBI. The Athletics scored eight runs in the game, with, according to the official records, the runs batted in by Jimmy Dykes (1), Foxx (1), Mule Haas (2), and Bing Miller (4). According to Retrosheet's detailed PBP narrative, there are no discrepancies with the official RBI numbers for Dykes, Haas, and Miller. However, as stated in the Retrosheet PBP for the third inning, Philadelphia scored its one run as follows: "Bishop walked; Haas out on a sacrifice bunt (pitcher to first) [Bishop to second]; Cochrane popped to shortstop; Kline threw a wild pitch [Bishop scored]; Simmons singled to first; Foxx walked [Simmons to second]; McNair forced Simmons (third unassisted)." Thus, Foxx did not have any RBIs in the game and his full-season total is 168, not 169, RBIs.
5. According to the Retrosheet Player Daily file for Joe Vosmik for 1935, Vomik amassed a total of 619 at-bats, one fewer than the 620 at-bats given in the AL's official DBD records. The discrepancy is attributable to the St. Louis vs. Cleveland game on June 03: The official DBD records show Vosmik with seven (7) at bats. The Retrosheet box score and PBP details show that Vosmik had six (6) at bats in seven plate appearances — (1) he doubled in the first; (2) he walked in the third; (3) he flied out to right in the fifth; (4) he flied out to right in the seventh; (5) he popped out to the catcher in the tenth; (6) he flied out to right in the twelfth; (7) he singled in the fourteenth. Thus, in actuality, Vosmik achieved a final batting average of .3489 (216 H in 619 AB), as shown in Table 1, not a final batting average of .3484 (216 H in 620 AB), as given in the official AL DBD records.
6. The details for Boudreau's six FO-RBIs are given here: (1) April 30 (second game) (5th inning) – "Boudreau flied out to right [Heath scored];" (2) May 31 (8th inning) – "Boudreau flied out on an unknown play [Keltner scored (unearned)];" (3) July 07 (1st inning) – "Boudreau flied out on an unknown play [Seerey scored (unearned)];" (4) July 13 (first game) (1st inning) – "Boudreau hit into a double play to center [O'Dea scored, Hockett out at third (center to first to third)];" (5) July 13 (second game) (4th inning) – "Boudreau flied out to left [Rocco scored];" (6) August 16 (8th inning) — "Boudreau flied out to right [Hockett scored]."
7. It is also noted that the Retrosheet PBP file for Doerr has one "unknown play" in which Doerr was credited with one RBI: July 20 (Boston at Chicago, 8th inning)—"Doerr out on an unknown play [Fox scored, B. Johnson to second]." According to the game account provided in the *Chicago Tribune*, "Fox did most of the damage against Maltzberger in the eighth, hitting a triple with the bases loaded and scoring on an infield out [by Doerr]."
8. It is noted that Retrosheet's "ML Leaders" file for 1945 does not include Cuccinello as the AL player with second highest batting average. The Retrosheet procedure for generating its list of the top four players uses the 1957 official rules, which require a minimum of 3.1 plate appearances per scheduled game for a player's team. [Tom Ruane, email to Herm Krabbenhoft, February 28, 2021] Thus, *according to Retrosheet*, 477 plate appearances were required for a player to qualify for the batting title (and be included in the list of the players with the four highest batting averages). However, Retrosheet's position is *not* in alignment with the "official rules" of major league baseball for the 1945 season. Actually, according to the official rules for major league baseball, there were *no* minimum requirements to qualify for the batting title; this was the situation for all seasons prior to 1950. The customary practice, however, was to award the batting championship to the player with the highest batting average — provided he played in at least 100 games. Beginning with the 1950 season, the official rules specified that "to be eligible for the individual batting championship of a major league, a player must be credited with at least 400 times at bat." Thus, Cuccinello, who played in 118 games and had 402 at bats would have been eligible for the individual batting title in 1950 — as well as in 1945. Indeed, several baseball encyclopedias [e.g., *The Baseball Encyclopedia* (ten editions, Macmillan), *Total Baseball* (eight editions, several publishers), *The ESPN Baseball Encyclopedia* (five editions, Sterling)] each show the top five AL batters for 1945 as follows—Stirnweiss (.309), Cuccinello (.308), Dickshot (.302), Estalella (.299), and Wyatt (.296).
9. Not surprisingly, shortly after it was announced that the sacrifice fly rule had been re-instituted [Hy Turkin, "Batters Get Break in Rule Change," *The Sporting News*, Volume 136, Number 16 (November 11, 1953), 1–2], the following was reported in *The Sporting News* [Volume 136, Number 17 (November 18, 1953), 14]: "Had the sacrifice fly rule been changed one year earlier, it would not have affected the American League batting championship, according to Hal Lebovitz of the Cleveland News. 'Al Rosen and Mickey Vernon hit six sacrifice flies in 1953, scoring runners from third base, and, therefore, Vernon would have remained ahead of Rosen,' Lebovitz wrote. 'Eliminating a time at bat each sacrifice fly, Rosen's average advances from .336 to .339. Vernon's jumps from .337 to .341.'"
10. Similarly for the 1953 National League batting title: Roscoe McGowan reported in *The Sporting News* [Volume 136, Number 18 (November 25, 1953), 6]: "Carl Furillo brought five mates home from third base for a potential batting average gain of four points, which would have made his league-leading mark .348." In the previous issue [J. Roy Stockton, "Rule Changes Please Players," *The Sporting News*, Volume 136, Number 17 (November 18, 1953), the following was reported: "Bob Broeg (*Post-Dispatch* baseball writer) furnished statistics on Stan Musial and Red Schoendienst to show the effect the sacrifice fly would have had on their 1953 batting marks. Musial, who hit .337, hit eight run-scoring flies, and if they had been sacrifices, Stan would have finished the season with .342. Schoendienst hit .342 and five run-scoring flies, if sacrifices, would have made his average .345." Schoendienst's official .342 placed second to Furillo's official .344.
11. Anthony Castrovince, *A Fan's Guide to Baseball Analytics* (New York: Sports Publishing, 2020), 4–7.
12. John Thorn and Pete Palmer with David Reuther, *The Hidden Game of Baseball* (Garden City, NY: Double Day & Company, Inc., 1984), 69; Alan Schwartz, "The Numbers Game," (New York: St. Martins Press, 2004), 165, 233; Bryan Grosnick, "Separate but not quite equal: Why OPS is a 'bad' statistic," beyondtheboxscore.com, September 18, 2015. Accessed January 20, 2021. See also: Tom Tango, "This is a step-by-step explanation as to why you should use some form of modified OPS, and not just OPS," insidethebook.com, February 07, 2007. Accessed January 20, 2021; Pete Palmer, "Why OPS Works," *The Baseball Research Journal*, Volume 48, Number 2 (Fall 2019), 43–47.

13. On Base Average (OBA) [the sum of (times on base via hits, walks, and hit by pitched balls) divided by the sum of (at bats plus walks plus times hit by pitched balls *plus sacrifice flies*)] was formulated by Branch Rickey and Alan Roth in 1954 and became an official stat in 1984; see: (a) Branch Rickey, "Goodby to Some Old Baseball Ideas," *Life*, August 2, 1954, 79–89; (b) Pete Palmer, "On Base Average for Players," *The Baseball Research Journal*, 1973, 87–91; (c) Ray C. Fair and Danielle Catambay, "Branch Rickey's Equation Fifty Years Later," Cowles Foundation Discussion Paper No. 1529, July 2005 (Revised, January 2007), Cowles Foundation for Research in Economics, Yale University, New Haven CT. It should be emphasized that on base average is *not* impacted by the varying Sac-Fly rules for the 1931–38, 1940–53, and 1954–2019 periods because (a) for the 1931–38 and 1940–53 periods, there were no sacrifice flies (i.e., RBI flyouts were at bats) and because (b) for the 1954–2019 period, sacrifice flies are included in the denominator of the OBA formula. For the exceptional 1939 season, the OBA league leaders were, as given on Baseball-Reference.com) Jimmie Foxx (AL, .466) and Mel Ott (NL, .449). It is pointed out that these OBA values were computed *without* including sacrifice flies — because sacrifice flies were *not* specifically tabulated in the official records: the official records only tabulated the sum of sacrifice hits (bunts) *and* sacrifice flies. Including Sac-Flies, as ascertained by examining the pertinent Retrosheet PBP narratives (5 for Foxx and 9 for Ott), in the denominator yields adjusted (true) OBA values of .462 and .441, respectively. According to my research, no AL player had a higher adjusted (true) OBA number than Foxx; likewise, no NL player had a higher adjusted (true) OBA number than Ott.

APPENDIX — Details for FlyOut RBIs (FO–RBIs) for Selected Players (1931–53).

Player (Year) [FO–RBIs]	FO–RBIs Details: Game [Inning (outfield position — L, C, or R)]
Dale Alexander (1932) [2]	8–02 [7 (R)]; 8–13(1) [1 (R)]
Jimmie Foxx (1932) [11]	4–26 [1 (L)]; 5–21(1) [8 (L)]; 6–10 [5 (L)]; 6–23 [5 (C)]; 7–03 [1 (L), 8 (L)]; 7–18 [1 (L); 7 (L)]; 7–30 [4 (L)]; 9–18(2) [5 (C)]; 9–21 [5 (C)]
Buddy Myer (1935) [7]	5–15 [5 (C)]; 6–01(2) [6 (R)]; 6–14 [2 (L)]; 6–16(1) [2 (L)]; 8–04 [1 (?)]; 8–22 [1 (R)]; 9–15(1) [3 (L)]
Joe Vosmik (1935) [9]	5–11 [9 (R)]; 5–22 [4 (R)]; 7–04(2) [7 (C)]; 8–09 [3 (C)]; 8–13 [6 (R)]; 8–17(1) [6 (L)]; 8–18(2) [2 (?)]; 9–01 [2 (R)]; 9–15(1) [3 (S)]
Lou Boudreau (1944) [6]	4–30(2) [5 (R)]; 5–31 [8 (?)]; 7–07 [1 (?)]; 7–13(1) [1 (C)]; 7–13(2) [4 (L)]; 8–16 [8 (R)]
Bobby Doerr (1944) [7]	4–28 [9 (C)]; 5–06 [4 (C)]; 6–11(2) [1 (L)]; 7–08 [2 (C)]; 7–09(1) [3 (R)]; 7–28 [3 (R)]; 8–25(1) [9 (C)]
Bob Johnson (1944) [11]	5–01 [7 (L)]; 6–14(1) [1 (C)]; 6–14(2) [1 (C)]; 6–22(2) [9 (C)]; 6–29 [4 (L)]; 7–13(1) [1 (L)]; 7–28 [1 (R)]; 8–13(1) [5 (L)]; 9–04(2) [8 (L)]; 9–19 [4 (R)]
George Stirnweiss (1945) [3]	6–05(2) [9 (R)]; 6–15 [2 (C)]; 6–23 [8 (R)]
Tony Cuccinello (1945) [4]	6–17 [7 (L)]; 7–31 [1 (L)]; 8–09 [7 (L)]; 9–07(2) [3 (R)]
George Kell (1949) [6]	4–21 [7 (?)]; 5–11 [6 (8)]; 5–15(1) [1 (L)]; 5–21 [4 (C)]; 8–14(2) [7 (C)]; 8–27 [5 (?)]
Ted Williams (1949) [7]	4–20 [1 (L)]; 6–07 [1 (R)]; 7–14 [5 (L)]; 7–27 [7 (C)]; 8–14(1) [2 (C)]; 9–02 [1 (C)]; 9–21 [5 (R)]
Jimmie Foxx (1935) [1]	8–04(1) [3 (C)]
Hank Greenberg (1935) [9]	5–23 [7 (C)]; 5–24 [1 (C)]; 6–15(1) [5 (L)]; 6–27 [1 (S)]; 6–28(1) [9 (L)]; 7–04(2) [8 (R)]; 7–06 [4 (L)]; 8–23 [7 (L)]; 9–18 [9 (L)]
Vern Stephens (1945) [9]	5–20(1) [1 (C)]; 6–22 [8 (R)]; 6–26 [3 (C)]; 7–16(2) [9 (R)]; 7–29(2) [8 (C)]; 8–05(2) [5 (C)]; 8–13(2) [4 (C)]; 8–19(1) [9 (?)]; 9–03(2) [4 (C)]
Stan Musial (1950) [3]	8–30 [4 (L)]; 9–14 [3 (R)]; 9–17 [9 (L)]
Andy Pafko (1950) [4]	5–21(2) [1 (L)]; 6–25(1) [9 (C,C)]; 7–19 [8 (L)]
Ralph Kiner (1950) [10]	5–20(2) [2 (L)]; 6–06 [6 (R)]; 7–01 [4 (R)]; 7–15 [3 (R)]; 7–19(1) [11 (C)]; 7–24 [1 (R)]; 8–12 [1 (L)]; 8–20(1) [6 (L)]; 9–10(1) [7 (C)]; 9–21 [6 (C)]
Jimmie Foxx (1939) [5]	5–03 [5 (L)]; 7–15 [9 (C)]; 7–16(2) [4 (C)]; 8–10 [1 (R)]; 9–03(1) [1 (R)]
Mel Ott (1939) [9]	5–04 [8 (R)]; 5–09 [3 (R)]; 5–19 [6 (R)]; 6–08 [1 (C)]; 6–23 [1 (L)]; 7–29 [5 (L)]; 8–12 [5 (L)]

NOTES

1. These FO-RBI details are taken from the Retrosheet PBP narratives; the outfield positions are Left (L), Center (C), and Right (R). For some FO-RBIs the Retrosheet PBP narrative states "player-A flied out on unknown play [player-B scored]." For these the fielding position is shown as a question mark i.e., (?).
2. For some FO-RBIs the fielder was an infielder; for these the fielding positions are abbreviated as follows — First (F), Second (S), Shortstop (SS), Third (T).
3. The FO-RBIs for Foxx (1939) and Ott (1939) were officially recorded as sacrifice hits; see endnote 13.

When the Fans Didn't Go Wild

The 2020 MLB Season as a Natural Experiment on Home Team Performance

J. Furman Daniel, III and Elliott Fullmer

The 2020 Major League Baseball season was unprecedented, as games were played without fans for the entire COVID-19-abbreviated schedule, creating a unique environment for study of the effect of fans on MLB team performance.

The season almost never happened at all. After the COVID-19 pandemic abruptly halted Spring Training and delayed Opening Day, players and owners squabbled for months over a plan to return to the field. As the virus continued to kill thousands each week and compromise the global economy, an agreement was finally reached to play 60 regular season games with significant scheduling and travel modifications, notable rule changes, and increased safety protocols. Teams would travel shorter distances than usual, playing games only against regional opponents. The National League (NL) would adopt the Designated Hitter (DH) for the first time. Regarding safety protocols, the most striking change was the exclusion of fans and non-essential personnel from all 2020 MLB games. With the exception of an April 29, 2015, White Sox-Orioles game played without fans due to rioting in the city of Baltimore, this was uncharted territory. This new reality produced a powerful consensus—seemingly everyone could concur that they missed fans in the ballparks.

While the circumstances of the 2020 MLB campaign were far from ideal for owners, coaches, players, and fans, the season does present a unique research opportunity. Home-field advantage has long been observed in all major team sports, including baseball. While the advantage in baseball is smaller than in other sports, an MLB team could historically be expected to win between six and seven more games at home than on the road in a given season (Moskowitz and Wertheim, 2011).[1] Over the past several decades, researchers have sought to explain this persistent phenomenon. While multiple explanations have been advanced, the most common centers on the effect of attending crowds. Cheering (or booing) fans, the argument goes, affect the performance of players or umpires, leading to advantages for the home team.

Because the 2020 MLB season was played without crowds, we are able to test the impact of fans on game outcomes through this unique natural experiment. If crowds are indeed the primary driver of home-field advantage, then we should expect home teams to perform more poorly in 2020 than they typically do. We examine all 8,188 MLB games played from 2017 through 2020 in an effort to assess whether the absence of fans reduced home-field advantage in 2020. To our surprise, it did not. Home teams continued to enjoy comparable success, winning 55.7% percent of their games in 2020. This figure was actually slightly *higher*—albeit not significantly so—than that observed in the three previous seasons. Through a series of multivariate OLS and Probit regressions, we also report that the unique travel circumstances associated with 2020 had no effect on home team performance. Predictably, home team quality did have a strong, positive relationship with on-the-field success.

Our work proceeds in several steps. First, we discuss the logic regarding why home crowds arguably *should* confer an advantage to MLB home teams. Second, we briefly address the relevant scholarly literature. Third, we present our methods and findings. Finally, we discuss the implications of our results, as well as some potential directions for future research.

FANS AND HOME-FIELD ADVANTAGE

The impact of fans on the outcome of professional sporting events has long been part of popular lore and conventional wisdom. To take an early literary example, Ernest Lawrence Thayer's 1888 poem *Casey at the Bat* is as much about the emotions of the crowd as it is about the failure of the title character. Indeed, the prospect of their hero having a chance to win the game transforms the atmosphere from a "pall like silence" to a "lusty yell" which echoed from "five thousand throats." The fictitious crowd is so invested in the outcome of the game that they even threaten to, "'Kill him! Kill the umpire!'...[A]nd it's likely they'd have killed him had not Casey raised his hand [and] [W]ith a smile of Christian charity...stilled the rising tumult;

he bade the game go on." While Casey ultimately strikes out and leaves the Mudville faithful with "no joy," the logic is brutally simple; the crowd has power and influence (Thayer, 1888).

In theory, the power to affect outcomes comes in two basic forms: 1) the ability to change the performance of players and 2) the ability to change the performance of umpires. Arguably, fans can use their cheers to either exert a positive energy or a negative one. When applied to players, positive energy would encourage them to play harder, have confidence in their own abilities, and know that they are loved—presumably all things that will result in improved performance of home team athletes. When applied to umpires, this encouraging form of cheering would provide positive reinforcement for calls that benefit the home team—something that would result in their players having increased success thanks to a systematic bias in their favor. Conversely, conventional wisdom would suggest that cheering also has more sinister or negative uses—those of negative reinforcement or coercion through peer-pressure. Fans booing players or umpires, for example, could worsen the performance of visiting athletes or influence the impartiality of officials in favor of the home team.

This theory has a simple and appealing logic for fans, players, and owners alike.[2] Not only is it intuitive that cheering influences the outcome of the game, but the belief that fans play their own role in determining the outcome of games helps maintain fan interest, merchandise sales, and attendance. While there are plausible theoretical and psychological explanations for it, does the evidence support the hypothesis that fan participation is the primary catalyst for home-field advantage?

LITERATURE

Despite the fact that millions of fans spend billions of dollars to attend live sporting events worldwide each year, their impact on the outcome of actual games was not rigorously tested until recent decades. The lack of serious study is the failure of both sports teams and academics. Until recently, sport franchises tended to be some of the least analytically inclined businesses, preferring to trust their scouts, coaches, and "insiders" to make decisions about how to construct and manage their teams.[3] What analytics they did conduct were proprietary in nature and thus not shared outside their limited circle for fear of other teams copying or exploiting their own methods. Similarly, until recently, few academics seriously studied sports in a rigorous manner and few peer-reviewed journals existed to validate their work and expose it to a broader audience.

The first major academic analysis regarding the impact of home-field advantage on team performance was published in 1977 by Barry Schwartz and Stephen F. Barsky. In this groundbreaking work, the authors concluded that there was a very strong, positive correlation between playing at home and team performance. The authors reported that home-field effects were most pronounced in "indoor" sports such as ice hockey and basketball and less pronounced in "outdoor" sports such as baseball and football. While this study had some methodological limitations, it made a critical

ED SHEAHIN/WASHINGTON TIMES/ALL PRO REELS VIA CREATIVE COMMONS/FLICKR

Juan Soto's family represented as cardboard cutouts at Nationals Park in 2020.

breakthrough for future researchers—home team advantages were due primarily to social forces from the crowd. Meanwhile, the authors concluded that factors such as visiting team fatigue and (un)familiarity with the home arena had no measurable impact on the outcome of games.

Schwartz and Barsky's research spurred a series of follow-on studies which generally supported their initial findings regarding a strong correlation between fan participation (e.g. noise level, attendance, behavior, etc.) and team performance. With the possible exception of unruly or disruptive fans (Thirer & Rampey, 1979), there is a positive correlation: the greater the fan participation, the greater the performance (Courneya and Carron, 1992; Carron, Loughead, & Bray, 2005; Armatas and Pollard, 2013; Goumas, 2014).[4]

In an effort to test a causal mechanism regarding *why* home crowds affected the outcome of games, research began to examine the impact of crowds on two different groups: 1) players and 2) officials. While it is incredibly difficult to measure the true impact of crowd noise on players' performance, the majority of studies suggest that crowds probably have little impact on the individual performance of players. Studies that examine repeatable actions such as free throws in basketball, shoot-outs in ice hockey, and field goals (from comparable distances) and extra-point kicks in football show remarkably little variation from athletes at home versus on the road (Moskowitz & Wertheim, 2011).

Some studies suggest that playing at home may lead to higher levels of testosterone and cortisol versus playing on the road (Neave & Wolfson, 2003; Carré, Muir, Belanger, and Putnam, 2006), yet the actual impact of these chemical changes on physical aggression and athletic performance has not been fully supported by scientific research (Jones, Bray, & Olivier, 2005). Moreover, these studies were primarily conducted on amateur ice hockey players, not professional athletes. Given the (literally) toxic and taboo nature of performance enhancing drugs in professional sports, it is unlikely that such research could be conducted on professional athletes.

While the impact of crowds on player performance is inconclusive at best, what about the ability of crowds to systematically bias officials? Again, the logic here is that officials may conform to the pressure of the home crowd by giving them favorable calls, or that they could use the initial reaction of the crowd as a heuristic short cut to rapidly make a difficult call under tight time constraints. One would expect that the larger the crowd, the greater the impact on officiating, particularly in cases of close or judgment calls such as penalties or fouls in a variety of sports, balls and strikes in baseball, and stoppage time in soccer. Indeed, evidence exists to support the hypothesis that a noisy crowd does impact the judgment of officials in a manner that benefits the home team (Downward and Jones, 2007).[5] A similar series of studies tested this hypothesis by comparing soccer games under normal crowd conditions with those played under no-noise conditions where officials watched games with headphones or without sound. The results showed that on judgment calls such as extra time or penalties, officials were much more likely to 1) reward the home team with extra time and 2) punish the visiting team with penalties in the presence of crowd noise than in no-noise conditions (Boyko, Boyko, and Boyko, 2007; Nevill, Balmer, and Williams, 2002; Unkelbach and Memmert, 2010).

The most scientific way to explore crowd effects is to compare officials' calls with a home crowd present to known cases where one was not present. This unusual situation actually occurred in the Italian Soccer League in 2006–2007 because of inadequate safety precautions in stadiums, as well as in various 2020 professional soccer leagues because of COVID-19. In the games played without crowds, a home-field advantage was still observed, but it was both substantively and statistically less than games in the control group played in front of fans (Pettersson-Lidbom and Priks, 2010; van de Ven, 2011; and Baldwin, 2020).[6]

While professional soccer has accounted for the plurality of studies on crowd effects, Major League Baseball (MLB) is an ideal candidate for this research because it has a large number of judgment calls in the form of balls and strikes which have a clear impact on the outcome of games. The most notable study to explore crowd effects on officiating in MLB appears in Jon Wertheim and Toby Moskowitz's popular book, *Scorecasting*. In a study analyzing over 1.5 million ball-strike determinations in 2002–08, the authors determined that the social pressure of the crowd systematically favored home teams. This finding was particularly pronounced in "high leverage" situations such as full counts, where the batter could either walk or strike out based on the call of the home plate umpire. According to the researchers, high leverage ball-strike determinations accounted for 516 more strike outs called against away teams and 195 more walks for home teams, enough to account for a "sizable fraction of the home team's success in MLB" (Moskowitz and Wertheim, 2011; Chen, Moskowitz, & Shue, 2016).

While this research was extremely rigorous, it could not test the impact of playing without a crowd. Indeed, until the 2020 MLB season, there was only one regular season game ever played without fans, hardly a sufficient sample size to draw any meaningful conclusions. With the 2020 season complete, however, there are now 898 games that can be analyzed to subject the crowd effects hypothesis to new scrutiny.[7] The unique features of 2020 games can also be used to explore some competing hypotheses regarding home-field advantage.

In addition to the impact of crowds on home team advantage, researchers have also found that road team fatigue from travel (Recht, Lew, and Schwartz, 1995; Goumas, 2013), as well as the ability of home teams to bat last (Simon and Simonoff, 2006) and pitch first (Smith, 2015), can also produce positive advantages for home clubs. Furthermore, teams constructing their rosters to exploit the unique dimensions of their home stadiums appears to have little or no effect on home-field advantage (Moskowitz and Wertheim, 2011).

DATA AND METHODS

Due to the COVID-19 pandemic, the 2020 MLB campaign was delayed nearly four months and consisted of only 60 regular season games (instead of the usual 162) per team. Games were played in teams' home stadiums, though fans were not permitted to attend. Instead, some organizations chose to place cardboard cutouts in some seats, particularly those most visible on television. While teams also experimented with artificial crowd noise, the typical cheers and boos that accompany home runs, errors, and controversial ball-strike calls were nowhere to be found.

Furthermore, the league altered team travel in an attempt to minimize the risk of contracting COVID-19. Teams played only against 1) other clubs in their division or 2) teams in the corresponding division in the opposite league (i.e. NL East teams played against other NL East teams and AL East teams only). For the first time, the Designated Hitter (DH) rule was applied to NL teams, meaning pitchers would no longer be required to bat. Games played as part of doubleheaders were shortened to seven innings, while a runner was automatically placed on second base at the start of all extra innings. The Toronto Blue Jays—denied permission to play in their home stadium by the Canadian government—were forced to play the entire season in a minor league park in Buffalo, New York. And on nearly two dozen occasions, feared or actual COVID-19 outbreaks caused home teams to play games in the away team's stadium.

While the 2020 season was less than ideal for all involved, the altered landscape offers convenient treatment and control groups. Some aforementioned explanations for home-field effects (e.g. batting last, stadium familiarity, the comforts of home) were unchanged in 2020. If these features are indeed major drivers of home-field effects, then we would not expect home teams to perform worse in 2020 relative to previous years. But if screaming fans are responsible for teams playing better at home—due to effects on either players or umpires—then any normal effects should be absent in 2020. Similarly, if travel fatigue typically hurts away teams, then the restricted travel schedule in 2020 would be expected to lessen—at least slightly—these effects.

Our first goal is identifying whether home-field advantage changed during the 2020 season. Data were obtained through Baseball-Reference.com, which includes dates, outcomes, and attendance figures for each contest. One-way ANOVA and Chi Square tests determine whether home-field advantage dropped in 2020 relative to each of the three previous seasons. We measure home-field advantage in two ways: 1) the mean run differential enjoyed by home teams during the respective years (*HTRunDiff*) and 2) the share of games won by the home team (*HTWin*). One could argue that if crowd effects matter, they should help determine winners and losers. This is particularly true if crowds matter most in high-leverage situations, as Moskowitz & Wertheim (2011) suggest. However, we include the run differential measure because it is also possible that empty stadiums impact team performance, but not in ways that cause significant changes in win rates.

Second, we conduct a series of OLS and Probit regression tests to better gauge the role of empty stadiums and other potential factors on home-field advantage. Our unit of analysis is each MLB game (N = 8,188) played 2017–2020. We again run models with two different dependent variables—a continuous measure noting the home team's run differential in a respective game and a binary measure of home team victory. Our primary independent variable is a binary variable noting whether a game was played without a crowd (*NoCrowd*). Because only 2020 contests were played without fans in the four years examined, this measure is effectively a binary measure for 2020 games. As we discussed, research has suggested that the mere existence of a crowd may not fully capture fans' effect on outcomes. Crowd size or density may also matter (Armatas and Pollard, 2013; Goumas, 2014). We therefore include specifications that consider both total attendance (*CrowdSize*) and the share of the park filled in each game (*CrowdDensity*).[8] In a typical season, a team with 10,000 fans may not enjoy the same home-field advantage as one with 50,000. If this is true, then it would follow that a drop from 10,000 to 0 in 2020 would not be the same as a drop from 50,000 to 0. Notably, our attendance variables capture tickets *sold* rather than the number of fans actually *attending* games (which teams do not announce). Nevertheless, these metrics should capture variation in attending crowds reasonably well.

Because research has also offered travel fatigue as an explanation for home-field advantage (Recht, Lew, and Schwartz, 1995; and Goumas, 2013), we include two variables designed to capture situations when the home team may be affected by travel factors. The first is a binary measure indicating whether the away team is an out-of-division opponent (*NonDiv*). In most cases, these opponents are required to travel further than division opponents. Even if they are traveling from a different city (as part of a longer road trip), this indicates that they have been on the road for an extended period of time, perhaps exacerbating fatigue effects. Because 2020 did not include out-of-division matchups (but previous years did), this variable should help isolate any effects of that year's unusual travel schedule. If this measure is significant and positive, we can gain confidence that home teams typically benefit from playing teams who have traveled further, likely due to increased fatigue. The second travel variable is a binary measure indicating whether the home team played a game on the road the previous day (*RecentTravel*). While away teams nearly always must travel, home teams generally do not. However, there are instances when home teams must return from an away series in another city before beginning a new series in their own park. In these situations, we should expect that travel fatigue would not be considerably different for the home team than the road team.

Not only were games played without a crowd in 2020, but there were 24 games in which the home team was forced to play in the visiting stadium. Most, though not all, of these instances were due to COVID-19 related game postponements. Furthermore, the Toronto Blue Jays were forced to play each of their home games at Sahlen Field, the team's Triple-A park in Buffalo, New York. If the comforts of home and/or park familiarity are valid explanations for home-field advantage, we would expect those effects to be absent in each of these cases. As a result, we include binary variables noting 1) home games played in visiting parks (*HomeTeamRoad*) and 2) games played at neutral sites (*NeutralPark*). The latter variable also captures three Houston Astros home games played in a neutral setting (in Tampa Bay) during Hurricane Harvey in 2017.

MLB rules arguably confer an advantage to home teams. First, as Simon and Simonoff (2006) have reported, batting last is an asset to home teams. In addition, interleague contests between American League (AL) and National League (NL) teams adopt the Designated Hitter (DH) rule, or lack thereof, of the home club. AL teams have played with the DH since 1973, though NL teams instead allowed pitchers to hit until 2020. Before 2020, we would expect both AL and NL teams to have an added advantage in home interleague games because their rosters were constructed in a way that matched the applicable DH rules. In 2020—just one month before the season began—the National League adopted the DH for the first time. Because this was too late to modify rosters in a meaningful way, AL home teams appeared to still benefit from DH rules in 2020 interleague contests, while NL home teams did not. We therefore include a binary measure for interleague games during 2017–20 in which the home team should be advantaged—AL-hosted contests in 2017–20 and NL hosted contests in 2017–19 (*InterleagueAdv*).

Finally, one of the most obvious predictors of a home team's success in a given game is the quality of its roster. While teams of all talent levels tend to perform better at home than on the road, better teams should have more success at home than poorer teams. Similar to Goumas (2014), we therefore control for each home team's division ranking at the time a game was played. All MLB teams belong to divisions consisting of five teams. To capture team quality, we include binary variables noting whether a team was in first, second, fourth, or fifth place before a particular contest (*FirstPlace, SecondPlace, FourthPlace, FifthPlace*).[9]

While we run specifications with additional variables (as discussed) to ensure robustness, our primary regression model can be expressed as:

$$y\,(\text{HTRunDiff.}) = a + \beta\,(\text{NoCrowd}) + \beta\,(\text{InterleagueAdv}) + \beta\,(\text{FirstPlace}) + \beta(\text{SecondPlace}) + \beta\,(\text{FourthPlace}) + \beta\,(\text{FifthPlace}) + \beta\,(\text{RecentTravel}) + \beta\,(\text{NonDiv}) + \beta(\text{NeutralPark}) + \beta\,(\text{HomeTeamRoad}) + e$$

FINDINGS

Figures 1 and 2 feature simple bar graphs demonstrating home-field advantage in MLB 2017–20. The graphics clearly suggest that the advantage did not decline in 2020, both in terms of the mean run differential or win percentage enjoyed by the home team, respectively. In fact, home teams appeared to perform slightly *better* in 2020. While run differential and win percentage

Figure 1. Mean MLB Home Team Run Differential (per game), 2017–20

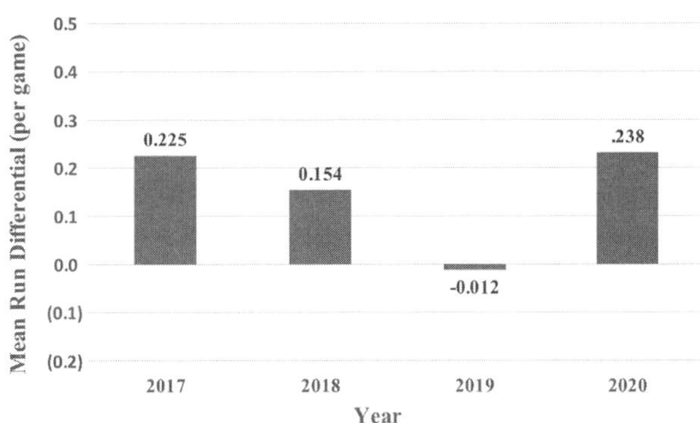

Figure 2. MLB Home Team Win Percentage, 2017–20

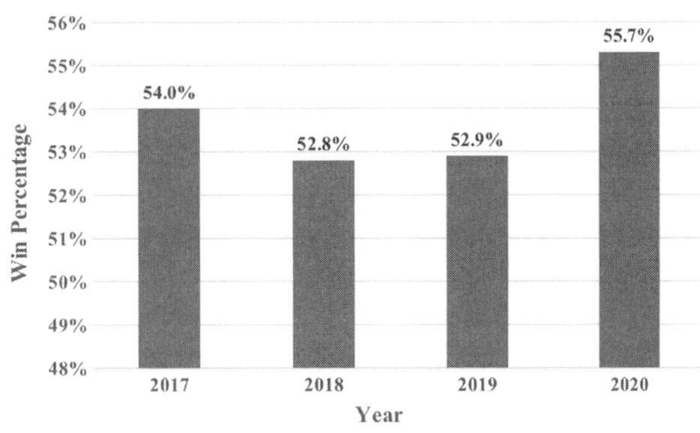

generally mirror one another, 2019 was a bit unusual in that home teams actually scored fewer runs per game despite winning nearly 53% of their contests. In fact, while all but six MLB teams had better records at home than on the road in 2019, just 16 had better run differentials at home. It appears that many MLB clubs won home games by smaller margins than they tended to lose them that season, suggesting that their run scoring was unusually efficient.

Table 1 presents a One-way ANOVA test that examines whether the mean run differential recorded by home teams significantly differed in any of the four years examined. Because the p value is 0.490, we can confidently assert that no significant differences are present. The dip observed in 2019 does not represent a statistically significant deviation from the other years we examined. More importantly for our purposes, 2020 did not feature a statistically meaningful drop or rise in home team run differential.

Table 1. Mean MLB Home Team Run Differential, 2017–20 (One-way ANOVA)

	2017	2018	2019	2020
Mean Run Differential (per game)	0.225	0.154	-0.012	0.238

P value: 0.490

Table 2 presents a Chi-Square test that compares the means of home team win percentage across the four years. With a p value of 0.356, we continue to report no significant differences between home team performance during the 2017–20 seasons. These findings are striking, as they indicate that the absence of fans in 2020 did not alter the strength of home performance in any discernible way.

Table 2. MLB Home Team Win Average, 2017-2020 (Chi-Square Analysis)

	2017	2018	2019	2020
Share of Games Won	0.540	0.528	0.529	0.557

P value: 0.356

Through more sophisticated regression models, we are able to assess the role of empty ballparks while accounting for other potential predictors of home-field advantage. Table 3 presents our findings using the home team's run differential as the dependent variable. In the first specification, with only the binary measure of empty stadiums included, we confirm the insignificant findings reported in the One-way ANOVA test. Home-field advantage was unaffected by the absence of fans in 2020. In the second test, with all covariates now included, we continue to report no relationship between the primary independent variable and home team run differential. In the third and fourth tests, we substitute our binary measure of crowd-free games for continuous variables capturing total stadium attendance and the share of the stadium that was full, respectively. While these values are always zero for 2020 contests, they vary considerably for 2017–19 contests. Neither variable registers a significant effect on home team performance, meaning that the existence, size, or density of crowds did not appear to aid home teams over the course of 8,188 games played during 2017–20.

Our full model produces other notable findings. Predictably, team quality is highly significant of a home team's performance ($p < .01$). First and second place teams are significantly more likely to enjoy large run differentials at home than lesser-ranked teams. Conversely, fourth and fifth place teams have lower run margins than higher-ranked clubs. The substantive effects are notable. In the second specification, a first place team is expected to have a run differential that is 1.4 runs greater per game than non-first place teams. Meanwhile, fifth (last) place teams are associated with a run differential 0.79 runs smaller than teams ranked higher in their respective divisions. More surprisingly, we report a negative relationship between games where the home team is advantaged in inter-

Table 3. Predicting MLB Home Team Run Advantage, 2017–20 (OLS Regression)

	(1)	(2)	(3)	(4)
Variables	HT Run-Diff.	HT Run-Diff.	HT Run-Diff.	HT Run-Diff.
No Crowd	0.108	0.044		
	(0.162)	(0.171)		
Interleague Advantage		-0.382**	-0.380**	-0.380**
		(0.154)	(0.154)	(0.154)
First-Place Team		1.441***	1.445***	1.451***
		(0.154)	(0.155)	(0.155)
Second-Place Team		0.720***	0.720***	0.718***
		0.156)	(0.156)	(0.156)
Fourth-Place Team		-0.540***	-0.542***	-0.549***
		(0.160)	(0.160)	(0.160)
Fifth-Place Team		-0.791***	-0.796***	-0.811***
		(0.161)	(0.163)	(0.163)
Recent Travel		-0.169	-0.168	-0.168
		(0.180)	(0.180)	(0.180)
Non-Division Opponent		-0.063	-0.067	-0.055
		(0.106)	(0.103)	(0.103)
Neutral Park		0.192	0.201	0.149
		(0.813)	(0.810)	(0.811)
Home Team on Road		-0.257	-0.245	-0.296
		(0.937)	(0.933)	(0.933)
Crowd Size			0.000	
			(0.000)	
Crowd Density				-0.139
				(0.178)
Constant	0.122	0.001	0.031	0.089
	(0.054)	(0.125)	(0.156)	(0.159)
Observations	8,188	8,188	8,188	8,188

**** p<0.01, ** p<0.05, * p<0.1*

league contests (due to the Designated Hitter rules) and home team run differential. This finding, which is significant with 95% confidence ($p < .05$), suggests that home teams in interleague games where a DH advantage exists (n = 979) are associated with run differentials 0.38 runs *smaller* than home teams in other settings. While this finding is a bit counterintuitive, it is possible that adjusting to new Designated Hitter rules is less burdensome for teams than we anticipated. Nevertheless, because interleague contests comprise a fairly small share of games in our data set, we encourage more scrutiny in this area.

Notably, we report no significant effects regarding travel in any tests. Home teams hosting non-division opponents see no increased run differential, as we anticipated might be the case. Furthermore, those home teams playing immediately after returning from a road game the day before were not disadvantaged. As a result, we cannot confirm the results of others (Recht, Lew, and Schwartz, 1995; Goumas, 2013) regarding the effect of travel fatigue on home-field advantage. Interestingly, teams playing "home" games in road stadiums or at neutral sites (e.g. the Toronto Blue Jays) were no less likely to record positive run differentials. We do caution, however, that the sample size of these cases is small. There were only 24 contests requiring home teams to play at a road park in 2020. Regarding neutral sites, cases are limited to all Toronto Blue Jays home games played in Buffalo in 2020 (n = 26) and three Houston Astros games played in Tampa Bay in 2017 due to Hurricane Harvey.

Table 4 replicates the previous tests, but substitutes a binary measure of home team victory as the dependent variable. Because of the dichotomous nature of the dependent variable, a Probit regression test is appropriate for each of these tests. Once again, we report no significant effect of a crowd, its size, or its percentage filled on a home team's success in a given game. Home teams were more likely to win in each of the four years we examined (see Figure 2), but crowds did not increase their likelihood of doing so in a statistically significant way. We again report significant associations between team quality and home team success. First-place clubs are 39 percentage points more likely to win home games than other clubs, while fifth-place teams are 25 percentage points less likely to win home games than higher-ranked teams. We also continue to find that home teams advantaged in interleague games performed a bit worse than they did in other contests. Mirroring our findings in Table 3, we report no relationship between travel conditions or teams playing away from their home parks and a home team's likelihood of victory.

CONCLUSIONS AND DIRECTIONS FOR FUTURE RESEARCH

Examining 8,188 MLB games over four years, we find no significant effect of crowds on home team performance. The presence of fans does not predict higher run differentials or likelihood of victory for host clubs. Even in 2020, when crowds were entirely absent from MLB parks, home-field advantage remained strong. Our findings are similar to those reported by Van de

Table 4. Predicting MLB Home Team Win Likelihood, 2017–20 (Probit Regression)

	(1)	(2)	(3)	(4)
Variables	**HT Win**	**HT Win**	**HT Win**	**HT Win**
No Crowd	0.053	0.042		
	(0.045)	(0.048)		
Interleague Advantage		-0.0941**	-0.380**	-0.0924**
		(0.043)	(0.154)	(0.043)
First-Place Team		0.392***	1.445***	0.398***
		(0.044)	(0.155)	(0.0i44)
Second-Place Team		0.197***	0.720***	0.197***
		(0.044)	(0.156)	(0.044)
Fourth-Place Team		-0.163***	-0.542***	-0.169***
		(0.045)	(0.160)	(0.045)
Fifth-Place Team		-0.255***	-0.796***	-0.267***
		(0.045)	(0.163)	(0.045)
Recent Travel		0.028	(0.168)	0.029
		(0.051)	(0.180)	(0.051)
Non-Division Opponent		-0.014	-0.067	-0.013
		(0.030)	(0.103)	(0.029)
Neutral Park		0.054	0.201	0.041
		(0.228)	(0.810)	(0.227)
Home Team on Road		-0.260	-0.245	-0.269
		(0.264)	(0.933)	(0.263)
Crowd Size			0.000	
			(0.000)	
Crowd Density				-0.078
				(0.050)
Constant	0.0812***	0.053	0.031	0.105**
	(0.015)	(0.035)	(0.156)	(0.045)
Observations	8,188	8,188	8,188	8,188

*** $p<0.01$, ** $p<0.05$, * $p<0.1$

Ven (2011), who reported that home-field advantage persisted when crowds were removed in Italian soccer contests. Try as they might, fans may have limited ability to impact their teams' success by influencing the abilities of players on the field or the impartiality of umpires. Homer Hankeys, Bleacher Bums, Tomahawk Chops, Rally Monkeys, and mascots may increase the baseball fan experience, but our findings shed doubt on their ability to change outcomes.

Our findings suggest, though admittedly do not prove, that home-field advantage may be caused by other factors. These include rule advantages that allow the home team to bat last (as reported by Simon and Simonoff) and to pitch first (as reported by Smith), the familiarity players have with the unique features of their home parks, or the comforts associated with being at home (e.g. having family nearby, sleeping in one's own bed, etc.). While we report that home teams performed no better or worse when hosting opponents traveling from further distances or returning from a road trip, the simple idea of "being home" may be more powerful than once believed.

While our study may deflate the egos of fans, it does provide a reassuring perspective about the quality of MLB play. Players and umpires are trained professionals who are extremely skilled at their jobs. They have only reached the highest level of their profession because they are able to excel under adverse conditions and they have thousands of hours of practice doing so. The fact that fans can expect such consistent quality of competition should give hometown rooters something to cheer about, even if those cheers do not matter.

Because our findings contradict the conventional wisdom and some previous research, we expect and encourage reinterpretation and revision of our work. For example, with additional time and access to data, it would be possible to replicate the aforementioned PITCHf/x studies conducted by Moskowitz and Wertheim (2011) and Chen, Moskowitz, and Shue (2016) for the 2020 MLB season. This would help provide additional evidence to support or reject their conclusions regarding the importance of social pressure on high-leverage ball-strike calls. Similarly, it would be interesting to investigate the decibel-levels and intensity of artificially produced crowd noises used by some MLB teams in 2020 in their home stadiums. This, however, would require access to proprietary information from the teams that will probably not be forthcoming. Finally, it is possible that 2020 was simply unique and that games played under similar conditions in later years would not produce the same results. One could argue, for example, that the burdens associated with travel in 2020 were unusually great, perhaps creating additional challenges for road teams. Given that MLB teams travel on private planes and bus charters, we are a bit skeptical of this explanation. It remains possible, however, that other features of the COVID-19-modified season—stress, family concerns, the late start of competitive games—affected players in ways that are unlikely to recur in future years. ■

References

Armatas, V., & Pollard, R. (2013). Home advantage in Greek football. *European Journal of Sport Science*, 14, 116–22.

Baldwin, B. (2020). Inside the numbers: How empty stands affect home-field advantage? *The Athletic*, posted online Aug 25.

Balmer, N.J., Nevill, A.M., and Williams, A.M. (2003). Modelling home advantage in the Summer Olympic Games. *Journal of Sports Sciences*, 21, 469–78.

Barry, D. (1995). *Dave Barry's Complete Guide to Guys*, New York: Random House.

Boyko, R., Boyko, A., and Boyko, M. (2007). Referee bias contributes to home advantage in English Premiership football. *Journal of Sports Sciences*, 25, 1185–94.

Carré, J., Muir, C., Belanger, J., and Putnam, S. K. (2006). Pre-competition hormonal and psychological levels of elite hockey players: Relationship to the "home advantage." *Physiology and Behavior*, 89, 392–98.

Carron, A. V., Loughead, T. M., and Bray, S. R. (2005). The home advantage in sport competitions: Courneya and Carron's (1992) conceptual framework a decade later. *Journal of Sports Sciences*, 23, 395–407.

Chen, D., Moskowitz, T., and Shue, K. (2016). Decision making under the gambler's fallacy: Evidence from asylum judges, loan officers, and baseball umpires. *The Quarterly Journal of Economics*, 131, 1181–242.

Courneya, K. S., and Carron, A. V. (1992). The home advantage in sport competitions: A literature review. *Journal of Sport and Exercise Psychology*, 14, 13–27.

Downward, P., and Jones, M. (2007). Effects of crowd size on referee decisions: Analysis of the FA Cup. *Journal of Sports Sciences*, 25, 1541–45.

Goumas C. (2013). Home advantage and crowd size in soccer: A worldwide study. *Journal of Sport Behavior*, 36, 387–99.

Goumas, C. (2014). How does crowd support contribute to home advantage in soccer? *Journal of Sport Behavior*, 37, 236–50.

Keri, J. (2011). *The Extra 2%*: How wall street strategies took a major league baseball teams from worst to first. New York: Ballantine Books.

Jones, M. V., Bray, S. R., and Olivier, S. (2005). Game location and aggression in rugby league. *Journal of Sports Sciences*, 23, 387–93.

Judge, J. (2020). Strike Zones in the Age of COVID-19. *Baseball Prospectus*, posted online, September 21.

Lewis, M. (2003). *Moneyball: the art of winning an unfair game*. New York: W.W. Norton.

Moore, J. (2015). "The Washington Nationals try to psych out their opponents with bad music." *GQ*, posted online, April 15.

Moskowitz, T., & Wertheim, L.J. (2011). *Scorecasting: the hidden influences behind how sports are played and games are won*. New York: Crown Publishing Group.

Neave, N., & Wolfson, S. (2003). Testosterone, territoriality, and the "home advantage." *Physiology and Behavior*, 78, 269–75.

Nevill, A., Balmer, N.J., and Williams, M. (2002). The influence of crowd noise and experience on refereeing decisions in football. *Psychology of Sport and Exercise*, 3, 261–72.

Pettersson-Lidbom, P., and Priks, M. (2010). Behavior under social pressure: Empty Italian stadiums and referee bias. *Economics Letters*, 108, 212–14.

Ranking all 30 MLB Ballparks. (2019). *NBC Sports Washington*, posted online July 9.

Recht, L. D., Lew, R. A., and Schwartz, W. J. (1995). Baseball teams beaten by jet lag. *Nature*, 377, 583.

Sawchik, T. (2015). *Big data baseball: math, miracles, and the end of a 20-year losing streak*. New York: Flatiron Books.

Schwartz, B., and Barsky, S. F. (1977). The home advantage. *Social Forces*, 55, 641–61.

Shanks, B. (2005). *Scout's Honor: The Bravest Way to Build a Winning Team*. New York: Sterling and Ross Publishers.

Simon, G., and Simonoff. J. (2006). "Last Licks:" Do they Really Help? *The American Statistician*, 60, 13–18.

Smith, D. W. (2015). Home Team Scoring Advantage in the First Inning Largely Due to Time. Presented at the annual convention of the Society for American Baseball Research, June 24–28, 2015.

Sports Reference LLC. Baseball-Reference.com – Major League Statistics and Information. https://www.baseball-reference.com. Sept. 15, 2020.

Thayer, E. L. (1888). Casey at the Bat. *The Daily Examiner*, June 3.

Thirer, J., and Rampey, N. (1979). Effects of abusive spectator behavior on the performance of home and visiting intercollegiate basketball teams. *Perceptual and Motor Skills*, 48, 1047–53.

Unkelbach, C., and Memmert, D. (2010). Crowd noise as a cue in referee decisions contributes to the home advantage. *Journal of Sport & Exercise Psychology*, 32, 483–98.

Van de Ven, N. (2011). Supporters are not necessary for the home advantage: Evidence from same-stadium derbies and games without an audience. *Journal of Applied Social Psychology*, 41, 2785–92.

Notes

1. Home-field advantage is highest in the NBA (60.5%), followed by the NFL (57.3%), the NHL (55.7%) and, finally, MLB (53.9%).
2. For a self-critical but illustrative example of how fans can believe that they have a direct impact on the outcome of games, see: Dave Barry's *Complete Guide to Guys* (1995), 181–83.
3. For excellent narrative accounts of how baseball teams were particularly resistant to data analytics, see: Michael Lewis's *Moneyball* (2003), Jonah Keri's *The Extra 2%* (2011), and Travis Sawchik's *Big Data Baseball* (2015). For a somewhat contrarian account of how one franchise, the Atlanta Braves, found success by matching traditional scouting approaches with analytical principles, see: Bill Shanks' *Scout's Honor: The Bravest Way to Build a Winning Team* (2005).
4. Some, such as Armatas and Pollard (2013), have found that crowd density (i.e. the share of a stadium that is full) is most important, while Goumas (2014) reports that total crowd size has the largest effect on home-field advantage.
5. In contrast, the effect of crowd noise appears to be less in sports without judgment calls, such as weightlifting and short-track speed skating (Balmer, Nevill, and Williams, 2003).
6. The one exception to this was the 2020 Bundesliga games, which showed no significant home-field advantage for games played without fans. For extensive data on the European Soccer Leagues, see: https://github.com/lbenz730/soccer_hfa.
7. One study (Judge, 2020), applying PitchInfo data from Baseball Prospectus, reported that the strike zone did not appear to advantage home teams more in the first two weeks of the 2020 MLB season when compared to the 2019 season.
8. MLB ballpark capacity data is provided by NBC Sports Washington (2019).
9. Our full data set is available upon email request.
10. Interestingly, in 2015, the Washington Nationals admitted to playing sad songs during visiting teams' batting practices in order gain an advantage. See: Moore, J. (2015). "The Washington Nationals try to psych out their opponents with bad music." *GQ*, posted online April 15.

A Minor Innovation

Uniform numbers in the minor leagues earlier than previously thought

Mark Stang

Photographic evidence has emerged that disproves the oft-cited narrative that the 1925 American Association was the first baseball league at any level to consistently number their players' uniforms. This article will present the photographs along with a brief history of uniform number usage in baseball.

The practice of using jersey numbers, which was in use among dozens of prominent college football programs as early as 1914, had a slow evolution in baseball. In 1916, the Cleveland Indians temporarily added numbers to players' left sleeves during the second half of the regular season. The following year, the Indians tried moving the numbers to the players' *right* sleeves. A brief wire service blurb dated March 29, 1917, reported that the Boston Red Sox and the Brooklyn Dodgers played a spring training exhibition game in Memphis, Tennessee, where both teams sported numbers on their players' sleeves. However, these experiments proved to be nothing more than a passing fad.

Sportswriter Tommy Rice, who covered the major leagues for The *Brooklyn Daily Eagle*, was an early advocate pushing the big league clubs to number their players. As early as the offseason of 1922–23, Rice's almost constant lobbying succeeded in getting the eight National League club owners to take up the matter at their annual Winter meetings. Though ultimately little came of the discussion, Rice would continue to beat the drum, and other baseball writers—notably Stoney McLinn and later syndicated columnist Billy Evans of The *Philadelphia Ledger*[1]—would consistently make the point in print that the fans deserved a better and more expedient way of identifying both the home and visiting players.

At least one other major league club thought the issue worth pursuing; the 1923 St. Louis Cardinals featured numbers on the players' left sleeves. It would prove to be a one-year dalliance and nothing further was seen of uniform numbers at the major league level for another six seasons. The practice of numbering players in the major leagues would not be adopted permanently until the 1929 New York Yankees and Cleveland Indians. It would take until 1931 for all eight American League clubs to follow suit, and the National League wouldn't catch up until the middle of the 1932 season.

This period of seeming indifference on the part of major league club owners prior to 1929 left the door wide open for others to step in. The result was that the minor league club owners pioneered uniform numbers, as they did many of the game's most fan-friendly customs (including bat day and the "knothole gang"). Recent research has uncovered significant photographic proof of minor league clubs adding uniform numbers to player jerseys several years prior to 1929. For example, we know that the Atlanta Crackers of the Southern Association began numbering their players in 1926. A vintage wire photo of the Crackers' Leo Durocher, his back turned towards the photographers' camera, has been seen (but not yet acquired) by the author. What is unknown as of the writing of this article is whether the other seven Southern Association teams followed suit, or was this simply a case of Atlanta going it alone?

Sportswriters in *The Sporting News*—and other wire service reports of the day—generally credit the teams of the American Association (AA) with debuting player uniform numbers at the start of the 1925 season. In fact, the December 11, 1924, issue of the "Bible of Baseball" contained the following note: "At a special meeting of the American Association owners, held in Hartford, just before the magnates left, it was decided by unanimous vote that all players be numbered on the field during the coming season. The players will wear the numbers on the sleeves of their shirts, which will correspond to the numbers on the program. The numbers are to be six inches high so they will be easily discerned from the stands." League president Thomas J. Hickey was quoted as saying, "The numbering system has become almost general with football teams and I see no reason why it should not help the baseball fan."[2]

A photo of pitcher Curt Fullerton of the St. Paul Saints clearly shows the results of the league-wide edict in the American Association (see Figure 1).

AUTHOR'S COLLECTION

Figure 1. Pitcher Curt Fullerton, 1925 St. Paul Saints.

Fullerton originally began the 1925 season in Boston as a member of the Red Sox staff. His first four years in Boston had produced a combined 10–32 record and, when he gave up a total of 11 runs in his first 22-plus innings of work in 1925, the Red Sox shipped him to the Saints in early May, where he spent the remainder of the season. The wire photo of Fullerton shows him wearing the number two (2) on his left sleeve. The back of the photo is date-stamped May 25, 1925.

But were the eight teams of the 1925 American Association really the first minor league clubs (at any level) to begin numbering their players?

The author has uncovered proof of at least two other minor league ball clubs far to the south of St. Paul adding uniform numbers to their players' jerseys. The first was the Fort Smith (Arkansas) Twins of the Class C Western Association. Slugging first baseman Jimmy Hudgens (who spent parts of the 1923–1925 seasons with Fort Smith) is shown in Figure 2 boldly wearing a rather large number 22 on his left sleeve.

Hudgens had a career season for Fort Smith in 1925, leading the league in several key offensive categories. He batted .389 with 63 doubles and produced 168 RBIs over a 150-game schedule. As a result, Fort Smith won 94 games and the league title. Hudgens's reward was a promotion to the Cincinnati Reds, who brought him to the majors for the final two weeks of the regular season. There is no date (stamped or written) on the reverse of the Hudgens photo, leaving open the possibility that Fort Smith actually donned uniform numbers *prior to* the 1925 season.

We also have proof that the Bloomington (Illinois) Bloomers of the Class B Three I League numbered their players in 1925. Pitcher Herman John Schwartje spent the 1925 season with Bloomington, where he compiled an 18–10 record for a team that won only 56 games and finished nearly 30 games out of first place. He is shown in Figure 3 as a member of the Bloomers wearing number 15 on his left sleeve. A career minor leaguer, Schwartje spent parts of 15 seasons toiling in the low minors, where he twice won at least 22 games. (After he did it a second time in 1922—winning 23 games for Class B Saginaw—he was promoted to Class AA Rochester of the International League the following season. It would prove the pinnacle of his pro career.)

AUTHOR'S COLLECTION

Figure 2. First baseman Jimmy Hudgens, 1925 Fort Smith (AK) Twins.

AUTHOR'S COLLECTION

Figure 3. Pitcher Herman John Schwartje, 1925 Bloomington (IL) Bloomers

AUTHOR'S COLLECTION

Figure 4.
Outfielder Ike Boone, 1923 San Antonio Bears

The final photo accompanying this article is that of outfielder Ike Boone. In Figure 4, Boone is shown wearing the uniform of the San Antonio Bears (Class B Texas League) with a large number five (5) on the left sleeve. The most important thing about this photo is that Ike Boone's only season with San Antonio was 1923. He played for Little Rock in 1922 and when he tore up the Texas League in 1923 (hitting .402 and leading the league in hits, doubles, triples and RBIs), his performance for the Bears would get him promoted to the majors to join the Boston Red Sox for the final 10 days of the regular season. Boone would spend the entire 1924 and 1925 seasons with the Red Sox.

Thus, we now have definitive proof establishing that at least one minor league team wore uniform numbers as early as the 1923 season, a full two years prior to the American Association's league-wide adoption of the same custom. Could there possibly be other minor league teams that also jump-started the custom a year (or more) in advance of San Antonio in 1923? I invite any interested SABR members to contact me with any information which might shed light on this topic. ■

Notes

1. *The Philadelphia Evening Ledger*: Jan. 13, 1923; Feb. 15, 1923 and April 13, 1923; "Billy Evans Says" syndicated column; Oct. 9, 1925.
2. *The Sporting News*, December 11, 1924.

The Kitty's Kentucky Return

The One-Off 1935 Paducah Red Birds

Michael Tow

The fifth life of the on-again, off-again Kentucky-Illinois-Tennessee (Kitty) League began in 1935. The first four attempts to establish rookie-level, Class-D professional baseball in the small cities of the Upper South and Midwest states of Kentucky, Illinois, Tennessee, and Indiana were unsustained from 1903 to 1924. While about a dozen players from these earlier inceptions of the league did advance to the major leagues, the Kitty League itself never lasted more than five years at a time.[1] Nevertheless, the "reorganization bug" continued to bite those who "insisted that the territory [was] ready to resume its place in organized baseball," and the Kitty League returned in 1935 for its longest phase to date.[2]

The new-for-'35 Kitty League brought Portageville (Missouri), Lexington, and Union City (Tennessee) into the league for the first time, while the league's return was welcomed in Jackson (Tennessee), Hopkinsville, and Paducah (Kentucky), three of the original Kitty League cities.[3] The 1935 season would give approximately 100,000 people access to professional baseball across parts of three states, and it would be the first time a team from Illinois was not in the Kitty, and the first time a team from Missouri was.[4]

Of the six cities competing in 1935, Paducah was the largest with a population of around 33,000.[5] Paducah is an old Ohio River town (established in 1827) in far western Kentucky, fifty miles upstream from where the Ohio terminates into the Mississippi River at Cairo, Illinois.[6] Local legend suggests baseball in Paducah is as old as the War of the Rebellion, having been brought there by Union soldiers from the northeast as they marched through Paducah on their way down to Vicksburg, Mississippi, in the summer of 1863.[7] Thirty-four years later, Paducah got its first professional team, the Little Colonels, when the city's street car company agreed to back an entry in the newly formed Central League.[8] That team, along with the Cairo Egyptians, would be the only two left in the black when the league faltered at the end of July 1897.[9] The financial resilience that kept the Little Colonels afloat would endure as Paducah fans continued to support the home team as three waves of the Kitty League crested and collapsed by 1924.[10]

After ten years without professional baseball, Paducah fans were believed to be ready to support a team again in 1933. B.B. Hook, Paducah pharmacist, baseball promoter, and owner of Hook Park (located on Paducah's north-west edge between North Eighth Street and the Ohio River), was so confident of the Kitty's resuscitation that he ordered fifteen new uniforms and scheduled a practice for a team that hadn't yet been formed.[11] Hook's hopes were for naught, however, as the Kitty was not revived and the city's team instead became the independent Paducah Merchants.[12] When the Kitty failed to return in 1934 as well, Hook again forged ahead and formed his own six-team league—the Little Kitty League—that played a seventeen-game schedule on Sundays and holidays starting June 10.[13] Finally, in late November 1934, the Kitty League made its official application to the National Association of Professional Baseball Leagues for a 1935 return.[14]

Reformation efforts gained two competent and capable organizers in January 1935 in Dr. Frank Bassett and "Honest John" McCloskey.[15] Bassett, the founder and three-time former president of the Kitty League, had sponsored the league's application to the National Association at Louisville the previous November, and afterward, spent his time gauging interest among the leaders of various cities in his "organization for the development of youngsters."[16] In late April, Bassett would again be elected president and vowed "not to have a repetition of the league failure 12 years ago."[17] McCloskey, once believed to be held back from being "the greatest manager of all time" by "players [who] lack the quickness and the brains to follow his orders," was a highly-respected baseball man who had founded the Texas League in 1887 and was now tasked by the National Association with the field work in Kentucky, Illinois, and Tennessee.[18] By month's end, the two had secured financial support from teams in the International League in exchange for those teams holding options over players of the Kitty League, and set the ground rules by which the Kitty would operate:

a guaranteed monthly team salary between $500 and $1000 divided among the fourteen players, no players with any prior professional experience, a minimum of three games per week, and a $500 bond from each team guaranteeing the team would play its schedule through the end of the season.[19] Many of the rules that guided the 1935 Kitty League were written in direct response to the issues that had led to the collapse of previous installments of the league.

Once McCloskey reported "unlimited enthusiasm" among potential players and fans in the cities he visited, organizers such as Hook set about bolstering the likelihood of their city being included in the new Kitty.[20] In early March, Hook believed he had secured assistance from the St. Louis Cardinals and agreed to cover the remaining costs himself as official sponsor of the team, greatly improving Paducah's chances of scoring a franchise.[21] Next, Hook began searching for a team manager and the funds to light Hook Park, estimated to cost $2500.[22] Hook believed the St. Louis Cardinals would provide him with a player from one of the organization's minor league teams to serve as manager, but neither of the two men reported in the *Paducah Sun-Democrat*—Wally Schang and Johnny Hodapp—ever managed in Paducah.[23]

On May 1, three days after the Kitty League was announced to be officially reorganized, forty "green youngsters" answered an invitation to try out for Paducah's yet unnamed team.[24] Immediately, a need for pitching was realized and interim manager George "Skin" Griffin identified players from his Paducah Merchants team whom he'd like to see audition for the city's Kitty club.[25] Over the next three weeks, Griffin continued to drill the growing number of young auditioners and work them into exhibition games as he determined who would make the final roster. Griffin desired to find and keep five pitchers on his fourteen-man roster.[26]

One week before the first game of the season, the Paducah team was named the Red Birds, either as a nod to the Cardinals' loose sponsorship or in hopes that Hook could secure future designation as a Cardinals farm team. One day before the first game, the opening-day roster was revealed: pitchers Bernie Walters, Aubrey Mitchell, Jett Mason, and Palmer Pinnegar; catchers Floyd Perryman and Gene Ruoff; infielders Bob Mason, Jenks Mason, George Cooper, and Roger "Sonny" Fields; and outfielders Pete Zimmerman, Louie Perryman, Connie Lee, and Griffin himself as manager and reserve infielder.[27]

Opening Day 1935 was twelve years in the making, and both excitement and expectations were high. Exhibition games had been well attended by Paducahans and well played by the Red Birds. *Paducah Sun-Democrat* sports editor Sam Livingston (named one of the league's official scorekeepers by President Bassett) wrote that the Red Birds could be a "title contender," but "must improve their hitting...to be able to win the pennant."[28] Right-hander Aubrey Mitchell was given the ball for Opening Day against the Hopkinsville Hoppers after Griffin's other choice, Bernie Walters, had tweaked his knee in an exhibition game three days before.[29] Mitchell pitched all nine innings in front of an estimated eight hundred fans, giving up seven hits and two earned runs while striking out ten.[30] The Red Birds only had two hits off Hoppers' starter Tucker Joiner, but after he left the game in the sixth inning with a sore arm, the Red Birds began to hit, scoring a run in the sixth, two in the seventh, and three in the eighth. The Hoppers added tension in the ninth inning when the first two batters singled then scored on a ground out and an error, giving the Hoppers four runs to the Red Birds' six. Mitchell remained in control, however, and ended the game by striking out the game's final batter. As good as Mitchell was on Opening Day, Bernie Walters was even better the next day.[31] Walters, a screwball pitcher, allowed only two hits through seven innings but gave up three in the eighth that, paired with two Paducah errors, led to three Hopkinsville runs. The Red Birds tied the game in the ninth, but the Hoppers took the lead for good on a wild pitch by Walters in the tenth inning. On Friday, Paducah amassed twelve hits but only five runs, winning another one-run game—and the opening series—against Hopkinsville.[32]

Through the Red Birds' first series, two areas of concern presented themselves: late-inning pitching and suspect fielding, both to be expected among young men playing professionally for the first time. In the first six innings of the three games against Hopkinsville, Red Birds pitchers had an excellent earned run average of 1.50. Beyond the sixth inning, however, that ERA rose to 5.25, which could be indicative of fatigue (pitchers' arms not fully conditioned after only three weeks of spring training) or a limited pitch selection (pitchers not being able to get outs with their secondary, or even tertiary, pitches against batters who have already faced them earlier in the game). The Red Birds also committed nine errors in the series, leading to two unearned runs in the opener. The poor fielding of the outfield led Sam Livingston to urge Griffin to "abandon his plans to have an outfield composed only of players who also can pitch, play first, catch, or mend broken bats and give Paducah's Kitty League team a genuine outfielder."[33] Given the constraints of a fourteen-man roster, Livingston's request would be hard to fulfill.

Two series later, the Red Birds were not improving and found themselves with five wins, five losses, and in need of help. On June 2, the day after the Red Birds scored nine runs—and still lost by five—it was announced that a pitcher and a slugger were to be added once the team returned from a two-game road trip to play the first-place Lexington Giants.[34] Later that afternoon, the Red Birds "suffered their customary late inning letdown," when the Giants scored two, two-out runs in the eighth off of Jett Mason, underscoring the team's needs.[35]

Manager Griffin rejoiced when rain washed out the game the next day, giving his pitchers an extra day of rest.[36] Since "there [was] little prospect...of any team running away with the Kitty League baseball championship," adding the right players this early in the season could allow any of the six teams to get ahead of the others.[37] With that in mind, team president B.B. Hook signed nineteen-year-old slugging first baseman Benny Sanders out of Marion, Illinois, left-handed starting pitcher Gerald Veach, a freshman at Southern Illinois Normal University from Simpson, Illinois, and former Paducah Merchants third baseman Harry Williams who hoped to play in the Red Bird outfield while he was home for the summer from the University of Tennessee.[38] To make room for these additions, Hook released outfielder Pete Zimmerman, utility player Gene Ruoff, and Nelson Hughes.[39]

The improvement brought about by these signings was immediate, propelling the Red Birds to win seven of their next eleven games. On June 4, back from the team's first road trip of the season, Harry Williams and Benny Sanders were both in the lineup as Paducah tried to distance themselves from Jackson, who trailed them in the standings by only half a game.[40] The two newest Birds "dazzled" with plays described as "sensational" and "polished," while Aubrey Mitchell remained undefeated with his fourth pitching victory of the season.[41] Moreover, Sanders "flashed more pep and more color than any ball player has shown in Paducah this year."[42] The next day Williams and Sanders combined to go 5-for-10 with four runs batted in to support Don "Lefty" Anderson's eight innings of relief pitching as the Red Birds won on successive days for the first time all season.[43] On June 9, eleven hundred fans saw Aubrey Mitchell defeat the Lexington Giants almost singlehandedly. In nine innings Mitchell allowed only two runs, struck out seven, drove in all three Paducah runs with two hits, and ended the game with an immaculate ninth inning by striking out all three Giants on nine total pitches.[44] It was the Red Birds' best game to date. The next day, Anderson bested Mitchell by allowing only one run in nine innings as the Red Birds played only their third game without committing an error.[45] Mitchell won his sixth game on June 16 and Gerald Veach won his first game the next day as the Red Birds collected fourteen hits against the Portageville Pirates.[46] During the two-week tear, the team's once problematic late-inning ERA improved by more than two runs and five Red Birds raised their season batting average to .300 or above as the Birds flew into second place.[47]

After the Red Birds' 7–4 run, they were the hottest team in the Kitty League and only a game-and-a-half behind the league-leading Lexington Giants on June 17. Then the Birds lost for a week straight. For whatever reason, there was a "jinx" on them during "nocturnal tilts."[48] One telling correlation was the number of errors they made in night games. In the four games the Red Birds played under lights the week of June 18—all losses—they committed fourteen errors that led to eleven unearned runs.[49] In those same four losses, opponents outscored the Red Birds by a total of only eight runs. Red Birds' pitching remained solid with a 2.43 ERA in the 37 innings of the four losses but the errors were too much to overcome. On June 19, Bernie Walters pitched through "wildness," but it was the "wobbly" defense in the field that allowed Jackson to score five unearned runs, and win 8–6.[50] After a rainout, Aubrey Mitchell tried for his seventh straight victory of the season on June 21, and despite allowing only one earned run in all nine innings, Mitchell took the loss as three errors allowed the Union City Greyhounds to score three unearned runs.[51] Two days later, on "Southern Illinois Day" at Hook Park (a promotion honoring the three Red Birds from southern Illinois: Benny Sanders, Gerald Veach, and Joe Grace), Veach "turned in a marvelous exhibition of pitching," but three unearned runs led to the team's fifth straight loss and pushed the Red Birds into last place.[52] Dissatisfied with the "skidding," Hook intervened for the second time in less than a month, suggesting lineup changes to Griffin, who "prepared for a shakeup of his club."[53]

The first change implemented by Griffin was to move recently-acquired outfielder Joe Grace to the leadoff spot. Grace had slugged his way onto the team nine days prior by batting .682 for the Anna, Illinois, State Hospital team.[54] In seven games batting third for the Red Birds, however, Grace was batting only .182. After being moved to the top of the lineup on June 24, Grace had ten hits in the next six games—four of them Paducah victories—while raising his batting average to .348. The last Paducah victory in that six-game stretch was also Bernie Walters's last game. The tough-luck loser of five well-pitched games, Walters's confidence was compromised and he "began to worry about his inability to win and lost his control."[55] Also released on the same day as Walters was Harry Williams who batted .230 in fifteen games for the Red Birds while playing left field and third base. The team was reluctant to release Williams, but granted him his release so he could accept a job with the Illinois Central Railroad.[56]

Although the Red Birds were in last place on June 30, they trailed the league-leading Lexington Giants by only three games.[57] None of the Kitty's six teams was dominant in the first half, and any of the six that could string together a handful of victories over the next eleven games could still take the first-half championship. The odds were favorable for the Red Birds; they would play eight of the remaining eleven games at home, ending the first half with three games against Lexington.[58] On July 2, Aubrey Mitchell "turned in another highly effective pitching exhibition" as he won his seventh game and moved Paducah one game closer to the first-half championship.[59] The next day Paducah played "raggedly," committing almost a dozen "boners" in what was arguably the team's worst game of the season.[60] Seven unearned runs twisted a potential 5–2 Red Bird victory into a 9–5 defeat against Hopkinsville.[61] In the first game of an Independence Day doubleheader, another unearned run in the twelfth inning spoiled 8⅓ innings of one-run ball pitched by Mitchell and the Red Birds lost, 2–1.[62] Losing the nightcap of the doubleheader eliminated Paducah from contending for the first-half championship, but, with three games remaining against Lexington, the Red Birds could stall the Giants while the Hopkinsville Hoppers, Union City Greyhounds, or Jackson Generals overtook or tied the Giants for the league lead.[63]

On July 8, the Red Birds played flawlessly behind Jett Mason, defeating Lexington, 2–1.[64] The following day, Griffin concocted an experimental lineup for the first game of a doubleheader that consisted of new shortstop Louis Bertoni, first baseman Ferrell, third baseman Milkovich, and the return of former Red Bird Palmer Pinnegar.[65] The experiment failed and the Red Birds lost, 15–2.[66] In the second game, Vollie Bishop made his Red Bird debut and held the Giants to two earned runs as the Red Birds won, 9–3, to close out the first half of the season. [67] By winning two of the three games over Lexington, Paducah finished the season's first half with a 20–24 record, half a game ahead of the last place Portageville Pirates.[68]

The Red Birds started the second half on July 10 playing "almost perfect ball" in a 5–2 two victory over the season's first-half champion Lexington Giants.[69] The Birds played every element of the game well; Clarence Owens's pitching was "steady," their "defensive work was the best of the season," and Joe Grace continued his great hitting against Lexington with an RBI-double and an opposite field "Ruthian smash" for the Red Birds' fifth and final run of the

AUTHOR'S COLLECTION

The Paducah Red Birds

B.B. Hook, Jr. is the child in the very front.

Front row (L–R): Joe Grace, Floyd Perryman, Venable Satterfield, and Louis Perryman.

Middle row (L–R): Lowell Green, Mel Ivy, E.R. Jones (more behind the row than in it), Robert Brown, Benny Sanders, and an unnamed child listed as "mascot."

Back row (L–R): Aubrey Mitchell, Vollie Bishop, Jett Mason, Gerald Veach, Don Anderson, Clarence Owens, and B.B. Hook.

afternoon.[70] As they had done a handful of times during the season's first half, the team again revealed its potential, and Sam Livingston called the nine who played that day "the best club [Paducah] has had on the field this season."[71] It would be the last time those nine played together. After the game, Louis Bertoni—who had become one of the team's "main cogs"—retired from baseball, citing as his reason the every-day strain on a knee he injured while playing football for Southern Illinois Normal University.[72] The next day, unearned runs again negated a good outing by a Paducah pitcher and after the loss, Milkovich and Benny Sanders were released.[73] On July 13, Griffin himself was released from managerial duties, but B.B. Hook wished to retain him as a utility player.[74] Griffin had played nearly every position in the infield and outfield, pitched, and was hitting .349—all at age 42. Under Griffin's lead, however, the team "never has been able to display a consistent winning spirit."[75] Sam Livingston was sympathetic, writing that "the situation was not ideal for Griffin. He did not have the material at hand he wished," which was another subtle dig at Hook trying to get by on the cheap.[76] Livingston would continue to lobby for Hook to raise the pay of his ballplayers, reminding him, "You get out of something what you put in it."[77]

Hook hired long-time minor leaguer Fred Glass as Griffin's replacement.[78] Glass was from just up the Ohio River in Golconda, Illinois, and had a remarkable minor league career in the United States and Canada.[79] In 1912, Glass had set a Central International League record when he pitched 29 innings in just three days for the Winnipeg Maroons, and, in 1914, Glass drew the attention of the Cleveland Naps when he was leading the Northern League with a .450 batting average as a pitcher-outfielder for the Superior Red Sox.[80] Superior released Glass before the start of the next season so he could manage Paducah's Kitty League team, but the league failed to organize for 1915 and Glass ended up playing for the Flint Vehicles.[81] Glass returned to Paducah in 1922 as a Kitty League umpire, and when the league again failed after the 1924 season, Glass became a sheriff's deputy in Golconda, where, in 1925, he apprehended E.R. "Kid" McGowan, who was implicated in the 1922 robbery of the Denver Mint.[82]

Glass joined the team in Union City on July 15 and vowed to not make any changes to the roster until he had watched a few games.[83] After the Red Birds squandered a four-run lead and lost to the Union City Greyhounds on his first night as manager, however, Glass "immediately sent Scout Ralph Bishop up into southern Illinois for some new ball players."[84] Over the next week, six new Red Birds debuted, all likely recruited in Illinois by Bishop. Those signed were catcher Mel Ivy from Marion, third baseman John Lutwinski from Harrisburg, Wilson, a first baseman, infielders Harry and Sam Wright of Brookport, and first baseman Jimmy Creek from Champaign.[85] In total, the Red Birds won only three of Glass's first nine games as manager, and found themselves right where they had ended the season's first half: a half-game out of last place.[86]

Through all of the roster inconsistency of Glass's first two weeks as manager, the one constant was the hitting of Joe Grace. Benched by Glass on July 17 after going hitless for three days, Grace blasted his way back into the lineup with three batting-practice home runs before the July 18 game against Hopkinsville, and, when the game started, he kept hitting.[87] Grace doubled and hit what would have been the game-winning home run that afternoon had Aubrey Mitchell not given up one himself in the ninth.[88] The next day, Sam Livingston remarked that Grace "probably will develop into the best hitter of all the Paducah players" when he pulls his hits naturally into right field (where left-handed hitters like Grace usually hit) rather than pushing them to the left side, which tends to greatly diminish a hitter's power.[89] Seeing Grace could hit for power, Glass coached Grace on how to hit more consistently to the right side and moved him to the fourth spot in the lineup, where a team's best power hitter tends to bat.[90] Grace responded with another double and another home run, but, for the Red Birds, it was another loss.[91] Undeterred, Grace kept hitting. He collected two hits in three at bats on July 20, one hit the next day, two hits both on July 23 and 24, another hit on July 25, and Grace hit his third home run in eight games on July 26.[92] In a little more than a week, Grace had become "by far Paducah's best individual attraction," and he was earning attention beyond Paducah as well.[93] On July 28, it was reported that the Philadelphia Athletics had made an offer to Hook for the twenty-year-old Grace, but Hook was reluctant to sell given Grace's value to his last-place team.[94] Grace stayed with the Red Birds and he stayed hot. On August 1, he singled, doubled, and hit a Kitty League-record three triples in a 10–8 win at Hopkinsville.[95] Grace would get two more hits on August 2 before his streak ended at fifteen games.[96] Grace batted .484 during his streak, and raised his overall batting average from .273 on July 15 to .337 on August 2.[97]

Through the duration of Grace's streak, which for a dozen games was matched by Floyd Perryman's own streak, the Red Birds won only six times. With an 8–13 record, they were in last place on August 2, five games behind the league-leading Portageville Pirates.[98] To add to the Birds' season-long struggle with errors, unearned runs, and late-inning losses were injuries to Sam Wright, Floyd Perryman, and Jenks Mason, and Harry Wright quitting the team after seeing his brother, Sam, sent to the hospital when he was bowled over by Portageville Pirates' 200-pound catcher Bill Scheele while fielding a bunt.[99]

By August 1 the Red Birds were considered out of contention for the second-half championship, and on August 5, Fred Glass was out of a job.[100] The timing of Glass's firing is interesting; the Red Birds had scored 29 runs in the three games before Glass was fired and won two of them. Hook simply said he was "not satisfied" with Glass, while Glass responded that there was "too much interference from the box office."[101] Hook cited Mel Ivy's popularity among his teammates when he named the catcher his new player-manager.[102] Glass returned to Metropolis, Illinois, and resumed managing the city's Hard Roads League team.[103]

The Red Birds fared no better under the twenty-year-old Ivy. Although Paducah was recognized as having the best pitching staff in the Kitty League, it was getting difficult for the hurlers to find victories when "they always have to play with anywhere from four to six errors behind them."[104] First-half ace Aubrey Mitchell hadn't won in eight straight starts dating back to July 2, and to further upend the defense, Jenks Mason, the club's regular second baseman, signed on to play softball with a team from Mayfield, Kentucky, once he healed from a late-July injury.[105] Five different second basemen were used in the first seven games under Ivy's management until the "sensational" Robert Brown secured the position.[106] Aside from Floyd Perryman and Joe Grace, the rest of the lineup wasn't producing much. On August 12, Perryman was batting .370, as he had done most of the season, and Grace hit a three-run home run as the Red Birds won for only the fourth time in the last twelve games, the extent of Ivy's tenure as manager.[107]

With fourteen games remaining, Hook hired the team's fourth manager right out of the stands. E.R. Jones was vacationing in Paducah watching the Red Birds and when he displayed "such a thorough knowledge of the game" to Hook, Hook hired him.[108] Jones had known some of the players on the Red Birds from his managing of an American Legion baseball tournament in Marion, Illinois, where many of the team's ten native southern Illinoisans had played. Jones quickly had the Red Birds playing their best baseball of the season. On August 20, Jones's second game as manager, Aubrey Mitchell shut out the Hopkinsville Hoppers on three hits to win for the first time in nearly two months.[109] The next day, Jones pinch hit for starting pitcher Clarence Owens in the eighth inning and knocked in the two runs that gave Paducah the win.[110] On August 23, every Red Bird in the lineup but Louie Perryman had at least one hit and the Birds beat Lexington.[111] A shutout of first-place Jackson by Gerald Veach followed on August 25 and Paducah crept .005 percentage points ahead of Lexington for fifth place in the league.[112] Two wins later and the Red Birds had their longest winning streak of the season at four games on August 27.[113] On August 29, an "untouchable" Veach allowed only three singles and Grace knocked in a run and scored the other as the Red Birds won their sixth straight over the Union City Greyhounds, 2–1.[114] Mitchell was unable to sustain the streak the next day and the Red Birds closed out August with a loss.[115] At Jackson on September 1, Jones put himself up to bat in the tenth inning with the bases loaded and again won the game with a clutch hit. On September 2, the last day of the season, the Red Birds played a split-park doubleheader against Union City, but without Floyd Perryman who had injured his shoulder in the game against Jackson. With Perryman out, Grace hitless, and eleven total errors, the Red Birds lost both games and finished the second half in fifth place with a 21–27 record.[116]

With the season coming to a close and teams looking to stock up on promising young talent, Hook began entertaining offers for his players. As expected, the three Red Bird All-Stars—Gerald Veach, Floyd Perryman, and Joe Grace—were highly desired. Veach led the Red Birds with a 2.43 earned run average and was named the best left-handed pitcher in the Kitty League.[117] The Memphis Chicks of the Southern Association were the first to show interest in Veach, but it was the National League's Boston Braves that gave Hook $1500 and the use of two pitchers for Paducah's 1936 team after Veach impressed Braves' manager Bill McKechnie at a tryout in St. Louis on September 5.[118] Veach was one of Boston's pitchers who "distinguished themselves" in spring training, and at only nineteen years old, he made the Bees' roster (the Boston Braves were renamed the Bees in 1936).[119] For two tantalizing months, the Bees gave Veach "a chance to see how it is done in the big show," but from the dugout.[120] He never made his major league debut and on June 15 was sent down to the club's Class B team in Columbia, South Carolina, and on to the Class-D Andalusia, Alabama, Reds where he went 8–1 with a 2.38 ERA.[121] Veach ended his professional baseball career after the

1938 season and returned to Southern Illinois Normal University.[122]

Floyd Perryman led the league in batting with his .359 batting average, prompting the Albany Senators to purchase him sight unseen from Hook for $500 and the use of two players.[123] In February 1936, Perryman joined the parent club Washington Senators' spring training in Orlando, Florida, and impressed manager Bucky Harris with his catcher's mitt, but not his bat.[124] Perryman hit so poorly that he fell from contention to be the Senators' third-string catcher and was reassigned to the Chattanooga Lookouts, the Senators' Southern Association team, as some questioned how he was ever a batting champion the year before.[125] At the end of spring training, Perryman was transferred to the Class-D Mayodan, North Carolina, Millers, where he played in 1936.[126] In 1938, playing for the Fort Smith, Arkansas, Giants, Perryman batted .260, fielded .989, and even won eight games as a pitcher, earning him the near-unanimous selection as the Western Association's most valuable player.[127] Perryman ended his career back in the Kitty League, playing for the Paducah Indians in 1941, and he was the Jackson Generals' first baseman on June 20, 1942, the last night of Kitty League play before the league's fourth phase folded due to financial woes in the wake of World War II.[128]

Joe Grace quickly made up for his slow start to the 1935 season, and just as quickly drew the eye of many suitors. In July, Hook turned down an undisclosed offer for Grace from the Philadelphia Athletics, and when the Jackson Generals offered cash and two players to rent Grace for the final two weeks of the Kitty League season, Hook again said no. Just five days later, on August 30, a scout from the Memphis Chicks was at Hook Park giving Grace a hard look, but before the Chicks could make an offer, Hook sent Grace to St. Louis to shop him to the Braves along with Gerald Veach.[129] The Braves did not make an offer for Grace at first, only agreeing to invite him to spring training in a few months.[130] On September 7, Hook received a phone call that the Braves agreed to purchase Grace for $1500.[131] A follow-up call from manager McKechnie on September 10, however, revealed that Commissioner of Baseball Kenesaw Mountain Landis had blocked the sale of Grace due to the Braves' deplorable financial condition (the Braves were only able to sign Veach when McKechnie put up the money himself).[132] In the meantime, Memphis made an offer of $500 for Grace but Hook refused to accept anything less than $1000.[133] On September 11, Hook received papers from Chicks owner Tom Watkins for the transfer of Grace, but Hook claimed the Braves already had an option on Grace.[134] Hook was buying time so the Braves could scrape together $1500, three times Memphis's offer. The Braves never came up with the cash and, on October 15, National Association President W.G. Bramham declared that a telephone conversation Hook had with Watkins constituted a sale, and Hook accepted the $500 from Memphis.[135] Grace batted .304 in three seasons with Memphis before making his major league debut with the St. Louis Browns on September 24, 1938.[136] By 1941 Grace had become the Browns regular right fielder and he batted .309 that year with the American League's sixth-best on-base percentage of .410.[137] In 1944, while the Browns were making their only World Series appearance, Grace was instrumental in the Navy winning the Armed Service World Series in Hawaii, batting .280 for the series, including a grand slam in Game Two.[138] Grace played two more years in the majors after the war, and ended his career with six seasons in the Pacific Coast League, batting .299 and earning the nickname "Old Reliable."[139]

Sports fans made 1935 a historic year in Paducah. As the Depression wore on, Paducahans turned to sports like never before. Retailers across the city reported a fifteen percent increase in the sale of sporting equipment and anywhere from twenty-five to fifty percent more people attended the city's football, baseball, golf, boxing, wrestling, and tennis events than in 1934.[140] When the gate receipts were totaled at Hook Park, the team had broken even, and the sale of Veach, Perryman, and Grace "netted [Hook] a nice profit for the season."[141] Hook vowed to learn from his mistake of the 1935 Red Birds being the lowest paid players in the league, and increased salaries for 1936 so that he may have a "more harmonious team."[142] In March it was announced the Paducah team would be affiliated with the Cincinnati Reds, and when Cherokee Ben Tincup was hired as the new manager in April, fans convincingly insisted it was "only proper" to call the team by its old name, the Paducah Indians.[143] On Opening Day, the Indians won big over the Mayfield Clothiers en route to the first-half championship and tied for best record for the 1936 season.[144]

Hook sold the team and ballpark to Holland Bryan and R.L. Myre in March 1937. The Kitty League would live its last life in Paducah from 1951 to 1955.[145] ■

Notes

1. Joshua R. Maxwell and Kevin D. McCann, *The Kitty League* (Charleston: Arcadia Publishing, 2012), 9; and Kevin McCann, "Kitty League 101," Kitty League (website), accessed May 24, 2020, http://www.kittyleague.com/features/kittyleague101.htm.
2. Sam Livingston, "Down Sports Avenue," *Paducah* (KY) *Sun-Democrat*, January 13, 1935: 10.

3. Maxwell and McCann, 9, 30–31; and Kevin Reichard, "Kentucky-Illinois-Tennessee (Kitty) League," Ballpark Digest (website), published November 4, 2008, https://ballparkdigest.com/20081104918/minor-leaguebaseball/news/kentucky-illinois-tennessee-kitty-league. See also "Minor League History: Kentucky-Illinois-Tennessee League (1903–1906 and 1910–1916)," *Dutch Baseball Hangout* (blog), published January 5, 2018, https://dutchbaseballhangout.wordpress.com/2018/01/05/minor-league-history-kentucky-illinois-tennesseeleague-1903-1906-and-1910-1916.
4. "Dr. Frank Bassett Works To Reorganize Kitty Loop," *Paducah* (KY) *Sun-Democrat*, January 2, 1935: 2; "Minor League History: Kentucky-Illinois-Tennessee League (1903–1906 and 1910–1916);" and "Minor League History: Kentucky-Illinois-Tennessee League (1922–1924 and 1935–1942)," *Dutch Baseball Hangout*, published January 15, 2018, https://dutchbaseballhangout.wordpress.com/2018/01/15/minor-league-historykentucky-illinois-tennessee-league-1922-1924-and-1937-1942.
5. "Dr. Frank Bassett Works."
6. Robert M. Rennick, *Kentucky Place Names* (Lexington: University Press of Kentucky, 1984), 224.
7. Randy Morgan, interview by Kate Lochte, *Sounds Good*, 91.3 WKMS-FM, August 11, 2015. Baseball historian Randy Morgan claims that baseball was brought to Paducah by "soldiers from the northeast," where "the game had been played in New England and New York [and] Pennsylvania areas" before the Civil War. In the interview, Morgan implies these soldiers played baseball at a fort (likely Fort Anderson) that the Union Army built just outside of Paducah. A thorough search of all fifty-one volumes of *War of the Rebellion: a Compilation of the Official Records of the Union and Confederate Armies* did not uncover any Union Army correspondence mentioning soldiers from the northeast encamped at Fort Anderson. However, a search of the National Park Service's collection of detailed regimental histories revealed just one regiment, the 34th New Jersey Infantry, as having duty at Paducah from August 28 to December 1864, and a handful of other various regiments from New York, Pennsylvania, Massachusetts, and New Jersey having "movement through Kentucky to Cairo, Ill., June 4–10, [1863], thence to Vicksburg, Miss." Though undocumented, it is possible baseball could have been brought to Paducah by soldiers in one of these units.
8. "Evansville's Managers," *The Sporting* News, February 6, 1897: 7.
9. "All Over Now," *Paducah* (KY) *Daily Sun*, July 26, 1897: 4.
10. See "Post Season Games Will Be Played," *Paducah* (KY) *Evening Sun*, August 18, 1905: 3; "Annual Revival Of Kitty Is In Order Just Now," *Paducah* (KY) *News-Democrat*, November 30, 1916: 6; and "New Baseball League Talked," *Paducah* (KY) *News-Democrat*, January 13, 1924: 1.
11. "Kitty League Baseball May Return Here," *Paducah* (KY) *Sun-Democrat*, April 19, 1933: 2.
12. "Youngsters Report For First Baseball Drill," *Paducah* (KY) *Sun-Democrat*, April 21, 1933: 10.
13. "League Formed For Baseball Competition," *Paducah* (KY) *Sun-Democrat*, June 3, 1934: 10; and "Little Kitty League Schedule Is Drafted," *Paducah* (KY) *Sun-Democrat*, June 5, 1934: 8.
14. Paul Mickelson, "Each Team Wants Something Free At Diamond Meet," *Paducah* (KY) *Sun-Democrat*, November 21, 1934: 2.
15. Sam Livingston, January 13, 1935.
16. Maxwell and McCann, 9; and "Dr. Frank Bassett Works."
17. "Kitty League Is Definitely Re-Organized," *Paducah* (KY) *Sun-Democrat*, April 29, 1935: 2.
18. Hugh S. Fullerton, "'Watch His Arm!' The Science of Coaching," in *The American Magazine* (New York: Crowell Publishing Company, 1911), 72: 469; and Sam Livingston, January 13, 1935.
19. "Kitty Loop's Reorganization Seems Certain," *Paducah* (KY) *Sun-Democrat*, January 30, 1935: 2; and Sam Livingston, "Down Sports Avenue," *Paducah* (KY) *Sun-Democrat*, February 1, 1935: 10.
20. "Progress Shown In Reorganizing Old Kitty Loop," *Paducah* (KY) *Sun-Democrat*, February 18, 1935: 2.
21. How much, if anything, Hook ended up getting from the Cardinals was not reported. Sam Livingston of the *Paducah Sun-Democrat* mentioned many times over the next few years that Hook had financed the 1935 team all on his own. The only assistance Hook may have received was hand-me-down uniforms from one of the Cardinals' minor league clubs. "Cardinals To Help Paducah In Kitty Loop," *Paducah* (KY) *Sun-Democrat*, March 6, 1935: 2; and "Round Ralph, Confident Mel Simons Will Give Paducah Good Ball Club, Urges Fans To Help," *Paducah* (KY) *Sun-Democrat*, April 2, 1941: 10.
22. "Cardinals To Help Paducah;" and Sam Livingston, "Down Sports Avenue," *Paducah* (KY) *Sun-Democrat*, January 24, 1935: 10. The location of Hook Park was determined using a 1936 Paducah map from the United States Geological Survey, https://www.oldmapsonline.org/map/usgs/5292838, accessed June 5, 2020, and Google Maps.
23. According to Baseball-Reference.com, Schang remained a player and caught thirty-nine games for the 1935 Muskogee Tigers. Johnny Hodapp's Society for American Baseball Research biography indicates he retired from baseball after the 1934 season and returned to Cincinnati to become a mortician. Sam Livingston, "Down Sports Avenue," *Paducah* (KY) *Sun-Democrat*, April 5, 1935: 12; and Bill Nowlin, "Johnny Hodapp," Society for American Baseball Research (website), accessed June 5, 2020, https://sabr.org/bioproj/person/ 3eff4e84.
24. "Kitty League Re-Organized;" and "40 Youngsters Report for Initial Drill of the Paducah Kitty League Ball Squad," *Paducah* (KY) *Sun-Democrat*, May 2, 1935: 12.
25. "40 Youngsters Report."
26. "40 Youngsters Report."
27. "Kitty League Season Will Open Next Week," *Paducah* (KY) *Sun-Democrat*, May 15, 1935: 6; Randy Morgan, *Paducah's Native Baseball Team* (n.p.: Randy Morgan, 2015), 84; and "Kitty League Season To Open Tomorrow," *Paducah* (KY) *Sun-Democrat*, May 21, 1935: 6.
28. Sam Livingston, "Down Sports Avenue," *Paducah* (KY) *Sun-Democrat*, May 20, 1935: 2.
29. "Kitty League Open Tomorrow."
30. "800 Fans See Paducah Capture Kitty Opener," *Paducah* (KY) *Sun-Democrat*, May 23, 1935: 10.
31. "Hoppers Beat Red Birds In Tenth, 4 to 3," *Paducah* (KY) *Sun-Democrat*, May 24, 1935: 12.
32. "How the Birds Won Friday," *Paducah* (KY) *Sun-Democrat*, May 26, 1935: 10.
33. Sam Livingston, "Down Sports Avenue," *Paducah* (KY) *Sun-Democrat*, May 26, 1935: 10.
34. "Paducah Baseball Club To Be Strengthened," *Paducah* (KY) *Sun-Democrat*, June 2, 1935: 11.
35. "Lexington Puts On Rally In 8th To Beat Paducah," *Paducah* (KY) *Sun-Democrat* June 3, 1935: 8.
36. "Jackson Arrives Here For Series With Griffinmen," *Paducah* (KY) *Sun-Democrat*, June 4, 1935: 6.
37. Sam Livingston, "Down Sports Avenue," *Paducah* (KY) *Sun-Democrat*, June 4, 1935: 6.
38. "Paducah To Be Strengthened."
39. Outfielder-pitcher Connie Lee, first baseman Robert Mason (both opening day starters), and pitchers Palmer Pinnegar and Chief Jackaway (or Jackoway) had also been released by June 12. According to Baseball-Reference.com, Mason played professionally again from 1937 to 1941. The *Paducah Sun-Democrat* mentions Ruoff and Hughes playing for teams in Paducah's semi-professional softball league after their release from the Red Birds, and, later, for the independent Paducah Merchants baseball team. Pinnegar joined the Merchants after his release, and returned to the Red Birds for one game on July 9, giving up nine runs in seven innings. "Portageville To Oppose Birds In Ladies' Day Fray," *Paducah* (KY) *Sun-Democrat*, June 12, 1935: 2.
40. "How They Stand," *Paducah* (KY) *Sun-Democrat*, June 5, 1935: 2.
41. "Williams and Sanders Help Mitchell Win," *Paducah* (KY) *Sun-Democrat*, June 5, 1935: 2.
42. "Williams and Sanders Help Mitchell Win."
43. "Paducah Whips Jackson, 7 To 6, In 11th Inning," *Paducah* (KY) *Sun-Democrat*, June 6, 1935: 12.

44. "1,100 See Mitchell Lead Birds To Victory," *Paducah* (KY) *Sun-Democrat*, June 10, 1935: 8.
45. "Birds Beat Lexington, 2 To 1; Sweep Series," *Paducah* (KY) *Sun-Democrat*, June 11, 1935: 2.
46. "Mitchell Beats Portageville For 6th Win," *Paducah* (KY) *Sun-Democrat*, June 17, 1935: 8; and "Red Birds Again Triumph Over Portageville; Lefty Veach Grants Only 6 Hits," *Paducah* (KY) *Sun-Democrat*, June 18, 1935: 8.
47. Sam Livingston, "Down Sports Avenue," *Paducah* (KY) *Sun-Democrat*, June 17, 1935: 8; and "How They Stand," *Paducah* (KY) *Sun-Democrat*, June 18, 1935: 8.
48. "Mitchell To Pitch For Birds At Union City," *Paducah* (KY) *Sun-Democrat*, June 20, 1935: 10.
49. "Jackson Wins In The Tenth," *Paducah* (KY) *Sun-Democrat*, June 19, 1935: 2; "Mitchell To Pitch;" "Union City Again Thumps Paducah Birds, 6–2," *Paducah* (KY) *Sun-Democrat*, June 23, 1935: 8; Sam Livingston, "Down Sports Avenue," *Paducah* (KY) *Sun-Democrat*, June 23, 1935: 8; and "How Birds Lost Friday Night," *Paducah* (KY) *Sun-Democrat*, June 23, 1935: 9.
50. "Mitchell To Pitch."
51. "How Birds Lost Friday Night," June 23, 1935.
52. "Veach Pitches Beautifully But Poor Support Enables Portageville to Beat Him," *Paducah* (KY) *Sun-Democrat*, June 24, 1935: 8.
53. Sam Livingston, "Down Sports Avenue," *Paducah* (KY) *Sun-Democrat*, June 24, 1935: 8.
54. "Kitty League," *The Sporting News*, June 27, 1935: 5.
55. Walters pitched at least one game for the Jackson Generals after leaving the Red Birds. Sam Livingston, "Down Sports Avenue," *Paducah* (KY) *Sun-Democrat*, June 27, 1935: 12; and "Portageville Wins," *Paducah* (KY) *Sun-Democrat*, July 3, 1935: 2.
56. "Portageville Wins."; Baseball-Reference.com shows Williams played twenty games with the Jackson Generals in 1940, his only other season in professional baseball.
57. "How They Stand," *Paducah* (KY) *Sun-Democrat*, June 30, 1935: 11.
58. Sam Livingston, "Down Sports Avenue," *Paducah* (KY) *Sun-Democrat*, June 30, 1935: 10.
59. "Burr Pierce's Homer With 2 Aboard Pulls Red Birds Ahead to Defeat Hoppers," *Paducah* (KY) *Sun-Democrat*, July 3, 1935: 2.
60. "Red Birds Play Raggedly and Lose to Hopkinsville," *Paducah* (KY) *Sun-Democrat*, July 4, 1935: 8.
61. "Red Birds Play Raggedly and Lose to Hopkinsville."
62. "Union City Wins Pair of Holiday Tilts from Birds," *Paducah* (KY) *Sun-Democrat*, July 5, 1935: 10.
63. "How They Stand," *Paducah* (KY) *Sun-Democrat*, July 8, 1935: 2.
64. "Lexington Falls To Paducah, 2–1, In Hurling Duel," *Paducah* (KY) *Sun-Democrat*, July 9, 1935: 2.
65. Louis Bertoni replaced Roger "Sonny" Fields—who had been the Red Birds regular shortstop all season—and hit .364 in three games with Paducah. Ferrell, whose first name is unknown, played only this one game with Paducah. Milkovich's first name is also unknown, and the Zeigler, Illinois, native replaced "Red" Davis at third base and hit .200 in four games. As stated above, Pinnegar returned for just this one game with the Red Birds after having been released in early June.
66. "Red Birds Drop No. 1, Trounce Lexington in 2nd," *Paducah* (KY) *Sun-Democrat*, July 10, 1935: 2.
67. "Red Birds Drop No. 1, Trounce Lexington in 2nd."
68. "How They Stand," *Paducah* (KY) *Sun-Democrat*, July 10, 1935: 7.
69. "Birds, Aided By Homers, Win As 2nd Half Opens," *Paducah* (KY) *Sun-Democrat*, July 11, 1935: 9.
70. "Birds, Aided By Homers..."
71. Sam Livingston, "Down Sports Avenue," *Paducah* (KY) *Sun-Democrat*, July 11, 1935: 8.
72. Livingston, "Down Sports Avenue."
73. "Three Bases On Balls And Three Errors Cost Tilt," *Paducah* (KY) *Sun-Democrat*, July 12, 1935: 10; and "Paducah Red Birds To Have New Manager," *Paducah* (KY) *Sun-Democrat*, July 14, 1935: 10.
74. "Paducah New Manager."
75. "Paducah New Manager."
76. Sam Livingston, "Down Sports Avenue," *Paducah* (KY) *Sun-Democrat*, July 14, 1935: 10; and Sam Livingston, "Down Sports Avenue," *Paducah* (KY) *Sun-Democrat*, June 6, 1935: 12.
77. Sam Livingston, June 6, 1935.
78. "Glass Named Manager Of Paducah Red Birds," *Paducah* (KY) *Sun-Democrat*, July 15, 1935: 2.
79. Upon his hiring as Red Birds' manager, the *Paducah Sun-Democrat* reported Glass pitched for the New York Giants from 1905 to 1907, but neither Baseball-Reference.com nor Baseball Almanac lists Glass on the Giants' roster for those years. According to Baseball-Reference.com, Glass began his professional career with the Jacksonville, Illinois, Braves in 1909.
80. "Fred Glass Has Exploded One Of The Theories Of Modern Baseball," *Winnipeg Tribune*, August 23, 1912: 6; and "'Nap' Scout Looks Over Fred Glass," *Winnipeg Tribune*, June 3, 1914: 10.
81. "Jesse Gilbert Is Baseball Head," *Paducah* (KY) *Sun-Democrat*, March 12, 1915: 6; and Baseball Reference.
82. "'Kitty' To Open Its Season In 4 Parks On Tuesday," *Paducah* (KY) *Sun-Democrat*, May 15, 1922: 2; and "McGown On Denver Bandit Gang in 1922," *Paducah* (KY) *Sun-Democrat*, June 13, 1925: 1.
83. "Glass Named Manager."
84. "Glass, Mason Are Put Out of Game As Birds Lose to Union City Outfit, 6 to 5," *Paducah* (KY) *Sun-Democrat*, July 16, 1935: 2; and Sam Livingston, "Down Sports Avenue," *Paducah* (KY) *Sun-Democrat*, July 16, 1935: 2.
85. The debuts of these six players were determined using the box scores reported in the *Paducah Sun-Democrat* from July 17–25, 1935. Wilson's first name is unknown. In 1935, Mel Ivy had not yet shortened his name from Ivanski. By early 1936, the entire Ivanski family from Marion, Illinois, began appearing as Ivy. The reason for this change is not known.
86. "How They Stand," *Paducah* (KY) *Sun-Democrat*, July 25, 1935: 10.
87. Sam Livingston, "Down Sports Avenue," *Paducah* (KY) *Sun-Democrat*, July 28, 1935: 8.
88. "Adams' Homer In Last Frame Whips Paducah," *Paducah* (KY) *Sun-Democrat*, July 19, 1935: 10.
89. Sam Livingston, "Down Sports Avenue," *Paducah* (KY) *Sun-Democrat*, July 19, 1935: 10.
90. Sam Livingston, "Down Sports Avenue," *Paducah* (KY) *Sun-Democrat*, July 21, 1935: 10; and "How Birds Lost Friday," *Paducah* (KY) *Sun-Democrat*, July 21, 1935: 11.
91. "How Birds Lost Friday," July 21, 1935.
92. Grace's hitting statistics are compiled from the box scores reported in the *Paducah* (KY) *Sun-Democrat* from July 21–27, 1935.
93. "Red Birds Will Play Lexington Here Tomorrow," *Paducah* (KY) *Sun-Democrat*, July 24, 1935: 2.
94. Sam Livingston, "Down Sports Avenue," *Paducah* (KY) *Sun-Democrat*, July 28, 1935: 8.
95. "Kitty League," *The Sporting News*, August 8, 1935: 7.
96. "How the Birds Won Friday," *Paducah* (KY) *Sun-Democrat*, August 4, 1935: 9; and "Grace's Streak Ends As Giants Beat Red Birds," *Paducah* (KY) *Sun-Democrat*, August 5, 1935: 6.
97. "Birds Hope To Break Their Road Mark Today," *Paducah* (KY) *Sun-Democrat*, August 4, 1935: 9.
98. "How They Stand," *Paducah* (KY) *Sun-Democrat*, August 4, 1935: 8.
99. Both Harry and Sam Wright left the Red Birds after playing just the one game and returned to the Beer Barons, one of Paducah's many semi-professional softball teams. Sam Livingston, "Down Sports Avenue," *Paducah* (KY) *Sun-Democrat*, July 21, 1935: 10.
100. Sam Livingston, "Down Sports Avenue," *Paducah* (KY) *Sun-Democrat*, August 5, 1935: 6.
101. Sam Livingston, August 5, 1935; and Sam Livingston, "Down Sports Avenue," *Paducah* (KY) *Sun-Democrat*, August 6, 1935: 2.
102. Sam Livingston, August 6, 1935.
103. "Metropolis Will Play Marion Today; Schneeman Is Gone," *Paducah* (KY) *Sun-Democrat*, August 11, 1935: 9.

104. Sam Livingston, "Down Sports Avenue," *Paducah* (KY) *Sun-Democrat*, August 18, 1935: 8; and "Hopkinsville To Play Red Birds This Afternoon," *Paducah* (KY) *Sun-Democrat*, August 11, 1935: 8.
105. Sam Livingston, "Down Sports Avenue," *Paducah* (KY) *Sun-Democrat*, August 11, 1935: 8.
106. "Skin" Griffin, Lake, Joe Grace, and Lauder each played second base from August 5 until Brown was signed on August 12. "Red Birds Win 5th Game In 6 Starts," *Paducah* (KY) *Sun-Democrat*, August 27, 1935: 2.
107. "The Birds at Bat," *Paducah* (KY) *Sun-Democrat*, August 18, 1935: 9; and "Veach Strikes Out 9 As Red Birds Win Over Union City, 9-2; Joe Grace Hits Homer," *Paducah* (KY) *Sun-Democrat*, August 19, 1935: 2.
108. Sam Livingston, "Down Sports Avenue," *Paducah* (KY) *Sun-Democrat*, August 26, 1935: 2.
109. "Mitchell Blanks Hopkinsville, *Paducah* (KY) *Sun-Democrat*, August 21, 1935: 2.
110. "Red Birds Again Win Over Hoppers," *Paducah* (KY) *Sun-Democrat*, August 22, 1935: 10.
111. "How the Birds Won Friday," *Paducah* (KY) *Sun-Democrat*, August 25, 1935: 10.
112. "Gerald Veach Shuts Out Jackson," *Paducah* (KY) *Sun-Democrat*, August 26, 1935: 2; and "How They Stand," *Paducah* (KY) *Sun-Democrat*, August 26, 1935: 3.
113. "Triumphant Red Birds To Return Home Thursday For Tilt With Union City Nine," *Paducah* (KY) *Sun-Democrat*, August 28, 1935: 2.
114. "Gerald Veach Untouchable In Series Opener," *Paducah* (KY) *Sun-Democrat*, August 30, 1935: 13.
115. "Birds Invade Jackson For Game Today," *Paducah* (KY) *Sun-Democrat*, September 1, 1935: 8.
116. "Union City Wins Last Two Games From Red Birds," *Paducah* (KY) *Sun-Democrat*, September 3, 1935: 2.
117. Sam Livingston, "Down Sports Avenue, *Paducah* (KY) *Sun-Democrat*, September 6, 1935: 12.
118. Sam Livingston, "Down Sports Avenue, *Paducah* (KY) *Sun-Democrat*, August 30, 1935: 13; and Sam Livingston, September 6, 1935.
119. "By Bob Dunbar," *Boston Herald*, April 2, 1936: 31.
120. "Pitcher Gerald Veach In One Year Made Way Up," *Andalusia* (AL) *Star*, August 27, 1936: 7.
121. "Kitty League," *The Sporting News*, July 2, 1936: 10; and Baseball-Reference.com.
122. Baseball-Reference.com; and "SINU Students to Complete Work by August 1st, 1941," *Murphysboro* (IL) *Daily Independent*, June 5, 1941: 6.
123. Sam Livingston, "Down Sports Avenue," *Paducah* (KY) *Sun-Democrat*, September 11, 1935: 2.
124. "Young Catcher From Paducah Wins Praise of Nats' Leaders," *Evening Star* (Washington, DC), February 28, 1936: C2.
125. "Young Catcher From Paducah…"; Wirt Gammon, "Catcher Floyd Perryman Is Turned Over to Lookouts by Washington," *Chattanooga* (TN) *Daily Times*, March 12, 1936: 11; and Wirt Gammon, "Lookouts Pack Up Their Togs This Morning and Move to Daytona Beach," *Chattanooga* (TN) *Daily Times*, March 10, 1936: 8.
126. The Millers, sometimes referred to as the Orphans or the Senators, had a loose affiliation with the Washington Nationals in 1936. "Southern League," *The Sporting News*, April 16, 1936: 12; and "International League," *The Sporting News*, September 10, 1936: 9.
127. John B. Foster, ed., *Spalding's Official Baseball Guide, 1939* (New York: American Sports Publishing Company, 1937), 289, 292–93; and "Perryman, Fort Smith Catcher, Most Valuable Player," *Arkansas Gazette* (Little Rock), August 21, 1938: 15.
128. Baseball Reference; "Barons Beat Jackson In Final Game Of Year," *Park City* (Kentucky) *Daily News*, June 21, 1942: 6; and "Players Scatter As Turbulent Kitty Folds For Fourth Time; Curtis Goes To Atlanta Club," *Paducah* (KY) *Sun-Democrat*, June 21, 1942: 8.
129. Sam Livingston, "Down Sports Avenue, *Paducah* (KY) *Sun-Democrat*, September 6, 1935: 12.
130. Livingston, September 6.
131. Sam Livingston, "Down Sports Avenue, *Paducah* (KY) *Sun-Democrat*, September 8, 1935: 12.
132. Sam Livingston, "Down Sports Avenue, *Paducah* (KY) *Sun-Democrat*, September 10, 1935: 6. See also "Fuchs Resigns As Braves Head," *Boston Herald*, August 1, 1935: 22; and Bob LeMoine, "Boston Braves Team Ownership History," Society for American Baseball Research Biography Project, accessed June 21, 2020, https://sabr.org/bioproj/topic/boston-braves-team-ownership-history/#sdendnote241sym.
133. Sam Livingston, September 10, 1935.
134. Sam Livingston, "Down Sports Avenue, *Paducah* (KY) *Sun-Democrat*, September 11, 1935: 2.
135. Sam Livingston, "Down Sports Avenue, *Paducah* (KY) *Sun-Democrat*, October 16, 1935: 8.
136. Martin J. Haley, "Browns Beat Chisox, 8–7, Then Lose to Knott, 3–2," *St. Louis Globe-Democrat*, September 25, 1938: 5C.
137. Baseball-Reference.com.
138. "Mize Leads Batters In Service World Series," *Honolulu Star-Bulletin*, October 2, 1944: 11; and Dan McGuire, "Grace Clouts Homer As Navy Wins," *Honolulu Advertiser*, September 24, 1944: 16.
139. Emmons Byrne, "Oaks Slug Seals, Move Up," *Oakland Tribune*, July 23, 1952: 40.
140. Sam Livingston, "Record Number Of Participants And Spectators Enjoyed Sports In Paducah During 1935; Desire To Play Considered Encouraging Sign," *Paducah* (KY) *Sun-Democrat*, January 1, 1936: 8.
141. "Record Number Of Participants…Encouraging Sign."
142. "Six Surviving Members Of Red Birds To Get Raises," *Paducah* (KY) *Sun-Democrat*, January 17, 1936: 14.
143. Seth Boaz, "Tincup To Manage Paducah Kitty Team," *Paducah* (KY) *Sun-Democrat*, March 17, 1936: 8; and Sam Livingston, "Down Sports Avenue," *Paducah* (KY) *Sun-Democrat*, April 3, 1936: 14.
144. Sam Livingston, "Hayes Hurls Indians To Win Over Mayfield," *Paducah* (KY) *Sun-Democrat*, May 20, 1936: 2; "Standings," *Paducah* (KY) *Sun-Democrat*, July 17, 1936: 10; and "Standings," *Paducah* (KY) *Sun-Democrat*, September 15, 1936: 2.
145. "Kitty League Baseball Team Is Assured For Paducah," *Paducah* (KY) *Sun-Democrat*, March 12, 1937: 12; and "Minor League History: Kentucky-Illinois-Tennessee League (1946–1955)," *Dutch Baseball Hangout* (blog), published November 4, 2018, https://dutchbaseball-hangout.blog/2018/11/04/minor-league-history-kentucky-illinoistennessee-league-1946-1955.

Miracle on Beech Street

A History of the Holyoke Millers, 1977–82

Eric T. Poulin

Once a very sparsely settled farming community, Holyoke, Massachusetts's geographic location on the banks of the Connecticut River was ideal for development, utilizing its ample source of hydroelectric power.[1] A group of four wealthy executives from Boston, about 90 miles to the east, believed the South Hadley Falls of the river was large and powerful enough to potentially fuel many large manufacturing plants.[2] This model of building industry on the banks of a large river had proven successful already in multiple other instances in Massachusetts, particularly involving the Merrimack River to the northeast.[3] The damming of the Merrimack had led to the evolution of the thriving factory towns of Lowell and Lawrence—both of which were already established as national cotton manufacturing giants—as the planning of the Holyoke Dam was commencing.[4]

Holyoke was incorporated as a town in the year 1850, and the construction of a dam on the Connecticut began shortly thereafter.[5] Immigrant labor from Ireland, Canada, Poland, Germany, and Italy was in no short supply. Holyoke truly thrived as a post-Civil War industrial city, making its mark most notably by producing high-quality paper products. The city's population would increase from a mere 4,600 in 1885 to over 60,000 people just 35 years later. At one point, there were nearly 30 paper mills in operation, as well as factories that produced woolens, cotton, thread, silk, and industrial machinery.[6]

However, as was the case with other cities that were established purely on manufacturing during the industrial revolution, times would not always prove to be prosperous. Newer technologies and cheaper foreign labor would soon render many of these once-thriving mills obsolete. The first of the major employers to depart the city was the Farr Alpaca textile mill, which liquidated in 1939.[7] Skinner Mill closed its doors in the late 1960s, although, as a slight consolation, the property site was eventually rehabbed and donated to the city to establish the now-popular Heritage State Park.[8] Throughout the 1970s, most other major employers followed this lead, departing the city or closing altogether. As factory after factory shuttered—taking with them the employment opportunities that were once plentiful—the fate of a once-mighty industrial center would soon be in jeopardy.

While the closing of the mills was obviously the major factor leading to widespread unemployment in the city (16.7% by April 1975)[9] and the concomitant social problems, a number of other factors also contributed. As the mills and the manufacturing jobs they provided became more of a scarcity, Holyoke also experienced a rather sharp increase of individuals entering the city looking for this exact type of employment. Throughout the first half of the 1970s, young servicemen would return home from the Vietnam War to discover that the jobs that had been available at the time of their enlistment were no longer in such supply. The guarantee of work opportunities that their parents' generation had enjoyed in Holyoke had seemingly disappeared.

The city also experienced yet another tremendous ethnic migration during these years, as a large number of people from Puerto Rico and South America came to Holyoke seeking a better future for themselves and their families.[10] Large ethnic migrations were nothing new to Holyoke—however, the employment opportunities that had been in great supply when the European and Canadian immigrants entered the city were no longer available. In fact, these migrants had the unfortunate timing of arriving at the exact period in the city's history that these manufacturing jobs were disappearing. Couple this with the usual difficulties that face non-white migrants upon entering the United States—including barriers of language and culture, as well as hostility from those already residing here—and a great many tensions would prove to be inevitable.[11]

This is the backdrop that the Holyoke Millers of the Class AA Eastern League began playing ball in during the 1977 season. Elected officials believed that a minor-league baseball team in the city would lead to an increase in tourism revenue for Holyoke (it was estimated by multiple sources that a AA-level team would lead to an additional $250,000 for a community in

1977).[12] Eastern League President Pat McKernan simply told city officials that if they could raise sufficient funds to complete necessary renovations to the municipally owned MacKenzie Field, he would deliver a franchise to Holyoke.[13] A range of $65,000–108,000 was given to complete multiple tasks, including refurbishing locker-room facilities, construction of a concession stand, and the possible resodding of the field, while removing a cinder running track that cut through the outfield grass.[14] As the city was in a bit of a down-and-out period, elected officials appeared willing to take a chance on something that could potentially reverse civic fortunes.

The city was able to muster the minimum $65,000 necessary to attract an Eastern League franchise. The Berkshire Brewers, a franchise that had been based in Pittsfield, Massachusetts 1965–1976, were convinced to depart the cozy confines of Waconah Park for the "Paper City" of Holyoke. League president McKernan held true to his promise to deliver a team to Holyoke, aided no doubt by his connections that still existed with the Berkshire team. (He had formerly been the franchise's president, a colorful tenure that included his wedding at home plate between games of a doubleheader, as well as an "attendance hunger strike," a promotion where he would fast on each home game day if the team drew fewer than 500 fans—no small feat, considering he weighed in at more than 350 pounds.)[15] Baseball fans were treated to an early holiday present, as city aldermen passed their final vote by a tally of 11–4 on December 21, 1976, to transfer the necessary funds to the Parks Department to bring minor-league baseball to Holyoke.[16] The new franchise would be named the Holyoke Millers—a tribute to the industrial past upon which the city was founded.

As the city prepared itself for its first-ever season of AA baseball, it also found itself embroiled in a national headline-making controversy. On a nearly nightly basis, suspicious fires ripped through old tenements and factory buildings, leaving residents completely on edge. As the cause of these blazes was going undiscovered, law enforcement officials dispatched a Special Arson Squad to investigate all fires within Holyoke, to assess if any were of criminal nature.

The Special Arson Squad would make its first arrest on April 13, 1977—the day the Millers played their first-ever game—a 15–2 exhibition victory against the neighboring University of Massachusetts in Amherst.[17] Right fielder and leadoff hitter Gary LaRocque blasted the second pitch of the game 335 feet down the right field line for a home run, and with that, the Holyoke Millers were born.[18]

Two days later, the Millers began their 1977 Eastern League regular season in Pennsylvania on a Friday night against the Reading Phillies. This would be the first of a nine-game road trip to commence the season—a scheduling abnormality that was by design, intended to give the Holyoke Parks Department sufficient time to complete the necessary renovations that MacKenzie Field needed to host professional baseball.

Meanwhile, back in Pittsfield (the city that had previously been the franchise's home), General Electric (the region's major employer) announced the layoff of 225 employees.[19] While Holyoke and Pittsfield were facing many of the same struggles at that time, there was seemingly no shortage of irony that these two events were occurring on the same day. Pittsfield's sad loss—for one day, anyhow—was contrasted with Holyoke's gain.

The starting lineup for the first-ever Holyoke Millers game was:

1.	**Gary LaRocque**	**RF**
2.	**Billy Severns**	**CF**
3.	**Ike Blessitt**	**DH**
4.	**Gary Holle**	**1B**
5.	**Jeff Yurak**	**LF**
6.	**Neil Rasmussen**	**3B**
7.	**Ron Jacobs**	**C**
8.	**Ed Romero**	**SS**
9.	**Garry Pyka**	**2B**
	Ron Wrona	**P**

Four hundred seventy fans (Reading officials had been hoping for 1500–2000) saw the young Millers build a 4–0 lead behind Wrona (one of the Millers' most experienced pitchers, despite being in only his second year of pro ball) through five innings. However, the Phillies awakened with seven runs in the sixth inning, three of which were unearned. They would ultimately drop all four games in Reading, on their way to a 2–7 road trip to begin the season. Holding leads seemed to be particularly troublesome for the new team, as they would blow multiple 4–0 leads against Reading, as well as a 6–0 advantage at Jersey City. Holyoke's bullpen would begin the season by dropping their first 11 decisions before a reliever would garner a single win.

The Millers were scheduled to make their home debut at Mackenzie Field on Sunday, April 24, 1977—an afternoon contest against the Waterbury Giants. Competition for fans on that day would be fierce, as the game would be directly competing with a live performance by the locally popular polka ensemble, The Larry Chesky Orchestra, who were performing that afternoon at Mountain Park (a mid-sized Holyoke amusement park that was a popular destination from the late 1800s until its closing in 1987). In some ways, the rain that would postpone the game was a blessing of sorts, as a poor attendance showing at a home debut opener as a result of a polka concert might not exactly inspire.

Rather, the Millers took to the field at MacKenzie the following evening before a raucous 2428 fans—who were treated to a back-and-forth affair that saw the home side overcome a 5–0 deficit, before falling, 7–5.[20] Future longtime major leaguer George Frazier would take the loss in relief. Designated hitter Ike Blessitt would provide the fireworks, bringing the Holyoke faithful to their feet, turning on a shoulder-high offering and blasting it 375 feet down the left field line for a game-tying two-run homer in the seventh.[21]

The Millers' team logo reflected the industrial history of the region.

Blessitt proved to be the Miller that would bring the fans the most consistent excitement, leading the Eastern League in runs batted in for 1977, and winning the fan vote as the Most Popular Miller.[22] His was an interesting story; while most members of the team were young prospects on the way up (Frazier and Romero both enjoyed lengthy major-league careers, while Jurak, Holle, Greg Eradyi, Doug Clarey, and Mark Bomback would all reach the show, if only for brief stints), Blessitt had already seen his career reach its pinnacle.

"The Blessitt One," as he was known to the MacKenzie faithful, had already experienced a brief call-up to the Detroit Tigers at the end of the 1972 season, going hitless in five at bats over four games. Blessitt was well known throughout Michigan, having been a high school four-sport legend growing up just outside of Detroit. However, he was reassigned to the Tigers' AAA affiliate during spring training of the following season, and was unfortunately involved in an off-field incident with manager Billy Martin in Lakeland, Florida, leading to the arrest of both men.[23] According to Martin, he was trying to prevent Blessitt from getting into a late-night altercation with another man in a cocktail lounge, taking the young outfielder out to the parking lot to calm him down. The Lakeland police arrived on the scene shortly thereafter, made racial slurs to Blessitt as they arrested him, while also apprehending Martin, who claimed to be an innocent bystander.[24]

Given Martin's well-documented history with numerous incidents of late-night barroom brawling (he was famously fired as manager of the New York Yankees for allegedly sucker-punching a marshmallow salesman in a bar at the end of the 1979 season[25]), the notion of him acting as a virtuous peacekeeper seems fictitious. Nonetheless, Blessitt would never reach the major leagues again following this evening in Lakeland.[26]

Blessitt's blasts would be a lone early bright spot as the inexperienced Millers stumbled badly out of the gate, winning only three of the first 18 games of their existence.[27] While victories were rare, the fan promotions you would expect at a minor-league ballpark certainly were not. The Millers held a "Guaranteed Win Day" (where fans would be admitted free of charge to the following day's game if the Millers were unable to prevail),[28] a "Mustache Night" (where 25-year-old general manager Tom Kayser promised to have his mustache shaved off if attendance surpassed 1500 for the game),[29] while hosting appearances by Hall of Fame pitcher Bob Feller, as well as Max Patkin, a.k.a. "The Clown Prince of Baseball." A "Beer Night" promotion was also considered, but never came to fruition.[30]

Nonetheless, something was clearly working—the Millers boasted the second-highest attendance figures in the Eastern League, drawing 61,171 fans for the season. They would rally to a respectable final record of 73–66, but would never realistically challenge the first-place West Haven Yankees, finishing 13½ games out of first.[31] The team went their separate ways after the season and, with minor league salaries being typically low, many would go to work for the winter months. First baseman Gary Holle returned to his home in Watervliet, New York, to work as a legislative aide for a state senator, while doubling as the color commentator for Siena College's basketball broadcasts. Outfielder Jeff Yurak would continue his education at California State University at Pomona, majoring in marketing. Pitcher Mark Bomback would return to his home in Fall River to work as a salesperson at a local clothing store.[32]

Perhaps the biggest accomplishment of the new team was the mere fact that Holyoke now had a galvanizing institution to bring it together, even as the arson-related problems kept the community on constant edge. By the end of May alone, the city had endured 17 multiple alarm fires that year.[33] In spite of all the efforts of the Special Arson Squad, the perpetrators of the majority of these blazes would never be determined. While New York City would ultimately gain some relief from their civic nightmare when David Berkowitz was arrested that August—ending the citywide fear of the Son of Sam murders—Holyoke experienced no such reassurance.

The Millers would open their 1978 season on the road at West Haven, dropping the first three games of the campaign to the Yankees. The home opener at MacKenzie on April 16 featured a ceremonial first pitch by Mayor Ernest Proulx, an offering that bounced multiple times before reaching the plate.

Based on the performance of the pitching staff during the year, Mayor Proulx could potentially have earned a spot in the rotation, as they posted the worst earned-run average in the Eastern League. In spite of the return of several fan favorites from the prior season (including the reigning EL home run champion Holle, along with Rasmussen, Yurak, and Bomback), the Millers greatly struggled to draw at the gate in 1978. An unusually cold and windy spring—even by Massachusetts standards—contributed to the reduced attendance, but the team's performance on the diamond certainly didn't help.

Rick Nicholson earned the first win of the season for the Holyoke nine on April 17 before 372 fans. Nicholson had been the top reliever in the New York-Penn League the previous season with the Newark Co-Pilots, posting a 5–2 record with 12 saves. This success was not replicated in Holyoke, as he compiled an ERA of 7.03 over 16 games.[34]

This would not be the lowest attendance figure of the season, as a May 2 contest against the Waterbury Giants would draw only 207 fans. Even the "Mustache Night" promotion couldn't entice fans to the ballpark, as the same event that drew nearly 2000 fans in 1977 would only draw 372 in the new year.[35]

In all, the honeymoon period between Holyoke and the Millers was apparently over. They drew 13,000 fewer fans than the previous season, as the team stumbled to a fifth-place record of 61–76. The MacKenzie faithful were able to enjoy a fine campaign from future major league outfielder Marshall Edwards, as well as a career year from Eastern League MVP Yurak, and a franchise-record 60 stolen bases by second baseman Steven Greene. As management had identified the 45,000 mark as being the "break-even" point

Gerald Ako, listed at 5' 8" and 165 pounds, went 6–4 with a 2.88 ERA in 44 games for the Millers in 1980, including five starts.

for attendance, the team managed to just scrape by in 1978.[36]

If the cliché about Rome not being built in a day is true, the 1979 Millers are certainly a prime example. The team improved its win total by a mere two games, while drawing 50,207 fans for the season—a modest improvement at best from the year before. This attendance number was surely aided by a mid-season appearance by the Famous Chicken—drawing 6,300 spectators (capacity at MacKenzie was listed at 4,100).[37] However, the groundwork was seemingly laid for bigger things in the future, as Harry Dalton had taken over as general manager of the parent Milwaukee Brewers, an executive with a keen eye for recognizing young talent. Almost immediately, more major-league-caliber prospects would don the Millers colors.

While four members of the pitching staff—Barry Cort, Sam Hinds, Larry Landreth, and Lance Rautzhan—would ultimately reach the big leagues, the most notable new member of the Holyoke nine would be twenty-year-old switch-hitting outfielder Kevin Bass. Bass would enjoy a fourteen-year major league career, highlighted by appearances in the postseason and All-Star Game in 1986 for Houston. His tremendous 1986 season would end unfortunately, however, as he struck out with two men on base in the 16th inning of Game Six of the National League Championship Series to end the game, sending the New York Mets to the World Series. As a young Miller, however, Bass enjoyed a respectable 1979. While his .263 batting average with eight home runs would be just the tip of the iceberg of his potential as a ballplayer, his Sammy Davis Jr. impersonation was already at a major-league level.[38]

Another item of note about the 1979 Millers was that they may have set an unofficial record for number of born-again Christians on one pro baseball team.[39] Of the 21-man roster, 11 players identified as having recently found the Lord. Catcher Bill Foley told *The Sporting News*, "I've never before seen this many on one team! I felt a void in my life that needed to be filled". Millers players filled this particular void with chapel services every Sunday and regular Bible readings throughout the season.[40]

The Millers faced some additional stiff competition for the local entertainment dollar throughout the second half of their season. After eight years of planning and negotiations, a million-square-foot shopping mall would open on July 5, 1979, in the Whiting Farms Road area of the city on the outskirts of town.[41] At the time of its opening, the promise of increased job opportunities and an expanded tax base seemed to be trumpeting a new era of prosperity for the city.[42] An unfortunate drawback of this new construction, however, would be the increased difficulty to attract business to downtown, as so many potential customers would instead opt for the convenience of one-stop shopping at the mall. Between the lack of businesses occupying downtown buildings, the ongoing arson fears, and an increase in crime as a direct result of unemployment, the center of the city became a very unpopular destination.

TCMA

KEVIN BASS OF

MILLERS

Switch-hitting outfielder Kevin Bass would go on to a 14-year major league career, including an All-Star Game selection in 1986 for Houston.

Meanwhile, back on the ballfield, the 1979 season proved to be a dress rehearsal of sorts for much bigger things to come as the 1980s commenced. But in many ways, the biggest shift for the Millers would not occur on the field at all, as young general manager Tom Kayser made headlines when he purchased the team from Spike Herzig and the Northeastern Exhibition Company at age 27.[43] The sale was announced a mere 24 hours before the Millers would open their 1980 season at MacKenzie against Reading. While an exact sale price was never announced, league officials stated it was less than the $45,000 an average Eastern League team was valued at in 1980. Sources say the sale price was closer to $30,000, as there was fear that another owner would buy the team and move it out of Holyoke. Kayser was seemingly given a bit of a hometown discount, as he was committed to ensuring that the team would stay put.[44]

The 1980 squad was, in a word, loaded. In addition to Bass and future big-league catcher Steve Lake, they possessed a pitching staff that featured MLB mainstays Doug Jones, Frank DiPino, and Chuck Porter. Rick Kranitz led the team with 13 wins, while closer Kunikazu Ogawa saved 16 games with an earned run average of 1.96.[45]

The featured attraction at MacKenzie that summer, however, was David Green—a prospect who had been dubbed "the next Roberto Clemente."[46] Green was the son of Edward Green Sinclair, considered one of the best Nicaraguan players of all time. The younger Green was a five-tool prospect, leading the Eastern League in triples with 19 while batting .291 and earning a spot on the Eastern League All-Star Team.[47]

Manager Lee Sigman's squad ran away with the Northern Division, finishing with a record of 78–61, a full ten games ahead of their closest competitors. They rolled into the playoffs against the Buffalo Bisons, with Green blasting the winning home run off Dave Dravecky in the clinching game to put Holyoke into the Eastern League Finals against the Waterbury Reds.[48]

In the finals, the Millers dropped the opener by a count of 3–2, but bounced back in Game Two behind a combined six-hit shutout by Kranitz and Ogawa to even the series.[49] In the winner-take-all Game Three, Doug Loman homered, tripled, and doubled while Chuck Porter threw a complete-game shutout as the Millers defeated the Reds, 7–0, to claim the 1980 Eastern League Championship before 2,717 fans.[50] It was a glorious night in Holyoke, as children danced on top of the Millers dugout to "We Are Family," the Sister Sledge

The Millers had their heyday under owner-GM Tom Kayser, who ended up selling the team to take a position in the Pittsburgh Pirates organization, and later became president of the Texas League.

classic that had become the unofficial anthem of the Pittsburgh Pirates during the previous summer. It would be the first professional baseball title for a Western Massachusetts team since the Springfield Giants won the Eastern League for three consecutive seasons 1959–61. The Giants of those championship years featured a number of future legends, including Manny Mota, Matty Alou, and Juan Marichal.[51]

The 1980 season of the Millers would prove to be the franchise's high-water mark. On December 12, 1980, the parent Brewers pulled off a blockbuster trade with the St. Louis Cardinals, trading David Green along with Sixto Lezcano, Lary Sorenson, and Dave LaPoint in return for future Hall of Famers Rollie Fingers and Ted Simmons, along with future ace (and *Major League* actor) Pete Vukovich.[52] Milwaukee also moved on from their affiliation with Holyoke, establishing their AA team in El Paso. The Brewers organization wanted out of the Eastern League—as the cold northeastern weather, sub-par ballparks around the league at the time, and the cinder track that ran through the outfield at MacKenzie Field were all factors leading to their departure.[53] The California Angels would fill the void left by Milwaukee—and although the new-look Millers would feature a number of future major leaguers, this would not translate to on-field success in 1981 or 1982.

In 1981, Holyoke rode the coattails of their championship season at the turnstiles, as they drew an all-time franchise high of 80,117. While the team got off to a strong start, they would end up faltering down the stretch, finishing a whopping 16½ games behind the first place Glens Falls White Sox.[54]

Speed was the name of the game for the Millers in '81, as future Angels mainstay Gary Pettis's 55 stolen bases would pace a team that would swipe a total of 151. Darrell Miller wore his last name on both the front and back of his jersey, splitting time between catcher and outfield—long before his two siblings Reggie and Cheryl would both be inducted into the Basketball Hall of Fame just down the road in Springfield. Dennis Rasmussen posted a record of 8–12, while showing flashes of potential he would later fulfill in the majors—all while living in what he believed was an illegal trailer park at the foot of Mount Tom.[55]

The biggest news around the Millers in 1981 would occur in early November, when team owner Tom Kayser announced he was offered a position as the Assistant Minor League Director for the Pittsburgh Pirates organization, and would be selling the team.[56] It ended up being a wise career move for Kayser, who would ultimately spend 25 years as the president of the Texas League, retiring in 2017.

A Holyoke-based group of executives led by City Alderman Hal Haberman were the early favorites to purchase the team, with an Eastern Massachusetts-based group also solidly jockeying for position.[57] In total, more than 30 potential bidders from as far away as Florida and California made inquiries about buying the team, before a different local group made a deal to purchase the Millers to keep them in Holyoke.

University of Massachusetts Political Science Professor Jerome Mileur recalled "having a few beers at the White Eagle Club" in Amherst with fellow UMass employee George Como (a systems analyst in the computer center) when they floated out the idea of purchasing the team from Kayser.[58] They recruited local heating oil businessman Ben Surner, and ultimately put in a bid of $85,000 to buy the Millers. The deal was announced on December 1, 1981.[59]

Unfortunately, the new ownership team stumbled early out of the blocks. The ownership group's first hire was general manager Larry Simmons, who would not make it to opening day before being fired.[60] The Eastern League establishment was cautious of the new ownership group, with longtime owner Joe Buzas directly asking Mileur at the Winter Meetings, "Why the hell would a college professor want to own a baseball team?" Mileur simply responded that he was a great fan of the game and had best of intentions.[61]

The team itself also struggled, as the Angels prospects failed to make an impact with the local fans, with attendance plummeting to just over 54,000. Oddly, the highlight of the season was not one that was readily apparent, as young author Domenic Stansberry had moved to Holyoke and was writing a murder mystery based on the Millers and Holyoke called *The Spoiler*. While Stansberry has had a moderately successful career in the interim, *The Spoiler* has remained out of print for many years, an apt analogy for the fate of the Millers.[62]

However, the biggest challenge the group would face was their rocky relationship with city officials. MacKenzie Field also doubled as the home baseball diamond for two of the high schools in the city, and there was increasing pressure from members of the community to ensure that their municipal field would be utilized by residents. Ultimately, it was decided that the Millers would not have access to the field for practice during the school year, as the teams from Holyoke High School and Holyoke Catholic High would be given priority. Additionally, the cinder running track that ran through the outfield would also be utilized by the track teams at these schools before the Millers.[63]

Public meetings between Millers owner Surner and Holyoke Mayor Ernest Proulx would become increasingly more contentious, and the team and city reached an impasse that could not be overcome.[64] The Millers would move to Nashua, New Hampshire and participate in the 1983 Eastern League season as the Nashua Angels.[65]

Coincidentally, one of the factors the ownership group faced in Nashua was a boycott from the community, who felt that the presence of the team was having a negative impact on attendance at youth baseball games. After four years in Nashua, Mileur had bought out both Surner and Como and the team was moved to Harrisburg, Pennsylvania, where the franchise has had a long and successful tenure. Mileur would ultimately retire from ownership in 1994, selling the team to the City of Harrisburg for four million dollars.[66]

While the Nashua Angels returned to play a single game at MacKenzie Field during the summer of 1983, it would be the end of professional baseball in Holyoke. Currently, the Valley Blue Sox of the New England Collegiate Baseball League play their home games at MacKenzie every summer. It seems hard to believe that Holyoke—given its lack of professional-level facilities—was able to be home to a AA team, even if only for six years. Clearly, the economics and atmosphere around minor league baseball have shifted so radically over the years that such a scenario would be impossible today—and it was honestly quite miraculous that it was able to happen then. ■

Acknowledgments

The author would like to thank the late Jerome Mileur for his insight, along with Ben and Jay Demerath III for making invaluable connections. Eileen Crosby and the staff at the Holyoke History Room were incredibly gracious with their time, as well as the great Tim Wiles and the A. Bartlett Giamatti Center for Research at the National Baseball Hall of Fame and Museum. Tom Kayser was very generous with his insight and information. Maury Abrams and Pumpkin Waffles provided tremendous support and perspective. Above all, eternal gratitude goes to Gabriela Stevenson for her editing, fact-checking, and overall determination to ensure the story of the Millers would be told.

Notes

1. Ella Merkel DiCarlo, *Holyoke—Chicopee: A Perspective*, Holyoke, MA: Transcript-Telegram, 1982.
2. Merkel DiCarlo.
3. Merkel DiCarlo.
4. Merkel DiCarlo.
5. Merkel DiCarlo.
6. Merkel DiCarlo.
7. Merkel DiCarlo.
8. Merkel DiCarlo.
9. Merkel DiCarlo.
10. Merkel DiCarlo.
11. Merkel DiCarlo.
12. Bill Doyle, "Eastern League President Favors Holyoke for Franchise," *Holyoke Transcript-Telegram*, December 3, 1976.
13. "City Needs Money For EL Team," *Holyoke Transcript-Telegram*, October 15, 1976.
14. "City Needs Money For EL Team."
15. Milton Richman, "Gate-Slim Pittsfield Boss On Hunger Strike," *The Sporting News*, July 10, 1971, 43.
16. "Aldermen Welcome Franchise," *Holyoke Transcript-Telegram*, December 22, 1976.
17. Michael J. Burke, "Special Arson Squad Makes First Arrest," *Holyoke Transcript-Telegram*, April 13, 1977.
18. "Miller Hitters Maul Minutemen Hurlers," *Holyoke Transcript-Telegram*, April 14, 1977.
19. "G.E. Eliminating 225 Jobs," *Holyoke Transcript-Telegram*, April 13, 1977.
20. Bill Doyle, "Millers' Debut Is a Success," *Holyoke Transcript-Telegram*, April 26, 1977.
21. Doyle.
22. "Blessitt Is Most Popular," *Holyoke Transcript-Telegram*, September 6, 1977.
23. Milton Richman, "Blessed Are the Peacemakers? Ask Martin," *The Sporting News*, March 29, 1973.
24. Richman, "Blessed Are the Peacemakers…"
25. Phil Pepe, "Yanks Wheel, Deal, and Squeal," *The Sporting News*, September 19, 1979.
26. Lee Thompson. "Former Detroit Tigers Outfielder Ike Blessitt Bringing His Big-League Story to Bay City for Bay Medical Charity Auction," Mlive, April 28, 2011, accessed August 31, 2021. https://www.mlive.com/sports/baycity/2011/04/former_detroit_tigers_outfield.html.
27. "Nothing Is Working for Failing Millers," *Holyoke Transcript-Telegram*, May 4, 1977.
28. "'Guaranteed Win Day' Starts Millers' Promotions," *Holyoke Transcript-Telegram*, May 6, 1977.
29. Bill Doyle, "Millers 'Shave' Bristol Sox, 8–7," *Holyoke Transcript-Telegram*, May 18, 1977.
30. "'Guaranteed Win Day' Starts Millers' Promotions."
31. Bill Doyle, "Millers Clinch Third Place," *Holyoke Transcript-Telegram*, September 3, 1977.

32. Bill Doyle, "Miller Players Are Ready to Bid Holyoke Farewell," *Holyoke Transcript-Telegram*, September 2, 1977.
33. Michael Burke, "Fire Destroys Main St. Block," *Holyoke Transcript-Telegram*, May 28, 1977.
34. Bill Zajic, "Hannon 'Curves' Giants," *Holyoke Transcript-Telegram*, May 3, 1978.
35. Bill Doyle, "Millers Pitching Collapses in Loss," *Holyoke Transcript-Telegram*, May 8, 1978.
36. The Baseball Cube, accessed August 31, 2021. http://www.thebaseballcube.com/minors/teams/stats.asp?Y=1978&T=10573.
37. Ray Fitzgerald, "His Vision on Target," *Boston Globe*, July 7, 1981.
38. Mike Downey, "Would Fans Respond to 'Bark Like a Dog'?" *The Sporting News*, October 27, 1986.
39. "Religious Millers," *The Sporting News*, August 11, 1979, 44.
40. "Religious Millers."
41. Pat Cahill, "Holyoke Mall Celebrates Its 10th Anniversary," *Sunday Republican*. July 16, 1989.
42. Cahill.
43. Garry Brown, "Want To Buy a Ball Club?" *Sunday Republican*. May 11, 1980.
44. Brown.
45. The Baseball Cube, accessed August 31, 2021. http://www.thebaseballcube.com/minors/teams/stats.asp?Y=1980&T=10573.
46. John Sonderegger, "Potential: The One Thing a Gimed David Green Couldn't Grasp," *St. Louis Post-Dispatch*, July 14, 1986.
47. Bill Doyle, "Holyoke Proves Itself," *Holyoke Transcript-Telegram*, September 6, 1980.
48. Warner Hessler, "Millers End Bisons' Year," *Buffalo Courier-Express*, September 1, 1980.
49. Bill Doyle, "Millers Force Showdown," *Holyoke Transcript-Telegram*, September 3, 1980.
50. Mike Bogen, "Millers Cop EL Crown," *The Morning Union*, September 6, 1980.
51. Garry Brown, "Springfield Marks 50 Years without a Professional Baseball Team; Is It Time to Take Another Swing?" MassLive, March 22, 2015, accessed August 31, 2021. https://www.masslive.com/living/2015/03/garry_brown_springfield_marks_50_years_without_a_professional_baseball_team.html.
52. Sonderegger.
53. "It's Spring Again," *Hampden County Enterprise*, April 13, 1981.
54. The Baseball Cube, accessed August 31, 2021. http://www.thebaseballcube.com/minors/teams/stats.asp?Y=1981&T=10573.
55. Owen Canfield, "Remembering the Eastern League," *The Sporting News*, May 9, 1985.
56. Barry Schatz, "Millers owner bows out; local businessmen want to buy team franchise," *Holyoke Transcript-Telegram*, November 5, 1981.
57. Schatz.
58. Author interview with Jerome Mileur, October 19, 2006.
59. Barry Schatz, "Millers' Deal to Keep Team in Holyoke," *Holyoke Transcript-Telegram*, December 2, 1981.
60. Don Conkey, "The Holyoke Millers: Sharp Decline in Attendance Just One of Many Problems Confronting New Management," *The Sunday Republican*, May 23, 1982.
61. Author interview with Jerome Mileur, October 19, 2006.
62. Domenic Stansberry, *The Spoiler: A Novel*, New York: Atlantic Monthly Press, 1987.
63. Barry Schatz, "Field Availability Is Snag between City, Millers," *Holyoke Transcript-Telegram*, October 14, 1982.
64. "Proulx Says Millers Should Be More Flexible," *Holyoke Transcript-Telegram*, October 22, 1982.
65. Milton Cole, "Nashua Votes to Take Millers," *Daily Hampshire Gazette*, December 7, 1982.
66. Author interview with Jerome Mileur, October 19, 2006.

The 1938–40 Québec Provincial League

The Rise and Fall of an Outlaw League

Christian Trudeau

In 2015, I acquired booklets containing scoresheets for all games played by the Québec City team in the 1938 and 1939 Provincial League. Handwritten neatly by somebody who was clearly involved with the team, these booklets contained tons of information, and led me to try to discover as much as I could about the league. The Provincial League has a storied history. It's better known for its 1948–52 period, during which it went from a top outlaw league, hosting so-called Mexican League jumpers and former Negro Leaguers, to a respected Class C league that was a top destination for Black players debuting in so-called "Organized Baseball" (teams and leagues affiliated with the National Association of Professional Baseball Leagues).[1] The 1938–40 version has received considerably less attention, but it offers the intriguing story of a league that sat outside of Organized Baseball, with all the chaotic opportunities that it allows, and dreamed of becoming a recognized league.

BACKGROUND

After the collapse of the Class C Eastern Canada League of 1922–23 and its follower, the 1924 Québec-Ontario-Vermont League, baseball in Québec was, to borrow the words of Merritt Clifton's pioneering work on Québec baseball history, quite disorganized.[2] In the 1925–35 period, baseball in the province never rose much above the industrial league level, with games mostly happening on weekends.

In 1936, a more organized league emerged and, as was often the case when a league started to expand, it was called the Provincial League, even though all of the teams were located within a 50-mile radius and much baseball was played elsewhere in the province. But the Provincial League was growing quickly: Its predecessor was strictly a Sunday league playing a 12-game schedule, with one team made up of Montreal police officers and another consisting of members of the Caughnawaga natives reserve.[3] In 1936, the schedule expanded to 30 games, and the league started with eight teams: two each in Montreal and Sherbrooke and single teams in Granby, Drummondville, and Sorel, as well as the Black Panthers, a traveling team acting as a sort of farm team for the Negro Leagues.[4] By season's end, the pairs of teams in Montreal and Sherbrooke had combined into single teams, but the season was otherwise a success.

League officials probably realized that the baseball market was limited in Montreal, where they had to compete with the International League's Royals. (When the Eastern Canada League and Québec-Ontario-Vermont leagues were in Organized Baseball in 1922–24, they were centered in Montreal, but the International League's Royals were in hiatus at the time.) As a result, for 1937, the Montreal team was replaced by one in Trois-Rivières.

As the Great Depression was slowly fading, the Provincial League took advantage to continue its expansion, doubling its schedule to 60 games. Sorel, as it had in the previous two seasons, emerged as playoff champion, even though it had dropped the pennant by a game to Drummondville. As a sign the caliber was improving, the Black Panthers, which were in the middle of the pack in 1936, fell to a dismal record of 10–50 in 1937, while the five other teams all had winning records.

At the time, rosters were still full of local, semipro, and college players, mostly from nearby New England. But more and more, these players were accompanied by veteran minor leaguers. The Drummondville Tigers—"Tigres" in French—were managed by Ted Veach, a 32-year-old right-hander who had fallen out of Organized Baseball in 1933 after a few years in B and C leagues and a tryout with the Montreal Royals. He dominated the Provincial League in 1937, and as a sign that the league's reputation was improving, he parlayed his performance into a contract with the Seattle Rainiers of the Pacific Coast League for 1938. Former major leaguer and Royals scout Herbie Moran took over the reins of Trois-Rivières at midseason and led the team to the finals. Sorel had built its championship team by snatching multiple players from the Class D Northern League: shortstop Ernest Olson, pitcher Ted Frank, and outfielders Jim Winn and Mike Sime.

With the Trois-Rivières team a success, the league added two new cities to the fray for 1938 with the Québec Athlétiques and the Saint-Hyacinthe Saints. The two additions, combined with the drop of the Black Panthers, moved the league's center of gravity eastward. Still, the league was compact. Teams traveled back home after games, and typically played a split-park doubleheader on Sundays, with each team collecting their own gate receipts. Table 1 lists the historical population for Provincial League cities. We can see the trade-off: The Provincial League eliminated competition by moving away from Montreal, then with a population approaching 1 million, but had to do business in much smaller cities (see Figure 1). It is, however, much easier to generate civic rivalries in smaller cities.

Table 1. Population in 1931, Provincial League Cities

City	Population
Québec City	130,594
Trois-Rivières	35,450
Sherbrooke	28,933
Sorel	19,320
Saint-Hyacinthe	13,448
Granby	10,587
Drummondville	6,609

Source: Les régions métropolitaines de recensement, Cahier 1, BSQ, 1998.

Another factor in the expansion of the league was infrastructure-related: Granby had built a stadium equipped for night baseball in 1934. As the 1938 season was about to start, three cities were waiting for new stadiums: Sherbrooke, Trois-Rivières and Québec City. While Sherbrooke built a standard wooden structure that burned to the ground in 1951, Trois-Rivières and Québec City built state-of-the-art stadiums that still stand. Trois-Rivières did most of the heavy lifting. A November 1937 meeting with Québec Prime Minister Maurice Duplessis, a Trois-Rivières native, sealed the deal. As recalled in 1984 by Gérard Duval, one of the managing directors of the team, they found a way to make the project a political winner:

> I approached his desk and laid out the plans for the future stadium. Mr. Duplessis was satisfied and asked about the cost. The Prime Minister was more hesitant about the total cost of $200,000 and wondered who would pay for such a large amount, for the time. A sudden inspiration made me answer that construction could be executed without machinery, by as many unemployed workers as possible, who could be given minimum wage instead of the food vouchers they were currently receiving. This suggestion pleased the Prime Minister, seeing the electoral potential of some 2,000 men out of work getting a job building the stadium.[5]

The prime minister liked the idea so much that the same arrangements were negotiated for the Québec City stadium. The 1938 season was delayed a few weeks for the three cities to have the time to complete the work. In Québec City, the selected land, a former swamp, needed serious filling and compacting, and after multiple delays the stadium was only ready for the start of the 1939 season, with a temporary park being used for 1938.

The two stadiums were worth waiting for. In the same 1984 interview, Duval recalls an American journalist describing the new Trois-Rivières construction as the "Yankee Stadium of the Minor Leagues." The stadiums were built with large locker rooms for both teams, underground tunnels, a permanent residence for security staff, and state-of-the-art draining and lighting systems.

Now, with four teams equipped for night baseball and higher gate receipts, the table was set.

Figure 1. Map of Provincial League cities

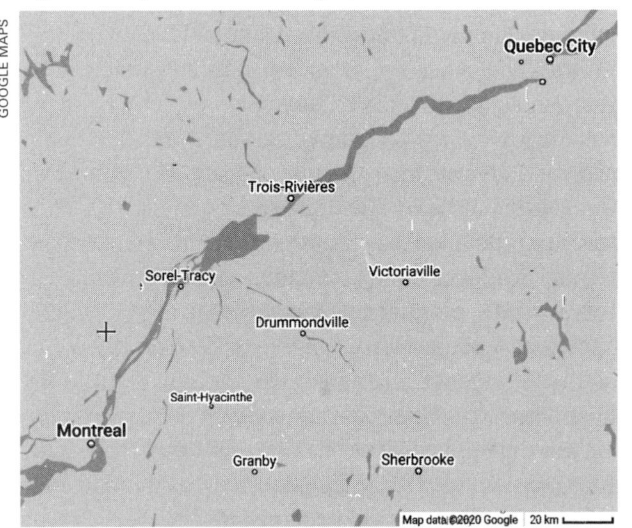

GETTING SERIOUS: THE 1938 SEASON

An arms race developed among the Provincial League teams as they spent to acquire experienced managers with wide networks. The Sherbrooke Braves poached former major leaguer Charlie Small from the Cape Breton Colliery League, based in Atlantic Canada. He brought with him many teammates and former league rivals. Drummondville and Trois-Rivières banked on former major leaguers recently with the Montreal Royals, pitcher John Pomorski and catcher Pinky

NATIONAL BASEBALL HALL OF FAME LIBRARY, COOPERSTOWN, NY

A former big-leaguer, Pinky Hargrave attempted to both manage Trois-Rivieres and catch, but his own ailments and a lack of other catching talent on the roster led him to resign.

Hargrave. Sorel and Granby both opted for a proven approach by making a 1937 player their manager. Sorel brought back Ernest Olson, while the Red Sox put Leo Maloney at the helm. Maloney had been hired the previous year from the nearby Can-Am League. The two new teams chose different directions: Saint-Hyacinthe hired first-baseman Jim Irving away from Sorel and made him the player manager, while Québec selected Billy Innes, known as the province's Connie Mack. Innes was a baseball lifer, but was only briefly a part of Organized Baseball, most recently 15 years prior in the Québec-Ontario-Vermont League.

Two divisions quickly emerged: Granby, Saint-Hyacinthe, and Sorel were doing well, while Québec City and Drummondville struggled. That left Sherbrooke and Trois-Rivières to battle for the final postseason spot. Both had replaced their managers after less-than-stellar starts.

In Sherbrooke, Tom Hammond, a teacher who had played football and baseball at Providence College and was well-connected with the New England semipro leagues, took over from Small, who stayed on as a player.[6] Hammond's turnaround of the Braves coincided with the rise of Paul Calvert, a 20-year-old right-handed pitcher from Montreal. The bespectacled accounting student might not have looked intimidating, but he threw gas, and over that season he became arguably the best prospect the province had ever seen. Legendary Yankees scout Paul Krichell tried but failed to sign him in August.[7] He recorded a 10–5 record with 127 strikeouts in 132 innings pitched in the Provincial League, finishing the season with three games pitched for the Montreal Royals and an invitation to pitch in front of New York Giants manager Bill Terry.[8]

In Trois-Rivières, manager Pinky Hargrave thought he could also handle the catching duties, but various ailments kept him on the sidelines, and he was left for a while with no real catcher available. Others took advantage, none more than Saint-Hyacinthe outfielder Joe Cicero, who in May consecutively stole second, third, and home in extra innings to win a game over Trois-Rivières. Hargrave, feeling that he was unable to fulfill his duties, eventually resigned. He was replaced by Lloyd Stirling, an Atlantic Canada native who had bombed as a pitcher with Drummondville earlier in the season and was now trying to transition to managing. Stirling was a character, constantly agitated on the bench or in the coaching box. This did not seem to go over well. At least twice, newspapers reported him being punched in the face, first by an opposing player, then by an umpire.[9]

Stirling acquired another colorful character, pitcher Jim Skelton, a regular of the New York semipro circuit. Skelton was signed after a masterful performance: He'd blanked the Philadelphia Athletics on four hits, striking out 10, in an exhibition game with his Alcion Park, New Jersey, independent team on July 7.[10] Three days later, he debuted in Trois-Rivières. Skelton had failed in Organized Baseball in the early 1930s and had been taking the train from Philadelphia every weekend to pitch in New York and New Jersey, where he was known as Jim Duffy. About 37 years old and overweight, Skelton had a trick up his sleeve, or more precisely, in his glove, where he kept a needle to give more movement to his pitches.[11]

Trois-Rivières newspaper *Le Nouvelliste*, visibly charmed by his larger-than-life personality, described him as a college professor, a cabaret owner, and a perfect gentleman off the field who was also the owner of a beautiful tenor singing voice.[12] Skelton won the hearts of the local fans with solid pitching performances, giving up only 27 runs in 86⅓ innings while compiling a record of 7–4. He entered local lore on July 24, when he pitched through stomach ailments to beat Granby before fainting in the clubhouse and being rushed to the hospital.[13] Four days later he was fine and back on the mound.

Skelton also had a part to play in the team's other big acquisition: outfielder Pete Gray. As recounted in William C. Kashatus's book *One-Armed Wonder*, Skelton and Gray arrived together by train in Montreal, where a team executive was to pick them up. Skelton had recommended Gray as an outfielder who can "hit, run and field like a mad fool." He had, however, failed to mention that Gray only had one arm. This was seven years before Gray's famous stint in the American League with the St. Louis Browns. The team executive almost fainted.[14]

Given that he was in town, Gray was given a chance and he made the best of it. After a quiet first game in Drummondville, he debuted in front of his new supporters on July 17, collecting a double and a single and stealing home. In his third game, he contributed a walk-off single. On July 30, he hit a ball over the fence in Sorel. He quickly became a fan favorite and the biggest draw in the league. People flocked to the games to see his one-handed swing and how he quickly removed his glove to relay balls back to the infield. He contributed solidly at the plate, hitting .306 with six doubles and the home run in 26 games, scoring 19 times.

For most of the second half of the season, it was a back-and-forth battle between Trois-Rivières and Sherbrooke for the fourth and final spot in the playoffs. The two teams were forced into multiple doubleheaders in the final days as they struggled to make up games lost to bad weather. Trois-Rivières entered the final day of the season half a game up on Sherbrooke. After being blanked in Saint-Hyacinthe in the afternoon, they travelled to Sherbrooke for a winner-take-all game in front of 3,500 spectators. Fittingly, Calvert and Skelton were the starting pitchers, and Gray was in center field and batting third. It was a good pitching duel, with Sherbrooke holding a 3–2 lead in the eighth when Skelton ran out of magic, giving up two insurance runs. Calvert struck out seven to lead the Braves to a 5–2 win and the final playoff spot.

Sorel (37–20) was heavily favored in the semifinals against Sherbrooke (30–30), and the logic prevailed, as Sorel won the best-of-five series 3–1. But the club had to work hard. The first game was decided by two runs, all others by a single one. Sherbrooke newspapers accused the league of favoring Sorel. Game Two, which was played in Sherbrooke, was rained out after six innings but replayed in Sorel, and the final game was decided by two close plays that went in Sorel's favor. The team had won the playoffs the previous three seasons, and accusations of favoritism were common.

Saint-Hyacinthe (34–23) swept Granby (37–25) in the other semifinal. After starting the season with a 13–1 record, the Red Sox had faded in the stretch. They suffered a big blow in August when the league was scouted by the Washington Nationals, After failing to convince Québec City third baseman Roland Gladu (.348, five homers, 32 RBIs) to sign, the Senators left with Granby's star second baseman, Mike Sperrick, who had been signed from the Can-Am League and was now going to Trenton in the Eastern League.

Sorel was led by second baseman Anthony De Nubilo (another player signed away from the Can-Am League, playing under the name of Tony Murphy), who hit .352 with 13 homers and 42 RBIs; first-baseman Nicholas Iarossi (.288, 6, 33 in 39 games, playing as Ross Nichols); and catcher Arthur Galen (.304, 4, 40).[15] Sorel had a strong pitching staff led by former major leaguer Roman "Lefty" Bertrand (11–3), Chuck Golinske (9–1), and Norman Bourassa (8–1).

Saint-Hyacinthe had a solid lineup built around center fielder Joe Cicero, who led the league with 14 home runs, 53 RBIs, and 25 stolen bases in 60 games. Other solid contributors were outfielders Mike Pociask (.296, 6, 45) and Red Dorman (.339, 2, 21 in 33 games), and manager/first baseman Jim Irving (.327, 0, 24). On the mound the Saints relied on their two winningest pitchers, Felix Andrus (13–4) and Bob Swan (12–7).

Sorel and Saint-Hyacinthe split the first four games of the best-of-seven championship series. Sorel outfielder Mike Sime, who had a solid .279–11–40 line in the regular season, collected the big hits and led his team to victory in the last two games. Sime exploded in the playoffs, hitting .447 with four doubles, a triple, five home runs, and 16 RBIs in 11 games. In Game Three of the championship series, he hit for the cycle with three home runs. It was the fourth consecutive championship for Sorel.

GOING FOR BROKE: THE 1939 SEASON

Overall, the 1938 season was successful, and no major changes were planned for 1939 other than expanding the calendar to 72 games. There was talk of a new stadium in Drummondville, but the deal was never sealed. Québec City's new stadium was finally set to open with the new season. A meeting between league president Jean Barrette and Frank Shaughnessy, his counterpart in the International League, was set to discuss the potential entry of the Provincial League in Organized Baseball, but nothing came of it.[16]

The big news of the offseason was Del Bissonette being hired to manage the Québec Athlétiques. Bissonette was well known across the province: Born in Maine to French-Canadian parents, he played amateur ball in Montreal before turning pro and returned to the

Montreal Royals after five seasons with the Brooklyn Dodgers. As he was turning 40 at the end of the season, he was expected to play first base only sparingly. One of his first moves was to sign outfielder Ernie Sulik, who had spent a year with the Philadelphia Phillies in 1936.

Not to be outdone by its rival, Trois-Rivières decided to hire a who's who of minor league stars. On the hitting side, while Pete Gray was not brought back, Trois-Rivières signed Dutch Prather, who would get to 2,000 hits and 200 home runs in his minor league career; Harlin Pool, a career .334 hitter in the high minor leagues who had also batted .303 in 127 games with the 1934-35 Cincinnati Reds; and Moose Clabaugh, who would collect 2,500 hits and 300 home runs in the minor leagues. They joined returning batting champion Paul Martin, as well as Phil Corrigan and Leo Maloney, poached from Granby. On the mound, the new acquisitions were Jake Levy, a 200-game winner in the minors, and By Speece, who collected 241 minor league wins and added five more in parts of four seasons in the majors.

While most of the other teams were satisfied with bringing back their 1938 players, the Granby Red Sox tried to keep up by signing Canadian outfielder Vince Barton, who had 133 Double A and 16 major league home runs, and their own 200-game winner in the minor leagues, Bud Shaney.

An early-season highlight was the opening of the new stadium in Québec City: 6,000 fans came to see a comeback, walk-off win against Trois-Rivières. On June 12, the Sherbrooke Braves elbowed their way into the festivities of the Canadian tour of King George VI and Queen Elizabeth. After nearly a month-long visit across Canada, the royal couple spent a few days in Washington and New York City and passed through Sherbrooke on their way to Halifax, whence they sailed home. While the royal visit to Sherbrooke was short, many made the trip to the city, which had organized a daylong event. The Braves lost to Trois-Rivières in the afternoon but won in 13 innings in a night game against Granby. Paul Calvert, a non-factor at that point because of a sore arm, pitched a complete game for his first win of the season. When the nightcap ended after midnight, fans poured into the Sherbrooke streets, where the party was still going on. That season's All-Star Game was also a big draw, attended by 5,000 spectators in Trois-Rivières.

Drummondville stumbled out of the gate, had a dreadful 5–22 record by the end of June, and were quickly out of the race, but the Tigres finished on a better note, led by the pitching of Art O'Donnell (7–2).

The other six teams were within striking distance of first place as the July 15 deadline to set their rosters approached. Trois-Rivières, unhappy that its costly acquisitions had not resulted in a runaway to first place, fired manager Stirling and replaced him with Jim Skelton. The team had already cut Pool after 20 games and did the same to Clabaugh just ahead of the deadline. To compensate, Trois-Rivières traded for Henry Bloch, first baseman and manager of Granby, and a few days later bought star Granby outfielder George Andrews outright. He would go on to win the batting title with a .332 average, along with six home runs and 48 RBIs. Saint-Hyacinthe countered by signing former major league pitcher Dutch Schesler.

Determined to keep its crown, Sorel opened its wallet to attract the star power hitter of the Can-Am League, Harry Powley, sometimes known as Bill. But there were two problems. First, Powley jumped his contract and was hidden under an alias. But instead of making up a fake name, he played as Allen McElreath, a real player who was with Chattanooga of the Southern League and Spartanburg of the South Atlantic League that season.[17] It is not obvious if the two players knew each other, but Powley claimed later he was offered $700 per month by Sorel, with part of the money coming from local politician and federal Public Works minister P.J.A. Cardin.[18] The second problem is that the addition of Powley came a few days after the July 15 deadline. The transaction was approved by league president Barrette, adding one more round of complaints about Sorel being favored by the league.

Sherbrooke, which was in first place as late as July 10, collapsed with a 7–27 record the rest of the way. First baseman Leo Marion (.314, 1, 42) was a rare bright spot. Paul Calvert (4–3 record, but mostly injured and ineffective) signed a contract with the Cleveland Indians in the offseason, on his way to the major leagues.

The remaining five teams fought valiantly for the four playoff spots. It was only in the final week that it became clear first place would be decided between Québec and Trois-Rivières, with Saint-Hyacinthe comfortably in third, leaving Sorel and Granby to battle for the final spot. After multiple rainouts, Trois-Rivières and Granby finished their seasons early, leaving Québec one game out of first place and Sorel one game back of fourth with two games each to play. They both won their first game, but on the final day of the regular season, they played against each other. It looked like bad news for Granby when Québec sent outfielder Sulik to the mound and then brought third baseman Gladu out of the bullpen, but somehow they did well enough to beat Sorel, 6–3. Just that quickly, Sorel's dominance was over. Powley, the post-deadline acquisition, was a disappointment, batting only .260 with three homers and 17 RBIs in 33 games, and DeNubilo, arguably the most valuable player in 1938, fell hard to a .245-3-32 line.

It soon became evident why the Athlétiques had sent other position players to the mound: Mike Schroeder (12–5 record) and Fred Browning (7–2) had deserted the team. While the beginning of World War II might have been a factor, it seems that some players were also exploiting the fact that the Provincial League, outside of Organized Baseball, had little recourse against players who felt they had the upper hand in negotiations. Schroeder and Browning disappeared for good, as did second baseman Fred Marcella of Granby, who had hit a crucial walk-off home run in the race for a playoff spot. Trois-Rivières pitching star By Speece (10–6) also held out for more money, a strategy that seems to have worked.

Québec City, in bad shape, was swept by Trois-Rivières in the best-of-three series to determine the pennant winner. In the playoffs, Trois-Rivières faced off against Granby. Even though they managed to sneak into the playoffs, the season had been difficult for Granby. The Red Sox claimed to have lost a considerable amount of money, to the point that they asked for emergency help from the city council, even after unloading Henri Bloch and George Andrews to Trois-Rivières. Off the field, pitcher Bill Kalfass was involved in an ugly story. A date with a local woman ended with her jumping out of his moving car, a statutory offense charge, and his release from the team.[19] Granby had managed a decent season, led by the outfield duo of young Howie Moss (.322, 11, 59) and veteran Barton (.286, 7, 55), as well as pitcher Hank Winston (12–7). But the Red Sox were no match for the star-studded Trois-Rivières team.

In the other semifinal, Saint-Hyacinthe took a 2–1 series lead over Québec City, but John Duncan and Glenn Liebhardt pitched the Athletiques to wins by scores of 4–1 and 5–3 to send them to the finals. It was the end of the line for another talented Saints team, led once again by outfielders Cicero (.316, 10, 49, 22 stolen bases) and Pociask (.331, 5, 52), and on the mound by Veach (12–5).

While waiting for its opponent in the championship series, Trois-Rivières played an exhibition game against the Montreal Royals, losing a 1–0 decision. Trois-Rivières was the heavy favorite for the best-of-seven final, with Andrews (.332, 6, 48), former batting champ Martin (.307, 1, 27), and Gene Sullivan (.301, 0, 33) leading the offense and Speece getting support from Joe Dickinson (12–7) and Jim Skelton (6–4) on the mound.

Québec City managed some extra-innings magic to take the first two games, winning both in the 11th inning. Pitcher Lou Lepine (6–7 in the regular season) got out of two bases-loaded jams late in the first game. The pivotal moment occurred in the fourth game, when Liebhardt (also 6–7) pitched a no-hitter to give the Athlétiques a 3–1 series lead. Trois-Rivières managed to win the next game in the 10th inning, but Lepine clinched the championship with another brilliant performance as Québec City won, 5–0. Helped by a timely rainout that covered the Athlétiques lack of depth, Lepine, Liebhardt, and Duncan did all they needed to replace the departed pitchers, on a team for which Gladu (.325, 5, 54) was the lone offensive star.

1940: A DISAPPOINTING JUMP TO ORGANIZED BASEBALL

With the payrolls ballooning faster than the attendance, teams spent the early part of the 1939–40 offseason claiming large deficits. One report claimed that the deficits totalled about $50,000 for the league.[20] Organized Baseball, with its structure, rules, and payroll limits, seemed like the solution to their problems. While in the past there had been a divide between small and big markets, now the majority was eager to join Organized Baseball, with only Sorel and Drummondville reluctant. Joe Page, who had set up the Eastern Canada League in 1922 and was its president, was asked to work his contacts to facilitate the process.

Discussions took most of the offseason, focusing on what class the league would obtain, which players would be ineligible, and which specific cities would be part of the league. The discussions dragged on all winter and were complicated by the opposition of the Montreal Royals, who in 1939 had become a farm team of the Brooklyn Dodgers. In late January, Dodgers president Larry MacPhail was in Montreal to visit his farm team and announced that the Provincial League application had been rejected by William Bramham, president of the National Association of Professional Baseball Leagues, which governed the minor leagues.[21] MacPhail also announced that Del Bissonette, who was in the running to become manager of the Royals, had been ruled out because of his stint in the Provincial League.[22] While MacPhail could decide who managed his farm team, his reach did not extend to the Provincial League, and league president Jean Barrette quickly replied that the application had been mailed from Montreal just the previous day and Bramham confirmed not having received it.

On February 3, Bramham officially accepted the league as a Class B circuit. Québec, Trois-Rivières, Sherbrooke, Saint-Hyacinthe, and Granby were confirmed, with Sorel out. Drummondville was still a possibility for the sixth franchise, but the league was exploring some intriguing options, including Lachine, on the Montreal island; Hull (now Gatineau), opposite Ottawa on the Québec side; Burlington and St. Johnsbury, Vermont; and Malone, New York.

As Organized Baseball granted veto power to a team within a 10-mile radius, it is not surprising that the Royals nixed the proposal for a team in Lachine. It was not until March 18 that Drummondville was reinstated as the sixth franchise. It's worth noting that Bramham was known for insisting on the sound fiscal and moral character of owners and leagues. The latter might explain why Sorel was out, while the former might be why Drummondville, the smallest town in the league, was on the bubble for so long.

Bissonette, having failed to land the job in Montreal, was back as manager in Québec City. Glen Larsen, a pitcher who'd taken the managing job in Granby midway through the 1939 season, was the only other returning manager. Jim Skelton had been scheduled to return as manager in Trois-Rivières, but given his ties to outlaw baseball, he was out. Instead, the team, which had previously gone without a nickname but was now known as the Renards, made a splash by hiring longtime major-league catcher Wally Schang. He'd been with Ottawa of the Can-Am league and had put on the shinguards more than 30 times during the 1939 season despite turning 50 in August. Two other former major leaguers and Montreal Royals, Doc Gautreau and Mel Simons, were named managers of Sherbrooke and Saint-Hyacinthe, respectively. Drummondville, late to the game, hired its former player (and former major leaguer) Charlie Small.

While a relatively large list of 1939 players were originally ineligible, arrangements were made to obtain reinstatements for most of those interested in returning, with a few exceptions, notably Granby's Howie Moss. Given their delayed return, Drummondville players were briefly made free agents, but the only loss was Butch Sutcliffe, who signed with Québec City. Sorel players, at least those eligible, were up for grabs. While Sherbrooke picked up most of them (infielders Ed Albertson and Red Durand, catcher Art Galen, and pitcher John Kimble), Trois-Rivières added an important piece in second baseman DeNubilo, who'd struggled in 1939 after his strong 1938 season. Outfielder Alex Pitko, who had cups of coffee in the majors the previous two seasons, also joined Trois-Rivières.

While the level of play seems to have been similar to the previous year, the crowds were thinning. If attendance of fewer than a thousand was a rare occurrence before, the league now often saw fewer than 500 paying customers. Bad weather, a constant flow of bad news from the war in Europe, and more games crammed into the same May-to-September time frame (80 per team, up from 72 in 1939, and 60 in 1938) were all factors. Locally, a strike in a textile mill in Drummondville forced the Tigers to move some games to nearby Victoriaville. The late start in organizing the Drummondville team led to some disastrous results. By mid-June, the Tigers sat at 3–15. On July 8, they folded with a 6–26 record.

Sherbrooke was doing fine at the end of June, with a 17–16 record, but the Braves were struggling financially and saw a change of ownership. The new owners fired Gautreau as manager and the team collapsed, going 8–15 in July and falling out of contention. On August 1, the Braves failed to meet payroll and also folded. The move coincided with 800 soldiers, a big part of their fanbase, moving out of town for training. Lucien Lachapelle, who had been the owner of the Sorel franchise, was in talks to save the team, but to no avail.

The league was left with four teams for the final month of the regular season. When it was announced that all four would qualify for the playoffs, interest and attendance dropped for the remaining games. All four teams started August with a shot at the pennant, but Trois-Rivières went into a tailspin and was quickly out. Saint-Hyacinthe finished on a 13–2 streak that allowed the Saints to win the pennant easily with a 48–30 mark, 4½ games ahead of Québec City.

The Saints were heavily favored in their semifinal against Trois-Rivières. If Joe Cicero had a down year by his standards (.284, 6, 49 with 20 stolen bases), Saint-Hyacinthe got strong years from George Andrews, who was picked up from Trois-Rivières (.339, 5, 32), and Stan Platek (.332, 9, 62). On the mound, Bruno Shedis (18–5), Bob Swan (10–6), and Dutch Schesler (7–5) all posted sub-3.00 ERAs.

The series kicked off with a split-park doubleheader. The first game, in Saint-Hyacinthe, was rained out. At night in Trois-Rivières, the Renards took the series lead as Shedis was outduelled by Art O'Donnell (8–13 overall), the former Drummondville ace who had been picked up by Trois-Rivières.

The next game, in Saint-Hyacinthe, was rained out twice, and having missed out on the large Labor Day weekend crowds they were expecting, the Saints were out of resources and forfeited the series. Apparently,

LIBRARY AND ARCHIVES OF CANADA/PUBLIC DOMAIN

Québec Prime Minister Maurice Duplessis, a Trois-Rivières native, approved the funding for league stadiums after being told they would be built by 2,000 or so otherwise unemployed workers in the region.

the team deficit was about $7,000 for the year, with losses of an additional $125 per day.[23]

The other semifinal featured the defending champion Québec Athlétiques and the Granby Red Sox. Québec was still led by Roland Gladu (.326, 8, 55) and 1939 playoff hero Lou Lepine (15–5), as well as by newcomer Bill Yocke (14–6). Granby could count on the most fearsome hitter in the league, Jim Walsh (.319, 17, 63), acquired in a trade with Jacksonville of the Class B South Atlantic League before the start of the season. The two teams split the first four games and Walsh hit a crucial home run for the Red Sox in the deciding game as John Kimble (12–11 between Sherbrooke and Granby) beat Yocke, 4–1.

In the finals, O'Donnell was dominant in Games One and Four as Trois-Rivières took a 3–1 series lead. The fifth game, in Granby, went into extra innings. In the 12th, the Renards scored twice on two Red Sox errors. The win went to Montreal native Jean-Pierre Roy, in the first year of a pro career that would briefly lead him to the majors in 1946. Roy was splendid out of the bullpen, allowing a single hit over six shutout innings and striking out nine. It was fitting that it was Roy, one of the few bright spots (10–8, 3.23 ERA) of this difficult season, who recorded the final out.

While the second half of their season had been difficult, Trois-Rivières had picked up important players along the way: Charlie Small came with O'Donnell from Drummondville, while catcher Galen joined from Sherbrooke. Pitko (.301, 12, 61) and 1938 batting champ Martin (.313, 1, 49) led the offense. The new team had not gelled during the regular season but manager Schang worked his magic when it counted the most.

THE BREAKUP

Soon after the season was over, league president Barrette resigned. He publicly stated that while he believed that the future of the Provincial League was in Organized Baseball, he thought that it would not be before the end of the war.[24] J. Emile Dion, president of the Québec Athlétiques, took over as league president, completing the rapid change in power across the league: Trois-Rivières and Québec City, who had joined the league in 1937 and 1938 respectively, were now fully in charge.

Of the three cities that did not make it to the finish line in 1940, Saint-Hyacinthe was the only one seriously interested in fielding a team for 1941. Once more, various other cities were considered, notably Hull, Sorel, and a few American cities on the border. Talks progressed through the winter, but in late March, with Granby and Saint-Hyacinthe hesitating and a disappointing meeting in Hull, Dion seemed about ready to give up.[25] The next week, along with representatives from Trois-Rivières, he attended a meeting of the Canadian-American League. On April 10, both cities were accepted into the league for 1941. The Provincial League was dead.

LEGACY

With little time before the 1941 season, Québec City and Trois-Rivières used many Provincial League players. The Athlétiques brought back Gladu, Yocke, and John Kosy, while local stars Roy and Martin, as well as Small, returned to the Renards. Québec City got the rights to Saint-Hyacinthe players and brought in three key ones: Joe Cicero, Bruno Shedis, and Bob Swan. Trois-Rivières was less successful with Granby players, but in 1942 they brought back one-armed outfielder Gray, while former manager Skelton scouted for them.

The other cities returned to local leagues, but after the war in 1946, Granby and Sherbrooke gave Organized Baseball another shot by joining the Class C Border League, with teams in Ontario and the state of New York. This did not go well. Long travel distances led to bulging deficits, and once again the Sherbrooke team folded before the end of the season.

The next year, both cities were back in a revived Provincial League, with Drummondville and Saint-Hyacinthe, but now also Saint-Jean and Farnham. The league quickly rose once again to become one of the top outlaw leagues. It received considerable attention in 1949, when it hosted players who should have been in the major leagues but were banned for having jumped to the Mexican League in 1946—players such as Sal Maglie, Max Lanier, and Bobby Estalella.

Table 2. Former major leaguers in the Provincial League

Player	MLB	Provincial
Vince Barton	1931–32	Granby 1939
Roman Bertrand	1936	Sorel 1938–39
Del Bissonette	1928–31, '33	Québec 1939–40
Moose Clabaugh	1926	Trois-Rivières 1939
Gowell Claset	1933	Saint-Hyacinthe 1938
Jake Daniel	1937	Granby 1939
Red Dorman	1928	Saint-Hyacinthe 1938
Doc Gautreau	1925–28	Sherbrooke 1940
Pinky Hargrave	1923–26, '28–33	Trois-Rivières 1938
Bill Kalfass	1937	Granby 1939
Glenn Liebhardt	1930, '36, '38	Québec 1939–40
Alex Pitko	1938–39	Trois-Rivières 1940
John Pomorski	1934	Drummondville 1938
Harlin Pool	1934–35	Trois-Rivières 1939
John Reder	1932	Sherbrooke 1938–39
Les Rock	1936	Sorel 1939
Wally Schang	1913–31	Trois-Rivières 1940
Dutch Schesler	1931	Saint-Hyacinthe 1939–40
Mel Simons	1931–32	Saint-Hyacinthe 1940
Charlie Small	1930	Sherbrooke 1938
		Drummondville 1939–40
		Trois-Rivières 1940
By Speece	1924–26, '30	Trois-Rivières 1939
Ernie Sulik	1936	Québec 1939
Butch Sutcliffe	1938	Drummondville 1939
		Québec 1940
Charlie Wilson	1931–33, '35	Sherbrooke 1938
		Saint-Hyacinthe 1938
Hank Winston	1933, '36	Granby 1939
		Trois-Rivières 1940

Table 3. Future major leaguers in the Provincial League

Player	Provincial	MLB
Paul Calvert	Sherbrooke 1938–39	1942–45, '49-51
Jim Castiglia	Trois-Rivières 1938	
	Drummondville 1939	1942
Joe Cicero	Saint-Hyacinthe 1938–40	1929–30, '45
Roland Gladu	Québec 1938–40	1944
Pete Gray	Trois-Rivières 1938	1945
Warren Huston	Trois-Rivières 1938	1937, '44
Howie Moss	Granby 1939	1942, '46
Jean-Pierre Roy	Trois-Rivières 1940	1946
Ed Walczak	Drummondville 1939	1945

Negro Leaguers were recruited starting in 1947 and by the next year the Provincial League became a prime destination for many veterans, including Terris McDuffie, Dave Pope, Buzz Clarkson, Silvio Garcia, and Chet Brewer. Drummondville, the laughingstock of the 1938–40 version of the Provincial League, spent a fortune to build a roster that could have competed with the top minor league teams and won the 1949 championship.[26] Most of these players were brought to Québec by Gladu, Roy, and Martin, now managing in the Provincial League after having risen through Organized Baseball during the war, with the first two briefly reaching the majors. Gladu and Roy, along with another local player, Stan Bréard, had also signed with the Mexican League before coming back home.[27] Former Sherbrooke pitcher Paul Calvert also made the trip back to the Provincial League in between major league stints.[28]

The jumpers were reinstated midway through the 1949 season, and the league joined Organized Baseball once again in 1950, with Québec City and Trois-Rivières reuniting with them in 1951. The league, originally keeping its outlaw roots, hosted many veterans and was focused on winning. It slowly became more entrenched in the traditional farm system before disbanding after the 1955 season.

Another obvious legacy of the league is the twin stadiums built in Québec City and Trois-Rivières that are still in use to this day. They have also linked the two cities' baseball histories. Together, they were part of the Canadian-American League from 1941 to 1950 (with a hiatus from 1943 to 1945), before jumping back to the Provincial League in 1951. They were together in a revived outlaw version of the Provincial League in the 1960s before jumping to the Double A Eastern League from 1971 to 1977.[29] After a long hiatus, professional baseball returned in 1999 when Québec City joined the independent Northern League. Trois-Rivières, which was part of the short-lived Canadian League in 2003, joined Québec in 2013 in a revived Canadian-American Association.

As a sign of things to come in the 1940s, the 1938–40 Provincial League had managed to show both how outlaw leagues can lead to out-of-control spending and how Organized Baseball was not a solution to all problems. Unfortunately, in the following years, much money was lost by team promoters who forgot that lesson. However, along the way, Québec baseball fans got to see some very good baseball.

MAJOR LEAGUERS IN THE PROVINCIAL LEAGUE

Tables 2 and 3 list of former and future major leaguers who spent time in the Provincial League. It is worth noting that the league also sent players to the NHL (Oscar Aubuchon of Saint-Hyacinthe and Fred Thurier of Granby); the NFL (Jim Castiglia of Trois-Rivières and Drummondville and Bob Trocolor of Drummondville); and the BAA, ancestor of the NBA (Nat Hickey of Drummondville). Tom Swayze (Drummondville, 1939) had a 20-year stint as head coach of the baseball team at the University of Mississippi. ■

Additional Resources

The main resources used were the Québec newspapers *La Presse, Le Petit Journal, La Patrie, Le Samedi, Le front ouvrier* (Montreal), *La Tribune* (Sherbrooke), *Sherbrooke Daily Record, Voix de l'Est* (Granby), *Clairon et Courrier de St-Hyacinthe, Drummondville Spokesman, Le Nouvelliste* (Trois-Rivières), *le Soleil et l'Action Catholique* (Québec). Baseball-Reference.com and *The Sporting News* player contract cards were the main sources used to identify players.

Rosters and statistics for the Provincial League are available on the author's website: https://lesfantomesdustade.ca.

Notes

1. Bill Young has done the most work on the 1948–52 period. His contributions include "From Mexico to Québec: Baseball's Forgotten Giants," *The National Pastime: Baseball in the Big Apple*, 2017; "Now pitching for Drummondville: the great Sal Maglie" and "Dangerous Dan Gardella fought for players' rights," *Québec Heritage News*, March–April 2005; and "Ray Brown in Canada: his forgotten years," *The National Pastime* 27, 2007.
2. Merril Clifton, "Disorganized Baseball–The Provincial League From LaRoque to Les Expos" (Toronto: Samisdat, 1982).
3. The 1935 league also featured an integrated team. See Clifton, "Québec Loop Broke Color Line in 1935," *Baseball Research Journal* 13 (1984), 67–68.
4. The team appears to be linked to Chappie Johnson, who sponsored African American teams in Québec on and off between 1927 and 1935.
5. Translated from French: "La construction d'un nouveau stade," *Le Nouvelliste*, July 7, 1984. A note on money: It's not always clear from newspaper archives what currency is being discussed in stories about Canadian baseball, but in this piece, except as noted, it's a good assumption that the currency is Canadian dollars, which were worth about U.S. $0.99 in 1938, $0.96 in 1939 and $0.90 in 1940, according to various sources. In turn, the U.S. Bureau of Labor Statistic's CPI Inflation Calculator says that a U.S. dollar throughout that period would be a worth a lille more than $19 in 2021.
6. At some point in 1939, the Sherbrooke team had six Providence College students or alumni: shortstop Johnny Ayvazian, pitcher Walter Morris, first baseman Leo Marion, and outfielders Chief Marsella and Jocko Crowley, as well as Hammond. See "Friars Baseball Stars Active During Summer," *The Cowl*, November 3, 1939.
7. "Trois-Rivières est battu 6-1 à Sherbrooke," *Le Nouvelliste*, August 20, 1938.
8. The tryout with the Giants did not go well. Calvert was brought to New York and asked to pitch batting practice. It rained most of the day, and "he pitched poorly when, after a long delay, he had an opportunity. Terry gave him his ticket to go back home and said he should have taken the Yankees' offer. See *The Sporting News*, October 27, 1938.
9. "Ripley slugged Lloyd Stirling," *Sherbrooke Daily Record*, August 17, 1938.
10. "Athletics thumped by Alcyon nine, 4–0." *Philadelphia Inquirer*, July 8, 1938.
11. "Necrology," *The Sporting News*, February 27, 1947, 27.
12. "Chronique sportive," *Le Nouvelliste*, July 19, 1938.
13. "En dépit d'une indisposition de Skelton Trois-Rivières gagne 6–4," *Le Nouvelliste*, July 25, 1938.
14. William Kashatus, *One-Armed Wonder: Pete Gray, Wartime Baseball and the American Dream* (Jefferson, NC: McFarland & Company, 1995), 47. Kashatus situates the story in 1942, when Gray came back to Trois-Rivières, now in the Canadian American League. Given that Skelton was on the 1938 team, and that Gray was still well known in Trois-Rivières in 1942, it makes more sense for the story to have occurred in 1938.
15. Players used aliases for fear that playing in outlaw leagues with suspended players might lead to their own suspensions. Some college players were also protecting their amateur status. Québec newspapers, especially those in French, sometimes blew these secrets, although often years later. Most often they would provide hints in the form of player bios, including teams played for and statistics. While very difficult to decipher back in the day, now, with easy access to minor league statistics, true identities can be found.
16. "L'ouverture de la Provinciale aura lieu le sept mai," *Le Droit*, April 18, 1939.
17. The subterfuge was not very successful, as Powley's actions were reported in *The Sporting News*, July 27, 1939. McElreath was declared permanently ineligible on June 4, 1947, for having been found guilty of inducing a fellow player to throw a game. Powley was on the ineligible list until 1947 after the Sorel incident.
18. "Between Ourselves," *Bridgeport Post*, August 29, 1948. This is an exception to the assumption that Canadian dollars are being discussed throughout this article. Powley was an American being quoted in an American newspaper, so he was probably referring to US dollars.
19. "Autre accusation contre W. Kolfass" [*sic*], *La Presse*, July 19, 1939.
20. "Dans le Monde Sportif par Oscar Major," *Le Samedi*, October 28, 1939.
21. "Les clubs de Jean Barrette dans le baseball organisé—Un fameux canard de MacPhail," *Le Soleil*, February 2, 1940.
22. Bissonette wrote a letter, published by *La Presse*, asking for an apology from MacPhail for having tarnished his name. In it, Bissonette claimed that he had always made sure that his players were released by their minor league team before signing them to a Provincial League contract. Confirming his claim, the list of ineligible players does not contain a single player from Québec. See "Protestations de Del Bissonnette," *La Presse*, February 5, 1940.
23. "St-Hyacinthe se retire du détail de la Provinciale," *Le Nouvelliste*, September 4, 1940.
24. "Jean Barrette abandonne la ligue Provinciale," *Le Droit*, October 22, 1940. In the same interview, Barrette also expresses some controversial opinions, questioning the love of French Canadians for baseball, as well as their business acumen.
25. "Québec veut s'affilier à la ligue de baseball amateur," *Le Droit*, March 21, 1941.
26. See note 1 for references on Bill Young's works on this era.
27. Bréard was too young to have played in the old Provincial League, but he starred with Gladu and Roy on the 1945 Montreal Royals. After his stint in Mexico, he managed Drummondville. Gladu managed in Sherbrooke, Roy in Saint-Jean and Martin in Saint-Hyacinthe.
28. A few more players came back, notably Joe Krakowski, an obscure outfielder with 1938 Granby, who managed Farnham in 1948–49. Former major leaguer Glenn Liebhardt, who had starred with Québec in 1939–40, resurfaced with Granby and Sherbrooke in 1949.
29. The spirit of the 1960s league was captured by a former player. George Gmelch, *Playing with Tigers: A Minor League Chronicle of the Sixties* (Lincoln: University of Nebraska Press, 2016).

Lang Ball

Forgotten Nineteenth-Century Baseball Derivative and Peculiar Kickball Ancestor

Chad Moody

The researchers at Protoball—the de facto authorities on baseball's ancestral and descendant games—unsurprisingly categorize the popular recreational sport of kickball as a baseball derivative.[1] But how did kickball originate? In *On the Origins of Sports: The Early History and Original Rules of Everybody's Favorite Games*, authors Gary Belsky and Neil Fine contend that kickball was invented around 1917 by Nicholas Seuss, a Cincinnati Park Board playgrounds director.[2] The World Kickball Association (WKA) disputes this commonly held belief, and instead posits this theory: "Emmett D. Angell is credited with the earliest known rules and diagrams describing a game very close to modern kickball in 1910 is his book *Play*. We believe the accreditation of Nicholas C. Seuss as the creator to be incorrect, he described the game seven years after Angell in 1917."[3]

The WKA is probably on the right track with its claim, but the truth might be found in a long-forgotten baseball offshoot known as Lang ball. Before we endeavor to probe this curious game, we should explore other kickball precursors.

Research indicates that Seuss brainstormed his creation earlier than commonly believed. "Prof. Suess [*sic*] of the North Cincinnati Turners has brought a new [kickball-type] game to Cincinnati," reported the *Dayton Herald* on January 29, 1907—some 10 years prior to the oft-credited origination date.[4] Called "kick base ball" in *The Playground Book* in 1917, Seuss's game resembled today's kickball with a notable difference of the ball being kicked either from a stationary position off the ground or via a drop or bounce kick; there was no pitching of the ball.[5] Additionally, fielders had no specific positional assignments and were all irregularly arranged within the diamond. And curiously, multiple baserunners could occupy the same base simultaneously. Rules specified the use of a basketball or volleyball.

As in Seuss's case, references to Angell's version of the game can also be found several years earlier than the typically cited creation date. Indeed, the University of Wisconsin physical education professor did formally document his game's rules in *Play: Comprising Games for the Kindergarten Playground, Schoolroom and College* (1910).[6] But six years earlier on April 25, 1904, the *Minneapolis Journal* reported that Angell was the inventor of "kicking baseball," which had been "tried and proved eminently successful in Wisconsin, Michigan and elsewhere."[7]

Despite preceding Seuss's kick base ball by at least three years, Angell's game much more closely resembled today's kickball, and was "played just the same as baseball, with a few exceptions."[8] As with baseball, the game featured typical fielding positions, including a battery, with the pitcher delivering the ball (a basketball) to the kicker.

Mystery solved? Well, not quite. In 1901, an organized game of "kickball" was played by youngsters in Chattanooga, Tennessee. "The game of kickball between the teams of the junior department of the YMCA and the First district school resulted in a victory for the First district with a score of 10 to 9," reported the *Chattanooga Sunday Times* on December 15, 1901. "This sport is creating much interest among the boys."[9] A few months later, a five-inning game was exhibited again by the junior members of the Chattanooga YMCA that featured "as much excitement as if it had been a professional game."[10] Pitchers were listed on the rosters, but catchers were not; therefore, it is inconclusive whether the ball was delivered to the kicker as in the modern game. Because the rosters featured typical baseball fielding positions, the game seems to most closely align with Angell's creation. However, the avid participation of members of the YMCA possibly suggests it to be a different game that stemmed from that same influential organization.

Over a decade before Angell's kicking baseball game was first referenced, physical education instructor R.A. Clark documented the basic description and rules of "Lang ball" in an 1892 edition of *Physical Education*, a journal affiliated with the YMCA. According to Clark, the game "was probably invented by Mr. C.G. Lang, who [at the time was] the physical director of the Y.M.C.A. gymnasium at St. Joseph, Mo."[11] Although no conclusive proof has been found to confirm Clark's assertion, evidence beyond the game's moniker does point to the validity of his claim.

Certainly, the Y itself was a veritable sports incubator in the late nineteenth century; basketball and volleyball were invented under its auspices at nearly the same time as Lang ball. And more specifically, Charles Gregory Lang is confirmed to have worked at the St. Joseph's Y in the early 1890s, and numerous newspapers across the country also credited him as Lang ball's inventor in subsequent years.[12] The highly educated and well-traveled Lang possessed the pedigree to invent and promote a novel game. "He was a thorough master of physical training in its every form, being a graduate in medicine and having had a two-year hospital experience," reported the *Trenton Evening Times*. "He was an all-around [YMCA] man, having been a physical director in large associations.... Dr. Lang had considerable experience in coaching and training athletic teams and his assistance in that line was of immense value."[13] And the *Trenton Sunday Advertiser* said: "In the opinion of leading association men over the country Dr. Lang belongs in the front rank of physical directors."[14]

Despite containing the earliest known reference to Lang ball, Clark's March 1892 article provides one of the most detailed descriptions found to date of the unusual game, complete with an artist's rendering of players in action. Conversely, on October 13, 1894, the *York* (PA) *Gazette* provided this concise—but proficient—summarization of Lang ball: "The ball used in this game is a round inflated foot ball [soccer ball]. It is batted with the soles of the feet, the batter at the time hanging from a bar [such as a horizontal bar utilized in gymnastics]. When the ball is served by the pitcher, he shoots out his legs and kicks it with both feet. Otherwise the game is base ball, the bases, runs, rules and scoring being just as in that game."[15]

One important fact missing in the brevity of the *Gazette*'s description was that as in modern kickball, baserunners could be put out when struck by thrown balls in a practice known as "plugging." Additionally, Clark's published guidelines allowed a light medicine ball to be substituted for the soccer ball and offered some gameplay flexibility: "Any number can play the game. One side may play against another, or the players may rotate as in 'one old cat.' "[16]

Clark did not exactly offer a glowing review of Lang ball in his article. "This game has not as many points of excellence as basket ball," he wrote. "In the latter, all the players are in brisk action at once, and during the entire game. In Lang ball it is mainly the runners who are active. Still, one game cannot be played all the time, and the game we have described makes a very pleasing variation from class work. In some places it has been played a great deal."[17]

Despite Clark's lukewarm attitude toward the game, newspaper reports in early 1893 indicated that Lang ball was avidly being played from New York to Seattle and many places in between. Originally conceived as an indoor game but soon also played outdoors, it was particularly "in great favor" inside YMCA gymnasiums, perhaps unsurprisingly due to its purported invention and promotion by that organization.[18] Not only played by children, the game also attracted more mature participants. "Lang Ball has been pushed with business men's class, more so than Basket Ball," reported physical educator W.T. Owen of his New Bedford, Massachusetts, gymnasium in an 1895 issue of *Physical Education*. "The abdominal work in Lang Ball has been found to be very beneficial."[19]

And in the mid-1890s, it became a well-received pastime among "fashionable" women attending the prestigious East Coast colleges of Cornell, Vassar, and Wellesley. "Moreover, it is just the game for women, for, while it includes all the health-giving features of baseball, it does away with the roughness and danger," opined the New Orleans *Daily Picayune* on April 12, 1896. "The batter runs no risk of being knocked senseless by having a hard ball crash against her skull, and the catcher does not fear for the safety of her pretty fingers."[20] In a perhaps humorous sign of the times, the women competitors were prohibited from wearing skirts because the long, flowing garments had increasingly been used to capture fly balls.

AUTHOR'S COLLECTION

Lang ball as played in 1892 as shown in Physical Education *1, No. 2, April 1892, page 32.*

Regardless of participants' sexes, the *Daily Picayune* story documented some of the most vivid accounts of Lang ball game play uncovered to date:

> The home plate in lang would vex the heart of the professional ballplayer with doubt. Reared above it is an ordinary horizontal bar attached to side standards, the same as in use in all gymnasiums. The girl at the bat leaps up from the ground and catches hold of the bar with her hands. The pitcher uses a big rubber ball, about six inches in diameter and as elastic as a tennis ball. She tosses the ball with the hope of hitting the girl at the bat. If she succeeds, it is counted a strike. If the batter kicks at it and misses, it is also counted as a strike.... No balls are counted against the pitcher, it having been found unnecessary, as even the poorest kind of a thrower is able to toss the ball somewhere in the vicinity of the plate.... A clever batter or kicker is seldom counted out on strikes. The ball offers a good target, and by swinging back the body at the right instant, and giving the ball a hearty kick, the sphere can be sent flying into the far field.... Home runs are of frequent occurrence, for on a very little kick a clever base runner can make the round of the diamond. The ball is awkward to handle, and cannot be thrown any great distance.[21]

NEW ORLEANS DAILY PICAYUNE

Lang ball was a popular alternative to baseball among women on East Coast college campuses in the mid-1890s.[49]

Curiously, the article is accompanied by an illustration of a kicker striking the ball with the top of her foot and/or toe, which differs from the typical description of the ball being kicked with the soles of the feet.

The popularity of Lang ball—or "hang ball" or "hang base ball" as it also was occasionally known—continued throughout the decade of the 1900s, but its luster quickly wore off. Exemplifying the larger trend, hundreds of University of Idaho students were surveyed in 1910 to select their favorite of 18 different sports; only Lang ball failed to receive a single vote.[22] Around the same time as Lang's sudden and untimely death from Bright's disease (nephritis) in the mid-1910s, his creation began to vanish.[23] Scant evidence of the game's existence can be found in the 1920s, and its swan song appears to be a brief mention in *Play Games and Other Play Activities* (1930) by physical educator Albert B. Wegener.[24] It might not be a coincidence that Lang ball's demise coincided with the rise of the kickball forerunners formulated by Angell and Seuss; however, it is not known for certain whether there existed a causal connection between the events. In any case, it is not inconceivable that these scholars consciously attempted to emulate or even supplant Lang ball when devising their rival games. The formal study of physical education and an associated exchange of ideas among its academic community in the United States flourished in the early twentieth century.[25]

Lang ball itself may have been influenced by another baseball derivative. Numerous publications of the day described it as strongly resembling the more popular sport of indoor baseball. The rules of the two games were nearly identical, although importantly, plugging was not allowed in indoor baseball. Born around four years prior to Lang ball at Chicago's Farragut Boat Club on Thanksgiving Day, 1887, indoor baseball, under its founder, George Hancock, quickly had official rules published and prominent leagues organized that drew many participants—and even big crowds. On March 12, 1893, the *Seattle Post-Intelligencer* bluntly called Lang ball "an adaptation of indoor baseball."[26] Indeed, at their inceptions both games were baseball derivatives rooted in the central idea of requiring larger and heavier balls to enable game play in confined indoor spaces. Indoor baseball later moved from gymnasiums to the outdoors and evolved into modern softball, thereby suggesting a surprisingly close familial relationship between the latter and kickball.

Some newspapers also alleged that Lang ball originated from old or even "ancient" games with a decidedly European bent.[27] But no obvious evidence to substantiate this claim can be found when consulting

Protoball's comprehensive kickball family of games, which are defined as "safe-haven games featuring running among bases, pitching, and two distinct teams (but no batting)."[28] All currently known European games in this family predating Lang ball initiated play through actions like throwing the ball or striking the ball with the hand; no actual kicking was involved. However, a clue to finding Lang ball's purported European roots can possibly be found in examining a key rule difference between it and baseball: plugging. The use of plugging (or "soaking") to retire baserunners was outlawed in baseball decades before the birth of Lang ball, yet somehow found its way back into the latter game. Exploring an age-old European game in the baseball family might reveal Lang's inspiration for resurrecting this bygone practice.

Played across Europe for centuries in different forms, a family of two-base, bat-and-ball baseball predecessor games known as "long ball" utilized plugging as an integral means by which to put runners out.[29] Not isolated only to Europe, long ball was heavily promoted by physical educators in the United States as a recreational activity in the late nineteenth and early twentieth centuries—the same timeframe that saw the advent of Lang ball. In fact, YMCA instructor James Naismith referenced long ball as one of the primary indoor games played in the early 1890s at the Massachusetts gymnasium in which he famously invented basketball.[30] Other physical educators of the day sang long ball's praises, with Henry S. Curtis, a prominent American playground movement supporter, specifically singling out plugging as a key advantage of long ball. "This game has the added charm over baseball of throwing at the runner," Curtis said.[31] And a Dallas school official called long ball "probably the best of all ball games for a large number of players in a limited space."[32] Additionally, evidence of long ball's possible influence on Lang may exist in another game promoted by the YMCA around the same time as Lang ball called "ling ball." Also described as a two-base, bat-and-ball game with plugging, ling ball sounds suspiciously similar to long ball.[33] Aside from some minor popularity in West Michigan YMCAs in the early 1890s and an unremarkable reference to the game syndicated to a handful of 1896 newspapers, further mentions of ling ball seem nonexistent, so the game appears to have suffered a quick and unceremonious death.[34] In any case, Lang undoubtedly would have been familiar with long ball (and/or ling ball) in his professional capacity.

From a personal perspective, it is not beyond the realm of plausibility that knowledge of long ball was passed down within the Lang family. Three of Lang's grandparents were natives of the heavily German-influenced Alsace region in France, where one-time German national pastime and long ball variant "das deutsche Ballspiel" (the German ballgame) was likely played. Now known as "Schlagball" in its more modern form, the venerable game is defined thusly on Protoball's expansive website: "Schlagball is an ancient sport that was one of the usual team sports from the beginning of the German gymnastics and sports movement in the 19th century, and until well after the Second World War enjoyed great popularity in Germany."[35]

Lending some credence to the German-heritage long ball theory, while simultaneously deepening the mystery, the January 2, 1906, *Hartford Daily Courant* reported on local YMCA members playing an "amusing and vigorous" game of Lang ball, which "originated in Germany and is as old as our national game."[36] However, this game was not exactly Lang ball, as evidenced by the *Courant*'s gameplay description: "It is similar to indoor baseball, although the ball is as large as a football and the players bat with the palm of the hand instead of with a bat."[37]

The game appeared to closely mimic Lang ball—including plugging—aside from the method by which the batter struck the ball. But it's unclear whether this was simply a case of mistaken identity or a deliberate alteration of Lang's creation that possibly borrowed from a game known as "German bat ball." A Schlagball variant in which the batter strikes the ball with an open hand and plugging is utilized, German bat ball was popularly promoted as a recreational activity for American children in the early twentieth century. And adding to the intrigue, in *The Practice of Organized Play: Play Activities Classified and Described*, Michigan-based physical education professors Wilbur Bowen and Elmer Mitchell suggested this about German bat ball: "In the fall of the year it is especially fitting to play the game with the batsman kicking the ball instead of batting it."[38] Although this was published in 1923, it opens the possibility that a kickball-type version of this long ball variant had been played in the United States and elsewhere much earlier.

Was long ball a key source of inspiration during the development of Lang ball? It would be speculative at best to say so, but it is worth considering when seeking to validate Lang ball's alleged ties to European games of yore. Interestingly, the English word "long" translates to "lang" in German and in the languages of several other European countries in which long ball was played. One of these countries is Sweden, from which the "old Swedish game of 'hang ball' " was revived as Lang ball according to the October 13, 1894, *York*

Gazette.[39] It is possible that "hang" and "lang" were linguistically confounded in this case, or that there was confusion with another game of reported Swedish heritage involving participants hanging from a horizontal bar known as "hang tag."[40] Between Lang ball, long ball, ling ball, and hang ball, the etymology here is curious to say the least.

Before proclaiming C.G. Lang the father of kickball, it should be mentioned that other baseball derivatives preceding Lang ball have been uncovered that feature kicking as a key element. In 1891, a Brooklyn street game called "kick the ball" was described by prominent ethnographer Stewart Culin.[41] Played on a typical baseball field layout, the game bore more than a passing resemblance to kickball, although there was no plugging of runners. Action began with the kicker booting either a small rubber ball or a baseball into the field of play from home plate; however, it is not documented whether the ball was delivered by a pitcher.[42] Minimal references to the game exist after this time.

And in the early 1880s, a new game, called "hildegarde," marketed toward females due to its minimized "danger and laboriousness," was described in several publications.[43] Stemming from England but quickly exported to the United States, hildegarde was described by the Minneapolis *Daily Minnesota Tribune* on September 23, 1883, as a "combination of football and cricket, [with] a big, soft ball being struck with a wide bat as well as kicked." Reporting on the game as played in New York, the *Tribune* said: "It is the kicking that will subject a girl to condemnation, but she will be able to stand it if fully convinced that she looks well at the exercise."[44]

Oddly, no mention was made of kicking being allowed by rule in Leonora's *The New Out-Door Games of Hildegarde and Ladies' Cricket*, published in 1881. In the game described by the pseudonymous author as a "combination of the noble old English one of Cricket with the popular American one of Base-ball," bats were used to strike the ball "as in Cricket."[45] Some news reports in 1883 corroborated Leonora's account of the game. "The latest thing in games is called hildegarde, and is a sort of cricket or rounders," reported the *Boston Daily Globe* on July 22, 1883. "It is played with a ball, bats, and wickets, but the latter are circular and some feet off the ground."[46] Other contemporaneous British accounts likened the game to a "curious hybrid of tennis, rounders, and cricket," likewise with no mention of kicking.[47]

As with many of the newly invented and promoted games from sports-crazed nineteenth-century England, hildegarde quickly "sank without a trace."[48] So despite predating Lang's creation, both kick the ball and the kicking variant of hildegarde appear to have only been games of limited shelf life isolated to the New York City area, thus leaving Lang ball as the likely progenitor of modern kickball—and arguably among the most peculiar of the baseball derivatives. ■

Acknowledgments

The author wishes to thank Alex Bentley of the Kautz Family YMCA Archives for her time and research assistance.

Sources

Ancestry.com, Archive.org, Chronicling America, GenealogyBank.com, NewspaperArchive.com, Newspapers.com, Paper of Record, and TheAncestorHunt.com.

Notes

1. "Kickball," Protoball, https://protoball.org/Kickball, accessed January 21, 2021.
2. Gary Belsky and Neil Fine, *On the Origins of Sports: The Early History and Original Rules of Everybody's Favorite Games* (New York: Artisan, 2016), 117.
3. "Kickball FAQ," World Kickball Association, https://kickball.com/faq, accessed January 19, 2021.
4. "Chicago Man Introduces Kicking Base Ball to Reds," *Dayton Herald*, January 29, 1907.
5. Mary E. Gross, Carl Ziegler, and Randall J. Condon, *The Playground Book* (Cincinnati: Cincinnati Playgrounds, 1917), 82–83.
6. Emmett Dunn Angell, *Play: Comprising Games for the Kindergarten Playground, Schoolroom and College* (Boston: Little, Brown, and Company, 1910), 71–72.
7. "Autos Called Animals," *Minneapolis Journal*, April 25, 1904.
8. Angell, Play.
9. "Game of Kickball," *Chattanooga Sunday Times*, December 15, 1901.
10. "The Y.M.C.A. Exhibition," *Chattanooga News*, March 4, 1902.
11. R.A. Clark. "Lang Ball." *Physical Education* 1, no. 2 (April 1892): 31–32.
12. *Year Book of the Young Men's Christian Associations of the United States and Dominion of Canada for the Year 1891* (New York: International Committee of Young Men's Christian Associations, 1891), 104; *Year Book of the Young Men's Christian Associations of North America for the Year 1892* (New York: International Committee of Young Men's Christian Associations, 1892), 92; "Sabbath School Institute," *Albany* (MO) *Weekly Ledger*, July 22, 1892; "A New Ball Game," *Buffalo Courier*, May 30, 1894.
13. "Dr. C.D. Lang Dies at Home in Iowa," *Trenton Evening Times*, January 30, 1915. The article uses an incorrect middle initial for Lang.
14. "Spicy Chat that Interests Athletes," *Trenton Sunday Advertiser*, December 16, 1906.
15. "Y.M.C.A. Athletics," *Gazette* (York, PA), October 13, 1894.
16. Clark. "Lang Ball."
17. Clark.
18. "Y.M.C.A. Athletic Notes," *Daily Standard-Union* (Brooklyn), June 22, 1892.
19. "Personals." *Physical Education* IV, no. 4 (June 1895): 62.
20. "Sports for College Girls," *Daily Picayune* (New Orleans), April 12, 1896.
21. "Sports for College Girls."
22. "Idaho Students Favor Basket Ball," *Spokane Chronicle*, November 5, 1910.
23. "To Ship Remains of Dr. Lang Here," *Trenton Sunday Times-Advertiser*, January 31, 1915. The article uses an incorrect middle initial for Lang.
24. Albert B. Wegener, *Play Games and Other Play Activities* (New York: Abingdon Press, 1930), 37.
25. Martha H. Verbrugge, *Active Bodies: A History of Women's Physical Education in Twentieth-Century America* (Oxford: Oxford University Press, 2012), 15–16.

delegates from throughout the Midwest met in Chicago and formed the Northwestern Association of Base Ball Players.[7] Member clubs in the new group were enjoined to report their match play to the Association and area vice presidents and corresponding secretaries were named. The convention adopted the NABBP's rules and regulations, excepting its ban on admission of members under 18 years of age. The *Philadelphia City Item* called for a Pennsylvania association, citing the Greater New York City bias shown at the NABBP convention, which had just declined to move the 1866 meeting to Philadelphia.[8]

The association movement would continue as the 1866 season progressed. The *Jackson Citizen Patriot* reported in April on a meeting of the Michigan State Base Ball Association.[9] The *Sacramento Daily Union* reported a meeting of Northern California clubs scheduled for August 17.[10] The list of state associations published after the season in the *New York Sunday Mercury* as existing or planned also included Maryland, New York, New Jersey, and "most of the Western states."[11]

"COUNTRY" CLUBS

When comparing 1860 (the last pre-war season) and 1865 (essentially the first postwar season), although there is not a remarkable increase in matches played, those matches are remarkably different in their distribution. Despite an increase overall of about 150 senior matches (between clubs whose players averaged 18 years of age or older) in 1865 over 1860, senior matches in Greater New York City were still in decline, from 252 in 1860 to 193 in 1865. At season's end, over 1300 interclub matches under the national rules appear in RIM for 1865, in 24 areas of the US and Canada.[12] Occasional trips by GNYC or Philadelphia clubs to the "country" continued to indicate a significant gap in skill; the GNYC champion was usually dubbed by the nationally distributed press as the national champion and was regarded as such in areas where NABBP rules had only recently been adopted.

What accounted for the gap in playing standard? An analytical sort who signed himself "Zeno," though nothing obvious relates him to that ancient Greek philosopher, laid out the question in the *Rochester Evening Express* of August 13. Noting that NABBP rules had been played in Rochester for six years, and that the locals were presumably as intelligent and athletic as those of GNYC, he ascribed the Rochester clubs' lower standard to deficiencies in training and leadership. The *Evening Express* also pointed out the necessity of raising Rochester's standard of play, remarking, "Manifest inferiority excites no feeling but indifference or contempt."[13] The *Jamestown* (NY) *Journal* reflected the general admiration for better standards of play by noting that a local 16–11 game "had a score that even city clubs would not feel ashamed of."[14]

How were country clubs organized? Nationally-distributed guides written by influential GNYC journalist and NABBP official Henry Chadwick published sample club constitutions for the benefit of new groups. Thus, the *Daily Evansville* (IN) *Journal*, printing the members of the first, second, and third nines of the local club, explained that this operation was "as per National Base Ball Regulations."[15] The *Spirit of Jefferson* of Charlestown in the new state of West Virginia provided a rare glimpse when it published the minutes of a business meeting of the local Stonewall Club. As a mid-season meeting, matters of annual importance—such as selection of officers and captains—were not on the docket, but financial matters were. The meeting approved the election of several honorary (non-players/donors?) members, appointed a committee to organize seating for ladies during "exercises" at the grounds, another committee to solicit contributions to cover expenses for a road trip, and passed a resolution to "tax" members to raise funds for incidental expenses.[16] In Rock Island, Illinois, the five clubs organized in the city consisted of age groups. The oldest enrolled men aged 18 to 25 (a senior club), another consisted of juniors down to age 12, and the other three of even younger boys.[17]

OPENING DAYS

Baseball in the 1866 calendar year began, as it had since pre-war days, with games on ice. Using modified rules, "ice baseball" was played with (usually) 10 players wearing skates per side, and a softer ball. The earliest reported game of "ice baseball" took place in Rahway, New Jersey, in December 1859, and this off-season recreation would continue into the 1880s. In the winter of 1865–66, ice games were reported in Rochester, Greater New York City, New York State, New Jersey, Philadelphia, and Chicago.

Play on dry land among "country" clubs also restarted with the new year. After an apparent hiatus following Thanksgiving Day, the Pacific and Eagle clubs of San Francisco undertook a best-of-three series for the state championship, a series delayed until February, when the Pacific toppled the Eagle, 32–18 and 35–15.[18,19] The pre-war Empire and Crescent clubs of New Orleans had also revived, and played on Sunday, January 7.[20] New Orleans and St. Louis were at the time the only prominent locations featuring Sunday matches. Clubs in such scattered outposts as Denver, Chattanooga, and Camden, New Jersey. were also reported in early March to have kicked off their seasons with intrasquad games.

Harvard's gentlemanly club, champions of New England, opened the grand match season in GNYC at the end of May by traveling to Brooklyn, where they lost matches to the Atlantic, Eureka of Newark, Excelsior of Brooklyn, and the Active of New York City, but impressed with their talent and *sang froid*.

BASEBALL'S BENEFITS (AND HAZARDS)

Would-be players and promoters of the game could find a wide range of opinions on the benefits and hazards of the game. The *Belvidere* (IL) *Standard* took an even-handed view:

> The ball used in this game is so hard that a good pair of buck (*n.b.*: buckskin) gloves are needed on the hands to escape bruised or dislocated fingers, and after making a hit with the bat, the candidate for a credit mark is obliged to make a circuit of about a quarter of a mile at the top of his speed; this comes under the heading of 'exercise', which it is, and without question, much better exercise than is afforded by Gymnasiums.[21]

The *Wheeling* (WV) *Daily Register* was more conventionally wholehearted:

> The exercise is not only beneficial, it is graceful and manly. It develops muscle and brings into play the whole physical frame. And then it is an out-of-door sport...The more ball players we have in this country the less billiard saloons and groggeries we will have.[22]

Others were not convinced. A widely reported item during the summer contained the recommendation that participating in sports might lead to contraction of cholera, which was widespread in 1866. "Violent exercise," as reported the *Cleveland Plain Dealer*, would lead to "the production of fevers and bowel diseases."[23] The *Raleigh Daily Sentinel* expressed its disapproval of Southerners spending time on amusements, noting that "Intellect, energy, frugality and hard labor will raise the South, and nothing else can."[24] And as incidents of Sunday ballplaying proliferated, stiff opposition was raised by the Sabbatarians and other religious groups, like the State Street Congregational Church of Brooklyn's Missionary Society.

AUTHOR'S COLLECTION

THE OFFICERS OF THE NATIONAL ASSOCIATION OF BASE BALL PLAYERS.
From the *Illustrated News*, July 21, 1866.

The 1866 NABBP officers. A spectacular success in popularizing its rules as the national standard for base ball play, the National Association of Base Ball Players had perennial issues with enforcement of restrictions on player eligibility and professionalism, and did not regulate championship competition.

The Society's diatribe warned that the game had turned from "a reasonable exercise into a moral contagion...insidiously diffusing and infusing itself into the minds and brains of thousands upon thousands of our young American people, from thirty years of age downward to little children...exhibiting a reckless abandon and mad ecstasy." The game could lead to not only physical injury, but "betting, swearing, quarreling, and fighting," neglect of gainful employment, and "demoralization of the mind."[25]

LEARNING THE GAME

New devotees of the NABBP game could also find both humorous and earnest advice on taking up the game. Presenting the result, including the box score, of the new home club's first interclub match, the *Cecil Whig*, of Elkton, Maryland, appended a helpful catalog of rules, fielding positions, and terminology, the progress of the game from inning to inning, and instructions for reading the box score.[26] An exposition in the *Richmond* (VA) *Daily Dispatch* was more analytical, if mistaken. Noting that the game was "copied in the main" from cricket, and recalling his boyhood adventures playing "cat," the *Dispatch*'s reporter paraphrases the NABBP rules directly, and in order, from a guide. Coming to the rule allowing bases on balls, he supposes that for Richmonders, being competitors but also heirs to Southern traditions of personal honor (as opposed, presumably, to Yankees), such an eventuality will not be required.[27]

Not all efforts to understand the game were a howling success. Invited to attend the first exercises of a new club, a correspondent to the *Western Reserve Chronicle* (Warren, Ohio) signing himself "GUEST" offered the following:

> The game being entirely new to most all present, the book on tactics had to be consulted first to find out how to lay off a field...This done, tactics was again consulted to find out what was an innings and what was an outings. This important fact being established, the game commenced in earnest, which consisted principally in the players running with their greatest speed 360 feet, stopping three times to change their base... The score was now footed up, and I learned that one side had 64 innings and the other side 67 outings, and the Umpire decided that the outings had won the game by three majority.[28]

THE SPREAD OF NABBP BASEBALL IN 1866

> "The base ball fever spreads through our community much more rapidly than cholera."
>
> —*Richmond* (VA) *Daily Dispatch*[29]

Not that the *Daily Dispatch* was complaining. In 1866, the year of the last of three major such epidemics of the century in the US (after 1832 and 1849), it considered the viral nature of baseball a "fortunate circumstance."

Over the course of the season, reports appear of the formation of clubs in 14 states in the west and south which had had no previous reported activity.[30] Additionally, the number of clubs in states where NABBP-rules baseball had been previously introduced multiplied, prewar clubs revived, and clubs playing other baseball codes converted, notably town ball clubs in the Cincinnati area.[31]

Local newspapers urged their towns' young men to start clubs. An editorial in the *Hancock Jeffersonian* of Findlay, Ohio, on July 13 laid out the reasons:

- Clubs have been organized in all the cities and towns of any note throughout the country.
- It affords a pleasant and healthful exercise to a class of young men who would, perhaps, otherwise lack an incentive to physical development.
- The rules of the game are simple and easily learned.
- We have an abundance of material for such clubs.
- Immense sport for both players and spectators.
- What we want in this day and generation is a return to out door sports. We live too much in the shade.[32]

In this case, the *Jeffersonian* apparently pled in vain; no further baseball items appear in its pages in 1866. And not all editors were so enthralled, for example the following from the *Lancaster* (PA) *Intelligencer*:

> The Harrisburg base ballers were here yesterday to show our boys how to do it, but we were compelled to go to press without any reports, and we are not sure that public will suffer much for want of a full report. If any limbs are broken or noses bruised we will inform the public by our next issues. The base ball business we think is overdone.[33]

More commonly, journalists merely wondered at the phenomenon, like a gentleman at the *Cleveland Leader*:

> ...we have a national game, peculiarly our own. Many of the matches of rival clubs awaken the deepest interest in the minds of the people. Representatives of the press travel hundreds of miles to attend these games, and their reports are looked for with as much interest as would have been excited a short time ago by the news of the defeat of an army, or the capture of a beleaguered city.[34]

The deep end of local dreams of achieving civic notoriety through baseball is represented by the fulminations (tongue likely lodged firmly in cheek) of the *Chestertown* (MD) *Transcript*:

> ...we look forward to the no distant time when the Chestertown Club will be known, dreaded, and admired throughout the entire country. When the famed *Athletics* and *Atlantics* will be compelled to "pale their ineffectual fires" before the meridian splendors of the Chestertown "*Ozenies*."[35]

Evidence also surfaced that the war had not left NABBP baseball shunned in the South as a feature of Northern society. Besides its revival in New Orleans, the *Charleston Daily Observer* commented favorably on the foundation of the Palmetto Base Ball Club in that citadel of succession.[36] The Palmettos moreover intended to play the national game: The *Philadelphia City Item* noted that they had requested information on organizing a club and on playing rules from the Athletic of Philadelphia. With the decline of summer heat in the fall, reports began to surface of the game's spread to new areas, with clubs also reported in Kentucky, Tennessee, Virginia, North Carolina, Alabama, and Mississippi.

The new rage naturally attracted some whose enthusiasm didn't last. The *Louisville Democrat* reported, as reprinted in the *Philadelphia Inquirer*, that "the base ball epidemic is abating," and they "hope[d] it will disappear."[37] And the *Bedford* (PA) *Gazette* complained that the local young men were now neglecting their baseball exercises in favor of watching the girls play croquet.[38]

PLAYING THE GAME

What were some experiences of "country" clubs in the field in 1866?

Deciding Who Could Play

The *Daily Iowa State Register* reported that the *DeWitt* (IA) *Observer* had castigated the new local club for refusing admission to a player because of his "African nationality…whereat every Copperhead in the place 'biled' over with the effervescence of malignity."[39] Age was another question. The *Rock Island Evening Argus* explained that the five organized clubs in the town of 5,100 (1860) were organized by age: One senior club with players age 18–25; another of age 12–15 "or thereabouts"; while the other three were younger.[40]

New Customs and Practices

For the benefit of new ballists all over the country, the NABBP rules were available in written form through guides and the nationally distributed sporting papers. Less known are the means by which unwritten practices spread, but spread they did. As they were in areas where the NABBP game was already established, umpires were "chosen at the grounds at time of play,"[41] if necessary by a coin toss if the clubs couldn't agree on a candidate.[42] Also continuing in the west was the custom of seeking a ruling from an umpire by asking for judgment.[43] One umpire reportedly commenced a game with the long-established call of "ball to the bat."[44]

A club in Iowa, the *Tipton Advertiser* reported, had decided to continue using the "bound" rule (batted balls caught on the first bound constituting an out), but had to adopt the "fly" rule (outs only on ball caught before bounding) for an interclub match, at the insistence of the other club.[45] Such delayed adoption of rule changes may have been the norm: *The Tennessean* (Nashville) noted that an umpire's calling of balls in a recent game was the first employment in the locality of that rule.[46] A detailed play-by-play recap in the *Buffalo Courier* reported a ground rule that a ball "over fence" was only good for a base for all runners, and that a baseman informed the umpire that he had not touched the runner on a steal attempt (an "exhibition of honor, not common in some clubs"), so that the umpire's out call was reversed.[47] Such precise and lofty considerations were undoubtedly beyond the purview of the more social and less competitive clubs, like the Blackstone of Louisville, each of whose players, the *Louisville Daily Courier* reported, at its exercises "has a small boy to run the bases for him after he bats the ball, while he sits down in the shade."[48]

The nationally distributed sporting newspapers were useful in resolving points of confusion by printing its correspondence from readers, as when *Wilkes' Spirit of the Times* informed a reader that "the man running to second base must be put out on that base, and not by a ball thrown to the base he has just left."[49]

Pitching

Nothing in the NABBP rules was more contentious than pitching, particularly the question, "What is a fair delivery?" The answer depended on the umpire. The *New York Sunday Mercury* reported in its extensive coverage of the Union of Morrisania club's venture into Connecticut that the umpire (Hall of Famer Chadwick, then a Brooklyn journalist and NABBP Rules Committee member) in one match strictly enforced the GNYC interpretation, while a local umpiring a subsequent match interpreted the rule much more liberally.[50]

Grounds

The *Sunday Mercury* also pointed out in the same article (immediately above) that even the nicest of country grounds weren't quite up to GNYC standards: at Norwich, the outfield was small, seats weren't provided for ladies, and the foul lines were not chalked, as the rules required.[51]

Being a new club sometimes meant coping with new grounds. The *Rochester Evening Express* reported the problems posed by the ground marked out by the new Star B.B.C.:

> First, it is rough, and any attempt to grade it will prevent the use of it for this season; second, the position of the sun with reference to the grounds

is bad; and thirdly, the large tree in the center of the Square interferes with the center fielder.[52]

Misbehavin'

The *Buffalo Commercial* chastised the "young gentlemen" of a ball club whose "profane and obscene language" had been complained of by neighbors of its grounds.[53] The lads' seniors could be worse: The *St. Louis Dispatch* noted the occurrence of a game during which "plenty of beer was consumed by both sides," climaxed by a "finale, when all hands went in for a free fight. There appeared to be a 'right smart' of scoring done by both sides...The whole transaction was disgraceful in the extreme..."[54] Particularly when, as in this case, the game was played on a Sunday.

Unaccustomed Scrutiny

Beyond putting a team's success (or lack of it) on display for family, friends, and the public in a numerically presented game summary, newspapers would occasionally print the story play by play. Given the newness of the game in some locales, reporters would note each play and add comments. The example in the *Janesville* (WI) *Daily Gazette* on October 15 is larded with descriptions of "weak" blows, complaints that runners did not "follow up," thereby not making as many bases as they should have, and other, obscure examples of contemporary slang ("lime and water").[55]

Mismatches

With (often) few clubs available for matches in their vicinity, country matches could have extremely one-sided results. The play by play reported immediately above detailed a Janesville loss to a Beloit (Wisconsin) club by a score of 61–9, which in the spirit of the time did not prevent the losers from providing the customary post-game hospitality.[56]

Banquets

When the sound and fury of competition had ceased, it was time to get down to having a good time. The *Leavenworth* (KS) *Bulletin* described the festivities following the locals' match with the Antelope Club of Kansas City, considered for the "championship of Kansas and Upper Missouri," as follows: "The boys were in the best of spirits at supper, and a great deal better than the best, afterward." After supper, speeches, and singing in the company of representatives of the press and prominent invited guests, all trooped off to the local Opera House.[57] Occasionally clubs added a more forward-looking program: the Diamond State club of Wilmington, Delaware, equipped a gym for its players' use.[58] Meanwhile, the *Louisville Journal* reported that the Olympic of Louisville was forming an offseason Literary and Debating Society.[59]

Spectator Behavior

Spectator behavior reportedly ran the gamut from exemplary to execrable, even in the same region. The *New York Sunday Mercury* coverage of the Union of Morrisania club's Connecticut trip noted above mentioned both fair-minded, polite behavior and rampant heckling. At all stops, cooperation by the local club members and police was necessary to clear the crowd from the field itself prior to the game.[60] Also in Connecticut, the *Waterbury Daily American* noted that near the end of one interclub match a spectator stole the game ball.[61] (The thief was nabbed.) Notably, only a single example of spectators leaving a one-sided match early can be cited, in the *Springfield* (MA) *Republican*, an eventual 68–20 loss for a team of locals in which the deficit was 35–12 after seven innings, and which ended as a four-hour marathon.[62] The collection of accounts of rude spectator behavior at a "country" match must be headed by the report in the *Urbana* (OH) *Union* that its locals' treatment at a match in Springfield included such "insulting and indecent" spectator behavior that a New Yorker in attendance was appalled.[63]

Uniforms

Whether because of their youth, or because uniforms were thought helpful in developing a team spirit, clubs that could afford to got themselves dolled up, like the Stonewall Club of Richmond, Virginia, who sported "pants [that] are red, and cut in the loose Zouave style; shirt white; cap red, trimmed with blue; a purple sash and morocco belt, inscribed with the letters 'S.B.B.C.'"[64] Many of course couldn't afford any such thing. The *Burlington* (VT) *Times* noted disdainfully that a visiting team was in full uniform, while the locals had only hats.[65]

Gambling

Gambling was endemic in American society, and was typically a feature of senior matches, such as one between the Mutual of New York City and the "country" Union of Lansingburgh, New York. The *Albany Morning Express*'s account emphasized the abrupt change during the game of the available betting odds as the game—a shocking upset by the Union—progressed.[66] An alternative form is spelled out in a match challenge printed in the *Boston Journal*: apparently just to make things more interesting, each side was to put up $100, to go to the winner.[67]

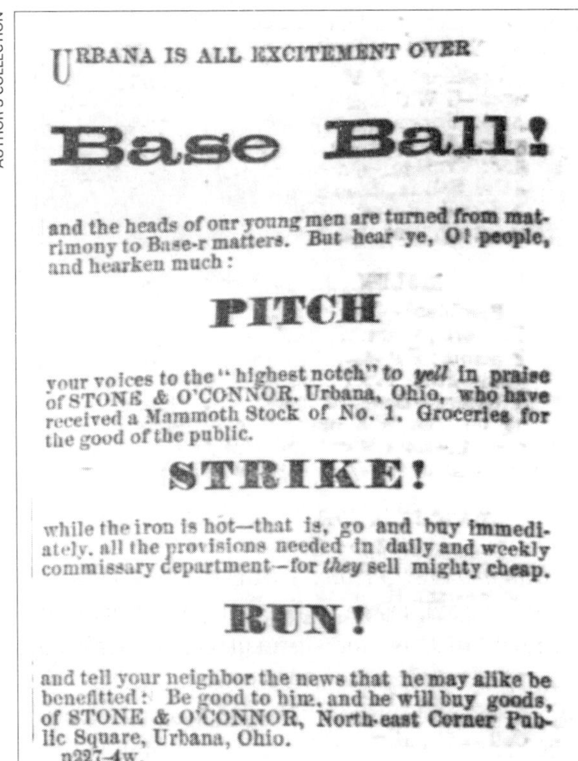

AUTHOR'S COLLECTION

Latching onto the boom of 1866, retailers all over the country drew attention by theming their advertising, as in this example from the Urbana (*OH*) Union *of August 22.*

TRIPS AND TOURS

The spring also brought a revival of plans for intercity trips and tours to the baseball hinterlands by prominent clubs. In 1860, perhaps taking its cue from the widely-publicized tour to New York State and Canada in 1859 by a squad of cricketers known as the "All-England Eleven," the wealthy Excelsior Club of Brooklyn—which had set its sights on wresting the unofficial GNYC baseball championship from the rival Atlantic of Brooklyn—sent its squad, beefed-up by promising recruits after the 1859 season, on a celebrated tour of New York State and later in the season to the South, vanquishing all comers and drawing large crowds and positive publicity. Occasional, more limited road trips continued during the war, but no similar tours were attempted. With peace, the Atlantic, the National of Washington, and the Athletic all planned extensive excursions.[68]

The lions and tigers of the game were not the only clubs eyeing the open road. "Country" clubs with little or no suitable competition in their locales looked to neighboring communities for opponents, both for variety and to stimulate local interest. Following the custom in GNYC of staging welcomes for out-of-town clubs, the host club and community would usually make its own effort to be hospitable, as in the following account of the visit of the Excelsior Club of Columbus, Ohio, to Circleville, about 27 miles distant:

> ...on the afternoon of Thursday last, several carriage-loads of Excelsiors (including the first nine) left town for the scene of action. When about two miles this side of Circleville the party were met with a deputation from the Eureka Club, the challenging party. After mutual handshaking all around, the party, headed by the gentlemen of Circleville, proceeded to their destination. They were escorted to the Pickaway House, where quarters were provided for them; soon after, supper was announced, to which ample justice was done. This over, the Excelsiors, under the escort of the Eurekas, were shown around their pleasant city and enjoyed themselves in various ways, passing the evening very pleasantly.[69]

A "pic-nic and dance" followed the game the next day, a 47 to 39 win for the Excelsior.

Neglect of hospitality, as was reported by a correspondent to the *Rochester Evening Express*, was correspondingly resented:

> Enclosed please find the score of a game played at Brockport, between the Churchville Club, of Churchville, and the Brockport Club...The game passed off very pleasantly, but after it was concluded the players went toward the Union House, and the Brockport players, *en route* quietly dispersed, leaving their guests to look out for themselves, who, after supper, departed for home, not one of the Brockport Club being present to extend any of the usual courtesies to their visitors. It is also customary, we believe, for the victorious club to receive a ball as a trophy of victory; and when we give the Brockport players another chance for such inhospitable treatment, it will be when there is no such place as "CHURCHVILLE."[70]

Churchville had thrashed their hosts, 61–36... which was no excuse for such rudeness.

Travel by train enlarged the territory in which an ambitious "country" club could search for suitable opposition. The Louisville Club of Louisville, champions of its city and—for lack of in-state competition—the champions of Kentucky, arranged a best-of-three match with the Cumberland Club of Nashville for the championship of Kentucky and Tennessee. The match was at times grandly proclaimed the championship of the South. The *Louisville Journal* dispatched a reporter to travel with the Louisville squad and a sizable contingent of Louisville ballists, other guests, and railroad officials, and printed the result. The party was seen off by other well-wishers. Traveling overnight to avoid the "dull and tiresome" 185-mile day trip, they enjoyed sleeping-car accommodations, in which their rows of seats were "transformed...(into) a regular succession of sleeping apartments with all the rich and elegant appointments pertaining thereto." The *Journal*'s reporter, who may have known little about baseball, was comparatively silent about the game itself, a 39–23 victory for Louisville, but he waxed eloquently and in detail about the generous hospitality afforded the travelers by the Nashville baseball fraternity.[71] The *Journal* didn't long remain satisfied, however. After witnessing a sloppily-played game shortly thereafter, the following appeared on August 24: "Why can't we have a match game with some Eastern club—the Atlantics or Athletics?"[72]

Even the first-class senior GNYC clubs could find this sort of baseball nirvana on tour. The Union of Morrisania was a club only on the fringe of GNYC but long-established and in 1866 a championship contender. Its tour of Connecticut included a memorable stop in Waterbury, described in the *New York Clipper*:

> ...a scene was presented to the delighted gaze of the Unions which will be remembered with pleasure for years hence. The Waterbury ball grounds are more extensive than any we know of, and in the picturesque surroundings of the field and in the natural facilities afforded for spectators to witness the proceedings of a match, this ground surpasses any in the country...back of the catcher's position were located rows of seats occupied by hundreds of ladies, the majority being among the fairest and best of Connecticut's daughters. Indeed, so brilliant an attendance of the fair sex at a ball match we never witnessed before... The game over (Union 71, Waterbury 11), the contestants returned to the hotel, and at 8PM. sat down to an excellent supper, speeches and singing being the order of the evening.[73]

Waterbury subsequently received offers to journey to GNYC to play, and made the trip in mid-September, playing three games. They posted one win, over the Eagle of New York City, one of the pioneer clubs but no longer first-class competitors.[74]

AUTHOR'S COLLECTION

The simultaneous crazes for base ball and ice skating spawned ice base ball, using base ball equipment and modified rules.

Touring clubs also scored national publicity. Games played by the Hudson River Club of Newburgh, New York, during its tour of western New York State were reported as far away as Iowa and as far south as Louisville. The Union Club of Lansingburgh's unexpected defeat of the Mutual Club, an annual GNYC championship contender, also enhanced interest when the Mutual traveled to Lansingburgh for a return match.

Road trips in the warmer South rolled on past the end of the season in the north, as the Mississippi Valley Club of Vicksburg visited New Orleans just before Christmas by yet another mode of transportation, river steamer, to play the more experienced locals for the championship of their respective states. They absorbed two one-sided defeats, but doubtless picked up valuable points of the game.

In end-of-season notes, two nationally distributed papers covering baseball extolled the effect of the tours. *Frank Leslie's Illustrated Newspaper* declared on November 24 that nothing else "had done so much to advance the popularity of the game,"[75] while the *New York Sunday Mercury* on November 4 lauded trips and tours for having "tended to bring not only the [base ball] fraternity, but men in all conditions and relations of life, together in the common bond of friendship."[76]

TOURNAMENTS

Tournaments were already a popular phenomenon in the 1860s, though baseball tournaments are recorded only occasionally before 1866. *The Pantagraph*, of Bloomington, Illinois, hosted a baseball tournament, having already recorded tournaments in chess, billiards, and fire-engine company races. For "country" baseball clubs, gathering three or more clubs for competition for a tournament championship was inseparable from civic boosterism.

The tournament announced for Rockford, Illinois, in June was typical, and one of the largest of its kind in 1866. It was promoted thusly in the *Chicago Tribune*: "This tournament promises to surpass any ever before held in the country—especially in the West."[77] Ten clubs from four states enrolled, with prizes galore, donated by civic-minded individuals, businesses, and groups. While the *Rockford Weekly Register-Gazette* concluded that "The Tournament ended with nothing to disturb its harmony and triumph,"[78] there was the matter of the championship final between the Excelsior of Chicago and the Bloomington of Bloomington, which the latter conceded without playing the game because they would have had to begin it immediately after playing their semi-final, while the Excelsior would be playing its first game of the day. Either the schedule was short one day, too many teams had been allowed to enter, or a second field should have been prepared.

As it stood, the Excelsior were awarded the championship prize without earning it on the field. The correspondent reporting on the tournament to *Wilkes' Spirit of the Times*, which published lengthy reports, claimed that "the Bloomington boys were satisfied with the laurels they had already won, and gracefully relinquished the first prize to the Excelsiors."[79] Unlikely as such magnanimity may sound, the *Pantagraph* presumably got the straight story from the club when it returned home to a serenade from Kadel's Silver Band and a parade (for those players "not too exhausted"). It reported on July 2 that the tournament format and schedule called for them to play both the Cream City Club of Milwaukee and the Excelsior back-to-back, and the club felt itself too tired and banged-up to do both, and so opted to only play the Cream City to decide second place, yielding first place.[80] Undaunted, the Bloomington club held a meeting a few days later and resolved to hold its own tournament—a four-day event, instead of three, as in Rockford.[81]

The glitch at the Rockford tournament was dwarfed by the tempest stirred by the 4-day, 13-club Western New York State invitational event in September in Auburn, convened to crown a champion of the northern and western parts of the state. First, the weather forced a two-week postponement to October 1. Six of the original 13 invitees dropped out; five replacements were found. A fifth day had to be added to the schedule. Finally, the winner of the gold ball designating the tournament champion, and the champion of most of New York State, was disputed. The *New York Clipper* summarized the situation thusly, probably the tournament sponsors' viewpoint:

> The award of the prizes offered by the managers of the tourney lately held at Auburn has given rise to a great deal of disaffection among some of the competing clubs, especially those from Rochester, who claim that as they were successful in every game played, they were entitled to the first and second prizes...and refused to play the final and Champion game unless both prizes were thrown in...the judges decided that the Niagara club, of Buffalo...should have a chance to compete in the closing game. The Rochester clubs refused and withdrew from the tournament...the silver ball (for second place) was therefore awarded to the Niagaras.[82]

Some tournaments were timed to be attractions at county agricultural fairs held in September or October. One particularly ambitious such event, held in Sussex County in New Jersey's northwestern corner, was announced in the *Trenton State Gazette*. While most tournament sponsors were content with crowning a county champion, silver-ball competitions were offered for all comers in order to crown county, regional, and state champions.[83]

Tournaments proved to be a country phenomenon. William Cammeyer's effort to stage a tournament among first-class senior clubs from Greater New York City and Philadelphia at his Union Grounds in Brooklyn petered out. Given that there were hundreds of clubs in the area, Cammeyer decided to name the clubs to play, and as the *Brooklyn Union* reported, "The clubs named to take part in the tournament gave it the cold shoulder, each giving some trivial excuse for not playing."[84]

BASEBALL IN BUSINESS AND CULTURE

A national game of baseball played under a common rule code emerged from a particular set of circumstances in a particular area, and the game returned the favor, finding its place in contemporary business and culture. As the national game spread in "country" areas in 1866, that contribution spread as well. Baseball's dominant contribution to the lives of its players and spectators was entertainment. The *Raleigh Daily Sentinel* praised the nightly diversion provided by clubs exercising on the Capitol square.[85] Game accounts in any detail invariably include the crowd's size and often its behavior.

Clubs could also be civic-minded: clubs in Urbana, Ohio, played a benefit game for the community band (which of course could then entertain at their games).[86] Clubs were also seen as an indicator of civic advancement: The *Daily Gate City* (Keokuk, Iowa), in noting the importance of sport to the public, opined that baseball games were one sign that "we are reaching a highly metropolitan state of civilization."[87] Cynics, reported the *Daily Illinois State Register* (Springfield), "insinuate that the spread of the (*baseball*) disease is very much encouraged by those interested in the pecuniary fortunes of the street railways", but dismissed the accusation as a "slander."[88]

That the baseball rules developed in GNYC, home of a nationally distributed sporting press, became the "national game" wasn't a foregone conclusion, but neither was it a coincidence. That press must be credited also with developing a demand for baseball as a source of both group exercise and public entertainment. "Country" newspapermen, however, were divided on the subject of baseball's newsworthiness. The *Daily Empire* (Dayton, Ohio) waxed sarcastic: "The *Journal* of this morning don't say a word on the important subject of 'base ball.' Some of it's [*sic*] most attentive readers are so uncharitable as to say they are greatly pleased with the omission."[89] The *New Orleans Daily Crescent* printed correspondence from a reader in Mobile blasting newspapers in general for covering such trivialities.[90] On the positive side, a journalistic milestone appeared in Nashville, where the Eureka Base Ball Club advertised a benefit game in a German-language newspaper, the *Tennessee Staatszeitung*.[91] "Country" journalists also began experiencing the delights of covering road trips. The account of the "local news" reporter of the *Rockford Daily Register Gazette* describes an experience far removed from the future grind of traveling scribes road-tripping with professional clubs: He traveled (by train and lake steamer) with other Rockfordians, was "taken in hand" at the destination (Milwaukee) and given a city tour which included (it being Milwaukee) an immense brewery (with samples). The return trip featured a reportedly riotous six-hour layover (as far as was possible in that "quiet city") in Kenosha, Wisconsin.[92]

An appetite among the public for yet more baseball news was detected in any case: a weekly covering Connecticut clubs, *Bat and Ball*, was founded, and its news found its way occasionally into the general press.[93] The *Louisville Daily Courier* noted a proposal for a similar local publication.[94] The *Trenton State Gazette*, for one, apparently inundated with requests to print the result of junior-club games, announced that it would henceforth charge $1 for the service.[95]

Though NABBP-rules baseball spread to southern cities from Richmond to New Orleans, barely twelve months after Lee's surrender was evidently too soon for a northern game to escape post-war bitterness entirely. The *Richmond Daily Dispatch* printed the reply of the Richmond Base Ball Club to a challenge received by the Union Club, also of Richmond:

> ...the Richmond Base-Ball Club does not desire and will not play the Union Club a single game. We are not, nor do we expect to be, members of the National Base-Ball Convention. Our reason: we are Southerners.[96]

The story was widely reported in the north. The *Daily Dispatch* later criticized the Richmond Club's attitude, even after learning that the Union Club was "entirely composed of "Federal officers" and stated that its attitude was not shared by other Richmond clubs.[97] The Richmond Club seems to have stuck to its guns; when the National Club of Washington (DC) visited later in the season, it played the Union and Pastime clubs, but not the Richmond.

Piggybacking on a fundraising format noted in the Philadelphia area, whereby charity events gave baseball equipment as a prize to the club receiving the most votes purchased at the event, a restaurant in Mifflintown, Pennsylvania, was reported to be offering the same for paying customers.[98] A rural ad writer whose work appeared in the *Star and Enterprise* of Newville, Pennsylvania, was far more adroit, crafting a three-verse baseball song mentioning local clubs and urging baseballists to buy at a local haberdasher's establishment.[99] More conventional ads settled for incorporating baseball jargon into the sales pitch.[100]

But by far the largest financial impact of the game in the "country" doubtless remained the dollars spent on gambling and wagers, as it had been from the sport's beginnings in the 1850s in GNYC. The correspondent to the *Detroit Free Press* from Lapeer, Michigan, reporting on the enthusiasm engendered by a recent match, cited as proof that "five to one could be had as often as desired."[101] The *Cleveland Plain Dealer* found it noteworthy that a club in Springfield, Ohio, had voted to expel any member found guilty of betting on a game.[102]

Two final miscellaneous incidents of cultural penetration can be noted: First, a conference of feminists in Albany listed the exclusion of women from the game among the "degradations" to which the "false laws of society" subjected their sex.[103] Finally, the "good old days" attitude had already arrived in Cazenovia, New York, where the local club planned an old-timers' game featuring past players "who won laurels in the early days of the game."[104]

BASEBALL HUMOR

Baseball has throughout its modern history been a laughing matter. Its early development, from 1845 to around 1865, by amateurs in social clubs combining play with social occasions perhaps got the ball rolling. In this amateur era, the first generation of American young adults were playing the game on a widespread basis and drawing a large, enthusiastic following, to the puzzlement of many and the amusement of others.

The newness of the sport as played under NABBP rules, particularly in "country" areas, obliged its proponents to explain the game to the public, a task in which writers of humor were happy to assist, after their own inimitable fashion. American newspaper readers of the 1860s were apparently unreasonably fond of the humble play on words, to which the English language, with its plethora of homonyms and homophones, lends itself admirably. No form of baseball humor was more common in the 1860s, as in the following example:

> Fired with the desire to promote the advancement of "our National Game", as much as it lies in my power, I have culled from my experience the following essential deductions, that may awaken the fraternity to a keener sense of the technicalities and "fine points"— so to speak, of the athletic sport. We do this in order that its future *bat*-les may be arranged upon some substantially equable *base*-is. You will observe that we *throw in* a few facts that may serve to put out some erroneous impressions that *run* in the heads of enthusiastic but mystified novices, who have caught the athle-*tick* mania.

- The regulation ball differs from the *bawl* of a teething baby.
- The *bats* are not nocturnal animals, although they may sometimes "fly."
- The pitcher is not composed of earthenware—nor does he use resinous gum to *pitch* the ball.
- The *base* men are not reprobates or always wicked.
- The *field* men are not scarecrows or farmers, and the strikers are not all blacksmiths or members of working men's associations.
- A good *catch* is not a swindle.
- A good *throw* may be done without a dice box.
- To throw the ball *home* does not require it to reach your residence.
- "*Going all out*" is not synonymous with strenuous effort.
- The *base tender* does not signify a *delicate base*; nor does *holding* your base require it to be raised from the ground.
- *Ruling a player out* is not done with a yard stick.
- *Stopping the ball* is not like the police arresting the manager and prompter at a masquerade.
- A foul *ball* is not allowed; but if caught the umpire may *bawl* "a foul."
- To *steal* a base is not felonious.[105]

So soon after the Civil War, humor with a military flavor also remained in vogue, as in the following game account:

> Companies 'C' and 'K', 5th New York State National Guards, played their long talked of game of base ball, at Jones Square, yesterday afternoon, and although most of the players had had no drill in base ball tactics, the performance was a very creditable one. Co. K is said to have had the best outside skirmishers, while Co. C seemed to have had better bases of operation. Ayers, at 1st base, captured twelve prisoners—four flying, and eight headed off by well-directed shots from the inside skirmishers. The rear guard (rear of the bat) was well attended to by both sides. Corp. Tuttle, of Co. C, made six shots and no misses, and Private Fulton, of Co. K, made seven misses and no shots.[106]

Great fun was had with accounts of games between "muffin" teams, unskilled players who were either social members of baseball clubs, or *ad hoc* groups, sometimes with a particular characteristic. These were "friendly" games in which inconvenient rules could be waived, such as in the match between two 13-man teams of "heavies":

> On this inning occurred the most extraordinary feat of agility your reporter ever witnessed. While one of the Naugatuck 300-pounders was running to the second base he encountered the City second baseman some ten feet from his base, which would have discouraged a smaller man, but his weight giving him courage, the Center man leaped over the head of the second baseman with the agility of an ox, and amidst a round of thundering applause cleared the intervening

> space of ten feet and landed flat on his base, a straddled base being charged against him for so doing. The world has never been jarred so since David slew Goliath...[107]

The same delight at the frailties of others could animate tales of injuries sustained, as in the *Jackson* (MI) *Citizen Patriot*:

> The usual amount of accidents occurred, the main ones being experienced by Paddock...who carried home with him a very sore finger and somewhat weak from loss of blood, and Hulin... who had quite a lively search for his wind, he being knocked down while fielding a ball.[108]

CLOSING CONTROVERSIES

Given the boom across the country, the 10th NABBP annual convention in December 1866 promised to exceed in geographic reach all those which had gone before it. The nationally distributed *New York Clipper* printed a notice that all proposed amendments to rules and regulations required submission to the NABBP Rules Committee by November 10, one month before the convention, and provided the rules governing admission to the Association.[109] The NABBP Judiciary Committee met on October 24 "to investigate charges made by the Irvington Club, of New Jersey, against the Active Club, New York" over use of ineligible players.[110] The *Philadelphia City Item* specifically called on its "country friends" to make application for membership and foretold strong action at the convention concerning the hiring and direct payment of players. Indirect compensation had long been a standard practice, but direct payment of salaries was contrary to NABBP rules. The paper had been campaigning against it all season.[111]

"Country" clubs began to hold meetings to consider membership and elect convention delegates.[112] The NABBP secretary, A.H. Rogers, in a letter published in the *Philadelphia City Item* (and elsewhere) noted that several such applications had already been received, from "as far west as Kansas."[113] The list of 93 clubs applying for admission printed in the *New York Sunday Mercury* included 70 from the "country," representing 15 states, and including the Pioneer, of Portland, Oregon.[114] The *New York Clipper* reported that over two hundred clubs would be represented in all;[115] with two delegates per club allowed, attendance would consist of 400 to 500 men. Recognition of "country" growth in the affairs of the NABBP also appeared in the *New York Sunday Mercury*'s call for the admission in some form to the new regional and state associations.[116] Returning to the subject immediately prior to the convention, it noted that while the NABBP's existing constitution did not permit the immediate admission of the associations, it expected that in 1867 membership status in proportion to the number of clubs represented would be in place, and foretold that the organization would in the next few years transform into a national body of state associations, citing as an indication of the need an estimate that existing associations enrolled over 300 clubs presently outside the NABBP.[117]

The convention began on the afternoon of December 12 at Clinton Hall in New York City. The *Sunday Mercury*'s tally in its post-convention report listed 209 clubs represented, including 129 from "country" areas. By the time the convention adjourned at 3:00 AM the following morning, those assembled had heard reports from the Judiciary Committee (which either dismissed or continued all complaints upon grounds of procedural irregularities), considered and passed several changes to its constitution, bylaws, and playing rules, elected officers for 1867, and resolved other routine housekeeping matters. Delegates from "country" clubs were appointed to the Rules, Judiciary, and Printing committees.

Also of import to "country" clubs was the change to the NABBP's constitution regarding state associations. Associations were required to represent at least eighteen clubs, and received two votes at the convention for each club represented. The *New York Sunday Mercury* considered that the result "will have the effect of at once creating such State Associations in every State of the Union."[118] The convention was reported, in less detail, in newspapers across the country. A post-NABBP convention of the regional Northwestern Association met in Chicago on December 19, noted the NABBP's action encouraging state associations, but voted against disbandment.[119]

Games continued in California and the South to the end of the calendar year, but for its part the *New York Sunday Mercury* offered a fitting conclusion on the status of the sport, emphasizing the magnitude of the expansion of "country" baseball in 1866: "North, South, East, and West, the game flourishes to an extent hitherto unprecedented, and it may now be regarded as one of the most popular 'institutions of this 'great country' of ours."[120] ■

Notes

1. Protoball.org, http://protoball.org/Bob_Tholkes%27_RIM_Tabulation
2. *When Johnny Came Sliding Home*, William J. Ryczek (McFarland & Co., Jefferson, NC, 1998), 57
3. "Base Ball," *New York Clipper*, March 17, 1866.
4. "Our National Game," *Philadelphia City Item*, March 17, 1866.

5. "The Base Ball Season of 1866," *Weekly Racine Advocate*, March 25, 1866.
6. "Affairs About Home," *Boston Herald*, November 9, 1865.
7. "Base Ball," *Chicago Daily Inter-Ocean*, December 7, 1865.
8. "Our National Game," *Philadelphia City Item*, December 23, 1865.
9. "Base Ball," *Jackson Citizen Patriot*, April 26, 1866.
10. "Convention of Base Ball Players," *Sacramento Daily Union*, August 4, 1866.
11. "Sports and Pastimes," *New York Sunday Mercury*, December 23, 1866.
12. http://protoball.org/Bob_Tholkes%27_RIM_Tabulation.
13. "Base Ball," *Rochester Evening Express*, August 13, 1866.
14. "Base-Ball," *Jamestown* (NY) *Journal*, September 7, 1866.
15. "Base Ball," *Daily Evansville* (IN) *Journal*, November 3, 1866.
16. "Stonewall Base Ball Club," *Spirit of Jefferson* (Charlestown, WV), September 4, 1866.
17. "Base Ball," *Rock Island* (IL) *Evening Argus*, November 12, 1866.
18. "Base-Ball Matters," *Wilkes' Spirit of the Times*, March 24, 1866.
19. "The California Base Ball Championship," N*ew York Clipper*, March 31, 1866.
20. "The City," *New Orleans Times*, January 10, 1866.
21. "A Base Ball Club…," *Belvidere* (IL) *Standard*, May 29, 1866.
22. "A Good Feature," *Wheeling* (WV) *Daily Register*, August 6, 1866.
23. "Violent Exercise and Cholera," *Cleveland Plain Dealer*, August 16, 1866.
24. "Base Ball Clubs," *Raleigh Daily Sentinel*, September 5, 1866.
25. "Sports and Pastimes," *Brooklyn Union*, December 3, 1866.
26. "Local Affairs," *Cecil Whig* (Elkton, MD), July 21, 1866.
27. "Base Ball," *Richmond* (VA) *Daily Dispatch*, August 31, 1866.
228. "Local and Personal," *Western Reserve Chronicle* (Warren, OH), September 12, 1866.
29. "Local Matters," *Richmond* (VA) *Daily Dispatch*, September 12, 1866.
30. http://protoball.org/Pre-pro_Baseball.
31. "Base-Ball Matters," *Wilkes' Spirit of the Times*, August 4, 1866.
32. "Base Ball," *Hancock Jeffersonian* (Findlay, OH), July 13, 1866.
33. "Local Intelligence," *Lancaster* (PA) *Intelligencer*, September 8, 1866.
34. "City News," *Cleveland Leader*, October 22, 1866.
35. "Base Ball," *Chestertown* (MD) *Transcript*, October 13, 1866.
36. "Local Matters," *Charleston Daily Observer*, May 24, 1866.
37. "Mail Gleanings," *Philadelphia Inquirer*, November 6, 1866.
38. "Local and Personal," *Bedford* (PA) *Gazette*, November 16, 1866.
39. "Iowa Items," *Daily Iowa State Register*, June 27, 1866.
40. "City Items," *Rock Island Evening Argus*, November 12, 1866.
41. "The CIty," *Leavenworth* (KS) *Bulletin*, May 28, 1866.
42. "Base Ball," *Philadelphia Sunday Mercury*, November 4, 1866.
43. "From Jacksonville," *Daily Illinois State Register*, May 31, 1866.
44. "Local and General," *Bradford* (Towanda, PA) *Reporter*, July 12, 1866.
45. "Editor Advertiser," *Tipton Advertiser*, August 2, 1866.
46. "The City," *The Tennessean* (Nashville), October 7, 1866.
47. "City and Vicinity," *Buffalo Courier*, August 8, 1866.
48. "Running the Thing into the Ground," *Louisville Daily Courier*, October 1, 1866.
49. "Base-Ball Matters," *Wilkes' Spirit of the Times*, August 18, 1866.
50. "Sports and Pastimes," *New York Sunday Mercury*, July 29, 1866.
51. "Sports and Pastimes."
52. "Local Intelligence," *Rochester Evening Express*, August 1, 1866.
53. "Brevities," *Buffalo Commercial*, September 1, 1866.
54. "Local News," *St. Louis Dispatch*, September 17, 1866.
55. "Base Ball," *Janesville* (WI) *Daily Gazette*, October 15, 1866.
56. "Base Ball," *Janesville* (WI) *Daily Gazette.*
57. "The City," *Leavenworth* (KS) *Bulletin*, November 17, 1866.
58. "Our National Game," *Philadelphia City Item*, November 24, 1866.
59. "Base Ball and Its Benefits," *Louisville Journal*, November 26, 1866.
60. "Sports and Pastimes," *New York Sunday Mercury*, July 29, 1866.
614. "Local Intelligence," *Waterbury* (CT) *Daily American*, September 11, 1866.
62. "The Base-Ball Matches on Saturday," *Springfield* (MA) *Republican*, September 10, 1866.
63. "City and County," *Urbana* (OH) *Union*, November 21, 1866.
64. "Local Matters," *Richmond Daily Dispatch*, August 22, 1866.
65. "Base Ball–St. Albans vs. Burlington," *Burlington* (VT) *Times*, September 15, 1866.
66. "Local Department," *Albany Morning Express*, August 29, 1866.
667. "Base Ball in New Hampshire," *Boston Journal*, September 1, 1866.
68. "Ball Play," *New York Clipper*, August 4, 1866
69. "Local News," *Daily Ohio Statesman*, July 2, 1866.
70. "Local Intelligence," *Rochester Evening* Express, July 18, 1866.
71. "Base Ball," *Louisville Journal*, August 3, 1866.
72. "Base Ball," *Louisville Journal*, August 24, 1866.
73. "Base Ball," *New York Clipper*, August 4, 1866
74. "The Excursion of the Waterbury B. B. Club," *Waterbury* (CT) *Daily American*, September 25, 1866.
75. "Our Base Ball Illustrations," *Frank Leslie's Illustrated Newspaper*, November 24, 1866.
76. "Sports and Pastimes," *New York Sunday Mercury*, November 4, 1866.
77. "N. W. Base Ball Tournament," *Chicago Tribune*, June 25, 1866.
78. "The Great Tournament," *Rockford Weekly Register-Gazette*, June 30, 1866.
79. "Base-Ball Matters," *Wilkes' Spirit of the Times*, July 14, 1866.
80. "City and County," *Pantagraph* (Bloomington, IL), July 2, 1866.
81. "City and County," *Pantagraph* (Bloomington, IL), July 9, 1866.
82. "Ball Play," *New York Clipper*, October 27, 1866.
83. "Base Ball Tournament," *Trenton State Gazette*, August 18, 1866.
84. "General City News," *Brooklyn Union*, September 10, 1866.
85. "General News," *Raleigh Daily Sentinel*, October 5, 1866.
86. "New Custom," *Cleveland Leader*, August 21, 1866.
87. "News Items," *Daily Gate City* (Keokuk, IA), September 1, 1866.
88. "Springfield," *Daily Illinois State Register* (Springfield), September 10, 1866.
89. "What's the Matter?," *Daily Empire* (Dayton, OH), September 11, 1866.
90. "Letter from New York," *New Orleans Daily Crescent*, November 16, 1866.
91. "Grosse Ball," *Tennessee Staatszeitung* (Nashville), September 22, 1866.
92. "Splendid Base Ball Match," *Rockford Daily Register Gazette*, August 25, 1866.
93. "Sundries," *Hartford Courant*, October 16, 1866.
94. "Town Trifles," *Louisville Daily Courier*, October 20, 1866.
95. "Base Ball," *Trenton State Gazette*, November 3, 1866.
96. "Local Matters," *Richmond Daily Dispatch*, October 2, 1866.
97. "Virginia News," *Alexandria Gazette*, October 9, 1866.
98. "Local Items," *Altoona Tribune*, May 5, 1866.
99. "Base Ball," *Star and Enterprise* (Newville, PA), August 18,1866.
100. "Groceries &c," *Urbana* (OH) *Union*, September 26, 1866.
101. "Base Ball Matches," *Detroit Free Press*, August 21, 1866.
102. "State News," *Cleveland Plain Dealer*, September 27, 1866.
103. "Woman's Rights," *Brookville* (PA) *Republican*, November 28, 1866.
104. "Town & Country News," *Cazenovia* (NY) *Republican*, June 13, 1866.
105. "Base Ball Definitions," *Mystic* (CT) *Pioneer*, September 1, 1866.
106. "Local Intelligence," *Rochester Evening Express*, September 7, 1866.
107. "Local Intelligence," *Waterbury* (CT) *Daily American*, September 13, 1866.
108. "Last Match of the Season," *Jackson* (MI) *Citizen Patriot*, November 12, 1866.
109. "Ball Play," *New York Clipper*, October 20, 1866.
110. "Sports and Pastimes," *New York Sunday Mercury*, October 21, 1866.
111. "Our National Game," *Philadelphia City Item*, October 27, 1766.
112. "Base Ball," *Burlington* (VT) *Daily Times*, October 27, 1866.
113. "Our National Game," *Philadelphia City Item*, November 3, 1866.
114. "Sports and Pastimes," *New York Sunday Mercury*, November 18, 1866.
115. "Ball Play," *New York Clipper*, October 20, 1866.
116. "Sports and Pastimes," *New York Sunday Mercury*, November 25, 1866.
117. "Sports and Pastimes," *New York Sunday Mercury*, December 9, 1866.
118. "Sports and Pastimes," *New York Sunday Mercury*, December 16, 1866.
119. "Base-Ball Convention," *Chicago Daily Interocean*, December 20, 1866.
120. "Sports and Pastimes," *New York Sunday Mercury*, November 25, 1866.

Runs, Runs, and More Runs

Pre-Professional Baseball, By the Numbers

Bruce Allardice

Baseball's post-Civil War period (1866–70) is vitally important to understanding the sport as we know it today. This era had significant changes in rules and equipment, and also saw the sport spread across the continental United States and into Alaska and Hawaii. The first openly professional club, the Cincinnati club, formed in this era, soon followed by others. Baseball progressed from a gentlemanly amateur sport to one increasingly dominated, in the newspapers as well as on the field, by professional players and teams.

Wholly professional baseball organizations began in 1871, with the National Association (NA). But the NA didn't burst forth from a vacuum, but rather evolved from the many amateur, semi-professional, and professional clubs in existence prior to 1871. One key to understanding the nine-club NA is to better understand the 8,000 clubs that came before it. And this especially applies to the subject near and dear to most SABR members—statistics. No previous study has analyzed via statistics how baseball was played in the five years prior to professional baseball organizations. This article hopes to fill that gap, answering such questions as: How many runs were scored in an average game? How many innings were played per game? How long did the games last? When and where were the games played? How did rule and equipment changes impact the game?

In this article I'll set forth the results of a first-ever statistical analysis of the baseball of this period. This research project analyzed all the games played under NABBP[1] rules for 1866-70 reported by the major baseball-covering newspaper of the time, the New York City-based *New York Clipper*. It also compares those numbers to games played prior to 1866.[2] Statistics regarding the pro game are well known from 1871 forward with the formation of the NA, hence the 1870 cutoff.

The 1866–70 data cover reports of 4,984 games,[3] with dates the game was played, scores, where the games were played, game times, and innings played. Not all game reports list all these items. A few lack detailed scores, some don't mention the innings played or date of the game, and many don't mention the time of the game. However, even with these gaps, the data are robust enough for valid analysis. The number of games per year averages almost 1,000, a number far greater than the games played per year in major league baseball during the 19th Century. Almost all these games were played by amateur clubs, a handful considered "first-class" (the country's top clubs, according to the sporting press) or semi-professional, but most truly amateur. The first openly professional team, the Cincinnatis, began play in 1869; several others followed in 1870. Data for "first class" amateur clubs, and professional clubs, are analyzed separately.

So what do the data tell us about amateur/semi-professional baseball in this era?

The general downward trend in scoring is obvious in Chart 1 and perhaps explained by factors mentioned below. There is an anomalous 1868–69 uptick in scoring, perhaps due to top clubs doing tours and playing mismatches against local clubs.

In the years 1869–70 professional teams often played, and roundly defeated, amateur teams. These mismatches reduced the disparity between overall runs per game and first-class clubs' runs per game. The 1870 professional v. professional scoring declined dramatically from 1869. Per below, this may be due to an equipment change (adoption of a "dead" baseball) and improvement in team defenses (also discussed below).

Table 1. Runs Per Game (RPG), 1866–70, by Year

Year	Games	Avg. RPG	Median[4] RPG	1st Class Club RPG[6]	Pro[5] Club RPG	Pro v. Pro RPG
1866	574	63.80	59.5	53.13	–	–
1867	562	65.01	60	62.84	–	–
1868	1054	55.86	50	45.25	–	–
1869	1271	56.01	50	51.63	48.9	43.6
1870	1523	48.97	44	47.23	36.8	30.4
1871						20.94[7]
Average		55.7	50.4			

Overall, runs per game in first-class games were less than in the average amateur contest, professional vs. amateur games less than that, and professional vs. professional lesser still. Professionalizing clubs clearly led to reduced game scores (and game times).

Baseball's rules have always been changing and evolving, and the 1860s saw a number of major rules changes. Some of these impacted scoring. The 1858 rules, now regarded as the starting point of baseball as we know it, were modified in 1863 and 1864 to restrict pitching and to ban the "first bounce out" rule. Umpires were allowed to call "strikes"—but rarely did so prior to 1866.[8] These changes all took a while to become standard practice. The changes resulted in a scoring binge for 1864 and 1865 (see below). However, as the game spread and the skills (particularly fielding skills) became more uniform, scores slowly declined. The rules changes made in the late 1860s were relatively minor and did not markedly affect the game statistics.[9]

Equipment in the 1860s was also ever-changing. The dramatic surge in MLB home runs 2016–20 has led to a welcome focus on the baseballs used in games. Studies have shown that recent balls have slightly different seams from past balls, leading (in one estimate) to fly balls traveling four feet further—increasing the number of home runs. Debate over baseballs in the 1860s was just as spirited, albeit less scientific. For 1868, the weight and circumference of balls was reduced and made uniform, but the elasticity of the balls—their interior composition—was not regulated.[10] Teams could, and did, choose the style of ball they desired for games. And until 1869, most baseballs contained over two ounces of rubber, making for a so-called "lively" or "elastic" ball. Newspapers printed numerous heated discussions about the difference between the lively and the dead balls, and the impact these balls had on scoring. In 1870 the *New York Clipper* linked the elastic ball both to increased scoring and to increased player injuries.[11] Many newspapers made the link explicit: Dead Balls = Fewer Runs.[12] Part of the reason scoring was less in first-class and professional games, compared to the general amateur game, was that the first-class clubs increasingly adopted the dead ball—against the wishes of the fans who, then as well as now, preferred the home run to the single.[13] Baseball pioneer Henry Chadwick repeatedly urged the adoption of the dead ball in his *Clipper* columns. The dead ball was formally adopted at the November 1870 baseball convention.[14] Scoring (at least among professional teams) declined accordingly in 1871.

Chart 1. Average Runs Per Game 1866–71

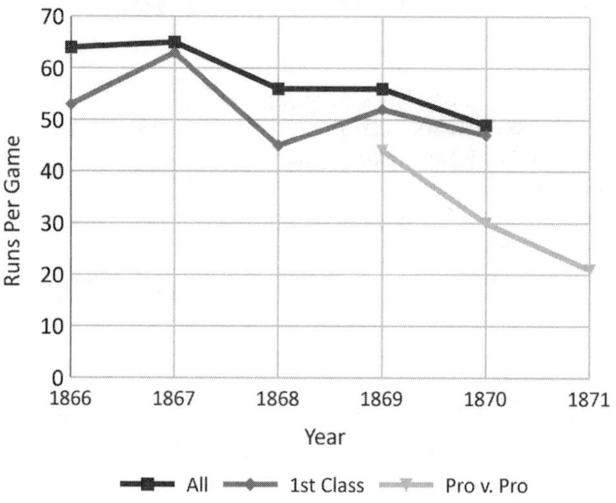

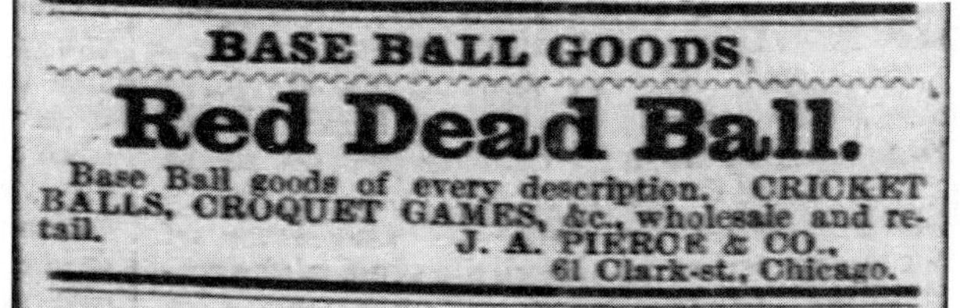
BASE BALL GOODS.
Red Dead Ball.
Base Ball goods of every description. CRICKET BALLS, CROQUET GAMES, &c., wholesale and retail.
J. A. PIERCE & CO.,
61 Clark-st., Chicago.

AUTHOR'S COLLECTION

Ad for dead baseballs in the Chicago Tribune, *August 17, 1870.*

The scoring decrease due to the dead ball could be dramatic. For example, the 1870 Chicago White Stockings switched from the live ball to the dead ball in mid-season. The club's games averaged 35 runs per game the first half of the season, declining to 23 runs (a ⅓ drop) in the second half. Their lowest scoring game of the year, a 9–0 shutout, was played with a dead ball. Looking at the team's head-to-head matchups that year with other professional teams (perhaps the best method for comparison), in eight of the nine instances where the White Stockings played a team more than once, the runs scored in the last game played was less than the first. The only exceptions were the games against Cincinnati, which already used the dead ball. In these nine head-to-heads, the teams averaged 35 RPG for first game, 23 RPG the last. A similar, if smaller, decline can be seen for the Mutuals of New York, who went to the dead ball starting July 6. The Cincinnati club, which always chose the dead ball, showed no such decline in its head-to-head matches.[15]

Baseball in the 1860s featured a batter vs. fielder contest, much more than the batter vs. pitcher contest we see today. Improvements in team defense in the late 1860s played a large part in the reduced scoring. While a few players started to wear gloves (more for protection than as an aid to fielding), what some historians have dubbed the "fielding revolution" relied more on fielders working together rather than as individuals. Baseball pioneer Harry Wright popularized, if he did not initiate, the fielding revolution during the

Chart 2. Comparison to RPG, 1858–70[17]

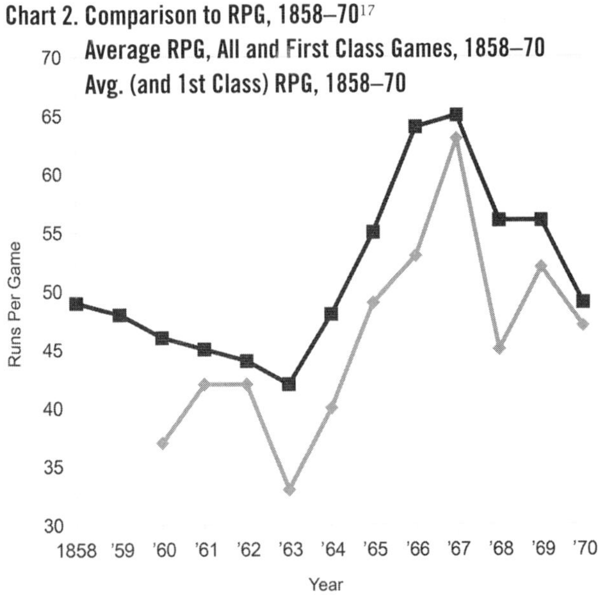

Chart 3. Median RPG, All Games, 1858–70

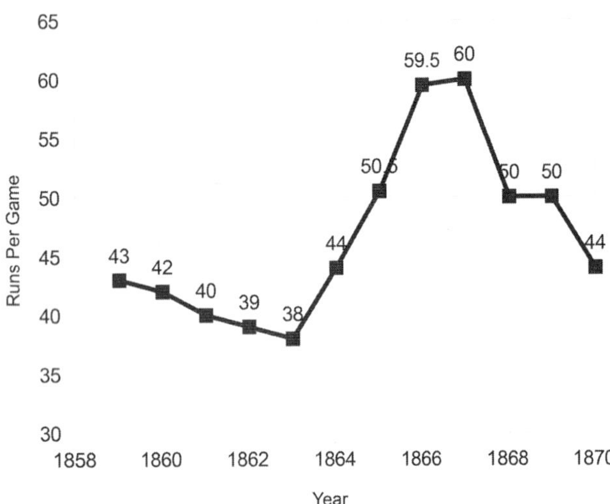

NOTE: The median RPG consistently tracks about 4–5 RPG less than the average RPG.

1869 tour of the Cincinnati club aka the Red Stockings. The thoughtful Wright had his players shift position, depending on the batter and the situation. He also trained his defenders to work together, to back up one another, to play defense as a team rather than as nine individuals. The astounding success of the Red Stockings soon led other teams to copy Wright's stratagems. This appears to have been an additional factor in the reduced scoring for 1869 and 1870.[16]

In the average game, one can see a huge disparity in RPG, from a yearly low of 42 RPG in 1863 to a high of 65 (1867). Scoring trends show three distinct movements: a steady decline 1858–63, followed by a dramatic upsurge 1864–67, followed by another decline 1868–70. As with 1866-70, scoring in first-class club games ran constantly lower than in games overall.

Since a statistical average score includes games with extreme highs and lows in scoring, perhaps a better measure of RPG is the median score per game, shown in Chart 3.

1847–57 RPG

For the curious, I studied all the game scores from 1847–57 listed on the Protoball database of early games. Games prior to 1858 were played under early, pre-nine-inning rules, and thus are not directly comparable to games from 1858 and after. The data nonetheless show a broad similarity to 1858-65 scoring, with 1847–57 games averaging 49 RPG. The average score was 30–19, with an 11 run average margin of victory.[18]

Table 2. High and Low Scores, 1866–70

Year	High Score One Team	High Total Both Teams	Low Score One Team	Low Total Both Teams
1866	135	156	1 (twice)	19
1867	124	165	1 (twice)	17
1868	116	164	1 (4 times)	16
1869	209	219	0 (8 times)	6
1870	157	167	0 (15 times)	4

With lower scores came closer games and more shutouts. The biggest blowout occurred in a June 8, 1869, game the *New York Clipper* headlined as "The Largest Score on Record," with the Niagara Club of Buffalo, New York, defeating the Columbia of Buffalo, 209–10. Evidently determined to humiliate their crosstown rivals, the Niagara scored 58 runs in the eighth inning alone. Despite the monster scoring, the game only took three hours.[19] In 1870, in a professional

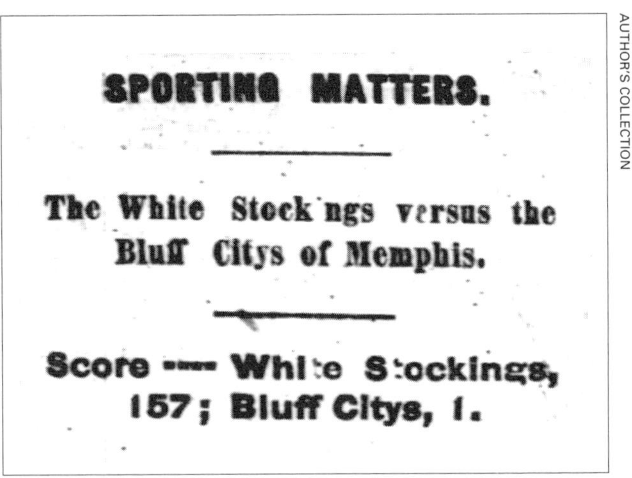
SPORTING MATTERS.

The White Stock'ngs versus the Bluff Citys of Memphis.

Score — White Stockings, 157; Bluff Citys, 1.

AUTHOR'S COLLECTION

Headline in the Chicago Tribune *from May 14, 1870. shows the lopsided score between the White Stockings and the top amateur club in Memphis.*

vs. amateur romp, the White Stockings of Chicago (pros) beat a hapless Memphis amateur team (which nonetheless claimed to be the champion amateur club of Tennessee), 157–1. Showing no mercy, the pros, already up 134–1, piled up 23 runs in the last inning, with their manager ordering, in the words of one newspaper, "the boys to go on with their rat killing."[20]

Table 3. Time of Games

Year	Avg. Time[21] (hrs)	Median Time (hrs)	< 9 Innings[22] (%)	> 9 Innings (%)	< 9 as % of All Games	Ties
1866	2.77	2.75	41.0	1.6	13.5	2
1867	2.63	2.5	26.6	0.9	11.2	5
1868	2.62	2.6	26.1	1.9	16.8	4
1869	2.65	2.6	34.5	2.0	17.8	6
1870	2.28	2.25	33.4	3.6	8.8	6

The shortest time for a nine-inning game—denoted by the *New York Clipper* as "the shortest regular game on record"—was an October 18, 1870, game between the Athletics and Stars, both of Brooklyn, which took only 1 hour, 5 minutes. The longest game time was 5 hours, 20 minutes—a May 1, 1866, game in Boston in which 144 runs were scored.

The reduced times in the later years were largely because of reduced scoring. There is no evidence that the players played "faster," though the umpires becoming more active in calling balls/strikes helped move the game along.

GAME TIMES, 1860–65[23]

For comparison, here are the average game times for nine-inning games 1860-65:

Year	Hours
1860	2.75
1861	2.99
1862	3.04
1863	3.22
1864	2.63
1865	2.73

As can be seen, game times increase until the 1864 rule changes go into effect.

To provide a modern-day comparison, MLB game times in 2019 averaged 3.17 hours (3 hours, 10 minutes). For all the complaints about the length of today's games, game times in 1863 were longer than in 2019… albeit in the 1863 context of much greater scoring.

Table 4. Number of Innings Per Game
Innings Per Game, for Games Where the Innings are Reported

Year	Avg. Innings Per Game	< 9 Innings (%)	> 9 Innings (%)	% of Games Where Innings Are Reported
1866	7.96	41.0	1.6	42.7
1867	8.31	26.6	0.9	42.7
1868	8.43	26.1	1.9	64.4
1869	8.27	34.5	2.0	51.4
1870	8.76	33.4	3.6	48.7

Table 5. Innings per Game, Assuming Games Where Innings Not Reported were Nine Inning Games

Year	Avg. Innings Per Game	% < 9 as % of all Games	% > 9 as of all Games	Ties (%)
1866	8.56	13.5	0.6	2
1867	8.70	11.2	0.8	5
1868	8.63	16.8	1.2	4
1869	8.63	17.8	1.0	6
1870	8.88	8.8	1.0	6

Nine-inning games become the in-practice standard by the late 1860s. However, as can be seen in Tables 4 and 5, a significant number of games didn't go the full nine. The rules since 1858 had mandated nine innings, but prior to 1866 clubs often ignored this. By 1870 the less-than-nine-inning games played became very rare, and were usually due to natural causes—weather, darkness, or one club having to leave town by a certain time.

The *Clipper* game reports often did not specify the number of innings played. For example, for 1866, less than half the game reports include the number of innings. The *Clipper* tended to report the number of innings only if it was other than nine. The variant reporting makes the calculation of average innings difficult, thus, I've calculated the average two ways.

Compared to today, there were very few extra inning games. Scoring was so high that games rarely ended nine innings in a tie, though it can be seen that as scoring lessened somewhat in 1869–70, the percentage of extra-inning games increases. The longest reported game was only 12 innings, a 14–13 game on August 29, 1870. Games ending in a tie almost disappear post-1865.

Using the average innings for all games has an impact on the runs per inning, 1866–70:

Table 6. Runs Per Inning (RPI), 1866–70, by Year

Year	Games	Avg. RPG	Avg. Innings	Avg. RPI	Normalizing RPI to 9 innings (RPG)
1866	574	63.80	8.56	7.45	67.05
1867	562	65.01	8.70	7.47	67.23
1868	1054	55.86	8.63	6.47	58.23
1869	1271	56.01	8.63	6.49	58.41
1870	1523	48.97	8.88	5.51	49.59
Avg.		55.7	8.70		

When adjustments are made for the innings played, the RPG shows the same trends as without the adjustments, though the increase from 1866 to 1867 is a bit less, and the 1870 dip in RPG is a bit greater.

LOCATION OF GAMES, BY STATE[24]

Overall, 59.4% of the reported-on games were played in the Northeast region of the United States. New York alone accounted for 28.3% of all games.

Using New York-New Jersey games as a proxy for Greater New York City (GNYC), 56% of games were played outside GNYC in 1866, and 67% in 1870. Many southern and western games involve tours of eastern clubs, playing and (usually) defeating the locals. Reporting of games in the south and the west increases after 1868, due largely to reporting of winter baseball games. Of the non-Northeast states, Ohio's totals are the only ones to compare to the northeastern states.

Sixty-two games in Canada were reported—more than in Michigan, more than in most U.S. states. Early baseball reporting had a surprisingly international, or at least North American, flavor.

Table 7. Number of Games, By Month

	1866	1867	1868	1869	1870	Total	% of Total
Jan.	2	2	1	2	11	18	0.5
Feb.	3	2	1	7	22	35	1
Mar.	1	4	2	9	20	36	1
Apr.	13	10	30	36	76	165	3
May	51	59	92	140	178	520	10
June	71	61	120	155	179	586	12
July	112	155	186	276	238	967	20
Aug.	121	124	265	232	289	1031	21
Sept.	81	81	213	192	294	861	17
Oct.	67	41	109	152	134	503	10
Nov.	45	20	32	51	61	209	4
Dec.	2	0	0	11	10	23	0.5

As can be seen, there are a lot more November games, and fewer April games, than today's Major League Baseball. July, August, and September were the core months, with over half (58%) of the games being played in these three core months. Much more than today, baseball in the 1860s was not the "Game of Summer" but rather the "Game of Fall."

CONCLUSION

With these data historians will be able to confirm, with hard numbers, previous assumptions about pre-pro baseball (most notably, that scoring was higher in the pre-pro era than in the professional era). The data also highlight noticeable changes from one year to the next in scoring and game times, as well as the spread of baseball from east to west. The analysis suggests that the pre-pro game of baseball never was static, but rather, ever-changing and ever-evolving, greatly impacted by rule and equipment changes—in many ways, more impacted by those changes than by the recent changes that impact today's game. ■

Notes

1. National Association of Base Ball Players, the governing body for amateur clubs.
2. The years 1858–65 are already covered in my article, "Baseball 1858–1865: By the Numbers," *Baseball Research Journal*, Spring 2020, 85–90.
3. 4,984 total entries, including a handful of games cut short because of rain.
4. The "median" of a set of numbers is that number where half the numbers are lower and half the numbers are higher.
5. "Professional" clubs as listed in the *Beadle Baseball Guide* "club averages" for 1870 and 1871, with professional games for the 1870 White Stockings of Chicago, Forest City of Rockford, and Maryland of Baltimore added. Includes the games the professionals played against amateur teams. At this time clubs jumped from "amateur" to "semiprofessional" to "professional," often in the same year. Authorities did not always agree on whether a club was "professional" or not. The 1870 Keystones of Philadelphia, for example, are listed as professional in some contemporary sources, amateur in others.
6. "First class" (top amateur) clubs as defined in the *Beadle Baseball Guides*. The 1869 *Beadle Guide* (covering 1868) listed only individual, not club, scoring statistics, so the postseason *New York Clipper* compilations are used as an analog. The numbers of "first class" games for each year are 1861:64, 1864:179, 1865:258, 1866:485, 1868:216, 1869:1138, 1870:570. 1867 numbers were calculated using *New York Clipper* end of year reports. Much "double counting" of games is included here.
7. By comparison, Major League Baseball games for 2019 averaged 9.66 RPG. On a side note, as pointed out by Douglas Jordan, if you only count "earned" runs, 1871 RPG roughly equal modern RPG. Douglas J. Jordan, "Eras of ERA," *The Sport Journal*, December 18, 2020. https://thesportjournal.org/article/eras-of-era.
8. Richard Hershberger, "Called Pitches," Protoball, July 23, 2014, https://protoball.org/Called_Pitches (viewed August 5, 2021).
9. Among the changes at this time were new rules on when an umpire should call a ball or strike, a rule confining the batter to a box, and rules confining pitchers to a box when delivering a pitch. See Richard Hershberger, *Strike Four: The Evolution of Baseball*, New York: Rowman & Littlefield, 2019, and Peter Morris, *Game of Inches: The Stories Behind the Innovations That Shaped Baseball*, Chicago: Ivan R. Dee, 2006, for more.
10. Hershberger, *Strike Four*, 122–23; Morris, *Game of Inches* 1:54; *Knoxville Press and Messenger*, May 7, 1868.

11. *New York Clipper*, April 16, 1870; July 9, 1870; October 29, 1870. See also Jack Bales, *Before They Were the Cubs*, Jefferson, NC: McFarland & Co., 2019, 50; Morris; Morris, *Game of Inches*, 1:53; *Brooklyn Union*, Dec. 6, 1869, Aug. 2, 1869. The core of the "dead" ball was restricted to one ounce in weight. Some "lively" balls reportedly had a 3-ounce rubber core—almost half their weight! Hershberger, *Strike Four*, 124.
12. Cf. *The Lewisburg Chronicle*, Oct. 7, 1870.
13. *New York Tribune*, July 28, 1870.
14. Morris, *Game of Inches*, 1:54.
15. Only games against other professional teams considered. Data from Marshall D. Wright, *The National Association of Base Ball Players, 1857–1870*, Jefferson, NC: McFarland & Co., 2000, 292–93. See *New York Herald*, July 27, 1870; *New York Clipper*, July 30, 1870. See also *New York Clipper*, Sept. 24, 1870, for an amateur club's scoring with the live vs. dead ball.
16. Hershberger, *Strike Four*, 116–18. While data on the quality of ballfields are lacking, it is safe to assume that better maintained ballfields also helped improve fielding and thus reduced run scoring.
17. For 1858–65 data, see Bruce Allardice, "Baseball 1858–1865: By the Numbers," *Baseball Research Journal*, Summer, 2020, 85–90. For the definition of first-class teams from 1866–70, see footnote 6. 1860, 1862 and 1863 first-class figures derived from Wright, *The National Association*. The numbers of games for those years are 1860:174, 1862:88 and 1863:128.
18. See Protoball website. Reported scores 1847–57 exist for 527 games, almost all in the Greater New York City area, and mostly in games by the Knickerbockers of New York, considered baseball's founding club.
19. *New York Clipper*, June 19, 1869; *Buffalo Commercial*, June 9, 1869.
20. *Chicago Tribune*, May 14, 1870.
21. Of games that have Times indicated.
22. Of games that have innings indicated.
23. Bob Tholkes, "Time of Game in the Amateur Era, 1860–65," October 2019 https://protoball.org/Length_of_Games,_1860-1865_1.0 (viewed August 5, 2021). The games sample here is small, and includes only nine-inning games.
24. Unknown state in a handful of games. The state-by-state breakdown can be found at www.protoball.org.
25. Of games that have months indicated.

Overall Offensive Performance (OOP)

Barry Hyman

We propose to measure overall offensive performance of a baseball player as the ratio of Bases Advanced to Outs Created. This new Overall Offensive Performance (OOP) statistic is deterministic, objective, readily calculated, and easily understood. OOP captures in a single number all aspects of offensive performance included in multiple, existing offensive stats, plus additional aspects not captured in any other offensive statistic. Among these additional aspects, OOP gives batters credit for advancing runners already on base and gives runners credit for taking extra bases on batted balls.

To provide the appropriate background, we first review existing offensive performance stats, including commonly used and lesser known deterministic stats, as well several probabilistic ones. Next, after pointing out some of the deficiencies in the existing stats, we introduce the rules governing the determination of the OOP numerator (Bases Advanced) and denominator (Outs Created). We then show how OOP may easily be incorporated into traditional scorekeeping, and close with sample calculations for four players.

EXISTING OFFENSIVE PERFORMANCE STATS

While there is a plethora of ways to measure offensive performance of baseball players, the statistics that are summarized here are those that are most relevant to overall offensive performance. Since the proposed OOP statistic is deterministic, we focus on other deterministic stats, i.e. those that describe the *actual* and *immediate* outcome of an individual player's offensive actions. Stats that compare or weight such outcomes relative to other outcomes (average player, replacement player, etc.) or different settings (eras, ballparks, etc.) are not addressed. Probabilistic stats that estimate or predict the eventual outcome of a player's offensive actions (runs, wins, etc.) are discussed only to the extent that they shed light on the proposed OOP stat.

COMMONLY USED DETERMINISTIC STATS

The most common measure of offensive performance is Batting Average (BA). One of the criticisms of BA is that it treats all hits equally, so it is combined with RBI and home runs to try to create a more comprehensive picture of overall offensive performance. Despite the shortcomings in this approach, not only are the league leaders in each of these categories lauded, but the "Triple Crown" is won by the player who leads his league in all three categories.

Sometimes additional measures such as runs scored and bases stolen are included in the description of offensive achievements. For example, the AP article announcing Jose Altuve as the AL MVP in 2017 included the following: "Altuve batted a major-league-best .346 in the regular season, hit 24 home runs with 81 runs batted in, scored 112 times, stole 32 bases... ."[1] Using this collection of five numbers to characterize offensive performance does not help us compare Altuve's 2017 performance with another (hypothetical) player who batted .340, with 20 home runs, 85 RBI, 105 runs, and 40 stolen bases. Let's call this the "Altuve problem" and our goal in this paper is to solve the problem using a single, easily calculated, deterministic measure of overall offensive performance. We begin by reviewing several other widely utilized offensive stats.

One commonly cited overall offensive performance statistic is Slugging Average (SLG) which gives proportionally more credit to extra-base hits and takes the following form, where TB is total bases:

$$SLG = \frac{TB}{AB}$$

Another widely used statistic is On Base Average (OBA) defined as follows:

$$OBA = \left(\frac{H + BB + HBP}{AB + BB + HBP + SF} \right)$$

OBA treats all hits (H) equally but also gives the batter credit in the numerator for walks and being hit by a pitch. In the denominator, OBA adds walks, HBP, and sacrifice flies (SF) to obtain total plate appearances, except for sacrifice bunts. (The argument used in the MLB glossary for not including sacrifice bunts is that "...it is rarely a hitter's decision to sacrifice himself, but rather a manager's choice as part of an in-game strategy."[2])

Recently it has become increasingly popular to add SLG and OBA together to produce On Base Plus Slugging (OPS). Slowinski argues that while OPS is a relatively quick and easy way to combine the ability to get on base (OBA) with the ability to hit for power (SLG), it incorrectly treats them as equal in value.[3] In addition, there is a major intellectual problem to combining SLG and OBA in this way because both the numerators and denominators of the two statistics represent different things. Keith Thompson characterized OPS as "...like adding apples and oranges."[4] Keith Law described OPS as "...a mash-up the way a toddler smushes two lumps of Play-Doh together and calls it a present for Mommy...."[5]

Even if we can overcome the intellectual problem of treating OPS as a mathematically meaningful measure of performance, it cannot be computed directly. To obtain it, we first have to compute both SLG and OBA, then add them together. So, from both an intellectual and computational perspective, OPS does not satisfy the desire for a single, simple measure of overall offensive performance.

LESS-KNOWN RELEVANT DETERMINISTIC STATS

Many other deterministic stats have been proposed to characterize overall offensive performance but have not been widely adopted in the mainstream media. The most interesting ones are examined in this section.

Secondary Average (SecA) was created by Bill James.[6] It is a modification of SLG that includes walks, stolen bases (SB), and caught stealing (CS) in the numerator and focuses only on hits for extra bases (TB-H). There are variations of SecA that include HBP and/or delete CS in the numerator.

In 1987 Richard Cochrane introduced Total Batting Average (TBA) that added SLG to BA, plus gives batters credit for RBIs (unlike the stats mentioned so far) and walks.[7] Here is his formula:

$$TBA=\left(BA+SLG+\frac{1}{2}\frac{RBI}{AB}+\frac{1}{4}\frac{BB}{AB+BB}\right)$$

A similar stat, Total Production Average, (TPA) was introduced in 1995, added runs scored (R), and took the following form, in which all plate appearances (PA) are included in the denominator:[8]

$$TPA=\frac{TB+BB+R+RBI-HR}{PA}$$

Recognizing the mathematical fallacy embodied in OPS, Mark Kanter developed a refinement called New Production (NewProd) where CI is catcher's interference.[9]

$$NewProd=\frac{TB+BB+HBP+CI}{PA}$$

Another approach to rectifying the OPS mathematical inconsistency is the Diamond Weight (DW) proposed by Barry Codell.[10] It takes the following form:

$$DW=\left(\frac{TB+H+BB+HBP}{PA}\right)$$

This approach was further refined by William Gilbert with his Bases per Plate Appearance (BPA), where grounding into double plays (GIDP) and sacrifice bunts (SH) are included.[11]

$$BPA=\frac{TB+BB+HBP+SB-CS-GIDP}{PA-SH}$$

Total Average (TA), developed by sportswriter Thomas Boswell, is the number of bases reached by a batter, divided by the number of outs created by the player.[12]

$$TA=\left(\frac{TB+HBP+BB+SB}{AB-H+CS+GIDP}\right)$$

Unlike BA, SLG, OBA, OPS, SecA, TBA, TPA, NewProd, DW, and BPA, which are essentially ratios of successes/opportunities, TA is a ratio of successes/failures—the approach used in OOP. (In principle, either approach could measure overall offensive performance.)

Another stat that uses the successes/failures ratio is the Base Out Percentage (BOP) which adds sacrifice hits (SH) and sacrifies flies (SF) to both the numerator and denominator of TA.[13]

$$BOP=\left(\frac{TB+HBP+BB+SB+SH+SF}{AB-H+CS+GIDP+SH+SF}\right)$$

Including SH and SF in the denominator is an important improvement since they both result in outs. Including them in the numerator is more interesting, though, because although sacrifice flies and sacrifice hits both represent success, BOP is the only stat discussed so far other than TBA and TPA that gives the batter credit for advancing a runner other than himself.

This failure to properly account for advancing the runners ahead of the batter is the basis for some criticism of the stats discussed earlier in this section.[14] And in a 2008 Fangraphs article, Brandon Heipp critiqued TA, BOP, and several similar stats, writing:

> "All of the base-based measures above ignore the existence of baserunners, and implicitly assume that all plate appearances occur in bases empty situations (or alternatively posit that the effects of a batter's actions on the other baserunners are meaningless in evaluating his performance). What if instead we look at how many bases actually are accounted for, on average, for each event?"[15]

But, as discussed above, BOP does in fact account for some of the runners on base by including SH and SF in the numerator and giving the batter credit for advancing them. Heipp's claim that he looks "at how many bases actually are accounted for" is immediately qualified by saying he does it "on average." While this is an improvement over other stats mentioned, there is a big difference between accounting for the bases actually advanced in an event and accounting for the average number of bases advanced in similar events. As we will show, one of the major contributions of OOP is tracking the actual bases advanced. In 2008, Bill James did introduce Player Baserunning as a separate stat.[16] However, it was not integrated with batting stats to arrive at a measure of overall offensive performance as OOP does.

In a 2004 application for a patent, Richard Kerns proposed to incorporate all actual bases advanced in the stat that he dubbed Offensive Average (OA).[17] Its basic form is as follows:

$$OA = \frac{BARAB + BARO1st + BARO2nd + BARO3rd}{AB}$$

BARAB = bases advanced by runner at bat,
BARO1st= bases advanced by runner on first,
etc.

While this numerator is an improvement over BOP, it credits all the bases advanced to the batter. OOP, on the other hand, assigns credit in a more nuanced manner.

While in its basic form, OA is a ratio of successes/opportunities, Kerns offers the option of adding an At-Bat Adjustment term to the denominator to include one or more terms such as CS, GIDP, and "any other factor deemed meaningful or useful by user." Such a modification would transform the denominator into a combination of opportunities and failures, thereby destroying the meaning of the ratio. Kerns's patent application was abandoned on July 31, 2006.[18]

Another deterministic stat that doesn't represent either a ratio of successes/opportunities or a ratio of successes/failures is Runs Created (RC).[19] Developed by Bill James, its original form is as follows:

$$RC = \left(\frac{TB * (H + BB)}{(AB + BB)} \right)$$

James developed several other versions of RC, the most well-known of which is the following, where IBB = intentional bases on balls.[20]

$$RC = \frac{[TB + .26(BB + HBP - IBB) + .52(SH + SF + SB)] * (H + BB + HBP - CS - GIDP)}{PA}$$

This expression discounts the value of terms such as BB and SB. As quoted by John Thorn in *The Hidden Game of Baseball*, James's justification for such discounts is that, "A stolen base advances only the runner" but "each...hit advances the batter...and anyone else aboard."[21] Thorn goes on to explain that "a walk cannot drive in a runner from third, as a single can, unless the bases are loaded."[22] This is another example of considering the value of advancing runners already on base.

It is important to emphasize that all of the stats mentioned so far except RC are deterministic and describe what actually happens as the immediate result of a player's offensive actions. On the other hand, while RC is deterministic, it is an empirical formula that estimates what will happen as the ultimate result of a player's actions. See Figure 1 for a typology of the deterministic offensive stats (including OOP) where the stats in the Partial category shown in Figure 1 include only either SB and/or RBI, SH, and SF as bases advanced.

PROBABILISTIC STATS

We now consider the category of stats that use large data sets and probabilistic considerations to estimate and predict the ultimate outcome of a player's offensive actions.

Figure 1. Typology of Deterministic Offensive Stats

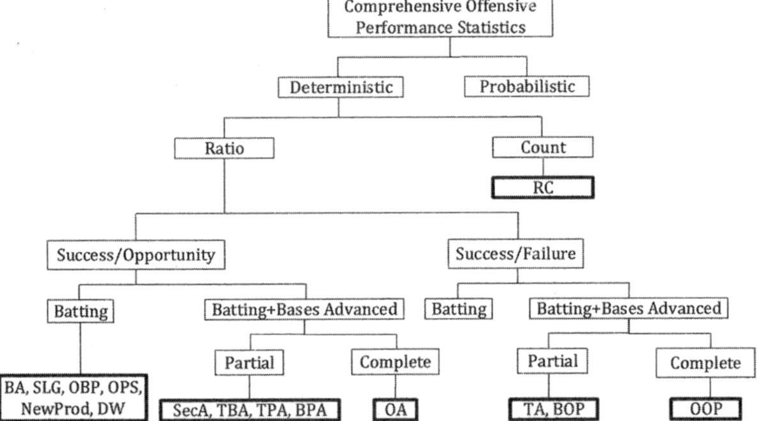

We briefly review some of these stats in this section, even though they are primarily of value to team managers and executives who use them to plan in-game and long-term team development strategy, estimate trade values, and negotiate salaries and contract terms. These stats are also of great interest to professional statisticians, baseball stats enthusiasts, and baseball history aficionados who use them to, among other things, distinguish between performance in home/away and day/night games, forecast future performance, and compare players from different leagues and eras. They are not easily accessible—in many cases not easily understandable—to the typical baseball fan.

However, there are several probabilistic stats that help to inform the way we calculate OOP, so we limit our coverage in this section to those stats.

A key data set that underlies many probabilistic stats is the Expected Run Matrix which lists the probability of runs scoring in an inning for every one of all 24 possible states of outs and bases occupied. Table 1 is Tom Tango's Expected Run Matrix for 1999–2002.[23] Consider, for example, the value of 0.953 associated with a runner on first and no outs. That number is obtained by knowing that during those four seasons, there were 44,552 times that MLB teams had a runner on first with no outs, and during those times teams scored 42,432 runs before the end of the inning. Therefore, on average there were 0.953 runs scored in an inning when there is a runner on first and no outs. A similar calculation is made to arrive at the other 23 numbers in the matrix.

Table 1. Expected Run Matrix (1999–2002)

		Outs		
		0	1	2
	None	0.555	0.297	0.117
	1st	0.953	0.573	0.251
Bases	2nd	1.189	0.725	0.344
Occupied	3rd	1.482	0.983	0.387
	1st and 2nd	1.573	0.971	0.466
	1st and 3rd	1.904	1.243	0.538
	2nd and 3rd	2.052	1.467	0.634
	All	2.417	1.650	0.815

These data can be used to determine Expected Run value of any offensive act. For example, if a batter doubles with the bases empty and one out, the Expected Runs increase from 0.297 to 0.725, an increase of 0.428.

Based on these data, Tango performed an extensive series of calculations and adjustments (spanning six tables and ten pages in his book) to arrive at this expression for Weighted On-Base Average (wOBA) for the 1999–2002 period:

$$wOBA = \frac{(0.72 * NIBB) + (0.75 * HBP) + (0.90 * 1B) + (0.92 * RBOE) + (1.24 * 2B) + (1.56 * 3B) + (1.95 * HR)}{PA}$$

In the wOBA formula, NIBB = nonintentional bases on balls, and RBOE = reach base on error.[24]

One feature that distinguishes wOBA from any of the previously discussed stats is that wOBA gives a player credit for reaching base on an error (although it does not distinguish between a one-base error and multi-base error). Fangraphs publishes a version of wOBA for every year; its version omits the RBOE term.[25]

Mark Pankin utilized the Expected Run Matrix concept to develop similar estimates of a player's offensive performance that include actions such as SB and CS.[26] Several others have applied the Expected Run Matrix concept to develop more comprehensive probabilistic baserunning stats such as Equivalent Baserunning Runs (EqBRR)[27] and Ultimate Base Running (UBR).[28]

Lee Panas makes the point that the addition of baserunning to batting statistics provides a more complete picture of a player's offensive production.[29] This type of data is incorporated into OOP as will be explained in detail in the following pages.

DEFICIENCIES IN EXISTING DETERMINISTIC OFFENSIVE STATS

Consider the following situations that are not captured by any of the deterministic offensive stats.

- With a runner on first, the batter hits a ground ball. If the runner advances to second and the batter is out at first, the result is better than if the runner is forced out at second while the batter is safe at first. None of the deterministic stats distinguishes between these two results.

- If a batter is out trying to stretch a single into a double, he is still credited with a base hit for that at-bat and is not penalized by any of the deterministic stats for creating the out.

- If a batter hits a single with a runner on base, unless the runner scores so the batter is credited with an RBI, deterministic stats (except for OA) do not give the batter credit for advancing the runner.

- If a runner scores from third on a fly ball out, the runner gets credit for scoring and the batter gets credit for an RBI and is not charged with an AB. However, if the runner advances from second to third on a fly ball out, neither the batter (except for OA) nor the runner gets any credit.

- There is no extra penalty for hitting into a double play in deterministic stats (except for TA and the refined version of RC) as compared to making an out.

We now turn to introducing a new stat that accounts for these and other deficiencies in existing deterministic offensive stats.

OVERALL OFFENSIVE PERFORMANCE

The offensive player's role is to advance as many players (including himself) as much as possible while creating as few outs as possible. We propose to capture this objective in Overall Offensive Performance (OOP) defined as:

$$OOP=\left(\frac{Bases\ Advanced}{Outs\ Created}\right)$$

This single, simple measure of offensive performance incorporates the bases covered by a player as a batter and a runner plus the bases covered by runners advanced by the batter. OOP also penalizes players for the outs they cause.

A fundamental rule underlying the calculation of OOP is that we must account for all Bases Advanced and all Outs Created. Detailed explanations for the numerator and denominator in OOP are provided in the next sections along with illustrative examples.

BASES ADVANCED

A player is awarded one point in the OOP numerator for each base advanced. Since there are multiple ways for players to reach first base and advance beyond first, the following subsections explore all of the possibilities.

Bases Empty. We start with the situation where the bases are empty and the batter advances to at least first base; we first examine reaching base on a hit, then reaching base via other means.

• Bases Advanced via Base Hits

The following points are earned by a batter for getting a hit when the bases are empty:

- The player who singles gets 1 point.
- The player who hits a double gets 2 points.
- The player who hits a triple gets 3 points.
- The player who hits a home run gets 4 points.

These point values are the same as those used in all the other deterministic offensive stats.

• Bases Advanced via Other Means

Remember that the fundamental OOP rule requires that we account for all Bases Advanced. A walk is treated like a single, worth one point in the numerator. This is the same approach taken by OBA, SecA, TPA, NewProd, DW, BPA, TA, BOP, OA, and the original RC. Neither the current versions of RC nor wOBA gives credit for intentional walks. Both TBA and the current version of RC include walks, but at a discounted value.

Being hit by the pitch should also be awarded a point. As with walks, reaching base by HBP is included in OBA, NewProd, DW, BPA, TA, BOP, OA, the current version of RC, and wOBA.

Batters who reach base on an error are credited with the points associated with the base reached. Many errors are the result of the fielder hurrying the play on a speedy offensive player. Other errors are the result of a judgement call by the official scorer and hence are not an objective statistic. OOP gives the batter credit as does Tango's wOBA, but all other stats mentioned above essentially charge the batter with an out. But since OOP requires that all outs be accounted for, it makes no sense to account for an out that has not occurred.

This discussion makes it clear that batters are given credit in OOP for bases advanced regardless of the mechanism by which they reach base. Thus, batters who reach first base by catcher's interference (included in NewProd) or dropped third strike also receive one point.

Runners on Base. Once a batter reaches a base as a result of a hit or other mechanism discussed above, he becomes a runner and can advance to subsequent bases in a variety of ways.

• Bases Advanced by Runners

When a runner advances in the absence of action by a subsequent batter, the runner gets credit for the bases advanced. Stealing a base is an offensive contribution and the runner is credited with a point in OOP, as is done in SecA, BPA, TA, BOP, OA, while a discounted point is awarded in the revised RC. The runner also gets credited if he advances due to an error on an attempted pickoff play, or advances an extra base due to a throwing error on his stolen base effort. A point is earned in OOP even if the base is advanced on catcher indifference, balk, passed ball, or wild pitch; James includes these as part of his baserunning stat.[30] So does Panas.[31] The basis for crediting the runner with such advances, as Panas says, is that "there is some evidence that such advancement is caused, in part, by baserunners distracting pitchers and catchers. Thus, good baserunners should benefit more from these events than poor baserunners."[32]

• Runners Advanced by Action of Subsequent Batters

If there are runners on base when the batter gets a hit, the batter gets the appropriate points for the bases he advances plus additional points for advancing the runners already on base. Here are some examples, with the points earned by the batter for advancing runners in front of him shown in italics:

- The batter who singles and advances a runner one base either from first to second, or from second to third, or scores from third, gets 1 + *1* = 2 points.
- The batter who doubles and advances a runner either from first to third, or from second to home, gets 2 + *2* = 4 points.
- The batter who triples with runners on first and third, gets 3 + *3* + *1* = 7 points.
- The batter who hits a grand slam, gets 4 + *1* + *2* + *3* = 10 points.

In each of the above examples, the runner(s) do not advance more bases than the batter.

Of course, there are situations where a runner advances two bases on a single (either from first to third or from second to home) or three bases on a double (scoring from first). Consider the following five circumstances under which these situations can develop:

1. The batted ball is a long hit or a hit combined with an error so that any runner, regardless of speed, could easily make it to the extra base.
2. The runner makes it to the extra base primarily on the basis of his speed.
3. A hit-and-run play is called by the manager so the runner breaks toward second at the manager's direction.
4. A runner approaching third is waved home by the third base coach.
5. With two outs and a 3–2 count on the batter, the runner(s) take off on the pitch and thus get a head-start.

The OOP rule requires that all the bases advanced be accounted for. So we have to decide who gets the credit for the extra base advanced, the batter or the runner? (We cannot give credit to either the manager or the coach.) A similar issue was addressed by Hal Stern, who assumed for his probabilistic model "that there are three types of singles (short singles, which advance all runners one base; medium singles, which advance all runners one base but allow a runner on second base to advance two bases; and long singles, which advance all runners two bases) and that the three types are equally likely."[33] That may be fine for a probabilistic stat, but we need a clear and unambiguous rule for OOP.

We have concluded that the credit for the extra base should always be awarded to the runner. This is supported by James Click who argues that "going from first to third or scoring from second on a single counts for just as much as stealing third or home."[34] This is the same approach taken by Bill James in his Player Baserunning stat. Panas used the same method in his probabilistic Bases Gained Above Average (BGAA) stat.[35] John Dewan also awarded the extra base to the runner and included estimated runs due to baserunning in his probabilistic stat Total Runs (TR).[36]

Runners can also advance as the result of the batter making an out. OOP gives the runner credit when he tags up and advances a base on a fly out, or advances a base on a groundball out in a non-force situation. This is similar to Panas's approach.[37]

OUTS CREATED

The OOP denominator is the number of Outs Created. As with Bases Advanced, there are multiple ways in which outs can be recorded.

The most obvious way, and the way captured by traditional stats, is the batter is out via a strikeout, fly out, or ground out. But consider the following ways of making outs that are not reflected in traditional stats, but are incorporated into OOP by applying the rule that all outs must be accounted for.

If a batter is out trying to stretch a single into a double, or a double into a triple, OOP gives the player credit for the bases he successfully reached but the player is also charged with an out.

If a runner unsuccessfully tries to advance from first to third or from second to home on a batter's single, OOP charges the runner with an out while the batter gets credit for advancing the runner one base. The same approach gives the batter credit for advancing a runner from first to third on a double but charges the runner with an out if he is thrown out at home. These rules complement the ones adopted in the previous section which gives the runner credit for advancing the extra base. Thus, we have a perfect symmetry: the runner is credited if successfully reaching the extra base and is penalized for the unsuccessful effort. Panas takes a similar approach, but since BGAA is a counting stat rather than a ratio stat, he deducts "from a player's bases gained total every time he is thrown out trying to advance an extra base on a hit."[38]

Similarly, this symmetry argument is applied to charge a runner with an out when he unsuccessfully tries to advance on a fly out or an unforced ground out.

A batter grounding into a double play is charged with two outs if the runner is forced. Another double play occurs when a runner takes off on a well-hit line drive or long fly ball that is caught and the runner is picked off before he can return to the base. We consider two situations. If the runner is either on first or all bases behind the runner are occupied, the runner is virtually obligated to head towards the next base or risk being forced out so OOP charges the batter with both outs. However, if the runner has the option to stay on his base because the base immediately preceding his is unoccupied, then the runner is charged with an out.

When a batter hits into a force play, there may be a temptation to award the batter a point for advancing to first in addition to charging him with an out. But, since there was a runner on first to begin with, all that happened is that one person on first is replaced by a different person on first and there is no advance.

While a batter gets appropriate points for advancing a runner from first on a sacrifice bunt, in accordance with the OOP rule the batter is also charged with an out.

If a runner successfully advances to a base, but then is tagged out because his foot comes off the base, the runner is charged with an out. Runners picked off a base are also charged with an out.

And if the runner is caught stealing, he gets a point added to the denominator. Runner interference, runner hit by the ball, running out of the base path, and illegal slide are further ways to be charged with creating an out.

KEEPING SCORE

One of the advantages of OOP is that managers, coaches, sportscasters, fans, and members of the media could use it to easily capture all of the ingredients of offensive performance during a game. Score-keeping systems vary, but most use a scoresheet containing a grid of square boxes in which the offensive performance for each player's at-bat is recorded. The preprinted content of the box and which additional information is entered by the scorer varies widely. (See Kern's patent application for his approach to tracking OA data.[39])

To illustrate one way OOP could easily be incorporated, consider the fairly complex preprinted box shown in Figure 2. It facilitates keeping track of balls, strikes, RBIs, errors, outs, etc., as well as details about the player's progress around the bases.

Without eliminating any of that information, OOP can be included by adding an outer dashed diamond as shown in Figure 3 that is subdivided into zones for each base which in turn are subdivided into two parts. The upper part of each zone is used to record the bases advanced while the lower part records the outs created.

To illustrate how to easily keep track of Bases Advanced and Outs Created, consider a hypothetical

Figure 2. Typical Preprinted Scorecard Box

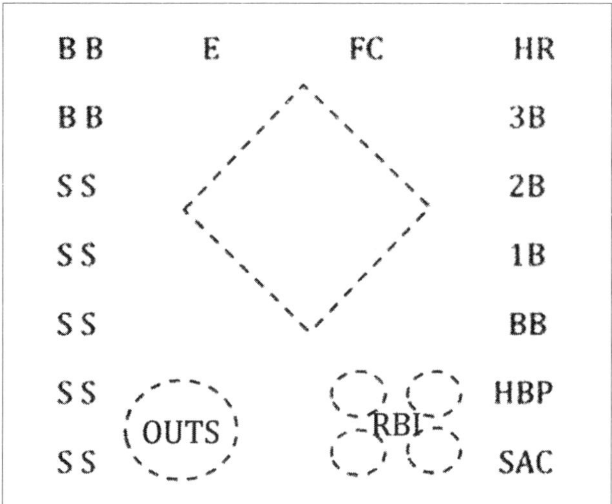

Figure 3. Scorecard Box for OOP

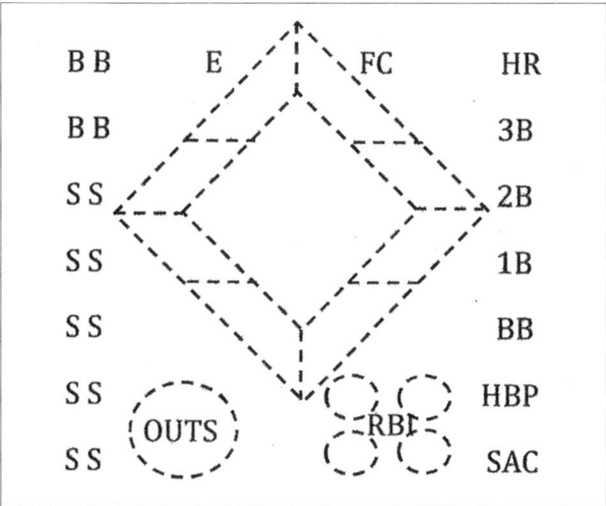

three-player segment of a scorebook shown in Figure 4. The only entries displayed are the values in the outer dashed diamond in order to focus on the application of the OOP rules, but narratives explaining the player's actions are added underneath each segment.

Figure 4. OOP Scorebook Examples

Player A

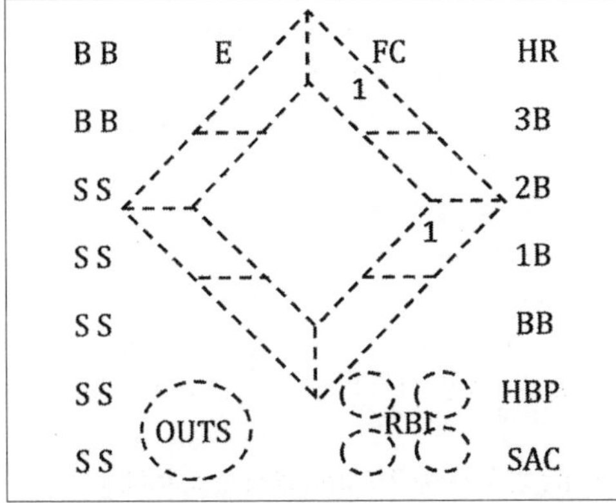

Player A singles (1 point), steals 2nd (1 point), advances to 3rd on a single by player B, and scores on a double by Player C. *[Bases Advanced = 2]*

Player B

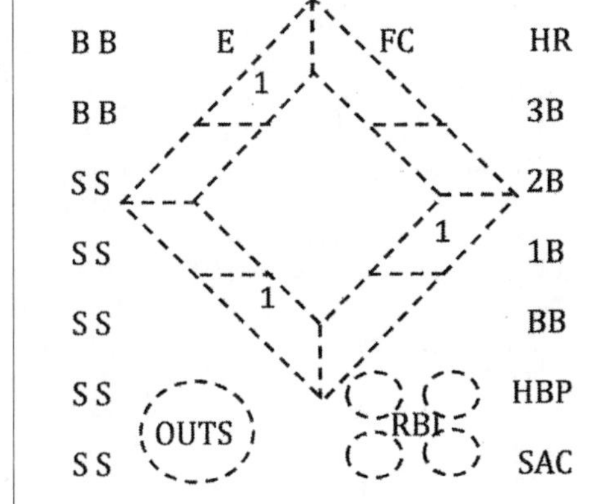

Player B hits a single (1 point) advancing Player A from 2nd to 3rd (1 point), and is out trying to score from 1st on a double by Player C. *[Bases Advanced = 2, Outs Created = 1]*

Player C

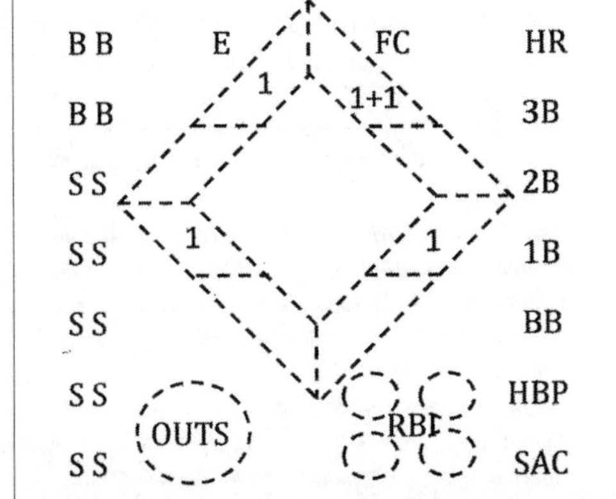

Player C hits a double (1 point for getting to 1st + 1 point for getting to 2nd), scoring Player A from 3rd (1 point), and advancing Player B from 1st to 3rd (1 point for advancing Player B to 2nd + 1 point for advancing Player B from 2nd to 3rd). *[Bases Advanced = 5]*

EXAMPLE OOP VALUES

While it is straightforward to develop new OOP data using a slightly modified traditional scorecard, developing historical OOP data is more difficult because not enough information is contained in traditional box scores. However, Retrosheet includes detailed complete play-by-play narratives of most games in the American and National Leagues from 1915 through 2020.[40] This is the source for our OOP data.

To get a preliminary feel for the range of numerical OOP values, we focused on the season-long performance of four players in 2001: Barry Bonds and Armando Rios of the San Francisco Giants, and Ichiro Suzuki and Dan Wilson of the Seattle Mariners. Bonds, a quintessential slugger, hit a record-breaking 73 home runs and was the National League MVP that year. By contrast, Ichiro led the American League in batting average, hits, and stolen bases, won the American League MVP, and was a quintessential speedster and small-ball player. The two superstars illustrate a vast difference. Wilson, the Mariners 2001 catcher, and Rios, Giants outfielder, were selected as prototypical average players.[41] These choices were based on Wilson's BA = .265 being close to the AL average in 2001 of BA = .267, and Rios's BA = .257 with the NL average in 2001 of BA = .261.

We calculated the 2001 season OOP values for these four players by applying the Bases Advanced and Outs Created rules to the play-by-play information in Retrosheet. See Table 2 for the results along with traditional stats.

Table 2. Sample OOP and Conventional Stats Values for the 2001 Season

	BA	OBA	SLG	OPS	OOP
Bonds	.328	.515	.863	1.378	2.644
Ichiro	.350	.381	.457	0.838	1.554
Rios	.257	.330	.465	0.795	1.320
Wilson	.265	.305	.403	0.708	1.057

Note that the OOP ranking of these four players is the same as their OPS ranking, although their relative standings can be quite different, for example:

$$\left\{\frac{Bonds}{Wilson}\right\}_{OPS} = 1.935,$$

$$\left\{\frac{Bonds}{Wilson}\right\}_{OOP} = 2.501.$$

While the OOP values are the result of many different ways a player accumulates Bases Advanced and Outs Created, it is instructive to consider other ways to interpret them.

For example, one straightforward interpretation of Bonds's OOP could be that for every out he caused, he hit the equivalent of at least a double (actually, it was closer to a triple).

A perhaps more intriguing result of our OOP calculations is that the OOP values for our two prototypical average players are in the range 1 < OOP < 1.3. This very preliminary result suggests that this range may indeed be the hallmark of an average offensive player. Of course, an important limitation on drawing such a conclusion is that our selection of Rios and Wilson was based on comparing their BA to the league average BA. What would be required to properly select prototypical average players would be to compare their OOP values to the league average OOP. But since no one has calculated the league average OOP (and we are not about to attempt such a Herculean feat), we are left, for the time being, with pure speculation. If enough other people hop on the OOP bandwagon, a meaningful database can be constructed to draw more definitive conclusions.

DISCUSSION

Once the few rules are learned, OOP is easy to understand and calculate. It captures in one number all of the ingredients of BA, OBA, SLG, and DW. Also, OOP accounts for SB and CS and GIDP that are part of the SecA, BPA and TA stats as well as the CI term in NewProd, SH term in BOP and RBOE term in wOBA.

In addition, OOP explicitly incorporates the batter's contribution to advancing runners ahead of him, without resorting to probabilistic analysis such as done in wOBA and other probabilistic stats.

Although OOP does not explicitly include RBI, it does serve as a surrogate. So, for example, in addition to the points a batter earns for the bases he covers, he also earns one point for scoring a runner from third on a single, double, triple, or home run. So in those situations OOP is accurately reflecting RBI. But OOP goes beyond RBI by crediting the batter two points for scoring a runner from second on a double, triple, or home run, three points for scoring a runner from first on a triple or home run, and six points for clearing the bases with a grand slam (in addition to the points the batter earns for the bases he covers). These additional points compensate for OOP not giving the batter credit for an RBI on an SF or an unforced ground out.

OOP incorporates a partial surrogate for runs scored because it only credits a player who scores from third on an SF or unforced ground out, from second on a single, from first on a double, or hits a home run.

This paper began by posing the "Altuve problem"—the difficulty in determining who is best within a group of offensive players by comparing their traditional stats (BA, HR, RBI, SB, etc.). We end it by claiming that OOP solves this problem by reducing each player's total offensive performance to a single number and thereby enabling the comparison. So when someone claims that the answer is OPS, we say oops, the real answer is OOP. ■

Acknowledgments

The author gratefully acknowledges the valuable comments received on a previous version of this document by Ray Baculi, Shawn Brinsfield, Glenn Drosendahl, Bob Pessemier, Jim Pfeifer, Harvey Sadis, Clark Swisher, and Betty Houchin Winfield. Their feedback has led to a much improved version.

Notes

1. Jake Seiner, "Altuve wins AL MVP, Marlins' Stanton earns NL honor," *Seattle Times*, November 16, 2017. https://www.seattletimes.com/sports/marlins-slugger-stanton-wins-nl-mvp-edges-reds-votto (accessed August 14, 2020).
2. "On-base Percentage (OBP),"https://mlb.com/glossary/standard-stats/on-base-percentage (accessed August 16, 2020). SABR prefers the term "On-base Average" (OBA) over "On-base Percentage" (OBP) since the stat is usually expressed as a three decimal term in the same style as Batting Average (e.g. .320), and not as a percentage (32%).
3. OPS and OPS+ I Sabermetrics Library, http://library.fangraphs.com/offense/ops (accessed July 16, 2021).
4. Keith R. Thompson, "What's Wrong with the OPS Analysis in Baseball," (persports.com) (accessed July 15, 2021).
5. Keith Law, Smart Baseball (New York: HarperCollins, 2017), 127.
6. Andrew Kneeland, "MLB Stat of the Week," Bleacher Report, May 20, 2002. https://bleacherreport.com/articles/24464-mlb-stat-of-the-week-secondary-average. Andrew Kneeland, "MLB Stat of the Week," Bleacher Report, May 20, 2002. https://bleacherreport.com/articles/24464-mlb-stat-of-the-week-secondary-average.
7. Richard M. Cochrane, "The Total Average Concept: Hitting, Pitching, Team Play," *The Baseball Research* Journal 16 (1987): 9–14, https://sabr.org/baseball-research-journal-archives (accessed July 21, 2020).
8. Eugene E. Heaton Jr. and Alan W. Heaton, "The Best Overall Batting Performance Measure-8 So Far," *The Baseball Research Journal* 24 (1995): 127–30, https://sabr.org/baseball-research-journal-archives (accessed July 21, 2020).
9. Mark Kanter, "New Production," *The Baseball Research Journal* 29 (2000): 102–04, https://sabr.org/baseball-research-journal-archives (accessed July 21, 2020).
10. Barry F. Codell, "DW: A Way to Truly Weigh the Diamond!" *By the Numbers, Newsletter of the SABR Statistical Analysis Research Committee* 5, no. 1 (1993): 4–6, http://sabr.org/research/statistical-analysis-research-committee-newsletters (accessed July 23, 2020).
11. William C. Gilbert, "A True Measure of Offensive Performance," *By the Numbers, Newsletter of the SABR Statistical Analysis Research Committee* 5, no. 2 (1993): 11–12, http://sabr.org/research/statistical-analysis-research-committee-newsletters (accessed July 23, 2020).
12. "Total average," https://www.baseball-reference.com/bullpen/Total_Average.

13. Barry Codell, "The Base-Out Percentage: Baseball's Newest Yardstick," *The Baseball Research Journal* (1979), https://sabr.org/journal/article/the-base-out-percentage-baseballs-newest-yardstick-2 (accessed August 17, 2020).
14. "Bases Fallacy," https://www.baseball-reference.com/bullpen/Bases_Fallacy (accessed August 20, 2020).
15. Brandon Heipp, "Bases and outs ad nauseum," https://tht.fangraphs.com/bases-and-outs-ad-nauseum (accessed August 18, 2020).
16. Bill James, "Player Baserunning," in Baseball Info Solutions, *The Bill James Handbook* 2008, (Skokie, IL: ACTA Sports (2007), 301–12.
17. US Patent and Trademark Office, United States Patent Application Pub. No: US 20050227793 A1, "Method, Apparatus, and System for Determining Player Effectiveness", Richard Dean Kerns, 2005, http://appft.uspto.gov/netacgi/nph-Parser?Sect1=PTO1&Sect2=HITOFF&d=PG01&p=1&u=%2Fnetahtml%2FPTO%2Fsrchnum.html&r=1&f=G&l=50&s1=%2220050227793%22.PGNR.&OS=DN/20050227793&RS=DN/20050227793 (accessed August 18, 2020).
18. US Patent and Trademark Office, Public Patent Application Information Retrieval, https://portal.uspto.gov/pair/PublicPair (accessed August 18, 2020).
19. "A Primer on Statistics," https://sabr.org/sabermetrics/statistics (accessed August 18, 2020).
20. "Runs created," https://www.baseball-reference.com/bullpen/Runs_created (accessed August 18, 2020).
21. John Thorn and Pete Palmer, *The Hidden Game of Baseball* (Chicago: University of Chicago Press, 2015), 50.
22. Thorn and Palmer, 50.
23. Tom M. Tango, Mitchel G. Lichtman, and Andrew E. Dolphin, *The Book: Playing the Percentages in Baseball* (TMA Press, 2006), 19–20.
24. Tango, Lichtman, and Dolphin, 30.
25. Steve Slowinski, "wOBA," https://library.fangraphs.com/offense/woba (accessed August 18, 2020).
26. Mark D. Pankin, "Evaluating Offensive Performance in Baseball," *Operations Research* 26, no.4 (1978): 610–19.
27. Albert Chen, "The Running Man," https://vault.si.com/vault/2009/07/27/the-running-man (accessed August 19, 2020).
28. Mitchel Lichtman, "Ultimate Base Running Primer," https://blogs.fangraphs.com/ultimate-base-running-primer (accessed August 20, 2020).
29. Lee Panas, *Beyond Batting Average: Baseball Statistics for the 21st Century*, 62, https://www.lulu.com/search?q=Lee+Panas&adult_audience_rating=00 (accessed July 25, 2020).
30. James, 302.
31. Panas, 63.
32. Panas, 66.
33. Hal S. Stern, Column Editor "A Statistician Reads the Sports Page: Baseball by the Numbers," *CHANCE* 10, no.1 (1997): 38–41.
34. James Click, "What if Ricky Henderson Had Pete Incaviglia's Legs?" in *Baseball Between the Numbers*, ed. Jonah Keri (New York: Basic Books, 2006), 116.
35. Panas, 63–67.
36. John Dewan, *The Fielding Bible-Volume II* (Skokie, IL: ACTA Sports, 2009) 393.
37. Panas, 64–65.
38. Panas, 64.
39. US Patent and Trademark Office, United States Patent Application Pub. No: US 20050227793 A1.
40. Retrosheet event files, https://www.retrosheet.org.
41. Rios was traded to the Pirates in late July 2001 but only played two games for them before suffering a season-ending injury.

Did Performance-Enhancing Drugs Prolong Careers?

David J. Gordon, MD, PhD

The 27-year span from approximately 1987 to 2013 is popularly called the "Steroid Era" because of the purportedly rampant use of performance enhancing drugs (PED), specifically anabolic steroids and (to a lesser extent) human growth hormone (HGH). Although steroid use in MLB dates as far back as Pud Galvin in 1889, the body-builder physique that steroids produce had previously been thought to impair the flexibility required for baseball rather than provide a competitive edge.[1] The use of illegal stimulants like amphetamines to gain an edge was commonplace before 1987, but did not create a stir because they did not bring about "unnatural" changes in body configuration and strength.[2]

Steroid use in baseball first gained visibility when Annie Leibovitz published photos of a shirtless Jose Canseco in *Vanity Fair* during his 40–40 season in 1988. Canseco's sculpted physique raised eyebrows. Concerns grew with a spate of 50-home-run seasons in the 1990s, capped by the epic Mark McGwire-Sammy Sosa race past Roger Maris's home-run record in 1998, and culminated with Barry Bonds's allegedly steroid-fueled late-career power surge in 2001–04.[3] The impact of PED use was reflected most visibly in the home run totals of hitters who used them.[4] The 50-home-run threshold had previously been reached or surpassed only 17 times in the first 70 years of the "live-ball" era (1920–89)—four times by Ruth, twice each by Jimmie Foxx, Ralph Kiner, Mickey Mantle, and Willie Mays, and once each by George Foster, Hank Greenberg, Maris, Johnny Mize, and Hack Wilson.[5] However, the 50-home-run threshold was reached or exceeded 29 times in 30 years (1990–2019) by 20 players (including four times each by McGwire and Sammy Sosa), and the 60-home-run threshold was exceeded six times—by Sosa (3), McGwire (2), and Bonds. Twenty-three of these 29 post-1989 50-home-run seasons occurred between 1995 and 2007; at least 13 of them were generated by known steroid users. Bonds hit more than 40 homers only two times (46 in 1993, 42 in 1996) before he supposedly began using steroids in 1999; he did so five times in 2000–04 at ages 35–39.

Apart from the undeniable effect of anabolic steroids on muscle mass and strength, which was responsible for the proliferation of 50-home-run seasons, the remarkable late career success of noted PED accusees Barry Bonds and Roger Clemens—who remained elite players in their late 30s and played through age 42 and 44, respectively—spawned a secondary narrative that PED use also prolonged careers. In a 2018 retrospective, Ben Lindbergh wrote, "There's the unusual aging profile that set that period apart, which would be consistent with the belief that steroids could aid in recovery. McGwire was in his age 34–35 seasons when he hit 70 and 65 bombs in back-to-back years; Barry Bonds was 37 when he hit no. 73. Their atypical aging pattern mirrored the overall major league landscape, which, when weighted by WAR, was heavily skewed toward oldsters to a greater degree than at any other time since the introduction of the DH."[6]

Analyst Bill James went even further: "One of the characteristics of the steroid era was that we had several dozen players who continued to improve beyond the normal aging time frame, so that many of them had their best seasons past the age of 32. This is historically not normal. In the post-steroid era we are returning to the historic norm in which players hit a wall sometime in their early thirties. But what does this mean? It means that steroids keep you young."[7] James provided no specific evidence for this startling conclusion, which drew considerable criticism, as did his prediction that by 2040–50 the normalization of anti-aging drugs will open the Hall of Fame gates wide for Bonds, Clemens, et al.[8] Only time will tell whether the latter prediction holds water, but we need not wait until 2050 to assess the premise that performance enhancing drugs arrest or reverse the deterioration of baseball skills with advancing age. In this article, I will present an in-depth historical analysis of how the age distribution of MLB players has changed throughout its history and will attempt to gauge the possible impact of PED on career longevity. Specifically, I will address two questions:

1. Was the average career longevity in the Steroid Era historically unprecedented, as Bill James claimed?

2. Were PED users more likely to remain productive into their late 30s and 40s than their non-PED-using contemporaries?

METHODS

These analyses encompass the following seven organizations: the National Association (1871–75), National League (1876–2020), American Association (1882–91), Union Association (1884), Players League (1890), American League (1901–2020), and Federal League (1914–15). (Data from the Negro Leagues are not yet sufficiently complete to include here.)

I have analyzed the age distribution of playing time—plate appearances (PA) for hitters and batters faced (BF) for pitchers—using the 2020 version of Lahman's Baseball Database, which is complete through the 2019 season. I added 2020 PA and BF data from Baseball-Reference.com.[9,10] I have analyzed the age distribution of WAR for hitters (WAR_H) and pitchers (WAR_P) using BaseballReference's STATHEAD analytic tool to count the numbers of players with WAR ≥ 2.0 in different age groups in 5-year intervals and to prepare historical lists of players with the most WAR accrued starting at ages 32, 36, and 40.[11]

For the purpose of my analysis of players who debuted between 1980 and 2000, I have defined PED to include anabolic steroids and human growth hormone (HGH), but not amphetamines and similar stimulants (which were in use long before the Steroid Era). PED users were defined as players who tested positive at any time for steroids, HGH, or masking agents (including leaked 2003 results), players who admitted (or whose spouses admitted) they used PED, and players implicated in the Mitchell Report or the Biogenesis Anti-Aging Clinic investigation.[12,13] I have also included three players (Bagwell, Piazza, and Ivan Rodriguez) whose Hall of Fame election was delayed by circumstantial evidence of PED use. Presumed PED users are listed in Tables 4–5 below.

Linear regression analyses relating WAR after age 35 (dependent variable) to purported PED use and WAR through age 35 (independent variables) were performed using the LINEST function in Microsoft Excel. Position players and pitchers were analyzed separately. Tests of statistical significance were based on the z-score (slope divided by its standard error) of the regression coefficient for PED use.

RESULTS

To establish a framework of what is "normal" in baseball, let us begin by looking at the age distribution of the nearly 17 million pitcher-batter confrontations and the nearly 20,000 2-WAR seasons in the seven organizations identified 1871–2020 (Table 1). I have taken 2 WAR (Baseball-Reference version) as indicative of a solid everyday player or member of his team's pitching rotation.[14]

Table 1. Distribution of Playing Time and 2-WAR Seasons by Age (1871–2020)

Age	Hitters		Pitchers	
	PA	$WAR_H \geq 2$	BF	$WAR_P \geq 2$
Group	(%)	(%)	(%)	(%)
< 32	79.08	80.57	80.77	79.11
32-35	16.03	15.44	13.82	14.69
36-39	4.89	3.62	4.20	4.71
≥ 40	0.62	0.37	1.21	1.49

Ben Lindbergh and Bill James were quite correct in characterizing baseball as a game for young men. Historically, roughly 80% of all PA and BF have gone to players under 32 years of age. Only 5.4% of PA and BF have gone to players over age 35. Although there are almost twice as many age 40+ pitchers as age 40+ hitters (1.2% versus 0.6%), both are rare. Similarly, roughly 80% of all 2-WAR seasons belong to players under age 32. While pitchers are more likely than hitters to hold their value beyond age 35, only 6% of 2-WAR_P seasons (versus 4% of 2-WAR_H seasons) occur after age 35.

So how does the Steroid Era compare to these historical norms? The percentage of PA and BF going to players at or above age 32, 36, and 40 are plotted in five-year intervals from 1871–2020 in Figures 1 and 2.

Figure 1. Trend in Age Distribution of PA (Hitters)

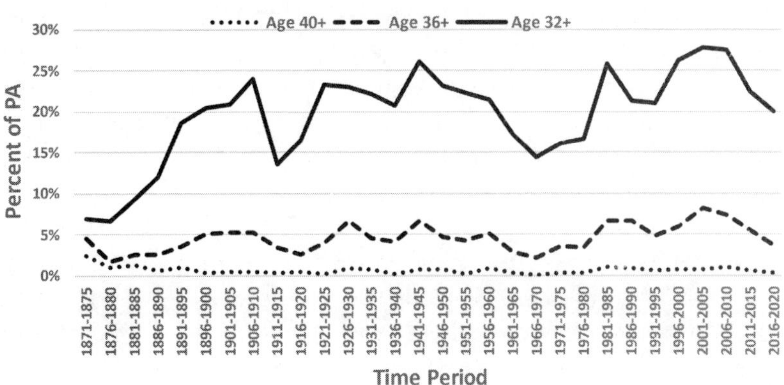

Figure 2. Trend in Age Distribution of BF (Pitchers)

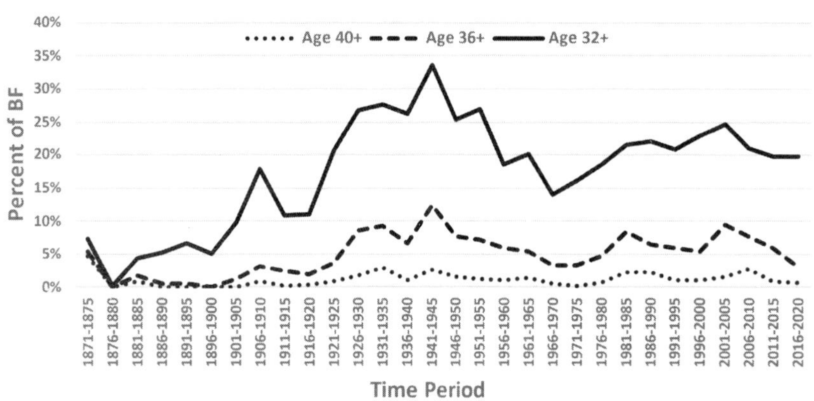

The age distributions for hitters and (to a lesser extent) pitchers did indeed skew somewhat older in the height of the Steroid Era (1996–2010) relative to the preceding or subsequent decades. But the broad historical trend is complex. First, there is a long-term linear trend toward gradually increasing prevalence of older players over time, especially in 1871–1925, paralleling the increase in life expectancy in US males from 42 to 58 years during this 54-year period.[15] Second and not surprisingly, the MLB population appeared to skew older in the war years (1941–45) and younger in periods of expansion. Third, the 1996–2010 "steroid peak" is but one of many peaks in the prevalence of older players and is not necessarily even the highest peak. The percentage of BF going to pitchers aged 32 and older was higher in 1926–55 than during the Steroid Era. While the percentage of PA going to batters aged 32 and older reached an all-time high in 1996–2010, it was relatively low earlier in the Steroid Era in 1986–95. Also, the difference between the 1926–55 and 1996–2010 distributions of PA is consistent with the underlying temporal trend toward an increase in older players.

While Figures 1–2 show that the Steroid Era was associated with only a small increase in the playing time going to older players, the quality of these older players is addressed in Figures 3 and 4, where the proportion of players with Baseball-Reference WAR ≥ 2 in the 32 + , 36 + , and 40 + age groups is plotted over the course of MLB history.

Again, while the proportion of solid everyday regulars and rotation starters contributing after they turned 32 was higher 1991–2010 than in the decades immediately preceding or following this period, there have been other times in MLB history when this proportion was even higher: 1906–10 and 1921–25 for hitters and 1921–55 for pitchers. The data again suggest a possible PED bump but nothing more. The extreme scarcity of older nineteenth-century pitchers with $WAR_P \geq 2$, which almost certainly reflects attrition due to extreme (400–700 IP) annual workloads, is also noteworthy.

Let us now look more closely at the 13 hitters (Table 2) and 26 pitchers (Table 3) who accrued at least 20 WAR after age 35. I chose age 35 as a cutoff, since there are too many players (125 hitters and 91 pitchers) with at least 20.0 WAR after turning 32 to list here and very few (no hitters and seven pitchers) with at least 20.0 WAR in their 40s. You can find the post-age 40 WAR of these players in the far-right column.

Figure 3. Age Distribution of Hitters with $WAR_H \geq 2$

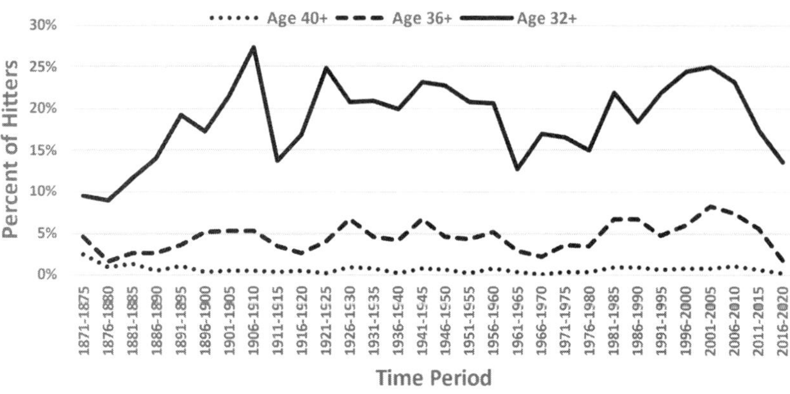

Figure 4. Age Distribution of Pitchers with $WAR_P \geq 2$

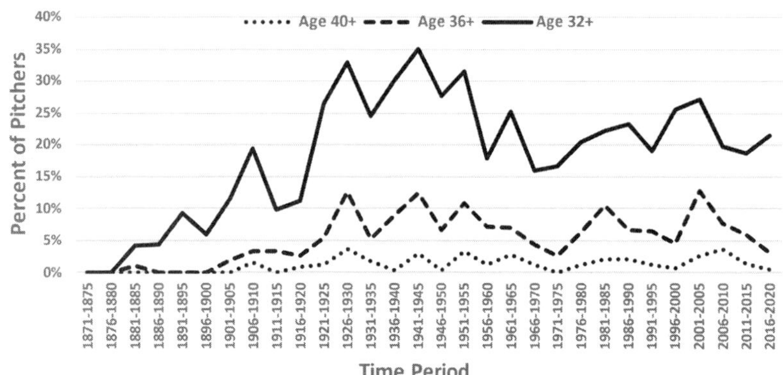

Table 2. Hitters with ≥ 20 WAR_H After Age 35

	Hitter	Age (Years)	WAR_H Age 36+	Age 40+
1	Barry Bonds	36–42 (2001–07)	51.4	8.0
2	Cap Anson	36–45 (1888–97)	36.4	13.8
3	Honus Wagner	36–43 (1910–17)	34.3	11.6
4	Babe Ruth	36–40 (1931–35)	30.2	0.1
5	Ted Williams	36–41 (1955–60)	29.5	2.8
6	Luke Appling	36–43 (1943–50)	27.9	13.4
7	Willie Mays	36–42 (1967–73)	27.0	8.2
8	Ty Cobb	36–41 (1923–28)	24.5	6.3
9	Hank Aaron	36–42 (1970–76)	23.4	2.5
10	Eddie Collins	36–43 (1923–30)	23.1	2.3
11	Edgar Martinez	36–41 (1999–2004)	20.9	3.0
12	Tris Speaker	36–40 (1924–28)	20.5	0.5
13	Joe Start	36–43 (1879–86)	20.2	7.9

Table 2 is dominated by elite Hall of Famers, who were exceptional in their 20s and early 30s as well as after age 35. These hitters were not immune from aging—their declines merely started from a very high performance level. The only non-Hall of Famers listed are Bonds and Joe Start, who was born too early (1842) to play in the majors until age 33. Table 3 is more diverse.

While Table 3 also includes several Hall of Famers (Randy Johnson, Young, Vance, Grove, Ryan, Spahn, Alexander, Rivera, etc.), they are joined by a similar number of knuckleballers (Niekro, Wilhelm, Hough, Leonard, Lyons, Niggeling), spitballers (Quinn, Perry, Faber), and others (Moyer, John) who relied more on guile than power and whose longevity derived from the minimal wear and tear on their pitching arms. **Bonds and Clemens are the only suspected PED users with more than 20 WAR after age 35**. The only other PED user with ≥ 15 WAR after age 35 is David Ortiz (18.6), whose only (rumored) positive PED test was in 2003 at age 27. Rafael Palmeiro (13.8), Nelson Cruz (13.3), Bartolo Colon (13.2), Andy Pettitte (12.5), and Randy Velarde (10.9), were the only other PED users with more than 10 WAR after age 35.

Our analyses thus far have looked broadly at historical trends in which the impact of PED is diluted by the far larger numbers of non-users. After all, as far as we know, steroids and HGH gained a foothold in MLB only in the late 1980s and even then were used by a minority of players. Only 5–10% of players were documented as using PEDs when MLB introduced random drug testing in 2003, and we have no hard evidence that the prevalence of PED use ever exceeded that level.[16] The next two tables represent a deeper dive into the players of the Steroid Era whose careers began

Table 3. Pitchers with ≥ 20 WAR_P After Age 35

	Pitcher	Age (Years)	WAR_H Age 36+	Age 40+
1	Phil Niekro	36–48 (1975–87)	57.7	25.4
2	Randy Johnson	36–45 (2000–09)	51.3	20.7
3	Cy Young	36–44 (1903–11)	48.4	23.3
4	Jack Quinn	36–49 (1920–33)	42.9	27.0
5	Roger Clemens	36–44 (1999–2007)	37.9	22.2
6	Dazzy Vance	36–44 (1927–35)	36.0	5.8
7	Lefty Grove	36–41 (1936–41)	35.9	2.8
8	Hoyt Wilhelm	36–49 (1959–72)	33.9	20.2
9	Nolan Ryan	36–46 (1983–93)	31.0	22.6
10	Warren Spahn	36–44 (1957–65)	29.3	12.3
11	Gaylord Perry	36–44 (1975–83)	28.9	10.2
12	Jamie Moyer	36–49 (1999–2012)	28.8	13.4
13	Dennis Martinez	36–44 (1990–98)	27.7	9.7
14	Charlie Hough	36–46 (1984–94)	27.0	10.0
15	Pete Alexander	36–43 (1923–30)	26.3	11.5
16	Dutch Leonard	36–44 (1945–53)	26.0	9.1
17	Curt Schilling	36–40 (2003–07)	23.6	4.0
18	David Wells	36–44 (1999–2007)	23.4	10.5
19	Tommy John	36–46 (1979–89)	22.9	6.5
20	Eddie Plank	36–41 (1912–17)	22.6	6.8
21	Babe Adams	36–44 (1918–26)	22.5	4.7
22	Ted Lyons	36–45 (1937–46)	22.1	7.8
23	Red Faber	36–44 (1925–33)	22.1	12.2
24	Mariano Rivera	36–43 (2006–13)	21.8	8.1
25	John Smoltz	36–42 (2003–09)	21.2	4.9
26	Johnny Niggeling	36–42 (1940–46)	20.5	5.9

in 1980–2000 and who accrued at least 10 WAR through age 35. (The 2000 cutoff was chosen to exclude all players whose careers are unfinished.)

Table 4 compares the average WAR_H accrued through and after age 35 by the 33 position players strongly suspected of PED use versus 296 position players not strongly suspected of PED use. On the average, the 33 PED users accrued more WAR_H (4.3 versus 1.3) than non-users after age 35, but they had also accrued more WAR_H (42.0 versus 26.6) through their age 35 seasons. Thus, the PED users—at least the ones we know about—were in general more productive through age 35 than non-users, although one cannot be certain whether this was *because* they used PEDs or whether they were just better players in the first place. In either case, if one wants to focus specifically on the *anti-aging* effect of PEDs, one must statistically adjust for the fact that players who were most productive in their 20s and early 30s were most likely to remain productive after age 35. This adjustment was done by using regression analysis to predict post-age 35 WAR_H as a linear function of WAR_H

through age 35 (Table 4) and subtracting this number from the player's actual post-age 35 WAR_H. After this adjustment, the average difference between PED users and non-users shrinks to 0.85 WAR_H (0.8 versus -0.1) and is not statistically significant (Z = 1.32, P = 0.19). Indeed, when Barry Bonds (who is something of an outlier) is removed from the regression analysis, PED use is associated with only a 0.26 increment in WAR_H after age 35 than non-users (Z = 0.28, 2-sided P = 0.78).

Table 5 shows the result of a similar analysis of the 232 pitchers who made their MLB debuts in 1980–2000 and accrued at least 10 WAR_P through their age 35 season. The adjusted post-age 35 productivity of the 12 such pitchers who were strongly suspected of PED use was compared to that of the 220 such pitchers who were not considered PED users before and after statistical adjustment for the WARP through their age 35 season.

Table 4. Position Players Suspected of PED Use— Actual versus Expected WAR_H After Age 35

PED Users	WAR_H Age ≤ 35	WAR_H after Age 35 Actual	Expected*	Difference
Barry Bonds	111.4	51.4	12.8	38.6
David Ortiz	36.7	18.6	2.8	15.8
Randy Velarde	14.0	10.9	-0.3	11.2
Rafael Palmeiro	58.1	13.8	5.7	8.1
Benito Santiago	22.1	5.3	0.8	4.5
Manny Ramirez	60.7	8.7	6.0	2.7
Gary Sheffield	52.9	7.6	5.0	2.6
David Segui	10.1	0.3	-0.8	1.1
Todd Hundley	10.9	0.0	-0.7	0.7
Hal Morris	13.4	0.0	-0.4	0.4
Wally Joyner	33.2	2.6	2.3	0.3
Jerry Hairston	13.2	-0.1	-0.4	0.3
Gary Matthews, Jr.	14.2	0.0	-0.2	0.2
David Bell	15.2	0.0	-0.1	0.1
Ken Caminiti	31.5	2.0	2.1	-0.1
Mark McGwire	57.7	4.5	5.6	-1.1
Paul Lo Duca	18.8	-0.9	0.4	-1.3
David Justice	39.0	1.6	3.1	-1.5
Mo Vaughn	27.1	0.0	1.5	-1.5
Rondell White	28.2	0.0	1.6	-1.6
Mike Piazza	56.4	3.2	5.4	-2.2
Jason Giambi	48.4	2.1	4.4	-2.3
Jose Canseco	41.8	0.8	3.5	-2.7
Miguel Tejada	46.0	1.1	4.0	-2.9
Troy Glaus	38.1	0.0	3.0	-3.0
Juan Gonzalez	38.7	0.0	3.1	-3.1
Bret Boone	25.0	-2.1	1.2	-3.3
Lenny Dykstra	42.5	0.0	3.6	-3.6
Matt Williams	46.3	0.3	4.1	-3.8
Chuck Knoblauch	44.6	0.0	3.8	-3.8
Jeff Bagwell	75.9	4.0	8.1	-4.1
Ivan Rodriguez	66.7	2.0	6.8	-4.8
Sammy Sosa	59.5	-0.9	5.9	-6.8
Alex Rodriguez	113.5	4.0	13.1	-9.1
Averages				
PED Users (N = 34)	41.5	4.1	3.4	0.7
PED Non-Users (N=295)	26.6	1.3	1.4	-0.1

* Based on linear regression equation Y= -2.16 + 0.1347*X, where Y=WAR_H after age 35 and X = WAR_H through age 35. This equation is based on 329 position players who made their major league debut in 1980–2000 and accrued at least 10 WAR_H through age 35.

Table 5. Pitchers Suspected of PED Use— Actual versus Expected WAR_P After Age 35

PED Users	WAR_p Age ≤ 35	WAR_p after Age 35 Actual	Expected*	Difference
Roger Clemens	100.8	37.9	18.4	19.5
Chuck Finley	49.5	12.5	7.9	4.6
Bartolo Colon	34.6	8.9	4.9	4.0
Kevin Brown	58.7	13.2	9.8	3.4
Andy Pettite	48.2	9.5	7.6	1.9
Paul Byrd	12.6	1.2	0.4	0.8
Ismael Valdez	24.5	3.3	2.8	0.5
Ryan Franklin	10.3	0.0	-0.1	0.1
Mike Stanton	11.4	0.0	0.1	-0.1
Bronson Arroyo	23.3	2.4	2.5	-0.1
Eric Gagne	11.7	0.0	0.2	-0.2
Denny Neagle	22.5	1.3	2.4	-1.1
Averages				
PED Users (N=12)	41.5	7.5	4.7	2.8
PED Non-Users (N=220)	21.6	2.1	2.2	-0.2

* Based on linear regression equation Y= -2.21 + 0.2043*X, where Y=WAR_P after age 35 and X=Y=WAR_P through age 35. This equation is based on 232 pitchers who made their major league debut in 1980–2000 and accrued at least 10 Y=WAR_P through age 35.

The impact of PED use on WAR_P after age 35 for pitchers was greater than that for position players, but fell slightly short of statistical significance. The 5.4 unadjusted difference in WAR_P after age 35 (7.5 versus 2.1) between the 12 PED users and the 220 non-users fell to 3.0 (2.8 versus -0.2) after statistical adjustment for WAR_P through age 35. Linear regression analysis, adjusted for WAR_P through age 35, showed that PED use was associated with a 3.0 increment in WAR_P after age 35 (Z = 1.82, 2-sided P = 0.07). When Clemens is removed from this analysis, PED use is associated with only a 1.67 higher WAR_P after age 35 than non-users (Z = 0.96, 2-sided P = 0.34).

Like many elite players, Bonds and Clemens are clearly outliers; there is little statistical evidence beyond these two players that alleged PED use broadly increased WAR after age 35. Since we cannot find good matches for Bonds and Clemens among their contemporaries, comparing the career WAR trajectories of Barry Bonds (Figure 5) and Roger Clemens (Figure 6) to two players of earlier eras (Willie Mays and Tom Seaver) with similar early career WAR trajectories is illuminating.

Figure 5 compares the annual season-by-season progression of WAR_H for Mays and Bonds. The two players performed similarly in their 20s. Mays then outperformed Bonds for ages 30–33. Bonds is assumed to have begun using anabolic steroids at age 34 (1999), but missed two months with an injury.[17] The 36–39-year-old steroid-enhanced version of Bonds far outperformed the 36–39-year old Mays. However, the two men performed similarly in their 40s, and their careers ended at about the same age.

Similarly, Figure 6 compares the annual season-by-season progression of WAR_P for Seaver and Clemens as a function of age. The two pitchers performed very similarly through age 33. Then, at ages 34–35, when Seaver was fading, Clemens suddenly surged to successive Cy Young awards. According to Kurt Radomsky's testimony, Clemens used PEDs in his 8.5-WAR_P age 35 season (1998), but we can only guess whether he also used PEDs in his 11.9-WAR_P age 34 season (1997).[18] In contrast to the Bonds-Mays comparison, Clemens outlasted Seaver and accrued 12.8 WAR_P at ages 42–44, after Seaver had already retired. But Clemens did not outlast some other great power pitchers, like his contemporaries Nolan Ryan and Randy Johnson, or the man (Cy Young) whose award he won seven times (Table 3).

DISCUSSION

Let us now return to answer the two questions asked at the end of the introduction.

1. The proportion of players who remained active and productive beyond their early 30s was indeed higher during the Steroid Era than in many preceding periods but was *not* historically unprecedented (Figures 1–4). Specifically, older pitchers—led by knuckleballers, spitballers, and other finesse pitchers—were more prominent in 1925–55 than at any time during the Steroid Era.

2. Although the Steroid Era data suggest that PED users tend to have outperformed non-users after age 35, this effect is modest at best and not statistically significant. The data are somewhat more convincing for pitchers than hitters, but the numbers are small and influenced by outliers like Bonds and Clemens. Moreover, due to the absence of a testing regimen before 2004, our information on who actually used PED and when exactly did they use them is incomplete and somewhat unreliable.

Performance-enhancing drugs are but one of many potential contributors to the historical fluctuation of the age distribution of MLB playing time, before, during, and after the Steroid Era. Other potential contributors include:

- **Pitcher usage patterns**: Nineteenth century pitchers, who routinely pitched 400–700 innings per season, rarely lasted into their mid-30s. The five pre-Cy Young pitchers who accrued at least 65 WAR_P— Tim Keefe, John Clarkson, Pud Galvin, Jim McCormick, and Old Hoss Radbourn—accrued a combined total of 0.5 WAR_P after age 35; none pitched an inning after age 36.

- **Improved general health and life expectancy**: The mean life expectancy at birth for US males varied between 40 and 45 years in 1870–90.[19] Although this statistic was heavily influenced by high mortality rates in infancy

Figure 5. Bonds versus Mays

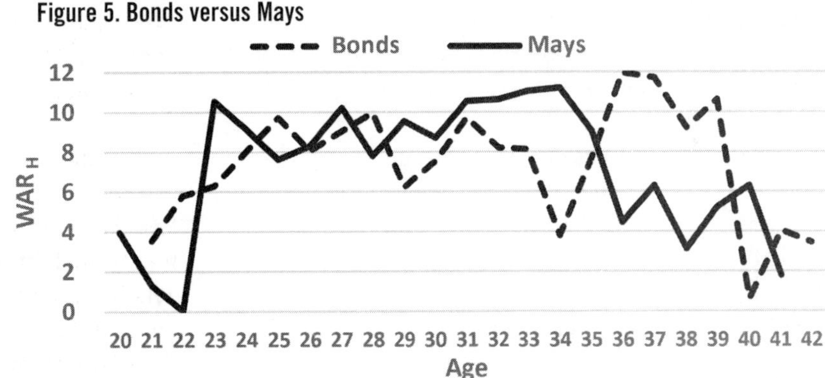

Figure 6. Clemens versus Seaver

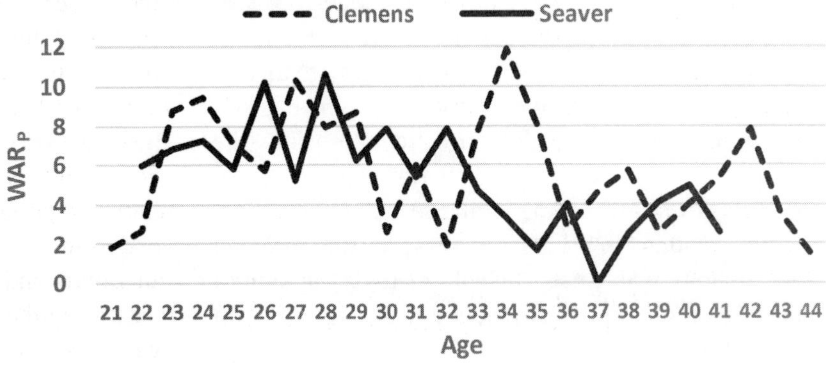

Clemens
Seaver
WAR_P
0 2 4 6 8 10 12
21 22 23 24 25 26 27 28 29 30 31 32 33 34 35 36 37 38 39 40 41 42 43 44
Age

and early childhood, a 40-year-old nineteenth century player was still much older biologically than a modern 40-year-old player. Indeed, Clarkson (47), Galvin (45), and Radbourn (42) were all dead by age 47, an age at which Phil Niekro, Jack Quinn, Hoyt Wilhelm, and Jamie Moyer were still getting major league hitters out. As life expectancy has increased by 35 years between 1870 and 2020, it is not surprising that the prevalence of older players has gradually trended upward.[20]

- **Improved medical and surgical techniques**: For example, before Dr. Frank Jobe operated on Tommy John in 1974, a torn ulnar collateral ligament spelled the end of a pitcher's career.

- **Expansion**: The prevalence of older players has tended to dip when there was a sudden influx of younger players to staff the new teams. This was most apparent when the Federal League was established in 1914 and eight new teams were abruptly added to the existing 16, but expansion may have also contributed to the drop in prevalence of older players in the 1960s and 1970s.

- **World War II**: The proportion of playing time allocated to older players spiked in 1942–45 when many younger players were serving in the military. However, this mid-century spike cannot be attributed solely to the war, since this proportion had been increasing since the mid-1920s and remained elevated into the 1950s.

- **Long-term free agent contracts**: Dave Cameron has suggested that the sharp decline in the proportion of playing time allocated to older players in 2011–20 may reflect MLB owners' growing aversion to offering multi-year deals to older free agents, more than the waning of the Steroid Era.[21]

While PED usage may have been a contributing factor in the higher-than-normal prevalence of older players in 1995–2010, their impact is modest at best. PED clearly made hitters better, but did not demonstrably prolong their careers. Barry Bonds's production spiked in his late 30s because that is when he had settled into an optimal conditioning program using "the cream" and "the clear." But his performance declined in his 40s just as Mays's performance had declined after he turned 40 in 1971. Lesser players like McGwire and Sosa, who probably used anabolic steroids throughout their careers, were less productive after age 35 than players who did not use PEDs (Table 4).

Pitchers are a bit different because their careers are often limited by the wear and tear on specific muscle groups and ligaments in their pitching arm and shoulder. HGH, which is said to promote recovery and healing without necessarily building muscle mass, features more prominently in the regimen of pitchers than of hitters who used PEDs. Still, aside from Roger Clemens, there is little statistical support for the proposition that PED users were more likely than non-users to remain productive after age 35 (Table 5).

The analyses in Tables 4–5 are of course not definitive, since we do not know for sure exactly who used PEDs, which drugs they used, and how long they used them. For example, I included Jeff Bagwell, who used androstenedione in 1995–97 when it was legal, but for whom the record gets murky after 1997. I did not include players who were the subject of uncorroborated steroid rumors after outlier seasons, like Brady Anderson (1996) and Luis Gonzalez (2001). Admittedly, our classification of PED users and non-users represents only best guesses based on public information.

One might argue that any association of career length with PED use could be at least partly attributable to the increasing likelihood of getting caught using PEDs the longer a player uses them. On the other hand, some players whom I counted as PED users (Sosa, Ortiz) may have stopped using them after testing protocols and penalties were implemented in 2004, so we really don't know whether PEDs could have prolonged their careers. Sammy Sosa's performance, for example, declined precipitously in 2003–05 (ages 34–36) after routine testing was implemented, while Ortiz's performance took off during those years. It is noteworthy in this vein that the prevalence of productive older players was *higher* in 2006–10, *after* testing protocols and penalties were in place, than in 1990–2000, when players were able to use PEDs with impunity. If PED use actually lengthened careers, one would have expected this effect to have diminished after 2004, when it became increasingly difficult for PED users to stay on the field—let alone remain productive—as they aged. For example, the late career productivity of Alex Rodriguez and more recently Robinson Cano were ruined by lengthy suspensions.

As a retired physician, I cannot help but comment here on the irresponsible marketing of anabolic steroids and HGH as "fountain of youth" or "anti-aging" drugs.[22] Indeed, the latter term even appears in the name of the Biogenesis *Anti-Aging* Clinic, which provided steroids to Alex Rodriguez and others 10 years ago. The legitimate use of testosterone and HGH to treat patients with low testosterone levels and pituitary deficiency, respectively, does not imply that they mitigate or delay the effects of aging or prolong life or justify their use by healthy young athletes. Just as insulin injections, which are life-saving in diabetes, would be dangerous and even lethal in persons without diabetes, anabolic steroids can be dangerous when misused.[23] Natural steroid supplements have gotten a partial pass from the US Food and Drug Administration (FDA), which requires only evidence of safety, not efficacy. However, the FDA has *not* endorsed the safety of the synthetic anabolic steroids that young athletes have injected, applied topically, or ingested in unapproved over-the-counter supplements to add muscle mass, and has warned of the potential for addiction, serious liver and kidney injury, severe acne, hair loss, irritability, increased aggression, depression, heart attack, stroke, deep vein thrombosis, and pulmonary embolism.[24] The wrecked lives and early deaths of steroid-abusing athletes Ken Caminiti and Lyle Alzado attest to the danger of these drugs and the falsity of steroids' promise of eternal youth.[25, 26]

In conclusion, although the last decade of the Steroid Era was temporally associated with a modest increase in the number of players sustaining productive MLB careers beyond age 32, it is not clear that PED were actually responsible for this increase. While rigorous training regimens incorporating anabolic steroids undoubtedly helped many players of the Steroid Era build muscle mass and strength and thereby attain inflated home run totals at all stages of their careers, there is no convincing evidence that they slowed the inevitable decline associated with aging. ■

Notes

1. Christopher Klein, "Baseball's First Fountain of Youth," History.com, 2012. https://www.history.com/news/baseballs-first-fountain-of-youth; Joe Halverson, "Pud Galvin: The Godfather of Juicing," Bleacher Report, undated, https://bleacherreport.com/articles/573866-pud-galvin-the-godfather-of-juicing.
2. Zachary D. Rymer, "Full Timeline of MLB's Failed Attempts to Rid the Game of PEDs." Bleacher Report, June 10, 2013. https://bleacherreport.com/articles/1667581-full-timeline-of-mlbs-failed-attempts-to-rid-the-game-of-peds.
3. Jose Canseco images, Bing image search performed Ocotober 11, 2021. https://www.bing.com/images/search?q=Jose+Canseco+Muscles&FORM=IRBPRS&=0.
4. B.J. Erickson, A. Yanke, B. Monson, A. Romeo, "The Effect of the Steroid Era on Major League Baseball Hitters: Did It Enhance Hitting?" *Journal of Sports Medicine*, Doping Stud 5: 161. doi:10.4172/2161-0673.1000161, https://www.hilarispublisher.com/open-access/the-effect-of-the-steroid-era-on-major-league-baseball-hitters-did-it-enhance-hitting-2161-0673-1000161.pdf.
5. Baseball-Reference.com, "Single-season leaders and records for home runs," https://www.baseball-reference.com/leaders/HR_season.shtml.
6. Ben Lindbergh, "How much of a role did steroids play in the Steroid Era?" The Ringer, September 28, 2018, https://www.theringer.com/mlb/2018/9/28/17913536/mark-mcgwire-sammy-sosa-steroid-era-home-run-chase.
7. Bill James, "Cooperstown and the 'Roids," Bill James Online, 2009, https://www.billjamesonline.com/article1160.
8. Jeb Stewart, "A response to Bill James' 'Cooperstown and the 'Roids,'" The Baseball Chronicle 2009, http://thebaseballchronicle.com/essays/response_to_bill_james.
9. Sean Lahman, Download Lahman's Baseball Database, http://www.seanlahman.com/baseball-archive/statistics.
10. Baseball-Reference.com, https://www.baseball-reference.com.
11. Stathead Baseball, https://stathead.com/baseball.
12. George J. Mitchell, 2007. "Report to the Commissioner of Baseball of an Independent Investigation into the Illegal Use of Steroids and Other Performance Enhancing Substances by Players in Major League Baseball," http://mlb.mlb.com/mlb/news/mitchell.
13. Michael Solomon, "The Biogenesis scandal explained," *The Guardian*, August 2, 2013, https://www.theguardian.com/sport/2013/aug/02/biogenesis-peds-scandal-explained.
14. Baseball-Reference.com WAR Explained, https://www.baseball-reference.com/about/war_explained.shtml.
15. Life Expectancy 1850-2000, University of Oregon, Mapping History: https://mappinghistory.uoregon.edu/english/US/US39-01.html.
16. Jack Curry and Jere Longman, "Results of steroid testing spur baseball to set tougher rules," *The New York Times*, November 14, 2003, https://www.nytimes.com/2003/11/14/sports/results-of-steroid-testing-spur-baseball-to-set-tougher-rules.html.
17. Mark Fainaru-Wada and Lance Williams, *Game of Shadows*. Gotham Books, New York, 2006.
18. Frederick C. Bush, "Roger Clemens," SABR BioProject. https://sabr.org/bioproj/person/b5a2be2f.
19. Life Expectancy 1850-2000, University of Oregon, Mapping History: https://mappinghistory.uoregon.edu/english/US/US39-01.html.
20. Macrotrends, US Life Expectancy 1950-2020, https://www.macrotrends.net/countries/USA/united-states/life-expectancy.
21. Dave Cameron, "The other big change in MLB's post-PED era," Fangraphs, February 4, 2016, https://blogs.fangraphs.com/the-other-big-change-in-mlbs-post-ped-era.
22. Harvard Medical School, "Human growth hormone and the search for the fountain of youth," Harvard Health Publishing, January 2015, https://www.health.harvard.edu/drugs-and-medications/human-growth-hormone-and-the-search-for-the-fountain-of-youth.
23. National Institute on Drug Abuse, "Anabolic Steroids DrugFacts," https://www.drugabuse.gov/publications/drugfacts/anabolic-steroids.
24. FDA Consumer Updates, "Caution: Body-building products can be risky," https://www.fda.gov/consumers/consumer-updates/caution-bodybuilding-products-can-be-risky.
25. Paul E. Doutrich, "Ken Caminiti," SABR BioProject, https://sabr.org/bioproj/person/ken-caminiti.
26. Mike Thomas, "Lyle Alzado's tragic story of lies, steroids, and his untimely death at age 43," Sportscasting, June 6, 2020, https://www.sportscasting.com/lyle-alzados-tragic-story-of-lies-steroids-and-his-untimely-death-at-age-43.

Community of Inquiry

A Blueprint for Bringing Baseball to African American Youth

Dave Ogden, PhD

From youth "select" baseball to the major leagues, the percentage of players who are African American has reached a historic low. As low as the percentage on 2020 MLB teams' 30-man rosters had ebbed (7.5 percent[1]), it is even lower among college players and youth players.[2] Scholars and pundits have offered reasons for, and solutions to, the decades-long disappearance of African Americans from the nation's ball fields. Their science-based solutions to address this demise rely on concepts in the social sciences and offer insights into African Americans' lack of involvement in baseball.[3] While those insights provide valuable theoretical guidance, they do not focus on the essence of the issue: Youngsters must be taught baseball to appreciate baseball. The literature lacks a pedagogical—or teaching-driven—approach in analyzing the paucity of African Americans in baseball.

Some organizations have tied baseball to other learning programs for inner city youth. Elementary Baseball in Washington, DC, for example, offered baseball instruction as a reward for participating in a literacy program mentored by judicial officials.[4] The approach proposed in this article extends educational principles into the teaching of baseball itself. This approach considers youth baseball as it is: a learning experience. It also provides ideas to increase interest in baseball by African American youth to the point that they graduate to higher levels of competition and subsequently to college and the professional ranks.

A fulfilling learning experience is needed to build the relationship between African American communities and baseball. An overarching educational paradigm incorporating interactive elements, called the Community of Inquiry, or CoI, would provide that experience. CoI emerged with the growth of online classes and technology in higher education,[5] and describes a framework for maximizing an individual's virtual learning environment, but has not been applied to interest or involvement in sports, much less baseball. When used as a lens to look at African Americans and baseball, CoI draws together theoretical perspectives from leisure studies, sport sociology, and cultural studies. Just as importantly, CoI offers a holistic approach by binding those perspectives and showing how they interact.

Individually, those perspectives have been discussed—some more than others—in the sports sociology and baseball research literature. The intent of this article is to add to the scholarship by examining the low number of African Americans in competitive baseball, previous research on the issue, and the coalescence under the CoI framework of theoretical perspectives from that research, all in an effort to understand factors affecting the likelihood of African American youth becoming engaged in baseball.

LITERATURE REVIEW

The concept, Community of Inquiry, as described by D. Randy Garrison, Terry Anderson, and Walter Archer, aims to provide a model to engage students through computer conferencing and to identify the elements necessary to optimize learning. The model reflects the basic tenets of learning as laid out more than 60 years ago by pedagogical scholar and writer, John Dewey. Dewey maintained that "the educational process has two sides—one psychological and one sociological" and "neither can be subordinated to the other."[6] Elaborating on Dewey's concepts in developing the CoI model, Garrison and colleagues describe the environment most conducive to a positive learning experience and the creation of a learning cohort.[7] Collectively, sports sociologists have described those same elements, but in different terms. The three conceptual "pillars" of the CoI are teaching presence, social presence, and cognitive presence. The pillars and concepts from the sports and leisure sciences and cultural studies covered by each pillar can be synthesized as follows.

Teaching presence. As perceived by Garrison and his colleagues, "direct instruction" is at the core of developing teaching presence. "Teacher immediacy" facilitates communication between teacher and student.[8] The teacher helps to shape the learning environment by setting "explicit and implicit structural parameters and organizational guidelines" and by enhancing "understanding through various means of assessment and feedback."[9] The teacher bears responsibility for "providing immediate and diagnostic feedback to student responses."[10] Baseball coaches do the same when they teach the game. Beyond skills instruction, though, coaches contribute to the social presence by serving as authority figures. They, like teachers, organize and construct the learning experience for their players and serve as accessible instructors.

The sports sociology literature and the mainstream media tend to focus on the importance of a coaching "presence," with the mainstream media quicker to point out the causes of the absence of that presence for baseball in African American communities. "The demise of the two-parent household and the passionate neighborhood volunteer coach have cut the connection between baseball and young blacks," Tom Verducci wrote in a 2003 article in *Sports Illustrated*.[11] Verducci's concerns have been echoed for years by journalists such as David Canton of *U.S. News*, who observed that "deindustrialization, suburbanization and mass incarceration....[have] had a disproportionate impact on black men and their community and are the major reason why the percentage of black baseball players has declined since 1981."[12]

That lack of role models stymies one of the CoI's most fundamental elements to teaching presence: "building understanding." Like the youth baseball coach and his players, "the teacher draws in less active participants, acknowledges individual contributions, reinforces appropriate contributions,...and generally facilitates an educational transaction."[13] Those transactions can't take place, according to the CoI paradigm, without a teacher who provides meaningful, timely, and personal instruction. Like the role of the teacher in a community of inquiry in building a "group consciousness,"[14] the coach assumes the responsibility of building cohesiveness among the learners or, if you will, a team mentality.

Social presence. The concept of social presence refers to fostering a feeling of community and interdependence among fellow learners. Garrison and colleagues say social presence depends on three elements: "emotional expression, open communication, and group cohesion."[15] Social presence can contribute greatly to learning when the participants "find the interaction in the group enjoyable and personally fulfilling."[16] Garrison said that "a sense of belonging" indicates that a participant feels comfortable with fellow learners. "[T]he more individuals know about each other the more likely they are to establish trust, seek support, and thus find satisfaction."[17] African American youth desire that same "sense of belonging" when playing a sport. Sports sociologists and educators agree that identifying with a group enhances the learning experience. Affiliation with peers and other "interpersonal" connections drive a youth's interest and desire to play a particular sport.

For a sport to attract a youngster, it must provide an opportunity to bond with peers.[18] That desire for affiliation with a social group rings true especially for African Americans. Steven F. Philipp—who has published widely about how "welcome" or "unwelcome" African Americans feel within certain sports—and Sherie Brezina found that African American youth, more often than "EuroAmericans," identify "social interaction" as one of the most important reasons for participating in a sport.[19] But parents, as another interpersonal connection, lay the groundwork for their children's interest in particular activities, and African American parents are most likely to steer their children to basketball over all other team sports.[20] When it comes to baseball, scholars Shaun Anderson and Matthew Martin claim that lack of parental involvement can kill a child's interest and chances of playing.[21] According to another study, parents from minority groups and lower socioeconomic levels are less likely than more affluent parents to support their children's sports activities.[22] Together, peers and parents (and other family members) create the social milieu and background that shape a student or young baseball player's learning environment. The player is ensconced in the social presence created by those groups.

Cognitive presence. This concept entails the "reciprocal relationship between the personal and shared worlds." Critical thinking shapes cognitive presence through "the integration of deliberation and action" and "reflects the dynamic relationship between personal meaning and shared understanding (i.e., knowledge)."[23] But the learning process takes place "within the broader social-emotional environment," as Garrison notes.[24] That is, students bring their own backgrounds and intrapersonal traits to learning experiences and learn from each other as they acquire new knowledge. The same can be said for youngsters who are exposed to a sport and the skills which must be learned to play it. Those intrapersonal traits, as defined by Stodoloska and colleagues, encompass "virtually any personal attribute that influences the way an individual views the world and the opportunities it offers."[25]

To whatever degree interpersonal relationships and social and cultural environment shape those traits, a youth looks for resonance between his self-image and the sport he decides to play. Researchers Brandon Brown and Gregg Bennett say this rings true especially for African Americans. Brown and Bennett contend that "African Americans [more so than other racial groups] must perceive a sense of congruence between their racial identity and baseball before choosing to consume the sport. This is supported by literature, as research suggests individuals will likely consume a product given the product possesses features that are representative of one's sense of self-identification".[26] Just as a student must acquire and synthesize knowledge and data to overcome "a state of dissonance or feeling of unease" when confronted with an intellectual or cognitive challenge (according to Garrison's description of "critical inquiry"),[27] a youngster must learn and then repeatedly practice the basic skills necessary to surmount the challenges of playing baseball. To what extent a youngster can find resonance between self-image and the sport will determine how much the youngster devotes to the sport, just as the student's cognitive presence determines the student's degree of and success in "critical inquiry".[28]

THE LOW NUMBER OF AFRICAN AMERICANS IN BASEBALL

In the 2020 Complete Racial and Gender Report Card, Richard Lapchick shows the disparity between the percentage of players who are Black in Major League Baseball (7.5 percent in 2020) and those percentages in the National Basketball Association and National Football League (74 and 57 percent, respectively). Numerous reasons for the disparity have been offered, such as authority figures encouraging African American youth to play sports other than baseball, more peer involvement in basketball and football, higher visibility of role models in those sports, and socioeconomic restraints. Regardless of the reasons, the 2020 MLB percentage marked the lowest since the first Racial Report Card in 1991.[29] That also marked a 60-year low (according to another study) when African Americans constituted 7.4 percent of players on 1958 major league teams. During the next 15 years, that percentage steadily climbed and remained above 17.4 percent between 1973 and 1987. The percentage peaked at 18.7 percent in 1981.[30] Since 2010, it has remained under 9 percent.[31]

The percentage of African Americans on NCAA Division I baseball rosters also remains mired in the single digits. Since 2010 that percentage has ranged between 2.5 and 4.1, the latter in 2019.[32] The percentage of African Americans at the highest levels of competitive youth baseball dips even lower. An 18-year study of youth select—or "travel team"—baseball shows that during the past decade (2010–19), the percentage of African Americans hovered between 2.1 and 3.6 percent (See Table 1). Overall, during the 18 years of primary research on youth select teams, less than 3 percent of the almost 10,000 players were African American.[33]

Table 1. Percentage of Players Who Are African American, 2010–20

Year	Youth Select Ball*	NCAA Div I**	MLB***
2010	2.4	2.8	9.1 (7.8)
2011	--	2.5	8.5 (7.9)
2012	3.6	2.6	8.9 (7.2)
2013	2.1	2.6	8.3 (6.7)
2014	2.2	2.8	8.2 (6.7)
2015	2.2	2.9	8.3 (7.2)
2016	2.2	3.3	8.3 (6.7)
2017	--	3.7	7.7
2018	2.6	3.7	8.4
2019	2.9	4.1	--
2020	--	--	7.5

* Updated from David C. Ogden, "Major League Baseball and the Framing of African Americans," 28th annual Cooperstown Symposium on Baseball and American Culture, June 2, 2016, Cooperstown, NY. Of the 5,608 players surveyed between 2010 and 2019, 143 (2.5%) were African American.

** Richard Lapchick, *2019 Racial and Gender Report Card: College Sport*, 54.

*** Richard Lapchick, *2020 Racial and Gender Report Card: Major League Baseball*, 36. Parenthetical percentages from Mark Armour and Daniel R. Levitt, "Baseball Demographics, 1947-2016," Society for American Baseball Research.

The data on teams were collected each summer from 2000 to 2019 (excluding 2011 and 2017) at regional and national youth select baseball tournaments in the Midwest. In all, 843 teams from 35 states and consisting of 9,783 players, ages 10 to 18, were surveyed. These tournaments included the Slumpbuster Tournament Series, considered the nation's largest select baseball tournament and held concurrently with the NCAA College Baseball World Series each year in Omaha and Lincoln, Nebraska, and Council Bluffs, Iowa.[34] Between 40 and 75 teams were surveyed each summer. As with the research by Armour and Leavitt, "skin color" was the "determining factor" in identifying African American players.[35] In this case, facial appearance also served as a determining factor. Printed tournament programs often featured names of players and team photos, as did banners some teams hung outside their dugouts. Those visual materials helped to identify Black players, possibly with a Hispanic background. When in doubt about the racial composition of the team, the researcher consulted a coach or parent for verification.

The low percentage of African American youths in select baseball presents a challenge for those intent on increasing the number of African Americans at higher levels of baseball. Select baseball differs from other forms of youth baseball such as Little League, YMCA, Catholic Youth Organization, and private youth sports organizations. Select teams usually are formed via competitive tryouts and play regionally and nationally against other elite competition.[36] According to research literature and even mainstream news sources, select baseball has become the prominent pool of talent for high school and college baseball. Select baseball's impact on major league rosters begins at the college level. A national study of almost 500 college baseball players found that 90 percent of them played in youth select baseball for an average of 6 years.[37] With college players now comprising more than 75 percent of those drafted by MLB teams, extrapolation of the results from the college baseball study shows that more than two thirds of those draftees played select ball.[38] Thus, youth select baseball initiated the majority of those draftees to high-level competition and served as the entry point to the talent pipeline that eventually leads to the major leagues.

Comparing the percentages of African Americans in the major leagues, college baseball, and youth select ball shows a "constriction" in the number of African Americans moving up that ladder of competition. (See Table 1) Increasing the number of African American youths in any type of competitive baseball doesn't guarantee that the number will increase at the college and major league levels, but at the very least, it would increase the potential pool of players moving forward. Major League Baseball has invested in urban baseball initiatives like RBI (Reviving Baseball in Inner-cities) and the Breakthrough Series. A model for teaching the fundamental skills and philosophy of baseball and addressing impediments to learning them could improve the results from these programs. The CoI can serve as a core for such a model.

COI AND STRUCTURING BASEBALL OUTREACH FOR AFRICAN AMERICANS

The CoI model offers a three-pronged approach for understanding and addressing the chronically low number of African Americans in baseball. Viewing the problem as a pedagogical challenge (i.e. the simple act of teaching a child to play and/or understand baseball) can address the larger relationship between African Americans and baseball. The CoI model integrates multiple considerations for narrowing the gulf between African American youths and baseball. Each presence—teaching, social, and cognitive—draws in threads of discussion from the research literature and observations by baseball writers. More importantly, CoI provides direction for identifying (or confirming) "best practices" for teaching baseball to youngsters, especially those with little or no exposure to the game.

Teaching presence. The role of coaches looms large, according to some research. Young African Americans in an RBI program told Stodoloska and colleagues that they grew to respect and admire their coaches.[39] African American youths participating in the RBI program said coaches shaped their baseball experience and facilitated learning baseball skills. The researchers concluded that "the support and encouragement from coaches and program staff were important factors" in keeping players engaged in RBI.[40]

In Verducci's 2003 *SI* article, he wrote that even more important than formal coaches were informal coaches, or "pied pipers."[41] Verducci was quoting the late John Young, a former major league player and scout and the founder of RBI who used the term "pied piper" to describe the men who voluntarily taught youngsters baseball in the South Central Los Angeles neighborhood where he grew up. Fathers usually served in that role, but as Verducci wrote, with the high number of fatherless households in the inner city, the role may go unfilled, and "Without its pied pipers, baseball, the more pedagogic game, suffers."[42]

MARY HOLT/MLB PHOTOS, COURTESY OF MLB

Player Bryson Graves receives encouragement from a coach during the 2021 WWBA Underclass World Championship. The Breakthrough Series, established in 2008, is a joint effort between USA Baseball and Major League Baseball aimed at developing players on and off the field through mentorship and instruction and is one of MLB's "diversity pipeline" programs.

To be effective, pied pipers must provide a consistent presence, not just for a few weeks in the summer. And for a community of inquiry to be effective, it must have "high levels of 'teacher immediacy.'"[43] For young baseball "students," that immediacy comes in the form of regular contact with a baseball mentor. Whoever serves as that mentor must have credibility (or "street cred") and youths must be able to identify him or her as part of their neighborhood or culture. Youths must consider that mentor as someone who understands the problems and pressures of living in impoverished neighborhoods or with those who are at the lower rungs of the socio-economic ladder. To be effective, that mentor should be a part of that local community or someone who has lived in that community.[44]

A few youth baseball mentoring programs have shown success by selecting coaches who spend considerable time in the community. Home Run Baseball Camps have followed that practice for years. Home Run Baseball founder John McCarthy described one of his young female coaches in Washington, DC: "She grew up alongside these kids. So when she goes into predominantly black neighborhoods, she takes no s--- from anybody. She knows exactly what's going on." That coach, like other Home Run Baseball coaches, will spend years following the development of the players who stay in the program. Such "immediacy" to instruction through frequent contact and familiarity between coach and player facilitate the player's development and growth, just as "teacher immediacy" facilitates a student's learning and sense of belonging in the CoI. McCarthy said that players who stick with the program "catch on fire for baseball. They're into it. They love it. They're competitive."[45]

Former New York Mets and Chicago White Sox manager Jerry Manuel has carried the concept of teacher immediacy a step further. He formed a nonprofit organization which, among other activities, works with charter school programs in Sacramento to teach baseball to Black children by letting them learn and play the sport as part of their regular curriculum. Manuel believes such measures can bring baseball back to the forefront of African American culture. "One of the pillars of our community was baseball," he said. "That baseball pillar has crumbled somewhat, but I still think that there's gonna be a surfing back, if you will, to where baseball comes back to what it was."[46]

Social presence. As with CoI, social and cultural ties have much to do with a youngster's propensity for seeking sports participation. As noted earlier, researchers most often cite peer groups and parents as the most influential in socializing and sanctioning sport for youngsters. Sociologist Anthony Giddens noted, "The generation of feelings of trust in others, as the deepest-lying element of the basic security system, depends substantially upon predictable and caring routines established by parental figures."[47] Shaun Anderson and Matthew Martin claim that when parents aren't involved, youngsters aren't likely to play baseball.[48] The RBI directors interviewed by Anderson and Martin said that getting parents to participate "is key" to getting African American youth on the baseball diamonds. One of the directors lamented: "Getting our participants [players] to and from games and getting our participants to and from the Urban Youth Academy hurts our growth. We need parents' help in this situation."[49] Providing transportation, helping their children find opportunities to play, and using discretionary time and money to encourage their involvement are among the ways parents can support their children's participation in baseball.

Peer influence also looms large in setting the social and cultural tone of a youngster's sporting experience. Stodoloska and her co-authors said the RBI players in their study "discussed feelings of closeness, connection, comradeship, pride, and enjoyment they experienced while interacting with their teammates."[50] As discussed earlier, research has established that for a sport to attract a youngster, it must provide an opportunity to bond with peers. Based on such studies, those who try to pique African American youth interest in baseball should consider the peer groups a youngster deems important. Being aware of what a youth's peer culture does and does not value can provide information for coaches in determining what may be most effective to teaching baseball.

In the absence of parental support, coaches can impact a youth's baseball experience beyond sustaining a teaching presence. As Stodoloska wrote, coaches "are particularly important for children with low self-esteem who depend on their encouragement and support."[51] In establishing a social presence, as explained by Garrison, the teacher (or coach) acts as more than just a purveyor of information. That person also acts as a partner, or collaborator, with the student in directing the discovery of new knowledge (or skills) and in helping students learn from each other. As CoI originators L. Randy Garrison and colleagues explain, "Collaboration is an approach to teaching and learning that goes beyond simple interaction and declarative instructions. Collaboration must draw learners into a shared experience for the purposes of constructing and confirming meaning."[52]

Based on the CoI perspective and research like that of Anderson and Martin, coaches of first-time players should consider spending as much, if not more, time with individual instruction as they do on group fielding and hitting drills. That means working with players one-on-one on the mechanics of fielding, hitting, and pitching, and relating to the players off the field, not just on the field. But coaches should also allot time for youngsters to apply their skills by playing with each other in a relaxed atmosphere, with the coach stressing adherence to that which was taught.

Cognitive Presence. Garrison notes that cognitive presence can be nurtured through a strong social presence, just as Dewey said that the psychological and sociological aspects of learning are two sides of the same coin. If the youngster can find cultural fulfillment with peers through baseball and, as Garrison might say, "personal meaning" in the "knowledge" gained from coaches,[53] then the youngster may internalize baseball participation to the extent to which the sport becomes part of the youngster's self-image. "That is, socio-emotional interaction and support are important and sometimes essential in realizing meaningful and worthwhile educational outcomes," Garrison and his co-authors wrote.[54] In such a case, repeated exposure to baseball may result in the youth incorporating the role of "baseball player" as part of his identity. This is particularly salient for African Americans, according to research by Brown and Bennett, because "minorities have a stronger sense of self-identification than other ethnic or racial groups... This is significant because a strong identity toward one's self will encourage behaviors that affirm identity characteristics."[55] As noted earlier, the "sense of [racial] congruence" is paramount in an African American youth's decision to play baseball.[56]

Incorporating a sport into one's self-identity goes beyond just learning the skills of the sport. Sports sociologist Jan Ove Tangen argues that even the venue where the game is played can have an intrapersonal impact. The venue itself can arouse excitement and anticipation for competition and provide comfort and confidence through the familiarity of the playing space. Tangen says research has "documented how people may feel affection for sport places and experience different qualities of the facility with beneficial consequences to their identity, health and so on."[57] The playing space is where the physical demands of the sport and the social and psychological attraction, or cognitive presence, meet and where the player reveals a part of his self-identity. From the CoI perspective, this sense of self plays within a larger "social-emotional" environment.[58] As several researchers have found, people feel "welcome" in some sports venues, but not in others, based on their own history (or lack of it) with the venue and the cultural significance they and friends and family place on the venue.[59] The venues which a youngster finds welcoming can spur his "purposeful thinking and acting" in growing into the sport. That allows the youngster to fuse "personal meaning and shared understanding (i.e. knowledge)" which Garrison said are necessary for cognitive presence.[60] Tangen says that for the youngster, the venue can elicit a fundamental question: "'Who am I?' Through repeated reflections such as this the identity of the individual develops."[61]

Stodoloska's research bears out Tangen's claim that the playing space itself bolsters a youth's cognitive presence when playing a sport. The African Americans in their study felt that the RBI program provided a safe place for them to learn the game and have fun with peers. Stodoloska concluded that "the desire to satisfy the need for safety may actually motivate some youth to increase participation in organized and supervised sport programs that provide safe havens in urban impoverished communities."[62] The researchers proposed that a youth's desire for a safe recreational place should figure into "future theoretical models" for attracting youth to baseball.[63] Making such space available and accessible should be a consideration when trying to root and grow baseball programs for inner city youth. Both public and private investments in neighborhood baseball fields are necessary to ensure that happens.

CONCLUSION

In the Community of Inquiry, teaching presence, social presence and cognitive presence intertwine. When applied to baseball instruction, teaching (coaching) presence "is essential in balancing" cognitive presence and social presence.[64] In looking at inner city youth baseball programs through the lens of CoI, the coach transcends his or her traditional role and becomes a pied piper, a neighborhood ambassador of baseball, and even a parental or trusted authority figure. In this role the coach attempts to connect culturally with novice minority players and to recognize the interpersonal influences on those players.

The coach also provides an accessible but safe environment for playing baseball. Having that trusted coach or mentor, an enclosed and secure playing field, supportive peers, and a growing familiarity with baseball can shelter a youngster, at least temporarily, from the grit of the inner city. While not as straightforward as it may sound, an effective youth baseball program that provides such an environment for nurturing an interest in the game can be built around the tenets of CoI.

The low percentage of elite-level players who are African American (from youth select ball to the major leagues) persists, despite programs aimed at increasing that percentage that have been in place for years. In the 2020 Racial and Gender Report Card: Major League Baseball, Richard Lapchick said that baseball organizations should "put a direct focus on continuing to grow the game in communities which do not have access" to baseball.[65] Major League Baseball formed the RBI program and other initiatives to do just that. But within the past few years, researchers contend that RBI has failed to develop long-term, meaningful relationships with many underserved communities, which "shows that MLB either does not care about developing these relationships or that MLB is not concerned about making changes within these communities."[66] While Lapchick sees signs for optimism,[67] the number of African Americans playing at high levels of competition remains stagnant.

Treating baseball as an individual learning challenge and incorporating the CoI model can be a tool for nurturing the game in baseball "deserts" and can allow baseball coaches and organizers to provide more immersive experiences for their youthful novices. On a larger scale, framing baseball as an educational activity allows youth baseball organizers to take advantage of other pedagogical research on enhancing the learning environment and improving student outcomes. Such an overview opens new possibilities for addressing the chronically low number of African Americans in elite youth baseball, and subsequently at college and professional levels. ■

Notes

1. Richard Lapchick, *2020 Racial and Gender Report Card: Major League Baseball*, The Institute for Diversity and Ethics in Sport (Orlando: University of Central Florida, August 28, 2020): 36, https://43530132-36e9-4f52-811a-182c7a91933b.filesusr.com/ugd/7d86e5_3267492245744522893b464512c42cad.pdf. Date accessed: July 3, 2020.
2. Richard Lapchick, *2019 Racial and Gender Report Card: College Sport*, The Institute for Diversity and Ethics in Sport (Orlando: University of Central Florida, June 3, 2020): 54, https://43530132-36e9-4f52-811a-182c7a91933b.filesusr.com/ugd/7d86e5_d69e3801bb8146f2b08f6e619bcddf22.pdf. Date accessed: July 3, 2020. Information on African American youth in baseball is based on a 2020 update of a report on a 15-year survey of youth select baseball teams. The report was given at an academic conference as cited: David C. Ogden, "Major League Baseball and the Framing of African Americans." Paper presented at the 28th annual Cooperstown Symposium on Baseball and American Culture, June 2, 2016, Cooperstown, NY.
3. For example, see David C. Ogden and Michael L. Hilt, "Collective Identity and Basketball: An Explanation for the Decreasing Number of African-Americans on America's Baseball Diamonds," *Journal of Leisure Research* 35, no.2 (2003): 213–22; David C. Ogden and Randall Rose, "Using Giddens' Structuration Theory to Examine the Waning Participation of African Americans in Baseball," *Journal of Black Studies* 35, no. 4 (2005): 225–45; Frank B. Butts, Laura M. Hatfield and Lance C. Hatfield, "African Americans in College Baseball," *The Sport Journal* 10(2007), http://thesportjournal.org/article/african-americans-college-baseball. Date accessed: September 12, 2011; Joseph Cooper, Joey Gawrysiak, and Billy Hawkins, "Racial Perceptions of Baseball at Historically Black Colleges and Universities," *Journal of Sport and Social Issues* 20, no. 10 (2012): 1–26; Brandon Brown and Gregg Bennett,"'Baseball Is Whack!': Exploring the Lack of African American Baseball Consumption," *Journal of Sport and Social Issues* 39, no. 4 (2015): 1–21.
4. John McCarthy, telephone interview, January 20, 2012.
5. D. Randy Garrison, Terry Anderson, and Walter Archer, "Critical Inquiry in a Text-Based Environment: Computer Conferencing in Higher Education," *The Internet and Higher Education* 2, nos. 2–3 (2000): 87–105.
6. John Dewey, "My Pedagogic Creed," in *Dewey on Education*, ed. John Dewey (New York: Teachers College, Columbia University, 1959), 20.
7. Garrison, Anderson and Archer, "Critical Inquiry."
8. Garrison, Anderson and Archer, "Critical Inquiry," 101–102.
9. Garrison, Anderson and Archer, "Critical Inquiry," 102.
10. Garrison, Anderson and Archer, "Critical Inquiry," 102.
11. Tom Verducci, "Blackout: The African-American Baseball Player is Vanishing. Does He Have a Future?," *Sports Illustrated*, July 6, 2003, 56–76.
12. David Canton, "Where Are All the Black Baseball Players?" *U.S. News*, July 10, 2017, https://www.usnews.com/opinion/op-ed/articles/2017-07-10/3-reasons-for-the-declining-percentage-of-black-baseball-players-in-the-mlb. Date accessed: May 18, 2020.
13. Garrison, Anderson, and Archer, "Critical Inquiry," 101.
14. Garrison, Anderson, and Archer, "Critical Inquiry,"101.
15. Garrison, Anderson, and Archer, "Critical Inquiry," 99.
16. Garrison, Anderson, and Archer, "Critical Inquiry," 89.
17. Garrison, Anderson, and Archer, "Critical Inquiry," 100.
18. Brian Wilson and R. Sparks, "It's Gotta Be the Shoes: Youth, Race, and Sneaker Commercials," *Sociology of Sport Journal* 13, no. 4 (1996): 398–427; G.G. Watson, and R. Collis, "Adolescent Values in Sport: A Case of Conflicting Interests," *International Review of Sport Sociology* 17, no. 3 (1982): 73–90.
19. Steven F. Philipp and Sherie Brezina, "Differences Among African Americans and Euro-Americans in Reasons for Sports Participation," *Perceptual and Motor Skills* 95, no. 1 (2002): 184–86.
20. Steven F. Philipp, "Are We Welcome? African American Racial Acceptance in Leisure Activities and the Importance Given to Children's Leisure," *Journal of Leisure Research* 31, no. 4 (1999): 385–403.
21. Shaun M. Anderson and Matthew M. Martin, "The African American Community and Professional Baseball: Examining Major League Baseball's Corporate Social-Responsibility Efforts as a Relationship-Management Strategy," *International Journal of Sport Communication* 12, no. 3 (2019): 397–418, https://doi.org/10.1123/ijsc.2018-0157. Date accessed: May 18, 2020.
22. Monika Stodoloska, Iryna Sharaievska, Scott Tainsky, and Allison Ryan, "Minority Youth Participation in an Organized Youth Sports Program: Needs, Motivations and Facilitators," *Journal of Leisure Research* 46, no. 5 (2014): 612–34.
23. Garrison, Anderson, and Archer, "Critical Inquiry," 98.
24. Garrison, Anderson, and Archer, "Critical Inquiry," 94.
25. Stodoloska, Sharaievska, Tainsky and Ryan, "Minority Youth Participation," 617.
26. Brown and Bennett,"'Baseball Is Whack!'," 6.
27. Garrison, Anderson and Archer, "Critical Inquiry," 98–99.
28. Garrison, Anderson, and Archer, "Critical Inquiry," 98–99.
29. Richard Lapchick, *The Complete 2020 Racial and Gender Report Card*, The Institute for Diversity and Ethics in Sport (Orlando: University of Central Florida, March 4, 2021):10, https://www.tidesport.org/complete-sport.

Date accessed: August 8, 2021. For further research on reasons for Africa American involvement in sport, see Othello Harris, "Race, Sport, and Social Support," *Sociology of Sport Journal* 11, no. 1 (1994): 40–50; and Douglas Hartmann, "Rethinking the Relationship Between Sport and Race in American Culture: Golden Ghettos and Contested Terrain," *Sociology of Sport Journal* 17 (2000): 229–53; Gerald Early, "Why Baseball Was the Black National Pastime," in *Basketball Jones: America Above the Rim*, eds. Todd Boyd and Kenneth L. Shropshire (New York: NYU Press, 2000), 27–50.

30. Mark Armour and Daniel R. Levitt, "Baseball Demographics, 1947–2016," Society for American Baseball Research, https://sabr.org/bioproj/topic/baseball-demographics-1947-2016. Date accessed: June 3, 2020. Armour and Levitt's percentages for African American players in the major leagues are consistently lower than those of Richard Lapchick's. Armour and Levitt surveyed the race of the approximately 11,000 MLB players on rosters between 1947 and 2016. As an example of the differences, Armour and Levitt found that 6.7 percent of those on the 2016 rosters, the last year they surveyed, were African Americans, compared with 8.3 percent reported by Lapchick. Lapchick's percentages include "Blacks or African Americans," while Armour and Levitt label their numbers as "African Americans." Lapchick does not define "Blacks" in his *2020 Racial and Gender Report Card.*
31. Lapchick, *2020 Racial and Gender Report Card: Major League Baseball*, 36. Armour and Levitt's research, however, shows that the percentage of MLB players who were African American varied between 7.1 and 6.7 percent from 2009 to 2016.
32. Lapchick, *2019 Racial and Gender Report Card: College Sport*, 54.
33. Ogden, "Major League Baseball and the Framing of African Americans."
34. "Omaha Slumpbuster Tournament," Triple Crown Sports, https://www.omahaslumpbuster.com. Date accessed: October 1, 2020. In 2019, 736 teams participated in the Omaha-area tournament.
35. Armour and Levitt, "Baseball Demographics, 1947–2016."
36. David C. Ogden, "The Welcome Theory: An Approach to Studying African-American Youth Interest and Involvement in Baseball," *Nine: A Journal of Baseball History and Culture* 12, no. 2 (2004): 114–22; Les Edgerton, *Perfect Game USA and the Future of Baseball* (Jefferson, N.C.: McFarland & Co., Inc: 2009).
37. David C. Ogden and Kevin Warneke, "Theoretical Considerations in College Baseball's Relationship with Youth Select Baseball," *Journal of Sport Behavior* 33, no. 3 (2010): 256–75. For further discussion on the link between youth elite baseball and college ball, see Charles Hallman, "Baseball is as White as Ever," *Minnesota Spokesman-Reporter*, June 12, 2019, https://spokesman-recorder.com/2019/06/12/baseball-still-as-white-as-ever. Date accessed: October 1, 2020; Edgerton, *Perfect Game USA and the Future of Baseball*, 39, 105–11; William C. Rhoden,"A Divide that Begins in Little League," *The New York Times*, May 28, 2007, D2.
38. J.J. Cooper, Carlos Collazo, and Jared McMasters, "Draft System Has Pushed Teams To Pick More College Players," *Baseball America*, June 7, 2019, https://www.baseballamerica.com/stories/draft-system-has-pushed-teams-to-pick-more-college-players. Date accessed: September 29, 2020.
39. Stodoloska, Sharaievska, Tainsky, and Ryan, "Minority Youth Participation," 621.
40. Stodoloska, Sharaievska, Tainsky, and Ryan, "Minority Youth Participation," 623.
41. Verducci, "Blackout," 56–76.
42. Verducci, "Blackout," 58.
43. Garrison, Anderson and Archer, "Critical Inquiry," 102.
44. David C. Ogden, "Wanted: Pied Pipers to Lead African Americans to Baseball," in *African Americans: Reviving Baseball in Inner City*, ed. Sharon T. Freeman (Washington, D.C.: AASBEA Publishers, 2008), 199–207.
45. John McCarthy, telephone interview, January 31, 2012.
46. Bradford William Davis, "Ex-Mets Manager Jerry Manuel Still Believes in a Better Major League Baseball," *New York Daily News*, February 14, 2021, https://www.nydailynews.com/sports/baseball/ny-20210214-pvtgdjdo2nadpnihf5usmntbim-story.html. Date accessed: August 7, 2021.
47. Anthony Giddens, *The Constitution of Society: Outline of the Theory of Structuration* (Berkeley: University of California Press: 1984), 50.
48. Anderson and Martin, "The African American Community and Professional Baseball," 408–09.
49. Anderson and Martin, "The African American Community and Professional Baseball," 409.
50. Stodoloska, Sharaievska, Tainsky and Ryan, "Minority Youth Participation," 620.
51. Stodoloska, Sharaievska, Tainsky and Ryan, "Minority Youth Participation," 617.
52. Garrison, Anderson and Archer, "Critical Inquiry," 95.
53. Garrison, Anderson and Archer, "Critical Inquiry," 98.
54. Garrison, Anderson and Archer, "Critical Inquiry," 95.
55. Brown and Bennett,"'Baseball Is Whack!'," 6.
56. Brown and Bennett,"'Baseball Is Whack!'," 6.
57. Jan Ove Tangen, "'Making the Space': A Sociological Perspective on Sport and its Facilities," *Sport in Society: Cultures, Commerce, Media, Politics* 7, no.1 (2004): 42.
58. Garrison, Anderson and Archer, "Critical Inquiry," 95.
59. Besides the previously cited work of Philipp, Brown and Bennett, Ogden, and Cooper, Gawrysiak and Hawkins, see Trevor Bopp, Robert Turick, Joshua D. Vadeboncoeur, and Thomas J. Aicher, "Are You Welcomed? A Racial and Ethnic Comparison of Perceived Welcomeness in Sport Participation," *International Journal of Exercise Science* 10, no. 6 (2017): 833–44, and Tangen's other 2004 article, "Embedded Expectations, Embodied Knowledge and the Movements that Connect," *International Review for the Sociology of Sport* 39, no. 1 (2004): 7–25.
60. Garrison, Anderson and Archer, "Critical Inquiry," 98.
61. Tangen, "'Making the Space'," 43.
62. Stodoloska, Sharaievska, Tainsky and Ryan, "Minority Youth Participation," 626.
63. Stodoloska, Sharaievska, Tainsky and Ryan, "Minority Youth Participation," 626.
64 Garrison, Anderson and Archer, "Critical Inquiry," 101.
65. Lapchick, *2020 Racial and Gender Report Card: Major League Baseball*, 3.
66. Shaun M. Anderson, "Diversity Outreach in Major League Baseball: A Stakeholder Approach" PhD diss., West Virginia University, Morgantown, 2016, Graduate Theses, Dissertations, and Problem Reports (5102), https://researchrepository.wvu.edu/etd/5102, 75. Date accessed: May 18, 2020. See also Anderson and Martin, "The African American Community and Professional Baseball," 411–12, and Maury Brown, "How Major League Baseball Lost the Soul of Baseball," *Forbes*, June 5, 2020, https://www.forbes.com/sites/maurybrown/2020/06/05/how-major-league-baseball-lost-the-heart-of-baseball/?sh=37c813c549a. Date accessed: October 1, 2020. Brown argues that any gains in African American RBI participants entering the professional baseball ranks could be offset by the downsizing of the minor leagues and MLB draft and the subsequent loss of college baseball scholarships.
67. Lapchick, *2020 Racial and Gender Report Card: Major League Baseball*, 9. Lapchick believes the MLB draft offers encouraging signs that the number of African Americans in the majors could be on the upswing. In 2018, almost 17 percent of the first 78 draft selections were "African-American/Black/African-Canadian." Between 2012 and 2020, almost 18 percent of first-round picks were "Black or African American."

Contributors

BRUCE ALLARDICE is a Professor of History at South Suburban College, near Chicago. Professor Allardice has written (and presented) numerous times on the Black Sox Scandal and on early baseball. His article on "The Rise of Baseball in the South" received an award from SABR for Best Baseball History article of 2012. He is currently editor of the SABR Origins of Baseball Committee Newsletter.

J. FURMAN DANIEL III is an Associate Professor in the College of Security and Intelligence at Embry-Riddle Aeronautical University. He is the editor of *21st Century Patton: Leadership Lessons for the Modern Era*, a co-author of *The First Space War: How Patterns of History and Principles of STEM Will Shape Its Form*, and author of *Patton: Battling with History*. He lives in Prescott, Arizona.

PETER DREIER teaches politics at Occidental College. **ROBERT ELIAS** teaches politics at the University of San Francisco. Their books, *Baseball Rebels* (University of Nebraska Press) and *Major League Rebels* (Rowman & Littlefield), will be published in April 2022.

ELLIOT FULLMER is an Associate Professor of American Politics at Randolph-Macon College. He is the author of *Tuesday's Gone: America's Early Voting Revolution*, as well as numerous scholarly articles on U.S. elections and voting behavior. He is an avid Philadelphia Phillies fan, and is proud to have watched MLB games at 36 different ballparks. He lives in Richmond, Virginia.

DAVID J. GORDON, MD is a retired biomedical scientist. He has previously published three articles in the *BRJ*, on the Deadball Era, Racial Equity in the Hall of Fame, and Competitive Balance in MLB. Dr. Gordon is also the author of a book called *Baseball Generations*, published in 2021.

BARRY HYMAN is Professor Emeritus of Mechanical Engineering and Public Affairs at the University of Washington. He started his career as an active baseball player at the age of 67. In the summers he plays in the Puget Sound Senior Baseball League. During the off-seasons he competes in the Men's Senior Baseball League and Roy Hobbs World Series tournaments. He is also a veteran of several Pro-Ball Baseball Clinics and Seattle Mariners Fantasy Camps.

FRANCIS KINLAW has contributed articles and poetry to many SABR publications since becoming a member of SABR in 1983. Having lived near Detroit in his youth, he came of age in a baseball sense as Al Kaline was achieving stardom in the major leagues. In the years that followed, he remained an admirer of Kaline as a man and athlete. He now resides in Greensboro, North Carolina, and writes extensively about baseball, basketball, and college football.

HERM KRABBENHOFT a retired organic chemist, has been a SABR member since 1981 and is the author of *Leadoff Batters of Major League Baseball* (McFarland, 2006).

CHAD MOODY is a nearly lifelong Detroit-area resident, where he has been a fan of the Detroit Tigers from birth. An alumnus of the University of Michigan and Michigan State University, he has spent 30 years working in the automotive industry. From his humble beginning of having a letter published in *Baseball Digest* as a teenager, Chad has since contributed to numerous SABR and Professional Football Researchers Association projects. He and his wife, Lisa, live in Northville, Michigan, with their dog, Daisy.

TOM NARDACCI was born in Rensselaer, New York, where he and his friends, unbeknownst to them, played sandlot baseball on the same Hudson Riverfront Park field where Roger Connor of the Troy Trojans hit major league baseball's first grand slam in 1881. Tom, a lifelong Yankees fan, is a collector of T206 baseball cards and primarily researches and writes about the Deadball Era. Tom earned his master's degree in strategic communications from Columbia University.

DAVE OGDEN, PhD is professor emeritus in the School of Communication at the University of Nebraska at Omaha. He has presented his research at the National Baseball Hall of Fame Conference on Baseball and American Culture, the Nine Spring Training Conference, and in the *Baseball Research Journal*, *Journal of Leisure Research*, and *Journal of Black Studies*. He is co-editor of three books on sports and reputation and co-authored the book, *Call to the Hall*.

ERIC T. POULIN is an Assistant Professor of Library and Information Science at Simmons University, where he directs their Western Massachusetts-based campus. He first joined SABR in 2002 after completing a Steele Internship at the A. Bartlett Giamatti Center for Research at the National Baseball Hall of Fame and Museum. This is his first contribution to the *Baseball Research Journal*.

MARK STANG is the author of nine books on major league baseball, including *Baseball By The Numbers* (Scarecrow Press, 1996), the definitive guide to major league uniform numbers. He can be reached at: markmstang@comcast.net.

ROBERT THOLKES of Minneapolis is a veteran contributor to SABR publications and to the journal *Base Ball*, concentrating on the game's amateur era (1845–70). Bob's past SABR activities include several years as an officer of the Halsey Hall Chapter (Minnesota), biographical research on major leaguers with Minnesota connections, and service as newsletter editor for SABR's Origins of Baseball Committee, and, beyond SABR, 20 seasons as operator of a vintage base ball club, the Quickstep of Minnesota.

STEW THORNLEY has been an official scorer for Major League Baseball since 2007 and a member of the MLB Official Scoring Advisory Committee since 2013.

MICHAEL TOW is a history and language arts teacher living in Seattle. Originally from southern Illinois, Michael is a former assistant editor of the *Journal of the Illinois State Historical Society*, and has over a dozen historical publications to his name. Michael has contributed to both the SABR Historic Games and Biography Projects, and is currently writing a book-length biography of Joe Grace. Michael can be reached at michaelctow@gmail.com.

CHRISTIAN TRUDEAU is a Professor of Economics at the University of Windsor. For the last 20 years, he has research Quebec baseball history. His findings are documented at sites.google.com/view/ligueprovinciale.

STEVEN C. WEINER, a SABR member since 2015, is a retired chemical engineer and a lifelong baseball fan. During his undergraduate years at Rutgers University, Steven worked in the sports information office and broadcast baseball and basketball play-by-play on WRSU radio. Steven obtained his doctoral degree in engineering and applied science from Yale University. Steven currently serves as assignments editor for the SABR Baseball Games Project with essay contributions in five SABR books. He volunteers as an in-classroom and virtual teacher at local schools.

ERIC MARSHALL WHITE, PhD, of Rocky Hill, New Jersey, is the Scheide Librarian and Assistant University Librarian for Special Collections, Rare Books and Manuscripts at Princeton University Library. He has published widely on Gutenberg and fifteenth-century European printing. This is his fourth contribution to SABR publications. The day his stepfather took him to his first baseball game, specifically to see Hank Aaron play, ranks among his fondest childhood memories.